The Phoenix Land

By the same author

The Writing on the Wall, the Transylvanian Trilogy:
They Were Counted
The Were Found Wanting
They Were Divided

Praise for Miklós Bánffy:

'One of the most celebrated and ambitious classics of Hungarian literature' – Jan Morris

'This epic Hungarian novel, absorbing both for its exploration of human nature and its study of the decline of the Austro-Hungarian Empire . . . weaves social and political themes into Bánffy's powerful tale' – *Daily Telegraph*

'A masterpiece. This very readable translation makes a wonderful book accessible to many more people' – *New Statesman*

'A genuine case of a rediscovered classic. The force of Bánffy's enthusiasm produces an effect rather like that of the best Trollope novels – but coming from a past world that now seems excitingly exotic'
– *Times Literary Supplement*

'Bánffy's masterpiece resembles Proust's [yet] he writes with all the psychological acumen of Dostoevsky'
– Francis King, *London Magazine*

'A huge, historical, romantic novel [with] good story-telling, solid historical background and enjoyable drama' – *Library Journal*

'Bánffy is a born story-teller. There are plots, intrigues, a murder, political imbroglios and passionate love affairs. His patriotic feelings are totally free of chauvinism, just as his instinctive promptings of tribal responsibility have not a trace of vanity' – Patrick Leigh Fermor

'A wonderful work, an elegy for a lost Middle-European Eden'
– Ruth Pavey, *Independent*

Miklós Bánffy

The Phoenix Land

The Memoirs of Count Miklós Bánffy

Including *Emlékeimböl – From My Memories*
and
Huszonöt Ev (1945) – Twenty-Five Years (1945)

Translated by Patrick Thursfield and Katalin Bánffy-Jelen
with an Introduction by Patrick Thursfield

A
ARCADIA BOOKS
LONDON

Arcadia Books Ltd
15–16 Nassau Street
London W1W 7AB
www.arcadiabooks.co.uk

First published in the United Kingdom 2003
Copyright © Miklós Bánffy 1932, 1945 and 2003
Translation © Patrick Thursfield and Katalin Bánffy-Jelen 2003

A catalogue record for this book is available from the British Library.

ISBN 1–900850–85–0

Arcadia Books gratefully acknowledges both the financial and practical
support of the Arts Council of England; the Hungarian Book Foundation;
Mrs Katalin Bogyay, Director of the Hungarian Cultural Centre, London; and
Magyar Magic – Hungary in Focus 2004.
We remain especially grateful to Vivienne Menkes-Ivry.

Typeset in Monotype Imprint by Northern Phototypesetting Co. Ltd, Bolton
Printed in Finland by W S Bookwell

Arcadia Books distributors are as follows:

in the UK and elsewhere in Europe:
Turnaround Publishers Services
Unit 3, Olympia Trading Estate
Coburg Road
London N22 6TZ

in the USA and Canada:
Independent Publishers Group
814 North Franklin Street
Chicago, IL 60610

in Australia:
Tower Books
PO Box 213
Brookvale, NSW 2100

in New Zealand:
Addenda
Box 78224
Grey Lynn
Auckland

in South Africa:
Quartet Sales and Marketing
PO Box 1218
Northcliffe
Johannesburg 2115

Contents

Introduction — vii
by Patrick Thursfield

From My Memories — 1
Part One: *A Wartime Coronation* — 1
Part Two: *Times Of Revolution* — 34

Twenty-Five Years (1945) — 183
Translator's Note — 185
Introduction by Miklós Bánffy — 187

Notes — 393
Glossary of People and Places — 407

In loving memory of
Patrick Thursfield, 1923–2003

ABOUT THE TRANSLATORS

PATRICK THURSFIELD and KATALIN BANFFY-JELEN are the translators of *They Were Counted, They Were Found Wanting* and *They Were Divided*, winner of the Weidenfeld Translation Prize 2002.

Introduction

by Patrick Thursfield

The thousand-year-old kingdom of Hungary, which formed the major part of the Austro-Hungarian Empire until the last Habsburg fled in 1918, was finally dismantled by the Western Allies under the terms of the peace treaties following World War I. Phoenix-like the Hungarian people survived the horrors of the war, the disappointment of the first Socialist Republic, the disillusion of the brief but terrifying Communist rule of Béla Kun and the bitterness of seeing their beloved country dismembered by the Treaty of Trianon.

This is the world that Miklós Bánffy describes in his two short books of memoirs. For some thirty years after Miklós Bánffy's death in Budapest in 1950 it might have seemed as if Hungary had gone into official denial that he had ever lived at all. As for his writings, they too might never have existed let alone have been hailed as a national treasure. At the time of Bánffy's death the post-war Communist government was at its most repressive; therefore, for the new rulers, the writings of any member of the former ruling class had never officially existed and, indeed, had been removed from the shelves of school and university libraries and were no longer offered for sale in the bookshops. Like their authors, they too might never have existed. Their significance, whether literary or political, was officially held to be of no contemporary value and so best forgotten.

In this climate of Communist political correctness, history was being rewritten according to the Party Line, and any digression from that was taken as at best subversive and at worst criminally traitorous. As a result of this short-sighted policy, several generations of young people of school and university age had no true knowledge of what had brought about the dismemberment of their once great and powerful country under the terms of the Treaty of Trianon, which had been imposed by the Western powers in 1920 and had been punitive rather than corrective of perceived injustice. These had the effect of arbitrarily replacing one set of ethnic imbalances with another in many ways as bad, if not worse, than those that had evolved over the centuries.

By the end of the nineteenth century the kingdom of Hungary, which for a thousand years had been the chief bastion of a Europe menaced by Turkish aggression, had become a vast multinational state whose peoples were of many diverse ethnic origins who spoke a myriad different languages and practised almost as many different religions. The existence of so many minority peoples, some of whom, to be sure, nursed dreams, if not of actual political independence, at least of some degree of autonomy, was to produce its own problems. However, it was not as simple as that. Western Hungary, which comprised the great Hungarian plain and formed the nucleus of the ancient kingdom of St Stephen, was bordered on all sides by very different provinces, each with its own ethnic minority, and some with more than one. To the east lay Transylvania, Hungary's largest province, in which the population was fairly equally balanced between those of ethnic Magyar origins and language and those of Romanian stock; and here it should not be forgotten that only a minority of these last were indigenous Transylvanians. Their numbers had been vastly increased in earlier years, especially in the eighteenth and nineteenth centuries, by waves of Romanian immigrants from the eastern side of the Carpathians. These had fled their native land to escape the savageries of Turkish rule. It must be remembered that, as a sovereign national state, Romania had not existed until the middle of the nineteenth century, when it become a principality, later upgraded to a kingdom and ruled by a German princeling.

It was at this time that learned discussion about the origins of the Romanian people with their Latin-based language so very different from those of their Magyar and Slav neighbours, took flight. Romanian and pro-Romanian scholars offered the view that they were the true descendants of the Dacians, who had inhabited the land when it formed part of the Roman Empire and who therefore predated the Magyar conquest of Hungary and especially of Transylvania.

This theory provided a convenient and timely argument to reinforce Romanian irredentist ambitions and as such was cynically used to foment discontent among the Transylvanian Romanians (the majority of whom were uneducated peasants) who until then had shown little sign of resenting being ruled by landowning Magyar aristocrats or government officials from Budapest. There were some, usually scions of those ancient landowning aristocratic families (of which Miklós Bánffy was one), who, while still loyal to the crown, cherished the hope that one day they could obtain some measure of independence for their formerly autonomous homeland. To the south lay the Banat in which there were more Serbs than Magyars in the districts just north of Belgrade, while only a mile or two further north there were more Magyars than Serbs. A little further west, but still to the south of central Hungary lay Slovenia, Croatia and Bosnia-Herzegovina. Directly to the West lay the Burgenland, with a mixed population of Hungarians and Austrians. There were more Austrians in the narrow strip of land closest to the Austrian border and more Hungarians in the equally narrow strip to the east; but, while the town of Sopron was predominantly Hungarian, elsewhere the two races were inextricably mixed.

To the north was Bohemia, populated mainly by Czechs, with a small minority of Germans in its northern region, while to the east the Slovaks formed the majority. In both these regions there was a substantial minority of Hungarians, particularly on the north bank of the Danube between the Austrian border and Estergom, and it was the same in the Nyitra hills to the north-east of Estergom, which now lie partly in the Czech Republic and partly in Slovakia. In 1921 it had all been handed over to the newly formed state of Czechoslovakia. As a result of the new boundaries laid down by the Allies, hardly a metre of the former borders of the Hungarian-ruled part of the former Austro-Hungarian Empire remained to her. These new injustices formed the basis of Hungary's post-1920 demand that the boundaries should be revised if justice were not only to be done but also seen to be done.

This was Bánffy's first preoccupation when he was appointed foreign minister in István Bethlen's government in 1921.

Much of the blame for the unjust redistribution of what had for centuries been Hungarian lands must be laid at the door of the baleful influence exercised at the Paris peace talks by the militantly pro-Slav British journalist, Seton-Watson. This meddlesome but influential journalist had battled tirelessly to reward the Czech leader Benes for his wartime support of the Allies with a high position in the new state of Czechoslovakia, 'gallant little Serbia' with Croatia; Slovenia and Bosnia, and the formerly insignificant little kingdom of Romania with the huge province of Transylvania, all of which cost Hungary well over half her former territory and two-thirds of her pre-war peoples. Hungary's despair and disillusion were most graphically explained by István Bethlen in a series of lectures given at the Institute of International Affairs at Chatham House in London's St James's Square in November 1933 and afterwards published in book form under the title of *The Treaty of Trianon and European Peace* (Longmans, Green and Co, London, New York and Toronto, 1934). Bethlen, who was also a cousin and remained a lifelong friend of Miklós Bánffy, had been in a unique position to discuss these problems, as he had been prime minister of Hungary from 1921 to 1931.

This was the world that Miklós Bánffy was to write about in his two short books of memoirs, *Emlékeimből – From my Memories* from 1932 and *Huszonöt Ev (1945) – Twenty-Five Years (1945)*, which had never been published before, since the manuscript had only been discovered after the fall of Communism among the Bánffy papers deposited in the Ráday Institute by his widow soon after his death in 1950. These two books describe a very different world from that into which Bánffy had been born in 1873 when Hungary had been at her greatest and when it had in effect been ruled largely by a privileged group of hereditary aristocrats.

From my Memories describes the death-throes of this world. The first part recalls those depressing days in the last months of 1916 when many men of clear sight had realized that the war would eventually be lost, and when all of Austria-Hungary felt that the death of the aged Emperor Franz Joseph signalled the end of an epoch.

In Budapest it immediately became imperative to crown the new monarch king of Hungary, since, according to the country's constitution, no parliamentary measures could be made law until there was a properly crowned and anointed sovereign to give his approval. This will explain why, in those desolate days when the casualty lists were daily growing longer and the capital was filled with the maimed and wounded soldiery returning from the front, anyone could have contemplated something so festive as the pomp and circumstance of a coronation.

Bánffy, as the scion of an ancient family whose father held an important office at court and who, moreover, had himself for some years been charged with responsibility for running the state theatres, was an obvious choice to organize the decorations and most of the other technical arrangements both inside and outside the coronation church. Part One of the book tells firstly of the hasty arrangements that had to be completed in a few weeks at a time when few people were available and the city was desperately short of almost everything that would be needed. He then goes on to describe the splendours and miseries of the coronation ceremonies on the last day of December 1916. Bánffy's account is written with compassion and understanding as well as with an eye to the ironic and occasionally ludicrous aspects of that beautiful but sad ceremony.

In Part Two we move on to the closing days of the war in October 1918, when the monarchy was overthrown in the so-called 'Aster Revolution' and in its place there was established a short-lived socialist republic with Count Mihály Károlyi – Bánffy's cousin and, when they were both younger, an intimate friend – as its first president. This in turn soon gave way to a Communist regime under Béla Kún. Bánffy, who had been in Budapest at the time of the Aster Revolution and who, along with István Bethlen and others of a like mind, was only too conscious of Károlyi's inadequacy and obvious inability to withstand the growing Communist threat, decided to go to England to explain, to any open-minded and influential people he could find, the menace to world peace that was inherent in what was happening in Hungary as a result of Allied policies. He decided to go, as a private citizen, at his own expense and under the auspices of the Szekler National Council, to London to raise support and sympathy for his suffering country. Before leaving in the first days of January 1919, Bánffy went to see Károlyi and, while explaining why he wished to go and also making it clear that he was not asking to be sent officially as he felt he would have more chance of success if he remained independent, obtained permission to take out the necessary funds.

At this point Bánffy takes the opportunity to insert a fascinating pen-portrait of the unfortunate Károlyi, which is different from all others as it is written by someone who knew the man intimately from the days of their shared childhood and school-days. In this it differs from most of what was later to be written about Károlyi both in its depth of psychological understanding and sympathy and in its freedom from the sort of sycophantic appreciation that pervades so much of what has been written about Károlyi by his wife and other admirers.

As it happens, Bánffy was never then to reach England as he found himself stranded in Holland with no money and, as a well-known aristocrat of independent means, was unable to return to Communist-ruled Hungary.

Bánffy's account of his adventures in passing through a Germany reduced to chaos by the Spartacist workers' revolt and finding himself so short of funds that he had to try to make a living as a portrait painter, is hilarious. When Béla Kun, in his turn, was forced to flee, and the Communist domination came to an abrupt and ignominious end, Bánffy received word to return from Bethlen, who was in Vienna heading a spirited group of exiles. He left at once for Austria. From there they would soon be able to go home and try to rebuild what remained of their shattered country.

Although written many years later when Hungary had suffered a second defeat in 1945, Bánffy still manages to keep up an urbane tone from which his good humour and irrepressible sense of the ridiculous has not been submerged either by the new tragedies to which Hungary had been subjected or by the bleak circumstances in which the book was written. When the war drew to a close the castle of Bonczhida had been reduced almost to a ruin, burned and looted by the retreating German armies as an act of revenge for Bánffy's attempt, made a year before, to persuade Romania, together with Hungary, to desert the Axis and sue for a separate peace. Countess Bánffy and their then teenage daughter, the future co-translator of her father's memoirs, had returned to Budapest because word had reached them that their townhouse had been occupied by the Russians and all their belongings thrown into the street. Miklós Bánffy had stayed in their Koloszvár house hoping to regain what was left of their forestry holdings from which their fortune derived. Although unsuccessful in this, he was prevented from rejoining his wife in Hungary because the frontier had been closed by the Romanian army. Nothing daunted, Bánffy, although his papers and archives had been destroyed by the German army, set to work to tell the story of his eighteen months as Hungary's foreign minister.

These were by no means uneventful and started after the fall of Count Pál Teleki's government following the first of the new young king's two failed attempts to return to Hungary to reclaim his throne in Budapest as a springboard from which to regain his other title as emperor of Austria. Teleki, who had not handled the attempted *coup* well, was forced to resign, and István Bethlen was appointed prime minister in his place. It was he who asked Bánffy to help him by accepting the onerous post of minister for foreign affairs.

Twenty-five Years (1945) tells the tale of Bánffy's period of office, starting with his first attempts to come to some agreement with the new neighbouring states so as to alleviate the minority problems brought about by the arbitrary fashion in which the Western powers had redrawn the map of Europe. These preliminary negotiations were brought to an abrupt end with King Karl's second and more serious attempt to return. Although this *putsch* also failed, and had its comic-opera aspects, it was nearer succeeding than the first and had more serious and long-lasting effects. The young king had been misled by unscrupulous courtiers who had told him tales of totally mythical support that would be forthcoming not only from the Western powers but also from the newly independent republic of Czechoslovakia. The Hungarian government under the self-appointed 'Regent' Admiral Horthy, a war hero who had been an aide-de-camp to the aged Emperor Franz Joseph, acted swiftly to stifle the revolt and so avoid a new Central-European war. However, it had a further and more deleterious result in bringing about an unbridgeable rift between the newly formed Legitimist Party and the supporters of Horthy's government. This deprived the country of the services of a whole generation of educated young men from the gentry and the great aristocratic families without putting anyone else in their place as candidates for government office or the diplomatic corps.

Twenty Five Years (1945) was published posthumously by Puski, Budapest in 1993 and later reprinted together with *From My Memories* in one volume. This contained a short foreword by Bánffy himself, a translation of which is included in this volume. I am indebted to the editors of both editions of *Twenty Five Years (1945)*, as their notes have been most useful to me in the writing of notes for this English edition.

In both these books Bánffy, who never failed to see the humorous side of any situation, however serious it might have been, uses a light and ironic tone, as if Puck's aside 'Lord, what fools these mortals be!' was never far from his mind (although in the kindest, most gentle way). It is clear that he reserved expression of his deepest feelings of love for his country, his reverence for honesty both in public and private life, his passion for the forests, rivers, meadows and wildlife of the mountains and valleys of his native land, his compassion for the unfortunate and exploited, his tolerance of folly or weakness, his disdain, almost amounting to hatred, of fraud and exploitation of the weak and powerless and, above all, his deep understanding and love of women, for his novels, especially the great trilogy *The Writing on the Wall*.

From my Memories was published in 1932, after Bánffy's retirement from active public life, partly through ill health and partly through disgust and disillusion at the treacheries and dishonesties of those who sought power for their own selfish reasons rather than for the good of others. Following the death of his father, Bánffy had retired to his home in Transylvania, the great and beautiful castle of Bonczhida only a few miles north of Koloszvár (now renamed Cluj-Napoca by the Romanians), and was devoting his time to writing. He, together with some others of like mind, founded a publishing house and spent much of his time in the encouragement of those Hungarian writers and painters who had remained in their home province after sovereignty had been transferred to Romania.

It is not clear when Bánffy started work on the great trilogy that told the tale of those crucial years from 1904 to the outbreak of the Great War in 1914. It seems to have been conceived many years before the author himself had returned to Transylvania and some years before he had produced the first volume of memoirs. Into it he poured all his feelings about Hungary and its people both humble and grand. Here he painted the picture of a great nation in decline, brought low by the folly and short-sightedness of its ruling class, to which he belonged and saw so clearly, unlike other writers who looked from afar but saw it only through the mists of envy or prejudice. As a chilling account of the folly of politicians and the blinkered vision of the rich and privileged, it draws much of its power not only from the fact that Bánffy knew this world from the inside but also because he wrote with a restraint that made his implied criticisms all the more powerful.

In 1981, when the Communists were still in control despite the cracks that were even then beginning to appear in many parts of Eastern Europe, Professor István Nemeskurty wrote a long article in a respected Budapest literary review in which he pointed out that if the state truly wanted the youth of Hungary to understand why their country had suffered so much between the wars, they should be made to read what had been written by a member of that former ruling class who had held power in those days and who had, in many ways, been responsible for Hungary's downfall. The writings of such men would provide a far more reliable idea of what had really happened than most of the works by officially approved proletarian writers of working-class background. In particular, he said they should read Miklós Bánffy's Transylvanian trilogy which, published in the 1930s, not only painted an unrivalled portrait of the social life and politics of those crucial years between 1904 and 1914 but was also a spellbinding tale by a master novelist who was worthy of comparison with Tolstoy and Lampedusa – high praise, indeed, especially from so respected a Hungarian critic.

Nemeskurty's reasoned enthusiasm led to the reissue in Budapest in 1982 of the first volume, *Megsámláltattál – They Were Counted*, and this in turn was followed in 1993 by a de luxe edition of all three books in one mammoth volume under the original general title of *Erdélyi Történet – A Transylvanian Tale* and more recently as *The Writing on the Wall* in an English translation of all three books as *They Were Counted, They Were Found Wanting*, and *They Were Divided*, published by Arcadia Books, London, in 1999, 2000 and 2001. A French translation of the first book came out in June 2002 and the second will appear in 2004.

Bánffy's great trilogy, even though the first two volumes came out in 1934 and 1937 and immediately went into several editions, was never previously translated into any other language, since the third book was not published until 1940 when the world was already wracked by war. Miklós Bánffy's daughter Katalin had long wanted to produce an English version of her father's most famous work, and this ambition was eventually to be realized with the collaboration of the author of this introduction.

One last diplomatic mission came in the darkest days of the war. I make no excuse for quoting here what I wrote in the Introduction to the English translation of the first books of the Transylvanian trilogy, *They Were Counted* for although Miklós Bánffy's *Twenty-Five Years (1945)* had only been written some two years after the events now described, that last posthumous work does not relate anything that took place after his return to Transylvania. I wrote then:

'On 9 June 1943, Bánffy went to Bucharest to meet the Romanian foreign minister, Georges Mironescu, in order to try to persuade the Romanians to sign a separate peace with the Allies and thereby forestall a Russian invasion and the destruction that a Soviet-imposed political revolution would inevitably bring about. Despite warnings from Hitler that he knew very well what was going on, both sides did agree to abandon the Axis, but there the agreement stopped. Romania, whose claim to historic rights over the whole region had brought about the transfer of sovereignty after the First World War, wanted the immediate return of Northern Transylvania, while Bánffy argued that it would be better to leave this question in abeyance until the war was over when the Great Powers would make a final decision.

'Bánffy's private dream, and that of many other Transylvanians at that time, was that this would be the opportunity for Transylvania once again to become semiautonomous as it had been in the seventeenth century. The return to Hungarian rule of the northern part of the province by the 1940 Vienna award had not been greeted by many important Transylvanians with quite the same joy that it had been in Budapest. What Bánffy and his friends really wanted was a measure of independence for their beloved country; and although he and the Hungarian Foreign Ministry both wanted to postpone a decision on the future of Transylvania, it was not entirely for the same reasons. Neither wanted to offer such a hostage to Fortune as would be a preliminary pledge to return those disputed lands to Romania. It was an agonizing choice, for Bánffy realized that unless both Hungary and Romania agreed to abandon the Axis, this dream would be forever unobtainable. Nevertheless, the negotiations were continued, and there was a further meeting between him and a Romanian delegation, this time headed by Iuliu Maniu. Once again the stumbling block proved to be the Transylvanian question, and negotiations were broken off on 23 June 1943.'

Everything that Bánffy had feared was now to come to pass. Romania and Hungary were invaded by the Russians, and Budapest was ravaged by the devastating siege of Budapest and the destruction caused by the last grim struggle between the German and Russian armies. Back in Transylvania the castle of Bonczhida was looted of its contents and set on fire by the retreating German army.

Now, ironically, some fifty years after Bánffy's death, and just as the importance of his name and work are once more becoming recognized, phoenix-like the castle of Bonzchida is being restored as a cultural centre by the Transylvanian Trust which, with English artisans and the patronage of the Prince of Wales, is now helping to restore some of the neglected national treasures of the ancient province of Transylvania.

From My Memories

Part One
A Wartime Coronation

◌ಲ Chapter One ಲ◌

It was nine o'clock on a cold November evening.

A few minutes before everything had been the same as on any other night in wartime. Very few people were to be seen in the streets, the theatregoers were in their places and those dining out snuggly indoors. The newsboys' shouts were stilled. One or two belated pedestrians hurried along the empty pavements, and there could occasionally be heard the clatter of horses' hooves from a passing hackney carriage. Apart from this . . . nothing. But at nine o'clock on this day a sudden excitement spread all over the city. People streamed out of the theatres, cinemas and restaurants, hurrying into the streets in silence, some of them still buttoning up their coats as they went, others muttering to each other in low voices. Everyone was going home and, as they went, they stopped in little groups, huddled in front of the news-paper stands where one single announcement was headlined in huge letters of black. On most evenings the people of Budapest, sick of the monotonous sadness of war news, would hurry past the depressing newsstands – but tonight they stopped to look and read. On this evening their minds were no longer preoccupied by the gentle panacea of crossword puzzles, nor by their fears of growing poverty: today, for a while, they put aside their daily anxiety for those on the front line, their fears and worry for hus-bands, sons and brothers who were prisoners-of-war, their anguish for the dead. Today all were overcome by the sense of a great national disaster, by the fear of what was to come and the terror of an unknown future.

What was drawing everyone to those brightly lit newsstands was the announcement of the death of Franz Joseph. Everyone knew that it must be true, and yet it seemed almost impossible to believe that the man whom few men living could recall ascending the throne, who had in himself enshrined the whole concept of the Austro-Hungarian monarchy and of the Hungarian kingdom, and who, for most of those who trudged the streets that night, had been a disembodied symbol rather than a real man of flesh and blood was now no more. The bald facts had to be faced: from this day there would be a new ruler – a young man that as yet few people knew anything about and that the old familiar sovereign who, although infinitely aged and infinitely mysterious, had been to all his peoples the unchangeable and ultimate arbiter of their lives, had finally said his last farewell.

From the police headquarters in the city messages were telephoned to order that all performances should cease in the theatres, cinemas and concert-halls, and that all restaurants should close. As it happened, these messages arrived after the news itself. The music had been stopped, the curtains rung down, and the people themselves were already on their way home. It had not needed a police order for the Budapest public to know how it should show respect for such news as this.

It had been the same for me. At noon that same day the news was spread abroad that the old king had taken a turn for the worse. That night I did not, as I otherwise always did, go to the opera but remained instead at the Kaszino Club, which was always in close touch with the office of the Minister-President. There I was sure to be contacted at once if there were any official instructions for whose dissemination I would be responsible. Immediately I had heard the news of the king's death I had telephoned to officials at the Opera[1] and the National Theatre, and both informed me that the news had already reached them, been announced from the stage and that by now most of the audience had left.

The next day was cloudy. Everything seemed darker than usual.

After the official obituaries and leading articles written to bid adieu to the old monarch came the details of his last hours: simple, dispassionate, crystal-clear – and as cold and as transparent as crystal too – just as he had lived his whole life. He had worked at his desk, as he always did, until he had finished everything he had to do. This was a discipline he had always

imposed upon himself, a duty he had performed daily. At the end
of each day there was no unfinished business to be later put in
order, and at the end of his life it was the same, even in his last
hours. Before he went to bed he took the document case in which
all those confidential papers that had been sent to him that day
were kept. His last words were as simple and unpretentious as his
life: 'I am tired.'

Only that – a phrase he might have uttered any evening during
the last half-century when he, the man who worked hardest of
any in the kingdom, retired to bed.

The funeral was held on the last day of the month.

I had hardly returned to Budapest after the funeral – and certainly had not yet rid myself of the disagreeable impressions
made by the chaotic arrangements inside St Stephen's Cathedral
– where the noise and tumult and confusion were all the more
unexpected because of the fastidious manner in which all state
occasions were usually handled at the court of Vienna – when I
was summoned to the meetings held to start preparations for the
coronation in Hungary. I had to present myself at the old royal
palace in Buda that very morning, 1 December.

We gathered in the anteroom of the Minister-President's
office. Present were several ministers, the chairman of the
Council for National Monuments, the chief of police, several
heads of various departments of the civil service ... and the
press.

Everyone was in a subdued mood, for all had heard the news of
a terrible train disaster that had occurred during the night on the
Brusk line. The express from Vienna, packed with people returning from Franz Joseph's funeral, had run head-on into a passen-
ger train going in the opposite direction. The morning papers
only contained a few lines about the disaster, but there was
enough to tell the world that there had been hundreds who were
badly hurt and at least thirty dead, among whom, it was almost
certain, must be counted Lajos Thallóczy, the eminent historian,
creator of Bosnia and a trusted confidant of the dead emperor.
Many of those at our meeting had had relatives returning from
Vienna that night, but no one knew whether it had been on
that train that they had been travelling. Each time that some

newcomer arrived at the meeting he would be quickly surrounded and asked what new details had become known. Although the atmosphere was calm and controlled, there was an underlying feeling of anxiety and fear . . . and each new arrival brought more horrifying and surprising details. It was a black day.

Around the table everyone sat with set expressions on their face, trying not to show that they all felt that this terrible accident occurring on the night of the old king's funeral, in the third year of war and almost on the eve of the new king's coronation, was a sinister omen. Everyone had the same thought, but no one put it into words lest it should be tempting fate.

However the time was passing and, whatever might have been in our hearts, there was work to be done and decisions to be made. Therefore, setting aside their gloom and personal anxieties, the members of the Council got down to their task. Firstly a committee of administration was formed and then the Council allocated certain specific responsibilities to various individuals. As for the past four years I had been directing the state-sponsored theatres, I was given the artistic direction of the ceremonies and responsibility for the street decorations as well as for the interior of the coronation church itself.

It was a fearful task, for all sorts of reasons. At first it was planned to hold the coronation before Christmas: then it was postponed until 28 December . . . and then postponed again until the thirtieth. This was the last date possible for it seemed that for the country's finance laws to be legally valid they must receive the royal assent, and, for the royal assent to be legally valid, the king must be crowned and in full possession of his prerogatives. We therefore had just twenty-six days in which to get ready, twenty-six days in the depths of winter, with snow, ice and frost and barely eight hours of daylight; and all this in wartime when the only available materials were those which happened by some chance to remain stored in the warehouses, and the labour was restricted to those artists too old or infirm to be defending their country upon some distant battlefield.

I was lucky with the artists and could not have wished for more willing or more competent assistants. Only at one point did I encounter any difficulty.

It was a tradition that at the coronation the country should offer the new ruler the symbolic gift of thousands of pieces of gold, the coins being placed for these purposes in an ornate coffer specially commissioned for each occasion (the gold itself appeared only briefly at the time of its official handing-over to the sovereign; it was returned to the state bank immediately after the ceremony). The case was ordered to be made by Bachruch the jeweller, and Professor Zutt, an art teacher, offered to provide the designs. His first sketches were dreadful, completely shapeless and undistinguished and no more Hungarian in style than if they had been done by some savage islander from Fiji. Of course Professor Zutt was from Switzerland and so probably thought that his ideas faithfully reproduced the old Hungarian local colour. Three or four times he was asked to produce new designs . . . and each time they were uglier than the last. After two weeks' struggle the jeweller announced that on that very day he would not undertake the work. I had no idea what to do. From sheer necessity I sat down and made a design myself, placing special emphasis on two silver angels to be modelled in relief and which I had no doubts would be superbly carried out, on time, by my friend the sculptor Ede Telcs.

Zutt lost his temper and returned in a pique to Switzerland.

Our workshop was established in Disz Square, in one of those large storage buildings pointed out by the big toe of Zala's statue of the angel. There, in front of the military memorial was our headquarters: workshop, offices, design shops, everything. It was unheated and very cold but magnificently lit from great high windows.

Inside life soon became quite unreal.

In the longest room trestle tables had been set up where the architects and designers Dénes Györgyi, Károlyi Kós, Pogány and sometimes Lechner made their designs and drew their plans on paper with giant rulers. On the high wall behind them young Lehoczky drew the outlines of coats of arms seven metres high. While all this was going on, the corners of the room were filled with craftsman kneading *papier-mâché* and making outsize plaster casts. In rooms nearby statues were being hurriedly run up on skeletons made of wooden lathes nailed together, and so quickly was the work being carried out that it seemed as if the figures were gaining weight as each day went by. At one end of the hall typewriters clattered without interruption. Nearby there were heaps of felt and samples of cotton and velvet and, beside them, boxes filled with modelling clay, slabs of plasticine, pails of plaster of Paris; and, to get from one doorway to another, one had to pick one's way between piles of glue-smeared strips of paper.

It was a weird mixture of medieval sorcerer's cavern and some disordered builder's shed, and if anyone unfamiliar with our work had come in unawares he must have thought he had stumbled into an asylum where raving lunatics were incarcerated and where each and everyone of them were indulging in their own private manias, absorbed in drawing, modelling, and hammering away while no one cared what they were doing or attempted to stop them.

In this sorcerer's kitchen my somewhat comic role was that of Head Cook who stuck his nose into every pan and sipped at every brew. This was all I could do, but do it I had to, for the ultimate responsibility for every detail rested with me, and I was sure to be blamed afterwards (as indeed I was) if anything did not go as planned. My task was to assemble and coordinate the whole, to bring harmony to every phase of the coronation, to provide the continuous frame in which the ceremonies were to be clothed. Accordingly I was obliged to put my finger into every pie, to meddle with every craftsman's concerns.

During these four weeks I lived only for the work in hand and therefore knew very little of what was going on in the world outside. Despite being a member of parliament, I really know very little about all the discussions that raged over the appointment of the Palatine whose duty was to carry the crown until it was placed on the king's head. This was not merely a battle of words. The opposition parties were so united in their determination that the post should not go to Tisza, who sprang from a family of the minor nobility, that they brought forth an archduke as a rival candidate. And when Archduke Joseph demurred and refused to be named, in view of the controversy, they put forward a hundred unexpected names, some of them of the most venerable elderly gentlemen of whose existence no one had

heard for decades and who must themselves have been astonished to read their names in the newspapers in such a connection.

Tisza's appointment was also attacked in other ways. Someone invented the slogan 'a Protestant cannot hold the crown' and
learned historians and lawyers were mobilized to produce evidence to clinch the matter. Rumour had it that a ruling would
come from the very highest ranks of the church and state to
prove their point. As it happened it was the Prince-Cardinal
Csernoch whose verdict settled the dispute; and decided in
favour of Count Tisza. When the Catholics demurred and
brought up the religious disqualification the cardinal silenced
them in his strong Slovakian accent, saying: 'I know best: I am
the cardinal!' As no one could think up any argument stronger
than that, the storm abated and was heard of no more.

At the time I knew very little of all this directly, for I was so
involved in a thousand different worries and running to and fro
from place to place and office to office that these things only
reached me like a far distant echo. The committee of administration had decided that all of the traditional ceremonies should
be carried out in the quarter of old Buda where the royal palace
was situated. However, no details were settled, and so I was given
the task of proposing where each of the different ceremonies
should be held.

There was no problem, of course, about the actual crowning:
that would take place as tradition demanded, in the Coronation
Church. Likewise St George's Square was the obvious choice for
the Ceremony of the Sword. I still had to find a place for the
moment when the sovereign has to take his coronation oath in
full view of the assembled populace. I thought that the most
beautiful site would be the Halasz Bastya – the Fishermen's
Bastion – which looked out over the whole city behind the
Coronation Church itself. Unfortunately, the chief of police was
nervous about a possible demonstration of outrage and declared
that such a place was impossible, as it could not adequately be
provided.

But how beautiful it would have been!

I envisaged the invited guests placed under the arches of
the outward curving wings of the bastions, the members of

parliament and representatives of the country districts grouped on the steps with their multicoloured local banners, everyone in traditional Hungarian gala costume and, lower down, beyond the statue of Hunyadi, there would be room for thousands upon thousands of ordinary spectators. Above everyone would be the balcony, and right in the centre, under the white wreath of intricately carved stonework and flanked by the Prince-Cardinal and the Palatine, the king would step out, his hand raised as he took the solemn oath. It would be a sublime moment, unforgettable too for the monarch himself as, St Stephen's crown upon his head, he appeared before his people to dedicate himself to their service. At his feet would be the Danube, behind it the sprawling capital and, further away, the great ocean-like expanse of the Hungarian Plain. If the oath could have been taken there it would truly have been given before the whole nation.

Since I was unable to carry out my dream I had to look for some other solution, and I at length suggested the votive column in Trinity Square on one side of which stands the Coronation Church. This was accepted and on the same day I sketched out draft designs for the balustraded podium, which Móric Pogány was to realize so brilliantly and which to this day shows off the great baroque votive column to such advantage. For the day of coronation the podium was constructed in wood, but this structure was afterwards rebuilt in stone and, unhappily, in so doing several small errors which had slipped into the original sketches failed to be eliminated and so have been perpetuated for all time in the permanent edifice.

The building of an artificial hillock in St George's Square for the sword ceremony presented few problems. Only the placing of the public stands round the square had to be settled. We looked up the dimensions of the one erected for the 1867 coronation and then made the top somewhat wider for I had been told by my father – and heard it from others too – that everyone had been filled with alarm and anxiety when Franz Joseph had taken his horse up the mound at an imposing gallop. With just two strides he reached the top and when, with St Stephen's Sword in his hand, he slashed to the north, to the east, to the south, and to the west – to the four corners of the world – his grey charger, confused by the cheering and the crowds and by the blasts of cannon-shot, reared up four times. Everyone nearby was afraid that the animal would jump clear over the balustrades and into the square below, but Franz Joseph had been a superb horseman who kept his foaming terrified steed turning upon the same spot, his hands, calming and masterful, close to the animal's withers, and his own bearing, cool and royal and fully in command, never for an instant changed or faltered.

The task that presented the greatest challenge was the decoration of the inside of the Coronation Church itself. With Jenö Lechner as chief designer, we selected the motifs of the decorations from medieval illustrated manuscripts and decided to clothe the entire interior of the church in dark red, which we felt would give the finest possible background to the multicoloured dresses and uniforms of the crowd who would fill every corner of the building. We ordered great bolts of the same material as would cover the church walls to drape the columns which, as they were covered with frescoes painted in a most stylish but agitated manner, would have clashed unbearably with the other decorations if left in sight. The builder of the church, old Schulek, was still alive and, having been the prime instigator of these murals, decided to be deeply offended, running everywhere denouncing us as 'vandals' and threatening to make an appalling scandal if an inch of his beloved frescoes was not to be seen. If I remember correctly, it was on the last evening but one before the ceremony that I received official 'advice' – although no actual order – that the drapery had best be removed from the columns.

I did not know what to do and certainly did not want to make any decision without having consulted Lechner who had been the originator of the whole scheme of decoration. He could not be found until late that evening, and so at the close of the performance, he came to see me in my box at the opera. Sitting side by side on the sofa in the little drawing-room behind the box we commiserated with each other at this last-minute interference in our plans. At last, resigned to the unfairness of life, we decided to go just once more and look at our handiwork for the last time before it was all changed.

It was eleven o'clock at night when we got there and found that the men were still hard at work, assiduously attending to last-minute details in the dimly lit church. They were bathed in a strange almost mythical atmosphere. We looked around. The ogival baldaquines over the two thrones, the drapes behind the altar and the sweeping folds of the material with which all the pillars had been swathed made the roof seem at an infinite height; and the dark-red velvet material contributed so much to this effect of sublime beauty, so human, so warm and yet so regal, that we realized that it would have been 'vandalism' indeed to do anything which might spoil it. On the spot I decided to change nothing and brave the consequences – for I was convinced that anyone who saw what we had achieved would agree that we had been right.

And so it turned out. The interior of the Coronation Church was the most successful of all our decorative efforts, and everyone who was there would never afterwards forget the effect it made. In the last week we had so much to do and were so feverishly busy that I hardly spoke to a soul who was not one of my fellow-workers. Even so, just before Christmas, news arrived, reaching even as far as me, which dampened everyone's spirits: it was the dismissal of Burian as minister of foreign affairs and his replacement by Czernin. After more than two years of war morale was not high, and the nomination of Czernin raised a spectre that most people hoped had been laid by the outbreak of hostilities. Those anxious rumours that had circulated in the years before the war, those sad indications of a doubtful future for the independence of Hungary suddenly seemed once more a dire possibility. It was as if the ghost of FF (Franz Ferdinand) had risen from its uneasy grave and become the rallying point for all those spirits who hate everything that was Hungarian and who had striven for some form of *Slav Imperium*. Czernin was the prophet of this movement and one of its first spokesmen. He had written a popular book on the subject and had been an intimate friend and confidential adviser of the dead heir, who himself is said to have declared that he would bring up his successor to follow his policies so that Hungarians would have him to reckon with for the next two hundred years. This saying was so well known that as soon as Czernin's appointment was announced it was heard once more on everyone's lips. It seemed as if there was truth in the old rumours after all. The effect was slightly modified when the Empress Zita, as queen of Hungary, at once asked to be accepted as president of the 'Pro-Transylvania' charitable organization as soon as she arrived in Budapest – but the damage had been done, and in many people's hearts the seeds of suspicion and doubt had once again taken root.

***

The coronation rehearsal had been timed for 28 December, the day after the royal couple had arrived in the capital.

The new king received me most kindly, saying that he remembered me well. As he spoke his face was suffused with a warm-hearted smile which did not leave his lips even when he was silent.

His manner was simple and sympathetic.

The rehearsal, behind closed doors, went smoothly.

In an hour it was over, and I was left alone. As I stood there, a 4,000-watt arc light hanging above the altar exploded in the heat. It had been hidden in the tent-like draperies above and it had burned brightly through the rehearsal. Tiny fragments of glass fell and covered the altar with needle-sharp little crystal daggers.

Something had to be done at once to ensure there was no repetition of the accident during the coronation itself. It was essential that the scene at the altar should be strongly lit – and it was obvious that we could not hope for a bright sunny day at the end of December. Therefore, following the chief-electrician's advice, a sheet of heavy glass an inch thick was rapidly polished and hoisted into position among the draperies overhead. This effectively protected the space below where the arc lights were hidden.

This decision nearly had a fatal effect on the following day.

This, however, was not the only last-minute change that had to be made. Late in the afternoon, when we had placed the holy crown in the nearby Loretto chapel, I received a message from the king's Master of the Horse who wanted to see me as quickly as possible.

I went to his office in the palace and he explained that it was the 'wish' of his Majesty that the giant coat of arms and supporting angels that had been mounted high above the main entrance to the palace and which were an essential part of the decorations of the adjacent St George's Square, should be taken down in case the king's horse should take fright at them and bolt! I murmured something to the effect that there was nothing to fear for these decorations were fixed some fifteen or twenty metres above the ground, well above the stonework of the great monumental palace gateway, and in any case could only be seen from afar. The Master of the Horse, himself an accomplished rider, merely shrugged his shoulders noncommittally and repeated what he had already said. It was all quite clear, and I promised that by morning there would be no decorations above the gateway.

However, this was not all. It seemed the king wished to mount his horse in front of the church without having to put his foot in the stirrup and swing himself into the saddle. It was therefore suggested that, during the night, I should have a sort of footstool made, with steps upon which the monarch would climb and whence he could slip into the saddle unaided.

This order was more difficult to put into effect. Had we been living in Vienna, with a choice of all the perfectly trained horses of the Marstall – the Royal Stables – at our disposal, we might no doubt have lighted upon an animal that could be relied upon to remain absolutely still beside such an unfamiliar mounting block. But we were in Budapest, capital of a nation of horsemen, a multitude of whom on the following day were expecting to see their newly crowned monarch leap into the saddle, his crown upon his head, on the steps of the church in which he had just been anointed. To place a little footstool where all could see it, a footstool whose only function must obviously be to help the king mount his horse, would have seemed to most of my country men inexpressibly ludicrous and would lead to odious comparisons and the sort of ribaldry undesirable on such an occasion. Some other solution had to be found, so after talking the matter over with the master mason, we decided to build a low wall on each side of the canopy, which had been placed above the church door.

Behind this a small flight of steps would be concealed. The wall was unusual, and otherwise quite without function, but the people in the square would think it had been placed there merely to enclose the church.

This little wall was quickly run up in a rather makeshift manner. Luckily there was no frost that night, and so by morning the cement had hardened and all was ready.

I arrived home very late. That night I slept little, as I wanted to be in the church early so as to be able to supervise any last touches that might be necessary.

It was just before four o'clock when I drove away from my house.

There was no sign of life in the inky darkness that enveloped the city. The only sound was that of the fiacre horses' hooves on the cobblestones. Here and there a lamp blinked in the darkness, solitary, forlorn . . . and yet how much brilliance and splendour, how much light would bathe the capital later in the day! I had dressed myself in traditional Hungarian gala dress, covered with a mass of gold braid. Looking out of the window of the hired cab my thoughts went straight to those thousands of my countrymen, my brothers, who were at that moment passing this winter's night in the mud, snow, and freezing cold of the trenches on the front line.

⚘ Chapter Two ⚘

It was still night when I entered the church by a little side door. To step from the darkness outside into the nave, which was now bathed in light gave me a feeling difficult to describe. It was rather like one of those marvellous moments recounted in legend when the tired hero, after battling his way through the horror of an obscure thorny wilderness, suddenly finds himself in the radiance of an enchanted castle.

The night before, when I had seen it last while giving final orders for the construction of the little wall outside the entrance, there had only been a few shaded lamps where the craftsmen were still at work. Now the whole church was ablaze with light.

In spite of the fact that I had discussed all the details – most of them several times – with my friend Professor Lechner and in spite, too, of having attended the rehearsal when the throne and their canopies and *prie-dieux*, the purple tent lined with white silk which hung over the altar, and the towering hangings of red velvet that draped the columns of the aisle, had all been in place, still, now, after another night of uninterrupted work had put the final touches of the great church's gala dress and the huge crystal chandeliers above sparkled with light, even I was surprised, indeed overcome, by the sublime harmony of the effect we had created.

On each side of the aisle, rising to the level of the windows above the side-chapels, rose banks of seats all covered with red velvet, and between the seats were narrow flights of steps all covered with the same red material. The double line of rising stands lent to the nave the aspect of a long open valley that was pervaded with a sense of expectancy as if it were waiting some long-awaited fulfilment. The church seemed to be stretching out its arms to welcome the festive throng who would soon be crowding to their places headed by all the members of parliament and, finally, the king. If the eye followed the line of the flowing drapes of the columns, their rich velvet folds as regular and as immobile as the pipes of some great celestial organ, to the soaring arches of the gothic vaulting so high above the great chandeliers, then it would finally come to rest on iridescent circles of white flames floating in the air like the haloes around the heads of medieval saints and filling every ogival curve of the stonework with a powdery radiance.

Somewhere high up on the banks of seats workmen were still hammering the velvet covering into place, while, behind the altar, seamstresses were stitching away hurriedly trying to finish the ceremonial cushions before the ceremonies began. The electricians, having just completed the reserve light-circuit, were carrying away their long ladders. There was very little time left, and anything that still needed doing had to be done quickly.

Very soon the ushers started to arrive. These were young men who would be responsible for showing the guests to their appointed places and ensuring that no unseemly scramble marred the dignity of the occasion. I selected a few of them to act as my personal runners who would keep me in immediate touch with the chief electrician who would be hidden from sight in the Bela III chapel, and some others to be posted outside in the square where they would stand like heralds to indicate which way the guests should go. Others I kept in reserve in case of unforeseen disaster.

After the ushers came the photographers; and with them was the painter Felix Schwormstädt, the eminent artist employed by the German magazine *Illustrierte* who was to be the only representative of the world press officially permitted to record the scene for posterity. The photographers were huddled together in the pulpit – which had been covered so that they could not be seen – and poor Schwormstädt had to squeeze himself somehow in behind the velvet curtain in which it had been shrouded. There was very little room for them all but, as the coronation was itself an official session of parliament as well as being a religious and state ceremony, neither he nor the photographers and their equipment would have been permitted in the aisles. Despite these difficulties Schwormstädt managed to do a magnificent job, and the painting that was reproduced in the next issue of *Illustrierte* was the only one that I ever saw that did justice to that splendid but fleeting pageant that had gladdened our hearts that winter's day so long ago.

Now the Keepers of the Regalia arrived in the church.

We had to place the crown and the other symbols of power and majesty in the Loretto chapel. There they had rested, each on its separate stand, on cushions which had been fitted with special fastenings to ensure that the sacred emblems could be carried in the horseback procession without risk of mishap.

This was the last time that anyone was to see the crown of St Stephen used for its essential purpose. It was a fabulous object not only for its historical associations and for the many legends that had become attached to it but also for its own sake, for it was a work of art unique in the world. Despite, or maybe because of, the fact that it is made up of two diadems, it has a wondrous and unexpected beauty. What was so surprising was the freshness of its enamels, as glowing and translucent as when they were first seen fresh from the hands of those unknown artists, goldsmiths, jewellers, and enamellists a thousand years before. Unbelievable, too, was the warmth and glow of its pearls – hundreds of them set in lines on every possible edge, still alive and radiant despite being kept for centuries in airless sealed cases. I remembered last seeing this fabulous object twenty years before on the occasion when Hungary celebrated the first thousand years of her history, and the crown had been displayed for three days in this very church. Then I had been one of the gentlemen appointed to stand guard around the sacred emblem of our monarchy and every detail of its shape and decoration were etched in my memory. Twenty years had gone by since the days of the millennium and now, with perhaps a more mature appreciation, I admired the great crown even more than I had before.

There was, however, another extraordinary object, also unique of its kind, among the 'clenodiums' – the sacred emblems of the state – this was the sceptre. When it first came into possession of the kings of Hungary is not known, although tradition also attributes it to the time of St Stephen. The ball is of crystal, as big as a man's fist, and rampant lions are carved all over it. It is Arab work from the eighth or ninth century, and the shaft and setting are of gold and are contemporary with the ball. It is an object to admire and ponder over. Whence did it come? How did it arrive in Hungary? What fate carried it from place to place and country to country and through what hands did it pass, what adventures had it known? The sparkling crystal above the golden shaft symbolized that above even the noblest of human values ruled the dispassionate clarity of the Word and Will of God.

It was now past seven o'clock and even though the women were still stitching away behind the altar and the ceremonial cushions were not yet ready to be put in place, the main doors had to be opened.

At once a stream of invited guests invaded the church.

Among the first was Móric Esterházy, the Minister-President elect.

I had just greeted him when the dark figure of a thin young man appeared alone at the top of the steps which led up to the main entrance of the church, silhouetted in the doorway against the light of the morning sky. He was dressed in a dark-green gold-embroidered tail suit and was holding his three-cornered hat under his arm. He moved forward and joined us and for a moment I did not recognize the man behind the finery, for I had previously only met him in the simplest of plain clothes. It was Czernin, the new minister for foreign affairs.

He asked me where he was to sit and then shook hands with Esterházy.

From the way he stood and moved, and from the knowing smile upon his face, I at once understood everything that was passing through his mind. It was as if he had said to Esterházy out loud for everyone to hear: 'See? I've made it! Now it's your turn. It'll come soon, you'll see!' In that one little moment I felt it so clearly that it was as if he'd spoken, and I was at once seized by the same anticipatory anxiety that so many others had felt as soon as Czernin's nomination to office had been announced. Once again I was filled with dread, fearing what so many others feared, namely that the gossip about Franz Ferdinand's prophecy was now brought to fulfilment. I tried to chase the thought away, telling myself that it would be madness at this critical time during the war to think of dispensing with Tisza, who alone among contemporary Hungarian statesmen had the greatness of soul and strength of character to carry the burden of the nation's survival. After the war perhaps . . . but now? No! It was impossible!

More people were flooding in, the men in splendid uniforms and the women in their elaborate best, and the seats in the tiered stands were beginning to fill up. Those few artists we had managed to fit inside the church – Alajos Strobl, Oszkár Glatz and the others – hurried to their allotted places high up under the windows on the right. The court ladies, those in waiting on the queen, arrived in a group and, dressed as they were in traditional Hungarian court apparel, it was as if a bevy of old family portraits had suddenly come alive. They wore fantastic diamond tiaras and diadems on their heads and their pearl and jewel-embroidered capes glittered like a cascade of rippling light. It was the last parade of Hungary's thousand-year-old history, a pageant that was never to be repeated and which will now never be seen again.

As we stood at the great doors telling everyone where to find their places I was suddenly accosted in French by a tall, broad-shouldered man in the uniform of a Hungarian general. It was the king of Bulgaria . . . and he was very cross indeed.

He would like to see the crown before he went to his place, he said shortly.

I led him to the Loretto chapel.

He inspected everything carefully, for he was a great connoisseur of all things artistic and a man of exceptional taste. In his total absorption in studying the Crown Jewels, for a few moments he forgot his anger. Then, turning back to me, he spoke passionately of how he had been insulted. He had been seated in the gallery of the oratorium, next to the little six-year-old crown prince; hidden away where no one could see him: he, the only foreign monarch who had the courtesy to come to Hungary for the coronation. He was very angry, repeating several times that he had been hidden away with a little child; where no one could see the presence of a foreign monarch, a traditional and long-time friend of Hungary who had come in these times of trouble to make a public gesture of alliance and solidarity. 'And this is all the thanks I get! This is how they treat me!' he said furiously.

It was extremely painful for me to listen to King Ferdinand's outburst, especially as only a year before he had received me in the palace at Sofia and had treated me with exceptional kindness and courtesy. I tried to explain that I had not been responsible for the seating arrangements and that, in any case, the little arch-duke Otto, as hereditary crown prince, was the highest ranking in Hungary after the king . . .

'That's all nonsense!' interrupted King Ferdinand. 'I know it's not your fault! But I know, too, whose fault it is. It's that camarilla at court . . . especially Montenuovo, who's always been my enemy. He would stop at nothing to humiliate me . . . he, and those others . . . they're my enemies, all right. Always have been. Always.'

Still trying to soothe him, I escorted King Ferdinand to his place in the oratorium gallery. There, however, although he was still fuming with rage, I had to take my leave. After more angry words he at last finished his tirade by saying: 'If I'd known it, I wouldn't have come!' Then, quite suddenly, he looked at me with a friendly smile and in a most charming way started to praise my ancient Hungarian dress as if to make it quite clear that whatever else he thought he didn't blame me.

I returned to the steps by the great doors and reached them in time to greet the little crown prince.

He was a lovely child; still at that time with golden-blond hair and rosy cheeks. Since then I have heard that his hair has turned dark, and that he greatly resembles his mother.

He was dressed in a resplendent brocade mantle, lined with ermine and decorated with egret feathers, his whole outfit having been designed by Benczúr, and in tiny shoes he tripped along hurriedly so as to keep up with General Count Wallis, whose finger he clutched in a tight little fist.

He was adorable as he moved swiftly through the crowd.

Now the officiating clergy all lined up outside the church to receive the royal couple, while in the Loretto chapel the Keepers of the Regalia and the standard bearers ensured that everyone with a part to play in the ceremony had been provided with the badge or clenodium they had to carry. Everyone was there except for Iván Skerlecz, the Ban[2] of Croatia, who was nowhere to be seen. Later he made the excuse that they would not let him in through the police cordon outside, but this sounded unconvincing in view of the fact that he made his appearance in the church during the coronation ceremony. His absence at the start however, caused a momentary delay in setting out the order of the procession and someone else – I forget who – had rapidly to be given the robe that the Ban should have carried for the royal carriage was even then drawing up outside the church.

I was unable to see the arrival of the king and queen, as I then had to hurry to reach my own place from where I could control the lighting. I was hidden, standing to the left and behind the throne, from where I could see nothing at all of the procession down the aisle. All I knew was that I could hear the roar of cheers from the crowd in Trinity Square outside the church and the bustle and stir as the royal couple approached their places. The congregation in the church, all now on their feet, so closed my view of what was going on that all I could see was the edge of the queen's throne and the outline of the steps below it.

Suddenly there was silence. Then the powerful fanfare of the organ announced that the king had arrived. In front of me the Chamberlain – it was my father – moved forward on the lowest step before the throne, staff of office in hand. Across from him, on the other side of the throne, the apostolic cross rose high on its long black shaft – the royal procession must be near at hand. I peered round, but the throne in front of me was still unoccupied. A few moments went by. Then the white figure of a woman appeared briefly in front of me, clad in lace and satin and wearing a crown of diamonds[3]. For a moment she was motionless; then she sank to her knees in a graceful movement that was both womanly and regal. It was a moment that touched the heart to see the queenly movement of this radiant woman as, her coronation mantel streaming out behind her, she bent over the purple prayer stool that had been embroidered with silver lilies and crosses. A long veil of white lace trailed diagonally from her head . . .

There was another peal from the organ, this time accompanied by strings and the voices of the choir.

The coronation ceremony began.

First there was the mass, the thousand-year-old Latin text interspersed with music and song, and sometimes merely by soft chromatic scales and melodies from the organ.

The king went up to the altar. Then he returned. Once again he moved up to the altar, but this time his shoulders had been draped in St Stephen's robe. Now the crown was placed on his head.

At that very moment a shaft of light shone through the window above the altar, a pale wintry ray, but sunlight nonetheless, transforming the scene into a magic shining picture. Facing me, seated under the high windows, were all the chief dignitaries of the Catholic Church, and the combination of the sunlight from the outside and the electric glow from the chandeliers banished all shadows, metamorphosing the multiplicity of ritual hieratic garments, the brocades of the all-white piuviales; the white, gold-embroidered mitres, the infulaes, all into one translucent crystalline, unreal, angelic fog. It was an unforgettable sight, even though it lasted but for one brief moment only, the moment when the crown was placed on the young king's head.

When Tisza stepped up to the altar, his tall slim figure standing high and straight, dressed in dark velvet; when he raised his right arm and waved his black hat three times in the air calling out with his manly deep voice: 'Long live the king!' the sun had already disappeared from the window above, never to be seen again.

The ceremony lasted for a long time, but for how long I could not possibly have said. In the resplendent, unreal, fairyland environment no one noticed the passage of time. There was music and song; incense rose in clouds and dissolved among the high vaulting of the church. The organ rumbled and sang and from outside could sometimes be heard the distant sound of a saluting cannon. Inside the church the constantly moving but silent groups of clergy moved solemnly in ritual observance, bishops sparkling in their formal robes stood hieratic and immobile as the ancient ritual moved to its inevitable conclusion, and one felt oneself living in a constantly changing but changeless, timeless dream. And when it ended, so it was like awakening from an enchanted sleep.

***

The king and queen retired to the sacristy, and the **great congre-**gation started to leave the church and take up their places in the square outside.

As the crowd inside began to disappear the ladies of the court and the ladies-in-waiting started to descend slowly from their places in the gallery on the left of the church. Now I could see them better. They came down, one by one or in pairs, down the steps from the gallery and into the centre aisle, all in dresses of gold and white and silver, studded with jewels and glittering like figures from ancient times suddenly come alive again, creating reality from imagination. Great family jewels, diamonds, pearls, emeralds and rubies adorned their heads in clusters of shining white and multicoloured precious stones, and from their shoulders long outer robes of velvet and brocade and ermine fell in soft folds to the ground behind them. As they moved slowly out of the church in procession they were accompanied by the softest of organ music as if the disappearance of all this beauty imposed silence in the now emptying basilica.

All at once, apart from those silent motionless officials who had not left their appointed places, the great church was empty. As when I had first come in early that morning all that was to be seen was the carmine of the carpeting and the red glow of the drapes which, after the pageantry of the last hours, now seemed almost severe.

From a door at the side, until now hidden by purple drapes, appeared the *equites aurati* – the knights of the Golden Spur – to receive the accolade from their sovereign.

There must have been about fifty of them, all officers coming from service in the front lines. Most of them were in iron-grey uniforms, faded, mended, with worn leather belts and blackened straps. One could see at once how old their boots were despite the fact that they had been vigorously brushed and polished to obtain an elusive and transitory shine. In the forefront were men with wooden legs, leaning on crutches, limping, knocking against each other, coughing and breathing heavily with the effort of movement. Through that side door and out into the glow before the altar there poured out all the sad grey tragedy of war to flood the space where a few moments before all had been shine and glitter.

Some of them, those who had been most cruelly wounded, sank down onto seats provided for them. The others, whom fate had left physically intact, lined up at attention in stiff military *garde-à-vous*. Their shirtfronts and tunics were stiff with medals and ribbons and orders, the outward symbol of their gallantry. No one spoke. They were all utterly silent, not a word passing between them. All of them just stood there, looking straight ahead with a stare that was both eloquent and at the same time passive. Their eyes were the eyes of men who, day after day, looked death in the face.

This indeed was an echo of the *Divina Commedia*, but in reverse order, the *Paradiso* then finally the *Inferno*.

In their lines they waited, standing or sitting, looking neither to the right nor to the left, like soldiers before a battle waiting for the word of command . . .

The king, crowned with St Stephen's crown and wearing St Stephen's mantel, came back into the church and ascended the throne. The first name was called out.

A grey broken ruin of a man pulled himself up on two crutches. An orderly rushed to his side to prevent him from falling and guided him forward. At the steps of the throne he faltered just as St Stephen's Sword touched his shoulder the ritual three times. Then somehow he was lifted to his feet and supported by his orderly as he tottered out of the church.

I could not stay to see the whole of the ceremony of investiture as I had work to do outside and was also only too thankful to be able to escape witnessing any more of the nightmarish scene. I went swiftly into the square.

Outside the square was by no means full and in many places there were spaces where the public might have gathered. Now the great hangings of coats of arms were no longer hidden by eager spectators. Somehow I felt it was rather like a large out-door ballroom in which the ball itself was something of a failure. The overwhelming effect brought by the presence of the great crowds was missing. How much more beautiful, and impressive, I reflected once again, it would have been on the Fishermen's Bastion. There, on the wide steps with the great curve of Albrecht Street and Park below, the whole city could have found a place and filled every nook and cranny with loyal crowds – and beyond, on the quay the Pest, hundreds of thousands of people could have witnessed the public swearing of the Oath which was, after all, the most sublime and important moment of the Hungarian coronation.

This oath was part of the very oldest of royal traditions. It must have originated in those nomadic days when the king was elected in an open space at the heart of the villages in which the people lived. The law was that the new king, holy crown on his head and regal cape on his shoulders, under God's free sky and in the sight of the entire population of the land, swears to keep and uphold and enforce the law. To maintain the law was the first and unalterable duty of the sovereign, who thereby protected his people, and it was to preserve this inalienable freedom that so many battles had been fought and so many hard-ships endured by the Hungarian folk over more than a thousand years . . .

In front of the church the procession formed up under the state canopy: firstly, the standard-bearers, then the great gold Hungarian coat of arms, the Lord Chamberlain and his suit, then the *barones regni* with their official emblems; and finally the young king.

They moved slowly over a three-coloured carpet to the centre of the square and then in stately procession mounted the steps behind the stone balustrade.

Even today I can still see them as they appeared on the high-est part of the eastern balcony. There were five, and none of them is still living today: Tisza with the text of the oath, Prince

Esterházy with the sword, and, between the Prince-Cardinal and the Archbishop of Kalocsa, the crowned king.

The cheering stopped, and the oath was read slowly, sentence-by-sentence. As each sentence was read out the king repeated the words loudly and in a clear voice. In his left hand he held the apostolic 'Pax' cross, and his right was held high to witness his oath before the people. He held his head high, and a youthful smile, unchanging and full of hope, was on his lips.

When the king and his immediate entourage had returned to the church all the members of parliament and the delegates from the provincial cities, counties and districts moved off towards St George's Square. Now the horses, all gaily caparisoned in multicoloured shabracks – those long heraldic saddlecloths we see in pictures of medieval tournaments – were led forward.

The first to mount were the archdukes. Then came the turn of the high court officials, or the deputies they had appointed to replace them, for only Endre Csekonics, the Master of the Table, my father, and the Ban of Croatia were prepared to do this *in propria persona*. There was not really enough space and this operation resulted in not a little confusion, partly due to the fact that the Ban, instead of carrying before him the golden sphere attached to its cushion as he should have done, handed it to his *écuyer*, who did not seem at all impressed at the honour of having to carry the symbolic golden apple – the *orszag almajat* – and simply held it in his hand as if it had been a football out of play. Many people were shocked at the sight. I suppose the man must have returned it later, but I did not see what happened, as I also had to hurry off to St George's Square. There too the place was not full, although admittedly the grandstands round the square and the artificial hillock at its centre took up much of the space.

Most of those present were gathered at the corner nearest to the royal palace, attracted no doubt by a most charming sight.

From a window on the first floor of the palace Queen Zita looked down on the square. She had stood the little crown prince, the Archduke Otto, in the windowsill and held him enlaced with one of her beautiful hands. They were alone, framed in the window, just the mother and her beautiful child. There was the dark-eyed queen with the diamond crown and, held in her arms, the golden-blond boy in his traditional Hungarian costume. It had not been planned, but nothing could have been more beautiful or more touching. In the square the cheering grew louder and louder as more and more people crowded in. The stands were full and men and women in gala dress swarmed all over the square. The multitude roared and, from her window, the queen nodded and smiled her acknowledgement of the applause. It was a scene of surging life when the blood is at its hottest – *vitam et sanguinem* – when all Hungarians present forgot themselves utterly in an expression of ardent patriotism.

There was so much noise in the square that we hardly noticed that the cheering was growing ever louder outside and that therefore the king must already be on his way from the parade square where the oath had been taken.

Everyone lined up so as to make way for the mounted procession. I was in the front row by the road, and there was so little space that the horses brushed against us all as they passed.

First of all came the high court officials riding side by side. Behind them Tisza rode alone, his dark-clad figure so sombre that it seemed black after the multicoloured parade of those who preceded him. I looked hard at his face, but the expression of his eyes could not be seen behind his thick glasses. However, the corners of his mouth were drawn into deep ridges as if he were subject to some unutterably bitter sorrow. His lips were pressed hard together tightly closed lest they should reveal some burning secret. I thought that he was like a man weighted down by the hopelessness of his task, by the pain and endless worry of a duty that could never ever succeed . . . I do not think that I have ever seen a more tragic face than that of Tisza as he rode through that cheering happy throng.

I stayed at the corner of the palace of Archduke Joseph and so was only able to see the sword ceremony from a distance. The mounted figure of the king suddenly emerged from the forest of banners in the square. Up the little balustrade hillock he rode. Then with the sword he slashed the air around him while a palace outrider in a green tail suit turned the horse to the north and east and south and west, to the four corners of the world.

A few moments later the steed was once more led down into the crowd and the figure of the king lost to sight among the ceremonial banners.

Not long afterwards the king became visible once again when, with the joy of a task well accomplished, he emerged from the crowd that surrounded him, waved a greeting to the figure of his wife at the window overhead and then quickly galloped away in the direction of the palace gates.

Everyone felt immensely relieved when his crowned head vanished through the great doorway, not the least because it was foolhardy to break into a gallop on that sloping slippery pavement, and the crowd, horsemen to a man, wondered what would happen if the charger were to stumble . . .

We next gathered in the largest reception hall of the palace. This was crowded not only with all those who had official commands to be present in the church and at the other two ceremonies but also with several hundred ladies who were expected to assemble here before being presented to the king and queen after their symbolic feast.

It was much more difficult to keep order here. All those who were waiting formed themselves into groups, some trying everything they knew to remain in the front rows, others refusing to move from the passages, and still more taking up their positions on the sofas that lined the walls. And, having selected their places, no one was prepared to move.

By now, most of those present were getting tired and obstinate and there were those who, spreading their legs wide, refused to move even from the established places of the officials of the court. My ushers were hard put to keep order, but somehow they achieved it and by the time the royal procession entered the hall most people were in their right places.

The royal couple, the two archbishops, the Palatine and the Prince-Cardinal took their seats along one side of a table that had been placed on a dais a few steps above the level of the floor.

Each dish was presented by the appropriate court official, by the chamberlains, members of parliament and certain magnates who approached the table in a long line. Only the gigantic roast, which had been cut from an ox roasted on the Vermezo, was brought up by the Chamberlain of the Table himself. At the lowest step of the dais he was handed the yard-long golden dish by the two lackeys who had carried it into the hall. It was very heavy, but somehow, given strength by his sense of duty and personal honour, he just managed the three steps, although it looked to all of us as if his legs would give way under him. Somehow, too, he managed to present the dish to the king, bowing as he did so.

The Chamberlain of the Wine filled the golden goblets.

The king toasted the nation, and everyone present responded with loud cheering.

This was the last official ceremony of the occasion, and immediately after it was over the court officials-in-waiting retired with the king and the members of parliament hurried down to the House so as to pass the necessary legislation confirming the act of enthronement and the consecration of a new monarch.

All the ladies and some of the men remained in the palace. At about half-past three Jekelfalussy and I were sent for and received in audience by the king. His Majesty thanked me most gracefully and warmly for my work. He did not seem in the least fatigued. When he dismissed us I went back to the drawing-room near the main staircase, knowing that those ladies who were to be presented would retire there after leaving the throne room and I wanted just once more to rejoice in the sight of such a pageant of beautiful women all dressed up in the panoply of jewels and trains.

A long table had been laid with a buffet meal in the drawing-room and, although I had eaten nothing for more than twelve hours, any fatigue was soon dispelled by a cup of tea and some slices of ham.

In the throne room, the *Defilier Cour*, as they called the ceremony of presentation, had already started. It had not previously been known in Hungary.

In order of rank, each lady to be presented enters the room. She walks to the throne where, on this occasion, only the queen is seated. The king stands behind her, and the crown prince, the little Archduke Otto, is at her feet. There, as the Lord Chamberlain has read out her name, she makes a low reverence and then walks back to the far end of the adjacent drawing-room.

When the ceremony started there were long waits between each lady, and where I was in the drawing-room there would be five or six minutes between the arrival of one lady and another. However the royal couple were anxious to board their train for Vienna no later than six o'clock and something had to be done to speed things up if the presentation of several hundred ladies was not to go on for hours. Accordingly they started to hurry them in, the chamberlains calling out, 'Quick! Quick! Hurry there!' until the ladies were scrambling in, now singly, now in groups, pushing up to the throne, and elbowing each other out of the way at the doors to the drawing-room.

Everyone was exhausted, for most had been in full evening dress since early in the morning, wearing tiaras or diadems on their heads and supporting the weight not only of their trains but also of the heavy gold and silver embroidery of the dresses themselves. Many had been up most of the night waiting their turn with some fashionable hairdresser.

Tired and faltering, pale with exhaustion and tottering under the weight of their finery, they came into the drawing-room and at once sank thankfully into the few chairs and sofas that lined the walls of the apartment. The room was by no means brilliantly lit; indeed it was rather dark, as not all the chandeliers had been lit. More light came in from the windows, for the lamps in the palace courtyard cast up a helpful glow through the shadows cast by the rain that had just started to come down.

In this poor light every vestige of beauty and pageantry was drained from these poor ladies. The silver veils looked merely grey, the gold-braid a dull black, even the jewels lost their sparkle. Makeup ran on the older faces, powder vanished. In the early evening light these formerly radiant creatures were a sorry sight.

***

I went home very late.

The city returned to its normal wartime aspect.

After the royal couple had left at the end of the afternoon, the evening was just like any other during the winter. The departure of the king and queen quenched all rejoicing and sense of occasion. Rumours and gossip started spreading at once. People whispered about imaginary ill omens, that the crown had been placed crooked on the monarch's head, and that he had stumbled just at the moment when he was reading the words of the oath . . . but all this passed me by. Only one thing did happen which could have provided food for this kind of gossip, but I do not think any one knew about it. The cathedral had only just emptied after the coronation when the inch-thick glass plate in the purple tent above the altar split in the heat and crashed like a giant guillotine to the altar and the *prie-dieux* below. However, no one was told about this except those who had work to do in the church on the following day and afterwards no one spoke about it.

Later in the evening the rain turned to snow and for a brief moment the white flakes lay on the pavements and glistened in the light of the street lamps. Then all turned to mud and slush, and everything returned to an all-enveloping greyness.

Already, on the very same evening of the coronation, the pageantry and colour seemed no more real than a half-forgotten dream.

From My Memories

Part Two
Times of Revolution

⚜ Chapter One ⚜

We were sitting at our regular Monday evening dinner table. This had started some years before the war when, on the first day of each week, the same group of friends would come together at Gusztáv Heinrich's table in a private room at the National Kaszino. Ferenc Herczeg, Andor Miklós, the playwright Ferenc Molnár, Jëno Heltai, Ambrus and myself were the regulars, while Géza Papp was a 'visiting member' who occasionally joined us. These had been enjoyable evenings devoted principally to serious literary discussions interspersed by amusing analysis of the day's news and laughter over the latest items of town gossip. Our evening meetings would pass quickly. With the war, however, the literary talk and the light-hearted telling of amusing anecdotes were dropped, and for the past six months everyone had been preoccupied with the news from the Front, and lately with growing worry at the general situation. Although our discussions had changed character during the war, they had been no less interesting, and it was at these dinners that we gained important insights from men of many different backgrounds: insights that were made all the more valuable coming, as they did, from so many viewpoints. As a result, we were lucky to be provided with an exceptionally true and vivid picture of those critical times. So, if one of us was away from the capital for some time – perhaps on some official mission or with the army at the Front – on his return he would hurry there as soon as possible knowing that he would find friends whose positions had kept them in the capital and who would therefore be fully informed about everything, whether it was public knowledge or a supposed secret, that had transpired during his absence.

When I returned from the eastern Carpathians to be greeted by the news of the Bulgarian armistice, I could hardly wait for the next Monday dinner.

The previous two weeks had been terrible. Everywhere there had been confusion and a general breakdown of order.

There were those who called for a message to be sent to President Wilson, others backed a direct approach to England. From the King-Emperor in Vienna decrees had been issued calling for all Austria-Hungary's peoples to form so-called 'national councils', thereby admitting the failure of parliamentary government while approving revolutionary movements. The effect was to destroy the last remnants of the admittedly crumbling authority of the central government. On our side of the Carpathians those happy words 'national councils' were seized upon everywhere and used to justify the public formation of similar national councils by the Romanian and Slovak minorities. Prime Minister Wekerle still called for the maintenance of the union of Austria with Hungary in the person of the monarch, while Mihály Károlyi demanded a complete break with Austria and Hungarian independence. Both sides consulted the law books and produced suitable texts to support their views. Meanwhile there had been an attempt on the life of István Tisza (the former prime minister) and a group of officers attacked some policemen in front of the National Theatre. Behind our lines on the Serbian Front, lawless gangs were creating havoc. It was rumoured that thirty thousand army deserters were in hiding in Budapest, while many a 'soldiers' and workers' council' was being formed on the Russian model. In parliament Károlyi openly supported revolution saying 'Take it as fact that I shall act!', and while many people made out that they did not understand what these words meant, the very next day the 'Workers' Party' joined up with some members of parliament, thus forming an impotent alliance in which everyone concerned was suspicious of their new allies and so was hopelessly irresolute.

The monarch in Vienna, or at his country place at Gödöllo not far from Budapest, gave constant audiences from which emerged new coalitions and governments that, like soap bubbles, burst as soon as they were announced. The atmosphere grew daily more heated, and there were those who took care that it should continue to do so. There were then many unscrupulous men who, for their own ends, did not hesitate to gamble with the lives of innocent young men: for example, by leading a demonstration to the royal palace in Buda regardless of whether the police would use force to disperse the crowd. 'To Buda, to the king!' they cried, although most people knew he was at Gödöllo and never came anywhere near Buda. The agitators had calculated aright. The government, demoralized and fatally weakened, nervously overreacted and ordered the police to cordon off the bridges and meet the demonstrators with drawn swords, thus adding fuel to the general exasperation as when kindling is thrown on the fire. Those who retreated unhurt proceeded to smash all the 'By appointment to the king' emblems on the city shops and smashed their windows. That same evening the 'National Council' was formed and supported by the majority since it was the only body to show any will to take control of affairs. All kinds of organizations, unions and people in authority, with baseless and futile confidence, hurried to join the Council with the same speed as moths rushing to a flame. Everyone was convinced that Károlyi would return from Gödöllo as Minister-President, and would then with great servility put on the robes of revolution.

This is what had happened on the previous two days, which seemed to have raced by like a film run at double speed. It was like the moment before being struck by a tornado when, with heart throbbing, one is overcome by a nerve-wracking sense of impending doom: so menacing are the tumbling clouds in the sky that first appear at the corners of the far horizon and then are suddenly above our heads, swelling and towering until they cover the entire firmament, cutting off all light and leaving only occasional gaps which at any moment will close up with a terrifying clash until the whole sky falls down upon us burying the whole world with it.

During those days this feeling never left us, and it was with a sense of deep foreboding that I went to our Monday evening dinner on 28 October 1918.

The latest news was only of delay, postponement and more talks.

On Saturday evening the king had taken Károlyi with him to Vienna arriving in the morning. There, Károlyi was told to wait at his hotel until he was summoned and, in the meantime, not to talk to anyone. Károlyi waited. Noon passed, and he still had no news. Finally he telephoned to the cabinet offices for instructions and was simply told to go home as he was not needed then . . . perhaps later in Budapest[4]?

Knowing Károlyi's passionate nature, I realized at once that he would not accept such a gratuitous insult without in some way hitting back. It was then certain that we must expect a violent outcome. Károlyi's arrival in Budapest would herald the storm to come.

At the Western Train Station a crowd of many thousands was already milling about. They had come from a huge public meeting outside the parliament building, called by the National Council where they had voted for the adoption of the Council's program. When the news came of Károlyi's imminent return the leaders at once suggested that they should all go there to greet the arrival of the evening express. The train came in. With deafening cheers and an air of celebration they lifted the 'Leader of the People'[5] onto their shoulders, passing him from hand to hand with outstretched arms. What happened next was strangely symbolic of his whole life to come. 'The crowd . . . took Károlyi not towards the usual exit but in the direction of the warehouses. The people were so overexcited that they had not noticed that they had carried Mihály Károlyi into a blind alley that ran between the warehouses and Váci Street and which was closed by a tall iron gate that was locked.' To turn back was impossible. The only way was to clamber over it and squeeze through the iron spikes on top. Mihály Károlyi scrambled through, but no one else. He was then carried off by the crowd milling around outside 'with much dangerous jostling and pushing . . . like a piece of driftwood tossed about by chance, he was propelled forward sideways by the force of that determined crowd.'

This happened on Sunday.

On Monday came the news that discussions were being held by Archduke Joseph in his capacity of *homo regis* (literally 'the king's man'): a thankless task that, with real self-sacrifice, he had accepted at this late hour in an attempt to make peace between the rival factions in the face of such heightened passions.

We discussed all this on Monday evening, weighing what seemed the most likely outcome; and also the most unlikely. At about ten o'clock we were just mulling over whether János Hadik had any chance of forming a government (an idea of which most of us had only just heard) and also the idea of nominating Archduke Joseph as Palatine (viceroy) when a waiter came in to call Andor Miklós to the telephone, saying it was very, very urgent.

Miklós left us at once. In a few moments he was back, unusually pale.

'There is a battle raging at the Chain Bridge,' he said. 'The men were ordered to shoot . . . many dead and wounded!' and left to hurry back to his editorial desk.

Jenö Heltai was with us, and we decided to see for ourselves what was happening.

Everything was quiet outside the Kaszino. There was nobody about in front of the National Council's headquarters in the Hotel Astoria just across the road where, on previous evenings, crowds had gathered to listen to speeches from the Council's spokesmen. We started off briskly towards the Chain Bridge, passing the Town Hall, down Bécsi Street and Harmincad Street. The streets were empty, and the only sounds we heard were our own footsteps. Then suddenly, at the corner of Gisella (now Vorosmarty) Square, we met a huge crowd. The whole square was packed with men, shoulder to shoulder. The reason we had noticed nothing and made this so unexpected was their total silence. There was something essentially dramatic and sinister about this mute voiceless multitude, something far more menacing than if they had all been shouting and noisy. There must have been several thousand men gathered there – and not a sound. Every window was dark except, far away at the corner of Váci Street, there were lights in the windows of the Károlyi party headquarters. Through those windows the outlines of men moving to and fro could vaguely be seen, and maybe some speeches were being made there, but this I do not know for certain as no sound reached us. We asked some men standing near us what had happened, but they did not answer. They just shrugged and turned away.

Then we decided to go to Jószef Square.

Only a few steps from there two lovers stood entwined, caring nothing for what was going on around them, perhaps even finding a good opportunity amid the general chaos. Oblivious to their surroundings and clinging tightly together they went on kissing happily.

Heltai laughed. 'That's Budapest for you!' he said as we hurried on.

On the far side of Jószef Square a barricade had been built, and the soldiers manning it would not let us through to the Chain Bridge. They were from a Bosnian regiment, and we heard later that they had been sent to replace the 32nd Infantry who had had orders to close Dorottya Street and Vigado Square but who had not only let the demonstrators though without a word of protest but also, in good part, left their own ranks and joined them. Now, however, every street leading to the Danube was closed by the loyal Bosnian regiment. Here again not a voice was to be heard, not even a command. The only sound was the rhythmic beat of the soldiers' iron-studded boots. That dark night was the last occasion when anyone was to hear the measured tread of the Imperial Habsburg army on the march.

‚ఴ Chapter Two ‚ఴ

It was only on the following day that we learned everything that had happened at the Chain Bridge.

From early in the morning Archduke Joseph had spent the day in his palace in the fortress of Buda, negotiating with various politicians in an attempt to form a government. Mihály Károlyi was due to join him in the evening. While he was there, István Friedrich and László Fényes, from their party headquarters, decided to lead the crowd that had gathered there – a crowd, it transpired later, that consisted mainly of workers from the out-lying districts of the city – up to the fortress to ensure the appointment of Károlyi as prime minister by a show of force. 'To Buda!' they cried just as they had on the previous Friday.

With their two leaders at their head, the mob moved off only to find that the army had blocked Dorottya Street and formed a solid cordon in Maria-Valeria Square. There they learned that access to the Chain Bridge was also barred by the armed forces. Nevertheless, everything went well with them at first. The first two lines of guards made no resistance and let them through, as did the soldiers at Ferenc-József Square. There were police guarding the entrance to the Chain Bridge, but they only put up a token resistance, and soon the crowd had broken through. There, just where the stone lions stand, was a line of gendarmes.

This was serious. Some men tried to climb up from the roofs of the warehouse that stood below and so get onto the bridge behind the gendarmes. At this point they were met by a round of rifle fire, while the mounted police charged the crowd with drawn sabres. Helter-skelter the mob turned to flee. Scared and distressed, the workers ran for their lives back to the protection of the Károlyi party headquarters[6], whence they had set out not long before.

As usual in such affairs, the leaders emerged unscathed, but there were three dead and some fifty wounded in that anonymous crowd which consisted largely of simple well-meaning factory workers. These were the victims. Ambulances took them to the Ritz where the hotel's entrance hall was transformed into a hospital ward to give them first aid.

That was the story of the battle on Monday night.

It was this demonstration, which had drowned in its own blood, that effectively made it impossible for Károlyi to be part of the proposed government even if – and this I do not know – he had been willing to do so. This was the immediate result of the demonstration, and there were those who said that it had been organized with precisely this end in mind.

For those like myself who had distanced themselves as far as possible from the witch's brew of politics, the next two days seemed to pass without any significant developments. But it was only the silence which precedes the storm: a silence full of disquiet for it was broken by the news that the machinery of state continued to disintegrate as the Budapest police force had gone over to the National Council!

In the streets the mob leaders were publicly embraced by those very police who, only the day before, had charged them with drawn sabres. It was in this climate that Count János Hadik formed his government, news of which was received everywhere with indifference, for I am sure that no one had any confidence in Hadik's selfless initiative.

***

Now followed the evening of the real revolution.

I had dined in the Kaszino, as I had most evenings in the last few weeks, although fewer and fewer people had been there, and it must have been about eleven o'clock when we left the club, being the last to do so. There were three of us, together with another friend who was escorting the old chairman of the Jockey Club. We had taken to doing this in the last few days, for recently a number of suspicious-looking men had been seen loitering in the streets – a phenomenon previously unknown in the centre of the town, and from time to time gunshots had been heard.

As soon as we stepped out of the Kaszino's front door it was promptly shut behind us. I glanced across the street towards the Hotel Astoria, which had been taken over as the National Council's headquarters, and it seemed that rather more people than usual were gathered there, although there were probably not more than one or two hundred. No doubt someone had made a speech from the balcony and just as probably there had been some cheering in the street; although as this had been going on for more than a week we had become used to it. Not far away the streets were as dark and empty as they always had been at this time of night. Then some shots were heard coming from the direction of the Danube, but there was nothing unusual in this. I was alone by the time I crossed Calvin Square, and it was then that I heard repeated firing from Ráday Street. This was unusual. The rapid sound of bullets hitting the steel shutters of some shop made a loud cracking sound, almost a sort of howl. Although I was not unduly worried because we had heard it before, on this night there seemed to be more of this crazy random shooting than ever.

After getting home I must admit that I slept soundly, although occasionally, when still half-asleep, I seemed to hear more rumbling of heavy lorries passing under my windows than on previous nights. However, since the street outside was the habitual route for deliveries to the market halls nearby, and the market cars had always rattled past noisily long before dawn, it did not seem to be different from any other night in the year.

It was only later that I heard what had happened early that morning. When my old valet called me he announced three things: my bath had been prepared, revolution had broken out, and Count Mihály Károlyi was now Minister-President.

Soon afterwards István Zichy came to see me and related what he had seen and heard outside in the streets, and together we went out onto Museum Boulevard.

Most of the shops were closed, and there were many people just standing about on the pavement. It looked as if all the

cleaners and domestic servants of the district were there, standing about in groups of five or six before each doorway, open-
mouthed and gaping, just as Zichy and I were doing along with
countless other citizens who had streamed out to gaze around in
wonder.

It was both interesting and amusing. Everyone seemed in festive mood, smiling and wearing white asters[7].

Enterprising youths from the suburbs were selling the flowers,
and should anyone dare to refuse to buy the friendly offers were
soon suffused with unconcealed menace. Resistance to these
offers swiftly melted away. However, very few did refuse for man
is a *Herdentier* – an animal that always follows the herd, a gre-
garious animal – and quickly follows its neighbour's example. It
may well have been us two, Zichy and myself, who alone failed to
pin on the symbolic flower, but this was not from mere contrari-
ness but because it went against our nature blindly to endorse
such trivial emblems. Anyhow, even without us, there were
plenty of asters to be seen on the passers-by, on the sightseers
standing in the doorways and decorating some shop windows,
just as there were on some heavy army weapon-carriers which
suddenly appeared among the crowd and just as suddenly rumbled away. Some of these were lavishly decorated with their rusty
sides, radiators and headlights garlanded with white flowers. By
contrast the army vehicles were packed with sooty-faced, heavily
armed soldiers. People ran alongside wildly as the great lorries
were driven directly into the crowd, regardless of anyone or anything that might be in their way. None could tell if they were
hurrying to some unknown goal or were roaming the streets at
random.

The crowd was in far too festive a mood to be worried by any
of this, nor did anyone seem to notice that among the many soldiers wandering about so aimlessly there were a number, heavily
armed, their tunics unbuttoned and dirtier than any I had seen
even on the worst days at the Front. Some seemed merely to be
seeking a sympathetic listener to whom they could explain in
hoarse voices, perhaps for the umpteenth time, what heroic
deeds they had done that night. There were others who, dead
tired, tramped mechanically on like the solitary ant who has lost

his way back to the heap and pauses, looking around in bewilderment. No one bothered about any of these men, even though they all carried loaded rifles and were hung with hand grenades. The crowd was in too festive a mood to be worried, indeed most of them seemed to rejoice in the soldiers' presence, as in everything else that day, for was it not the same for them as for everyone else? All that anyone could take in was that the terrible war was over, that now there would be no more flour tickets and food rations, and that peace would come again, at long last peace, wonderful peace. No worries, no anxiety clouded their exuberant joy, for did not every danger and every misery belong to the past, that evil past which must now be utterly forgotten? From this very day the future would hold nothing but brotherly love and friendship . . . and peace, wonderful peace.

Zichy and I, who also saw these soldiers from whom every vestige of discipline seemed to have drained away, were filled with trepidation at the thought of what would happen if this disintegration spread to the whole of the armed forces. For a while we saw nothing encouraging, but then we were faced with a wonderful example of enduring discipline and courage, a beautiful act that only we had witnessed and would remember.

A young officer appeared in the middle of the street, with some men, perhaps eight or ten, lined up behind him, all apparently from different units. Seeing that one of the aimless armed soldiers I have described was leaning against the railings of the Museum Garden, he stopped his little troop and walked over, alone, to speak to the man. He passed just in front of us. His emblem of rank had been wrenched off his helmet, he wore no officer's sword tassels, and the stars had been ripped from his collar; but these humiliations had left no other mark on him and there was something serious and dignified about the way he carried himself. In a friendly voice he called upon the lounging soldier to join the little troop he had gathered around him. 'We have to return to barracks,' he said. 'The revolution is over. Now all we need is a little order, a little solidarity.' He added that if he were needed he would remain with the others . . . but there was also such a thing as duty. Now was the time for discipline . . . With words such as these, and without giving an order or asking to be obeyed, he just talked to the man quietly and resolutely.

The soldier obeyed.

This young officer then collected three or four other men who had been standing about in the same way, formed them up with the others and marched them all off in the direction of Károlyi Boulevard.

'What a man!' said Zichy. 'If only there were more like him . . . then, perhaps . . . '

We turned into Lajos Kossuth Street and there we met several acquaintances. Among them was Miklós Vadász, the well-known designer, who was sporting a huge aster in his lapel and had about him a somewhat comic air of self-importance, making out that he was a secret revolutionary and hinting that it was he who had brought it all about. As it turned out it was not only he but everyone else we met who, according to the character of each, exhibited the full range of pleasure from radiant ecstasy down to a sort of modest relief which could be described as a 'post-extraction joy' or 'Thank God it's out at last', which, of course is not much but still in its way a sort of joy.

The general euphoria was not really surprising. Everything that the general public knew about Károlyi tended to invite their trust and gave them hope. Just before the war he had made no secret of travelling to France and America, openly admitting that this was a political mission. When war broke out he left New York for home but was for a while detained in France. Finally the French government let him go without his having to attempt to escape. He then stopped in Switzerland before returning to Budapest[8].

Back in Hungary he proclaimed his support for a rupture with Germany and a separate peace with the Allies. Later he was to declare that Hungary should lose no time in accepting President Wilson's terms. That he never seemed to waver in his publicly declared attitude, at least not so the general public would notice, (as, for example, when he volunteered for the army, or when Romania's entry into the war provoked a fierce chauvinist reaction in Hungary), may have puzzled many of those who did not know him well.

Some of his intimate friends, however, knew that Károlyi had relations in France and what was more significant, had held political discussions with Poincaré, who had once acted for him as a solicitor. This was enough, in those last ominous weeks and months, for more and more people to see in him not only the one politician who seemed always to have been right but also possessed powerful links with (and maybe even definite promises from) the Allies, who could bring about an end to the already all too evident menace of the nation's imminent destruction and so somehow lead the country to the other side of the political Ocean, just as the Czechs and Poles had already done. Even the lawsuit brought by his cousin, Imre Károlyi[9] seemed to confirm what they thought just because the two men had been in such close touch. Surely this meant, the general public assumed, that it was precisely this relationship which proved that Imre's accusations were true; and so, if it were true now, when the destruction of the Central Powers was only a matter of days away, how much more faith should be put in Mihály if he were indeed a secret agent in the pay of the French? The example of the Czech Kramarz strengthened this view, since the latter had been tried for treason in Austria, recently set free and had now re-emerged as spokesman for the newly independent republic of Czechoslovakia.

In the course of that first week of the revolution I met many men who analysed these events with cool logic. Furthermore, an army of eager gossip-mongers was to be found everywhere, who heard everything from 'reliable' sources, and these men, who now announced with joy that providence had sent Count Károlyi to head the government, were the very same who, a few months before, had related with wicked glee that the 'traitor' Károlyi was about to be arrested. This was one of those times when one needs a lot of brotherly love not to loathe one's fellow men.

So passed the first morning of revolution in a general out-pouring of joy. Everywhere was heard the cry: 'our bloodless floral revolution!'

And indeed that first day was bloodless, and all the firing heard during the night was only due to high spirits. No one was hurt, not even General Lukacsics who had been called 'Bloody

Lukacsics' as he had ordered ten or so deserters to be shot as soon as he had been put in command of the Budapest garrison. Arrested, like all the other senior officers in the capital, he had been taken to the Hotel Astoria, dressed in civilian clothes, and let out the back door.

Amazingly enough there was no resistance anywhere or incident of any kind. Even today[10], with the benefit of hindsight, it is difficult to understand how everything passed so smoothly. This cannot be explained solely by the fact that the night before, General Lukacsics had telephoned King Karl for instructions and he, always kind-hearted, had said that no blood was to be shed; nor because, as came to light later, all the telephone lines (including the secret ones) had been taken over by the revolutionaries. Some people later suggested it was because Hungarian officers refused to fire on their fellow Hungarians, but this does not explain it either, for neither the officers of the Kommando-Korps, nor many other army leaders were any more Hungarian than the men under their command, most of whom were *Soldatenkinder*, born into military families in which the tradition of serving in the Dual Monarchy's forces was handed down from father to son. Such men had hardly any connection with Hungary, for their only 'homeland' was the Austrian army. What was common to them all was a shared ideology (which, incidentally, was to prove to be both their strength and their weakness while ensuring that the dual army was one of the Habsburg monarchy's strongest supports) made up of such artificial notions as the *Kaisers Rock* and the *Portepée Ehre*[11], and this made it all the more extraordinary that all those disciplined officers, from humble depot commanders to those of the highest rank, should now forget their most cherished ethic and give up their arms when faced with threats and orders from mere civilians or disobedient soldiery. Was their passivity caused by the lack of orders from above? Was that why they did not automatically reach for their own weapons? I admit that theirs was the wisest course; but were they all wise? How was it that the tradition of never permitting an insult to the *Kaisers Rock* – which in times of peace was so fiercely upheld that an unwise remark or harmless gesture could provoke a duel as an 'affair of honour' – was now forgotten by them all?

However, one thing did cast a chill over that evening on the day when the sun had shone and 'bloodless' revolution was being celebrated everywhere with white aster flowers in full bloom.

This was the assassination of István Tisza.

The news spread like wildfire through the city, and as it did the universal merriment was stilled and the crowds started to melt away. Those few who remained would speak quietly to each other, whispering the news and moving swiftly on so as not to have to reveal what they felt. It was as if the flames of the guns that had killed the man whom many people, both friend and foe, had considered great had acted as a flash of lightning had laid bare the sinister truth.

The revolutionary idyll ended at that moment.

Tisza's funeral was to be at four o'clock on the following day. At half-past three I set off but was met by a friend coming away. He told me that the funeral was over and that it had been held before the time announced as it had been feared the mob might try to prevent the last respects from being paid because there were those who had threatened to desecrate the corpse of a man who had been so hated.

***

Tisza's tragic death at once put an end to the public rejoicing, but the people's confidence in the new order, and in particular in its leader, was eroded more slowly. The first disappointment came when the new cabinet was announced and, instead of an exciting bevy of new names, sparkling with talent and promise, which everyone had expected, the list of ministers held no surprises. Of course, the public's hopes had been essentially naive since by then most men of experience and integrity had long been antagonized and so, in the inevitable atmosphere of distrust and disillusion it was a matter of '*Woher nehmen und nicht stehlen?*'[12] Even if Károlyi had wanted to do otherwise, he found himself bound to make the choice from members of his own party.

Even so, the first list of ministers was not complete. No one wanted the post of minister of justice. This gave rise to a tragicomic little anecdote that was soon repeated all over Budapest and caused much amusement. It was recounted that all morning and most of the afternoon Károlyi had tried in vain to find someone willing to occupy the velvet seat of the minister of justice. This was serious, as Károlyi was desperately anxious to take over the government without delay. Nothing was to be done, however, and so Károlyi, with his incomplete band of proposed ministers, set off for Buda to present them to Archduke Joseph. In the funicular they met, by chance, one Károly Sladics who held a senior post at the ministry of justice. Why not offer him the vacant post? someone suggested, and to their relief and joy, he accepted; and so, by the time the old funicular car had rattled its way to the top, the cabinet list was complete. But not for long. Just as they were walking across from the station to the archduke's palace a newsboy came rushing over to them yelling out the news of Tisza's murder and offering them printed leaflets with all the details. Some of the little band bought them and then, just as they were saying they had better get a move on so as not to keep the archduke waiting, they looked around for the future justice minister – he was nowhere to be seen, vanished into thin air. No one had seen him go, and no one knew where he had gone. He had just slid away and vanished, and was never seen again.

This humorous little tale was characteristic of those days and, although perhaps not completely accurate in detail, essentially true[13].

Later on someone was found for the post, but everyone's feeling of disappointment remained. The new ministers were largely unknown, except perhaps to a few in obscure circles in the capital. What was worse was that none of them had any practical experience in the fields for which they were now to be responsible. They had never held executive posts in any civic or governmental department. On the contrary, they were armchair theorists or journalists who ranged from honest but donnish scientists and dreamers to that familiar type, those coffee-house prophets who had passed their days in playfully solving all the world's most complex problems while sitting at their desks or at the marble tables of popular cafés. The only exceptions were the Socialists for whom leadership of the trade unions had proved a good schooling, and so they alone of the new government had any idea of the effect new measures might have on real people when they passed into law.

It was therefore only to be expected that once such men had seized power, which they had done from the first day of the revolution, the whole edifice of government would gradually begin to wither away.

❧ Chapter Three ❧

The story of the October Revolution is not really the subject of these purely personal reminiscences. It is neither my intention nor my calling to write any more about it. Everything that I know of those days stemmed either from the newspaper accounts or from the unverifiable tales told to me by acquaintances. Even afterwards I never studied any of the official documents, and as far as the Károlyi case was concerned, all I knew was the published verdict. Therefore all I can recount of what actually happened in those troubled times was learned from the point of view of an onlooker; and very few of those events had any personal significance for me. My memories can offer only a fragmentary picture, and so their only value can be as source material for historians of the future who wish to write about this period after a long interval of time; and their interest, perhaps, will be underlined by the fact that these pages come from the pen of a man who tried always to avoid bias.

Impartiality is not necessarily a virtue; rather it is a question of character. At any rate it has always been a part of *my* character, so ingrained that I feel I was born with it as an inherited characteristic which was to be developed by many experiences during my time as a diplomat. Then I was apt to make mistakes by involving myself in the affairs of people whose ideas always held such a fascination for me that I would joyfully try to imagine myself in their shoes. Perhaps, too, it is part of a writer's makeup to collect facts, to analyse human nature and, by trying to enter the minds of others, to understand the significance of a strange association of apparently contradictory ideas. But once one does that, impartiality becomes a necessity, because only thus can one decide with clarity whence, and under what

influences, could this apparently strange and illogical action have
stemmed. Only with impartial analysis will the motives become
clear, even when they seem to contradict each other, and then one
can see what – after an agony of suppressed internal battles and
hesitations – has given birth to a decision that at first had seemed
beyond all reason. Such apparently illogical actions are almost
never inspired by a single motive. They spring from an unknown
number of threads, perhaps thousands of them, some forgotten,
some unconscious, some consciously suppressed or not admitted, which when collected and spun together have formed a conclusion, however considered or unconsidered it may ultimately
seem. It is like the myriad tiny wells and springs, underground
streams and insignificant little rivulets of water emerging from
far and wide, seeping out from swamps or caverns of rock-
crystal, surging forth from the dark underground or oozing
through rotting vegetation until, bursting from a cleft in the
rocks, they all unite and merge imperceptibly together then,
tumbling down to the valley, they achieve their ultimate purpose
and are transformed into a mighty river.

Among those who played a part in those uncertain days, I was
closely related only to one: Mihály Károlyi. Destiny had somehow placed him right at the centre of affairs. I think I knew him
better than anyone else, for not only was he a near relation but,
what is more important, we had also been close personal friends
since early childhood. I was seven and he was six when we first
met, and there sprung up between us an almost brotherly affection that lasted and bound us together well through our stormy
teenage years. Indeed it was to last long afterwards – even when
our careers and adult lives kept us more and more apart, and our
characters were becoming evermore different. Finally our very
different points of view and understanding of what was important in life were to bring about a complete rupture between us.
Nevertheless, we remained on the intimate terms born of our
childhood together, even at a distance and although we rarely saw
each other after his marriage and during the war. Brothers, even
if they have very different characters, can be like this; the bond
remains even if fate has sent them on widely separate paths. The
old intimacy is never entirely lost.

From his earliest childhood there were the most varied opinions about Mihály Károlyi's character and abilities. Even today in 1932 people still hold wildly differing views, some believing him to have only a most limited understanding and modest talents and to be little more than a power-hungry adventurer; others – although nowadays these are growing fewer and fewer – see in him some kind of noble prophet. To my view both these opinions are wrong, and so I will try to describe him as I personally see him, not as a politician but as a man. And to do so I will have to show not only what he became but also go back to where he started, so as to establish, if I can, whence came those early impressions that were to motivate his actions over two decades, actions which were ultimately so fatal as to land him where he is today[14].

A man's character is only formed after the impressions of childhood and early youth have become blended with the indefinable and hidden influences both atavistic and of more immediate heredity. When, like soft clay, the newborn human spirit has been first fashioned by the firm hand of the modeller and then allowed to set and harden, this is the moment the final character emerges, fixed for life. While the part played by heredity will always remain elusive and uncertain, the influences of a man's early years are not difficult to unfurl if we know where to seek and consider seriously what we find. I must therefore go back many years to start this search, and I fear it may prove a lengthy process.

Károlyi was a child of first cousins, and it is possibly this which resulted in his being born with a harelip and cleft palate, and so weak and puny that no one thought he would survive for long. His mother was already suffering from tuberculosis when he was born and was to die scarcely three years later.

The two orphans she left were cared for by their grandmother, who was also my aunt. She surrounded the child with constant care and careful nursing. He had to be shielded from everything, for everything harmed him. He was like a hothouse plant, so weak and pale that it had to be sheltered even from the slightest breath. Until he was fourteen years old one could hardly understand what he said; but then old Professor Bilroth from Vienna was induced to try a hazardous operation on his palate, which at least made it easier for him to enunciate his words more clearly. He then had to learn how to speak properly and, showing much willpower, he achieved this by endless exercises, daily repeating words and phrases ever more loudly until his speech was so improved that it became almost, although never quite, that of those born with a normal palate. This built-in physical handicap was to remain with him for life: never admitted, sometimes, perhaps, temporarily out of mind, but nevertheless always there, like some congenital stigma.

Thus we can find already present from birth some of the most important formative elements in building the young Mihály's character. One of these was the physical handicap that which was to inspire Mihály's lifelong battle to prove himself as good as anyone else – the spirit of 'I'll show you!' – a battle of willpower that had always to be waged in silence. It is terrible to think what it must mean, in the life of a small boy, to have to fight every day of one's life to overcome a genetic handicap. Furthermore, one can but imagine the feeling of humiliation at being forced to wage this constant battle just to arrive where every other child starts. This is the other most important outside influence in forming the young Károlyi's character.

Of course, something of this only appeared occasionally in his early days. When it did, it was to have all the more acute an effect. It was even a humiliation for the child to realize that he was given special consideration because he was physically so much weaker than other children. His faults would be forgiven him because of this very fragility; and all this because he was an incomplete being, almost a cripple. Things would happen that would all at once bring these ever-present feelings to the surface as a vivid and wounding reality. This would be provoked, for example, on the rare occasions when he found himself with other boys, usually relations of his own age, adolescents who, filled with an arrogant joy in their own strength, barely concealed their contempt for a weak undersized boy of their generation who had a speech defect to boot. This situation was graphically described by Ferenc Molnár in his novel *Boys of Pál Street*.

Such an experience must always be both painful and troubling. On a boy who has led a secluded life, cosseted and protected like a hothouse plant, it will have a far greater effect than on those who have already have had a normal exposure to the hardening experiences of everyday life. In Mihály's case, it was also provoked when I, never particularly athletic myself, forgot how much weaker he was and put him to shame in some boyish wrestling or other gymnastic activity. Although I remember how careful I was, when we were small boys, not to let this happen, once or twice in all those years of our youth, I grew careless. I understood then what I am writing about now.

I have now described the most important factors that were to result in three of his most marked characteristics – his 'I'll show you!' reaction to the cruelties of fate and the humiliations they provoked; the hothouse atmosphere in which he had been brought up protected from all contact with real life; and thirdly, the fact that, because he was an orphan burdened with a severe physical handicap, he had all his life been treated as the most important person in the narrow little world of which he was the central figure.

We have just described the internal spiritual effects of his social background and physical condition. Now we should examine the external visible ones.

Firstly, there was the cultural atmosphere of the house in which he was raised, and its particular political and social aura.

I write 'particular' because the intellectual life of that family home was permeated by an exaggerated veneration for the ideology of the party that fought for Hungary's independence in 1848 and consequently for the strong anti-Austrian and anti-Habsburg feelings it inspired.

This atmosphere was personified by the master of the house, Sándor Károlyi, and his wife Clarisse, both of whom belonged to that generation that had lived through Hungary's fight for freedom and the years of oppression that had followed. Both they and their contemporaries had enthusiastically imbibed in their youth the heady notions of self-sacrifice enshrined in the political slogans of the 1840s, but, protected by their wealth and social position, they were never personally to experience the devastation and misery caused to so many by the revolutionary war. Of course, they had suffered many anxious moments, witnessed scenes of high drama and endured much sadness and worry; and therefore the pain those past days recalled for them was mingled with a sense of romantic excitement and the sparkle of heroic battles. What sorrows they had were those of their youth and, although kept alive, were only enshrined in some scintillating golden web of memory.

Count Sándor Károlyi had been an officer in the hussars at the age of seventeen and later – so it was said – had been an active participant in the Komárom Conspiracy[15]. His father, the old István Károlyi (whom I never knew) was imprisoned for years at Olmütz and Kufstein for having himself raised the regiment in which his son Sándor had served[16].

Sándor's wife – my aunt and Mihályi's grandmother on his mother's side – had two brothers who fought on the Hungarian nationalist side. There were many exciting tales told about their escape and time spent in hiding. As a teenage girl she had lived with my grandparents at the house on Széchenyi Square opposite the 'New Building'[17] in Budapest, to which they had retired in 1850 after the storm. Sometimes at dawn there could be heard the crackling of gunfire from the fortress-like barracks just across the square's gardens. This meant that an execution was taking place, probably of some martyr to the Hungarian nationalist cause, although, except on one occasion, they did not know for sure who it was. The exception was when they executed Prince Voronievsky, who, on the eve of his death, had somehow managed to get a message to my grandmother and her daughters[18]. He had known them in Kolozsvár when he had been with the army of Bem. It was said that he had been in love with my Aunt Clarisse, and that that is why the message had been sent to them. It asked for their prayers, as his turn would come on the following day!

One can only imagine what traces such memories can leave.

Mihály's other grandmother, wife of Count György Károlyi[19], was a frequent visitor at Föth during his uncle Sándor's time. She was much older than my aunt Clarisse, and one could sense that those revolutionary times held no romantic aura for her but rather were a cruel and unforgettable reality. She hated Franz Joseph and everything Austrian and German. It is said that she had always been a woman of passion. She had also been very fond of her brother-in-law, Lajos Batthyány who had been arrested in her apartment[20].

Haynau stepped in and signed the death warrant. After Batthyány's death she went abroad and did not return until after her husband's death, which took place years after the 1868 Compromise. Abroad she was a famous hostess, filling her drawing-room with Hungarian political exiles; but any of these who applied for an amnesty and went home were at once branded as traitors. Under her influence, her sons were to take part in all sorts of *émigré* plots against the Habsburgs. I knew her as a silent woman with a hard mouth from which issued hard cruel words. We children were all afraid of her.

All that I have just recounted should explain the passionate pro-1848 partisan feeling that pervaded the Károlyi house and spread from the masters, through the children, even to the domestic servants. In some ways it is surprising that so late in the nineteenth century the Károlyi family should have remained so *'kuruc'*-minded, more so than most other aristocratic families[21].

This was in some measure true for many of the aristocratic families, although after the 1868 Compromise most of them took this stand only as a sort of *'fronde'* of the greater magnates against any form of government, who were apt to treat the flaunting of such opinions as a kind of sporting amusement. In fact 'they only did it to annoy!'[22]

This rebellious attitude did not arise because many of their estates lay far from Vienna, in the eastern part of the country, but because, as a consequence of the family habit of often marrying their cousins, they had fewer relations abroad than had those families[23] who lived further to the west. There were, as it happens, many important Hungarian families, many of them Transylvanian, who had fewer foreign ties but who were nevertheless by no means as chauvinistic as the Károlyis. Despite all the other influences, what was, in my opinion, a far more potent memory in the Károlyi family was the legacy of the part played by their ancestor, Baron Sándor Károlyi, the *'kuruc'* general who played a leading part in making the peace of Szatmár.

From the beginning of the nineteenth century, when Hungarian nationalist feeling began to take formidable shape, most historical writing began to be significantly coloured by this view of the nation's history and has remained so to our time. It is not difficult to understand how our historians were unable to free themselves of the bias created by the national struggle for freedom from the authoritarianism of Vienna and why this bias should have continued so long. It was finally checked by Kálman Thaly, who declared himself the 'Chronicler of Prince Rákóczi'. The effect of this one-sided reporting of our history was that any important figure tainted with sympathy for the 'enemy' (i.e. the Habsburgs) was either only cursorily mentioned or else severely maligned. Historical impartiality was almost totally lacking, as was any attempt to put Hungarian matters in context with events outside our borders. Without such historical comparisons events in Hungary are barely comprehensible. Our historians would write as if Hungary was a solitary island in an ocean of Nothingness, or as if they inhabited a world that contained nothing but Hungarians. (The term 'the Hungarian Globe' was invented to mock this sort of thinking.) In the second half of the nineteenth century this feeling came to infect an entire generation who were to believe it passionately. This same generation, who were to brand Görgey as a traitor, naturally declared Sándor Károlyi to have been many times worse. Nobody then bothered to ask themselves what would have happened if Görgey had not capitulated at Világos; nor did they recall that the Peace of Szatmár was most advantageous not only for Hungary but perhaps also for Rákóczi had he accepted it. 'Generals Görgey and Károlyi were both traitors!' was everyone's opinion, and Károlyi was censured the most because, while Görgey only just escaped execution, Károlyi was rewarded with grants of land. This was the 'historical truth' taught in our schools, and that is where I first heard of it.

It seems likely that all this must have had a deep-seated effect on the descendants of the '*kuruc*' General Károlyi; and it may well be that it was in exaggerated chauvinism that they sought justification and absolution for their ancestor.

I do not know this. It is only presumption. However, I do know that for Mihály himself the Treaty of Szatmár was a sore point, especially when he learned what his teachers and guardians – indeed everyone by whom he was surrounded – believed. We spoke of it occasionally, and it was always as of something ineradicably shameful, barely even to be admitted.

Everything I have just written concerns only the invisible forces that were continually present and influenced him, so that it was as if a stealthy process of capillary action determined Mihály's motivation. His uncle Sándor (mine too by marriage) was the most important and lasting influence in the formation of his opinions and convictions.

Sándor Károlyi was the founder of the Hungarian Co-operative Movement. He was a magnificent man, completely selfless and without personal ambition. He was intensely patriotic and wanted only to be of service to his countrymen. He was filled with youthful energy and even in old age would express his opinions with almost warlike energy. He was exceptionally well read and had a truly global vision.

I shall never forget how, on so many evenings, standing with his back to the fire, he would talk to us: two growing youths in our last years at school and first at university. He was a wonderful talker, often using paradox with many unexpected twists, explaining brilliantly the problems of the world and its economy. He would use much fantasy in his exposition of an almost utopian vision, and his deep erudition and passionate expression held for us a special magic. I can recall, even now, how he stood there, in front of the fireplace in his somewhat sombre study, always with his hands in his pockets. His short, thick, bristling hair seemed to have a halo round it caused by the light of two wall brackets behind him. With his legs spread wide apart, he would sway slightly from side to side as if impelled by some inner rhythm. He had a hard ascetic face with a firm chin ending in a pointed beard, and his thin lips, although often giving a hint of a smile, were set in a somewhat cruel line. He seemed to be without pity, either for himself or others, while his general demeanour was that of a man burdened with some deep mystery, the mystery of an ancient conspirator. He never spoke about himself, and many times, as we listened to him, I was to ponder upon how little we knew about him, either of his secret and passionate past, or even of what might have still remained with him. Only occasionally did we stumble over some fact, hitherto unmentioned, which would throw light on otherwise hidden depths. For example, I once discovered by chance that Sándor Károlyi, that devout Catholic aristocrat, had once been a freemason. This must have come about because many of the conspiracies in the cause of national freedom had been organized through the Masonic lodges. It was whispered that at the time of the Klapka-Komárom Movement he had himself shot dead one of the leaders of the secret organizing committee who had betrayed their cause. According to another version he had merely assisted at a duel whose details, at the time of writing, have not yet come to light.

I also learned another unexpected thing about him. When Alajos Károlyi, who had been Austro-Hungarian ambassador in London, died and, as was the rule, his insignia of the Order of the Golden Fleece was returned to the emperor, Franz Joseph sent word unofficially to Sándor Károlyi that he intended to offer it to him, the rule being that it could never be held at the same time by more than one member of the same family. Károlyi replied that before the monarch distinguished him with his family's highest order he ought to know that it was he who financed Lajos Kossuth in his exile by sending money to him, ostensibly from the booksellers as the proceeds of his books since he knew the old revolutionary would never otherwise have accepted it. Károlyi wrote that he did not feel it right that he should accept the Habsburg's highest decoration when he was ensuring a comfortable old age to the dynasty's greatest enemy. The offer was then withdrawn. It was, however, a measure of the old emperor's fair-mindedness that after Kossuth's death he at once sent the insignia of the Golden Fleece to Sándor Károlyi.

I would ponder on these things while I was in that dark room listening spellbound by the brilliance of his talk. He was imbued with the French manner of thought, so different from the German works of political economy with which, nevertheless, he was perfectly familiar. His talk scintillated with humour, using all kinds of jokes and bizarre anecdotes to add spice to the driest of themes. He often spoke in broken sentences that, although not always finished, still maintained a unity of sense and faith. Hundreds of differing subjects would meet and find a place in what he would tell us. The world believed him to be essentially conservative and pro-clerical, and to a certain point this was true, although he differed in many ways from others of the same mind, who would have listened in astonishment if they had been present at those dissertations in front of the fireplace when he talked about his own special enthusiasms such as the OMGE (the National Hungarian Agricultural Society) and the Hangya Central Cooperative Society and credit-unions. Sometimes he would hold forth about the future, prophesying the transformation of the world we knew, the disappearance of great estates – even of personal property – and the eventual realization of new social doctrines of which, in his view, the best for all humanity would be based on cooperative lines. This, he postulated, was the only form that he hoped would finally emerge from the mists of time.

These evening performances had the effect of stimulating our imagination, partly perhaps because of their rhapsodic delivery and daring content. His sparkling words would evoke in us heady trains of thought, no matter what great world subjects were being dissected. Maybe because it was he, the personification of the true oligarch and lord of Hungary's greatest private fortune, who was foreseeing the future success of radical ideas – even to their compulsory adoption – and emphasizing that in a cooperative system lay our only salvation that we saw something very touching in him, even if this view held also something of affectation. The paradox would be underlined when he, as he sometimes did with conscious self-irony, included cruel biting criticisms of that very society of which he himself was one of the chief pillars.

These gymnastic displays of fantasy and extraordinary ideas formed a deep impression on us both, and we would listen for hours sunk deep in great leather-covered armchairs.

It was at this time, under the spell of Uncle Sándor's ideas, that I wrote a short essay on the credit-unions in Transylvania, as my uncle's views had had the immediate effect of crystalizing for me their possible implications for the land of my birth. Unfortunately, later – it was my own fault – I was to separate myself from the circle over which my uncle presided.

Sándor Károlyi's early teaching was to have more lasting effect upon Mihály who, as I was often to remark, due to his exceptional birth and circumstance, was later to become a political leader. When he became chairman of the OMGE and principal spokesman for the radical Independence Party, I frequently heard echoes of Uncle Sándor's utopian ideas for the world's future, although in other forms – and unfortunately with quite other effects – than he would ever have imagined. All the same it is equally clear that in Mihály there was a clash of many opposing ideologies and that he believed in them all with equal passion. One of these was an ineradicable Hungarian patriotism, another a hatred of all things German; and a third the inward-looking 'Hungarian Globe' mentality which I have already mentioned; and yet in contrast he believed firmly in the ideal of world citizenship, and the germs of all these beliefs had been bred in him years before in the memories of Uncle Sándor's talk – but the sown seed brings different harvests depending on ground upon which it has fallen[24].

When Mihály was growing into a young man, he left his grandparents' house and went to live in the Károlyi Palais in Egyetem utca in the old quarter of Pest[25]. He had a huge allowance – two thousand crowns a month – although this barely covered the cost of keeping his twelve horses. I understand that in his will, Mihály's father had indicated that he wanted his son to be brought up as a horseman. The five hundred or so crowns that were left for him to spend were quite inadequate to pay for the style of living expected of a young man in his position, owner of vast country estates as well as the great townhouse, with all the claims so many people had on him. This was the time we both first joined the Kaszino Club.

In those days the Kaszino was not the somewhat sleepy club it was to become after the Great War. Then it throbbed with life. Nightly there was lavish entertaining in what was one of Budapest's most expensive eating-places. There was continual *cigány* music and social revelry in the great rooms on the ground floor, while upstairs, on the first floor, there was gambling for enormously high stakes.

In such surroundings five hundred crowns soon disappeared, and in such surroundings too, it was impossible to call a halt. The only way to avoid spending money was to stay away. This, however, required the steadfast character of a Cato, and neither of us had such a character. Soon we were drawn into the game and, no matter whether our luck was good or bad, somehow we always had money, from our winnings or from moneylenders.

As far as I was concerned, this phase did not last long as I was soon sent first to Fiume and then *en poste* abroad. Afterwards I only weakened once or twice, but Mihály, who had inherited a truly immense fortune as soon as he came of age, continued without a pause.

It was in those last years, when we were nearly always in each other's company, that Mihály's character was finally fixed forever. And it was then that those peculiarities, which had hitherto been suppressed, started to emerge for all to see.

One of these was daredevilry, which must have had its roots in his childhood when he had been so overprotected. From this sprang the assertive spirit of 'I'll show you!' of which I will give two examples.

The one I recall now happened at the end of the 1890s in Vienna, when he insisted on going up in a newly designed balloon whose inventor wanted to try it out for the first time. This inventor, I understand, had created a balloon that, if one wanted to come down, had to have the skin torn. The balloon would then transform itself into a parachute and, according to its eminent inventor, gently deposit the passengers on the ground. Mihály Károlyi and a friend, Stanislaus Deym, volunteered to fly with him at their own risk so as to try out this excellent invention. The takeoff went well, and the wind took them way over the borders of Bohemia. Then the inventor ordered them to climb out of the basket and cling to the lowest part of the net which covered the balloon and which was much wider than the basket itself. So there they were, at a height of one thousand metres, hanging by their hands alone and with nothing between them and the ground. A charming situation! Then the inventor tore the hull, upon which balloon, basket and its three passengers dropped like a stone to the ground – how far and how long it took, no one knew. Despite all this, the experiment was in one sense a success since no one was killed; but not much of a success, for all three were found unconscious in a field and carted off to a hospital in some neighbouring town. I well remember how astonished his uncle Sándor and my aunt Clarisse were when they received a telegram from Mihály, whom they had thought was in Vienna, saying that he was in Budweis, that he had flown there and was well. I don't think he ever entertained them with the balloon trip's more delightful details, nor anything of the famous inventor.

I was with him on the occasion of the second adventure. We were both staying at Abbazia with our families when we heard there was to be some famous party that night in Fiume.

Abbazia, just down the coast, was a favourite winter retreat for the Hungarian aristocracy. I do not recall if it was to be a masked ball or some informal hop-and-skip dance. We didn't tell anyone, but that night when all the others had gone to bed, we went down to where there were small sailboats kept for hire by those who wanted to go bathing up the coast. We woke up the boatmen; but no one was willing to take us as far as Fiume because there was a strong wind over the Quarnero and the red warning flag was hoisted above the mole. However, nothing would daunt Mihály and he finally, for a horrendous sum of money, persuaded one of the men to take us across; and so off we went. By the time we were barely four hundred metres from the shore the wind had become so strong that we would have capsized if we had not hauled down the sails of that miserable little boat and rowed instead. We rowed, all three of us, all night, arriving at Fiume some time after dawn when all the revelry had long been over. I was never so close to drowning.

Wildly excessive daring characterized all his activities. He drove a car at breakneck speed, in spite of only seeing with one eye, and having to wear glasses at all times. Twice he was picked up for dead and suffered from severe concussion. He hunted, bought prize-winning show-jumpers and started to play polo, which is a dangerous game even for good horsemen, and Mihály was a poor rider and violent with it. That he survived at all was due only to the fact that from a puny child he had grown into a big strong man.

All these characteristics were caused by his innate need to play with fire, seeking danger so as to show everyone not only that he was not weaker or more awkward than other people but, on the contrary, was outstandingly courageous and, indeed, braver than anyone else, and especially to show those who had looked down upon him in childhood that he could now do better than any of them. So that everyone should marvel, he made a point of being different from others, unusual, and a man to be feared. It was also important to him that by will alone he could overcome all difficulties and cope with any challenge. It was all 'I'll show them!' and stemmed from that pampered childhood when everything was permitted to him. All his life, from a baby, as a child and then as a young man growing up, he had been the centre of everything. As a grown man with an immense fortune and surrounded by flatterers, how could he have turned out differently?

With such a background and upbringing, reared in an hothouse atmosphere of abstruse confusing ideology, itself far removed from reality by its heady mixture of violent chauvinism and ideals of international cooperation, and violently self-willed withal, he stepped onto the platform of Hungarian politics.

At first he surprised everybody with his energy and his determination to get his own way. However, little by little he became wilder and wilder and more and more unpredictable, veering off in unexpected directions and down dangerous unexplored paths . . . on and on he went but never as a leader imbued with new ideas but rather one who was carried away by bombastic slogans and by the dizzying height of the role in which he had cast himself.

***

The government was lavish with numerous declarations during the first hours of the revolution. Among so many, the most famous was the message issued by Károlyi on the 2 November, which he addressed 'to all the nations of the world' no less and in which he declared that Hungary was now a neutral state and from that day on was at peace with the whole world.

'As of today Hungary is a neutral state!' shouted all the newspapers in black type on their front pages, and their more gullible readers were all thrilled, saying to themselves: 'We are neutral! How wonderful! How marvellously simple! We've said it, and immediately it is so. What a wonderful statesman that Károlyi is. Fancy knowing just what everyone longed for!' They had the example of those happy neutral states before them who had not only avoided the bloodletting but also had grown so rich that they were now the envy of all. 'Let the Germans, the French, anybody, everywhere, go on fighting! It's of no matter to us! We are not interested any more. Perhaps it will even do us some good. Perhaps we can even make some money from it, like the other neutral states!' the poor things were saying happily to each other.

Perhaps some wise rabbi of the ancient faith was the only man who, sitting in his room in the Orczy court of Budapest's old ghetto, surrounded, I imagine, by copies of the Talmud, torahs, and other holy books, would have smiled at the thought of this folly. What is this sudden transformation of a state that lost the war into a neutral power, the holy man may have reflected, but a legacy of an old ceremony still practiced by some orthodox Jews? According to their custom, when a family member is sick and likely to die they send for the rabbi. He, in his turn, does away with the dying man's name (let us call him Moise) by pronouncing the words: 'You are no longer Moise. No one here is called Moise; from today your name is Ephraim.' This is necessary so that, when the Angel of Death enters the house and calls to the dying man 'Moise! Come with me!' they can reply: 'What Moise? There is no Moise here. Moise must be somewhere else!'

'But this sick man here in his bed,' asks the Angel of Death, 'isn't he the Moise I seek?'

'Oh no!' they can all reply truthfully, 'This is Ephraim, with whom you have nothing to do!'

So the Angel of Death can only say, 'Excuse me', take his leave and seek Moise elsewhere. Echoes of this arcane custom could well have occurred to our old rabbi as he pondered the Károlyi government's message to the world, smiling ruefully as he weighed up its historical significance while possibly even despising it a little as just one more example of the goyim, as so many times in the past, once again following an archaic Hebrew tradition.

We should not be surprised, therefore, that this noisy declaration of neutrality by Károlyi was received with confidence and joy not only by the general public, who in those days understood foreign affairs even less than they do today, but also by those who had some claim to know better. Today we know everything that followed. We know that Károlyi's foreign contacts were to prove quite worthless, with the result that he was completely uninformed about the power and also the real condition of the victorious nations, and so his bold enterprise was not solidly based on any security of contract either by an exchange of official documents or even by a verbal promise. His ideas were all based, on the other hand, on erroneous suppositions which sprang, like empty phantoms created only in his own mind in the likeness of some wishful theory, from some visionary fantasy by which all nations were now ready to embrace and love each other – and were prepared to do so with unthinking haste so as to be prepared for some imminent apocalypse.

This is the only reasonable explanation for all the Károlyi government's actions, from the first days of power until the last moment when they handed over that power to the Communists. It can only have been a firm conviction that world revolution was even then about to break out at once, immediately and everywhere. They gambled everything on this single ticket, on this one possibility – just as a punter at the races will risk his entire fortune on the win of a single horse or on just one number at roulette. All their decrees, including those 'people's laws' they were to issue, came from the convictions of just ten men that this idea was not fantasy but reality, never for a moment understanding that they would be valid only if such a dream actually came to pass. In all other circumstances their actions would prove at best harmful and at worst fatal. But none of this bothered them, so hypnotized were they by this single improbable theory. They cared nothing for any other ideas; indeed, they did not even consider the possibility of anything different.

This degree of recklessness and ignorance could only have been believed possible by anyone who did not know the new leaders well and, especially, Károlyi himself. Indeed, anyone who witnessed the confidence with which they publicly expressed their guiding principles, who heard the decisiveness with which they declared their infallibility and sensed the Olympian height from which they smiled down in pity on any mere mortal who might voice some warning or hint at misgivings, could be forgiven for taking it as read that behind all this self-confidence there had to be some secret agreement with the Great Powers, probably starting with France, and that, for the new Hungarian government, everything they were doing today was but the first phase of a plan that, once successfully achieved, would be followed tomorrow by untold benefits for all. That no one then realized what was actually happening is difficult to credit today; but it must be accepted that those new leaders were truly extraordinary. As it turned out, they managed to destroy everything that would have ensured the nation's real strength. The minister of defence saw 'no need for soldiers' while the minister of finance declared he would raise taxes to a level 'the world has never seen'! They adopted a whole sheaf of contradictory slogans which could be brandished in coffeehouse debates to confound their hearers but which, when put into effect, proved merely destructive of essential institutions. It was as if they had all eaten from the 'Tree of Ignorance'! The foreign minister named only one ambassador: Roza Bédi-Schwimmer was to be sent to Bern – a woman to Switzerland, whose government was at that moment engaged in a battle over female suffrage! Of course, she was not received. Similarly, as soon as the minister for finance had declared his intentions all capital went into hiding or disappeared abroad. At the same time, although the minister of defence's speech was generally applauded, the army melted away.

Even those highly disciplined army divisions that returned in good order from the Italian Front, disintegrated as soon as they were across the Hungarian border. Examination of the details of how the army was to dissolve itself so disastrously reveals ever more inane stupidities. Once the government had declared its policy of disarmament, officials were sent to the border posts to await the arrival of the troops and to direct them, still fully armed, back to their home villages. Thus, instead of being disarmed, the men still possessed their weapons and were free to fire them off at will, which they did to conduct whatever vendettas they had a mind to. All violence went unpunished, for the old officials no longer had any authority and the new government's agents no power. And, with no one possessing either power or authority, there was anarchy everywhere.

That anarchy spread so rapidly was characteristic of the times. One result of this was that, when Károlyi wanted to go to Belgrade to attend the armistice discussions, nobody, not the government, nor the ministry of defence, nor even the commanding officer of the Budapest garrison, could find the twenty or thirty men needed as guards on the special train. As a last resort, they were forced to turn to the Soldiers' Council, which was gracious enough to furnish the necessary guard. This happened on 6 November, barely a week after the glorious revolution when Károlyi's personal halo was as yet untarnished[26].

This trip to Belgrade was to prove the Budapest public's first great disappointment.

Everyone had assumed that Károlyi would be received as a welcome friend. This belief had been fed and nourished by the government itself who had assured the public that that 'good Mihály Károlyi' would go to Belgrade and bring back news that Hungary's threatened borders would remain intact. It was just about this time that I remember seeing a poster at the corner of Kristoff Square on which was a poem extolling the great success of the Belgrade mission. It was a sort of ballad in antiquated language purporting to be by that 'good Mihály Károlyi' himself and telling how he had faced the enemy all on his own. In spite of the government's general gullibility, I do believe that there could have been reason for this. When the so-called Diaz Armistice had been signed by Austro-Hungarian representatives in Verona, it had been specified that the Hungarian armies should withdraw only as far as the existing Hungarian border, no further. Therefore it may well have seemed justified to prophesy the good news the mission would bring back. They may well have assumed that General Franchet d'Esperey would not be empowered to go further than the terms to which Diaz had put his signature. Therefore, it was safe to attribute this success to the new order. However, their calculation was wrong. The reason was simply that Károlyi, playing the part of the representative of newly independent Hungary, never identified himself with the contract made by the Dual Monarchy's military leaders but insisted on starting new negotiations. But new negotiations could entail new conditions, and this is what happened in Belgrade. The new conditions were much harsher for, in between the signature of the Diaz Armistice a few days before and Károlyi's trip to Belgrade, the Hungarian army had disintegrated. The new defence minister's remark about not needing soldiers had its effect here too. It is clear that the French commander of the Allied armies knew all about it and probably knew better than did Budapest what it meant; and so, if he was to be enabled to discuss new terms, it meant that these could be infinitely tougher and more cruel than those they replaced.

Apart from this fatal error, there were plenty of other blunders, starting with the mistaken belief that if now everybody worldwide was a revolutionary, it would do well for the Hungarians to show it. Accordingly, they appeared in informal clothes before the French general who had dressed himself in full gala uniform to receive them. What made matters worse was that a number of newspapermen[27] had accompanied the delegation – which would not have mattered if everything had gone well. However, what did matter was that some French officers took one look at the little group, asked who these people were and were told that they were only the delegation's secretaries. This lie was discovered by a Serb officer before the French general came in.

What resulted is well known. Shamed and humiliated, disappointed in all their rose-coloured hopes, Károlyi and his delegation returned from Belgrade. In vain did they try in the next day's papers to make something positive out of Franchet-d'Esperey's advice for everyone to follow Count Károlyi, but the damage had been done with the shattering effect that the public's rainbow dream of hope which had so heartened everyone at the end of October disintegrated, disappeared until suddenly there was nothing. Nothing remained of it, not even a memory.

❧ Chapter Four ❧

The Eastern Train Station was packed with people. In the great hall, the waiting rooms, the long corridors, and on all the platforms covered by the gigantic glazed vaulting, there was a huge crowd of people milling about, pushing, struggling. There was very little light, and in the darkness of that winter evening one could sense rather than see the mob around us. It was 31 December 1918.

They were nearly all men, mostly clad in dirty ragged uniforms. Some had their rifles, which they repeatedly banged on the ground. Among them were a few civilians, and here and there a frightened woman was to be seen crying and beseeching the people to let her by as she had to get home by morning because of her husband, or a sick child . . . for the love of God, please would they let her through? But almost no one paid any attention, and if one or two let her by the next would push her back roughly or would stand their ground, legs spread wide, or shrug their shoulders unconcerned – man's unkindness to man is always made worse by the dark.

I only once saw a worse mob at the station. It was night then too, but everything was brilliantly illuminated. All around were recruits in their thousands, newly called to the colours by general mobilization: It was in the first week of August in the year 1914. I was on my way to join my regiment in Transylvania. Even the streets outside the station were thronged with men hurrying to join their comrades. Most of them were working-class, with kitbags on their shoulders. There were a few gendarmes on the sidewalks outside the station, while inside some non-commissioned officers were trying to marshal the crowd into some order. With the men there was a mass of women, wives, sisters, sweethearts who all wanted to remain with their men-folk until the last possible moment and who, desperately frightened, clung to their arms and shoulders. Some of them were just crying silently, while others called out to let their men pass because, Dear God, they'd shoot him if he hadn't reported to his unit by the morning, for such things were then still firmly believed. Many of the men were drunk, and one of them nearly attacked me as I was trying to get through the crowd. I was dressed in ordinary country clothes and was carrying on my shoulder my Mannlicher sporting rifle in its hard leather case. All of a sudden a man next to me with big whiskers and blood-shot eyes started to shout, 'Look! The gentlefolk are going shooting while we go to war!' I tried to calm him down, saying I was off to enlist too, and that we were both going the same way, but he went on shouting just the same. Some others nearby pulled him away, and somehow I was able to move on; but even when he was far behind me I could still hear him shouting: 'The gentle-folk go shooting to amuse themselves! Shooting!'

The mood of the crowd had changed. Four years before everyone had been hurrying straight to the trains: all going in the same direction. Now many of them were milling about, while others stood around lazily or sat down, lolling on baggage or piles of sacks. It looked as if many of them had already been waiting for days, and that no one knew how long it would be before they were able to travel. With all this delay the angry tired crowd would all of a sudden start to whirl about without any apparent goal, so that people were carried along, turning from left to right, treading on those who were lying down and upsetting the ones who were seated. It was just like floodwater making whirlpools over unknown depths until the swirling muddy waters above pile up any debris they may meet.

The four of us had great difficulty getting through the crowd, even though Miklós Vadász, who was forging our way ahead, was a most powerful fellow. How he did it I never knew, but it was he who organized our whole trip even to getting us a First Class compartment for three people, which at that time was miraculous, a gift from Heaven. He even found a porter who in some mysterious way managed to get all of our luggage onto the train.

After struggling on in front of him, pushing our way in single file through the mob, we were guided by some railway official through the former royal waiting rooms (the velvet-covered sofas and chairs now under dust-covers) to the platform where a carefully guarded compartment awaited us. Everything was wonderfully organized by our guide and when we had settled in he received our thanks with a modest and mysterious smile. My thanks were especially warm, as I realized that all these favours had not been done for me but for Andor Andorján, who was a close friend of Miklós Vadász while I only saw him at art committee meetings and through my connection with the *Est* newspaper.

The man said his goodbyes and left, while we settled down to sleep if we could.

We were tightly squeezed into our little compartment, for where our feet should have been was the mountain made by Mrs Andorján's luggage, a mountain because she was going back to her home in Paris and was bringing out all she could. After a long and complicated struggle getting all this into place, we managed to contrive some sort of bed for the lady and a somewhat more limited space for ourselves. Then we were able to settle down and wait – no one knew for how long – until the train started.

The most important person in our compartment was Mrs Andorján's dog Lolotte: her comfort came first. Lolotte was a strange animal, one of whose parents seemed to have been some sort of ratter while the other was certainly a dachshund. A fox terrier, out of wedlock no doubt, came in somewhere, and she also seemed to have a dash of pointer in her. One grandparent must have been a pug. From this multiracial mix had emerged Lolotte, six inches high, long-bodied and weak in the limbs, very odd-looking with a tail shaped like a trumpet, a small head and a tiny pointed nose, pointer's ears and a white-spotted coat. She was swathed in cushions. She was also so overweight that when she begged she could have remained upright forever – a short little column supported by her own fat.

Her character was not a sweet one. She growled and barked and also bit, although not very successfully since her teeth were so bad. In spite of it all, I have to admit she was a nice creature of whom I later grew very fond.

We also had to arrange a bed for *that* Very Important Person; and more than that, it had to be a bed that was to her liking and that she would consent to use! This was not easy, but in the end we succeeded.

We waited. The corridor was thronged with people, and sometimes quarrels would break out, loud altercations conducted with hard words by tired men, occasionally broken by some woman's voice raised in endless complaint or by a child crying. Then again someone would try to force their way into the crowded carriage only to be pushed back by all those already on board who suddenly stopped quarrelling among themselves and joined forces to repel a common enemy. Then we could hear the sound of running steps as the disappointed boarder chased down the platform hoping against hope, poor man, to find a place somewhere else on the train.

Slowly everything became quieter, although one could still hear, on the platforms, the rumbling uneven throbbing of countless feet as the crowd milled to and fro.

We remained motionless for a long time.

No other trains arrived, and I fancy that none departed. Under the vast glazed vault the only movement was that of the crowd. There were plenty of men, but few trains. Sometimes we could hear an engine in reverse, shunting aimlessly it seemed, in and out of the station, blowing its whistle and puffing out clouds of steam and smoke, before backing out again, and all was still once more.

It came almost as a surprise when at last we seemed to be under way, with much hesitant jerking and some heavy jolts, for we could feel that the engine could hardly cope with so many carriages all crowded with passengers. After more rumbling and a noise like thunder . . . and several false starts, we really did begin to move. After noisily crossing a series of points at last we began to hear the familiar three/four rhythmic clicks as we were carried through the night to worlds of unknown turbulence.

***

We all tried to sleep. I leaned back and closed my eyes, but sleep did not come. Out of the unceasing rhythm of the wheels below us there rose up sharp and painful memories of those last few weeks, which had been so filled with menace and foreboding, with every day a new fear and a new anguish. And to these thoughts was added the awful uncertainty about what I might encounter on my journey.

All sorts of questions rose up to haunt me. Could it be true that the whole world was on the brink of revolution? Could it be that after our revolution in Budapest I was now heading for similar upheavals abroad? Had those four terrible years of war led only to a universal destruction of order?

The Hungarian press had been full of stories of revolution breaking out everywhere, mostly issued by the government's press office. I tried to recall some of them. On 8 November, I remember it was, they told how there had been a Bolshevik uprising in Zürich which, the story went, had spread to the whole canton. This one happened to be true, although no one told us of its suppression, nor that after a few days the other cantons had firmly finished it off. Then, in December, we had learned that in Berlin one Liebknecht had attempted a Communist takeover under the name of 'Spartacus' from which the government in Weimar had only managed to extricate itself by some intricate bargaining. Other stories concerned uprisings and army mutinies in France and Italy, where whole regiments were said to have hoisted the Red Flag!

No one knew if these stories were true, as few foreign papers reached Budapest. We read these stories with profound reservations, especially those about those countries who had won the war, since everyone knew that Károlyi's politics were firmly based on his belief that revolutions would break out everywhere.

We did not know much more about what was happening in Vienna. All that was certain was that the Socialists were in power and that those feeble politicians that the revolution had banished from their velvet-covered bureau chairs had been swept away God knows where.

At home in Budapest we were faced with a disturbingly imprecise picture of what recent events had brought about. It was like the multifarious little segments of a mosaic, which had to be fitted together to form the finished picture. All those spontaneous, enthusiastic public demonstrations were long past, while members of the new government tried to restore general confidence by slandering their enemies while praising themselves. The last of these festivities was to be the declaration in parliament, and to those gathered in the square outside, that Hungary had become a republic. After that, nothing. And so it was not long before it turned out that whenever there was a public demonstration, it was not for Károlyi but against him.

At this final mummery it was clearer than ever before – far more so than on that evening of revolution earlier in October – how the unrelenting grind of the war had deadened all feelings of faith and confidence in men's hearts, and that these qualities had now been replaced by a general sense of timidity and passivity. On that first night of revolution the people of Budapest were still alive, ready to express their opinions freely, with zest, pleased surprise and enthusiasm. This was no longer true today, principally because the government (the 'People's Government', as they liked to be called) had now taken to handling all matters in a tamer, less assured manner.

Desperate to avoid being accused of achieving their aims by force, they decided to consult the leaders of both Houses of Parliament. The president of the Upper House, Gyula Wlassich, insisted on strict application of the law. He declared that by law the parliament could only be dissolved by established legal procedure. Therefore his powers extended only to adjourning the House for an indefinite period. He persisted in this view, partly out of sheer captiousness, for it was clear that the consultation was a mere formality, but also, and this was more important, because in those troubled times it was essential, if possible, to maintain the principle that the rule of law should be inviolate and that one should not humble oneself before an upstart power.

This was a rare virtue in those days and much appreciated.

The Speaker of the House of Representatives took another line. It must be admitted that his situation was trickier. The mandate of the House as then composed rested on the 1910 elections and had later been extended by the emergency powers voted because of the war. This was probably the reason why the

Speaker now suggested that the House of Deputies should at once declare its own dissolution, and that this action should be voluntary and not imposed by force.[28]

Thinking about all this, as the train rumbled on, I recalled how the Fehérváry government[29] had dismissed the House of Deputies in 1906. The Fehérváry government was lawful in form, although the fact that its members were in the minority made it unconstitutional – and what indignation had broken out then! What a commotion was then heard from all those members, whether on the right wing or the left, who were offended by a proposal to bypass the law! To carry it off, the chamber had to be occupied by the military, and all opposition stamped out by the resounding clatter of soldiers' boots as they formed up in lines, blocking all the corridors and exits. This is what had been needed then to flout the law.

Now, in 1918, not even a show of force was needed. Everywhere the mood was fatalistic, almost suicidal, as if hara-kiri were inevitable. Let us surrender our country's most treasured traditions; we must be resigned to our own destruction! And that act of national suicide could not have been more complete.

There is a legend of Gül Baba that at the end of his life, impelled by desperation, he destroyed the rose garden that had been his life's work and upon which, since early youth, he had worked with loving care. Some such desperation must have worked its spell upon the Speaker, Károly Szász, on that fatal day in Budapest when he not only declared himself for voluntary dissolution but also failed to mention the recently assassinated István Tisza, the former Minister-President, who had set the precedent (although against the will of many), which had enabled Károly Szász to find himself in his present post. Not only that; he also tried to prevent anyone else from speaking a few reverent words in memory of Tisza.

It may be that he was afraid that if he did not mention the former Minister-President then others would shame him by doing so themselves.

I had it directly from Kunó Klebelsberg that before the meeting he had asked Szász if he was going to mention Tisza, and that the reply had been that it would not be 'timely'.

'Then I will do so. I shall ask to be heard before the minutes are read.'

'Then I will refuse my permission!'

And so it happened. Klebelsberg rose to his feet, but Szász appeared not to notice and quickly adjourned the session.

Even in Japan there is no more perfect act of hara-kiri: the only difference is that there they die of it.

In the last resort the only reasonable explanation can be found in the general neurasthenia that was then so prevalent.

While all this was going on some men of the 'new order' gathered in the House. Some female friends of mine had got tickets for reserved places in the public gallery and, as my post at the opera did not come to an end until 18 November and I had been obliged to stay on in Budapest, I arranged to go with them so as to see what was going on with my own eyes. The members of the Károlyi government, together with the representatives of the National Council and the trade unions, sat on the long dais that backed onto the Danube side of the Chamber. The session was presided by János Hock, that notorious priest, who sat in the middle of them. At that moment he was the effective head of the government of Hungary, and so presided over a meeting that, with no legal mandate, could speak on behalf of, and decide the fate for, the whole country.

The Chamber, which is much bigger than the great cupola above makes it seem, was by no means full. The seats in the centre were sparsely occupied, while in the wide corridors behind the pillars, we, the spectators who had come to gape at the proceedings, were able to move about at will.

Hock spoke first. He, who on most occasions had proved himself a most accomplished demagogue, speaking with a wit and brilliance that could even make his political opponents vote as he wished, now spoke with surprising ineffectiveness as he tried to be majestic, gloating and unctuous all at the same time. And as he spoke he lifted his hands as if giving a blessing, those same hands that had grubbed about in so many kinds of dirty work.

As I watched him the chief impression I had was of a cheap unshaven comedian trying to play the Archbishop of Canterbury in a Shakespeare play. Sitting there in the centre, with the face of a Lombroso, he brought to mind some events of many years before.

After that memorable day in 1904 – it was 18 November – when Tisza tried to use force to overcome the obstructionism that was holding up all parliamentary business, the House met again on 13 December. Then the opposition stormed the Speaker's podium, beat off the armed guards, and once alone in the chamber started to wreck everything in sight like a horde of unruly children. They destroyed everything they could lay their hands on and started to make a pile of all the broken furniture – desks, armchairs, shelves, the Thonet chairs of the stenographers and the wooden rails of the parapets – in the semicircle in the centre of the floor. When there was nothing left to break up, they stopped and just stood about laughing. Then Hock came forward and climbed onto the pile of wrecked furniture with a triumphant smile on his face. He sat there like a ravenous scavenging crow. There was something infinitely foreboding about him, as he sat there in his black clothes, back straight and head held high. One or two people called out 'Bravo, Hock!' and some even clapped him[30].

I was reminded of all this when I saw the same man once again sitting at the centre of an unhappy scene. But the corpse-hungry crow was now triumphing over more than broken furniture.

After Hock, there were others who would now speak at length, although they were addressing an audience that showed little signs of interest. When the establishment of the republic was announced it was presented as 'the will of the people' but only greeted by a few half-hearted cheers. Then there were more speeches, all repeating the familiar slogans in the same tired phrases with not a single original thought amongst them – and all this time the public in the corridors behind the pillars were chatting among themselves, while in some discreet embrasures some of the women were happily flirting and no doubt arranging amorous rendezvous, for Budapest, no matter what, is always Budapest.

At long last it was all over, and we could comfortably go home. Outside the square was deserted[31].

This was the last comedy to be mounted by the Károlyi government, but one could already sense that we had only reached a way-stop on the slippery slope in front of us. It was clear that there was no longer any unity among those who had at first welcomed the revolution. This was clear from the way in which one speaker would be applauded only by those on their own side of the House, while the next seemed to please only those on the other. The following weeks were to confirm this impression.

Day by day the radical socialists gained more and more ground while the middle-class ministers resigned their offices one after the other, only to be replaced by nonentities even feebler and less effective than themselves. All that carefully planned poisoning of people's opinions that the government had worked so hard to achieve was finally to bear fruit, and on that day the real revolution broke out.

It was on 12 December that the army revolted, this time against Károlyi. The soldiers of the Budapest garrison, armed with rifles and hand grenades, stormed the Royal Palace. There were thousands of them. They also brought up some cannon, which were pointed directly at the ministry of defence[32] and surrounded the Minister-President's office. No one could enter or leave either building. From one of the windows of the Royal Palace, a man called Pogány addressed the crowd 'in the name of the Military Council' and sent an ultimatum to the 'People's Republic'. Aiming at taking over Albert Bartha's post as minister of defence, he demanded Bartha's head on the pretext that Bartha was planning to organize groups of officers which, although it is true they might have helped to restore order, were anathema to the 'People's Army'. The whole of Szent György Square was full of soldiers, all shouting at once; and not only Bartha but also Károlyi found themselves prisoners in their offices nearby. Some government officials tried to parley with the soldiery from the balcony of the Minister-President's office – and I believe that Károlyi himself tried to speak to the crowd more than once – while others also tried from the ministry of defence. Despite the deafening noise everyone was doing their best to cajole the armed mob into starting negotiations or at least to listen to what was being said to them. Only one Hungarian officer had the courage to try to tell the men where their duty as soldiers lay. He was a broad-shouldered young infantry captain from the General Staff. He stepped out onto a balcony, climbed onto the parapet and, in a voice that could be heard right across the square, yelled: 'Go stop our enemies from invading our country!'

Others on the balcony pulled him back and dragged him into the building. Then, with much explanation and no little demagogic apologia, they went on trying to calm the soldiers down.

All this I heard later that same afternoon from eyewitnesses I trusted. The news put me at once in mind of a scene in Ferenc Herczeg's play *Byzantium*. When the news is brought that the invading Turks are streaming into the imperial palace, one Leonides turns to the doomed assembly of nobles and says, 'Let us pray!' whereupon the Patriarch at once replies: 'Let us not do anything which might offend them.' Indeed *Byzantium* was a most prophetic play.

Noon was long past, and still the cannons were pointed at the ministry of defence, and the besieging soldiery were still shouting and uttering fearsome menaces. Envoys from both sides were coming and going with new points for negotiation and exchanges between Károlyi and Mr Pogány. Finally, after a long delay, the government yielded and promised Bartha's dismissal and Pogány's appointment as minister of defence. Then those excellent soldiers of the Budapest garrison went triumphantly home to be praised by some of the following day's papers for having won their battle by shouting at unarmed civilians.

All this happened on 12 December. Two days later the metal workers declared for Communism.

***

Leaning back in my seat, motionless and with eyes closed, my thoughts wandered back to another incident that had occurred in the last week or two, this time more comical than tragic. On the day following the army's revolt news of a dreadful conspiracy raced through the city. The horror of it! It seemed that one of the Queen-Empress Zita's brothers, Prince René of Bourbon-Parma was in hiding in Budapest and had been there secretly for at least ten days. Ten whole days? What could he be doing? Surely nothing less than planning a counter- revolution? What could he be cooking up except a dreadful bloodbath in which all the leaders of the Revolution, along with their principal aides, would at once be slaughtered? People were running about, pale-faced with horror, distributing the awful news. The first man had only heard about it, the second knew for certain, while the third had seen with his own eyes that secret agents and hangmen were hidden everywhere, only waiting for the signal to start massacring innocent citizens. Then Parma was found and subjected to a daylong interrogation. Suddenly all the terror was blown away in a storm of laughter. It turned out that his was a purely private visit to pursue an amorous adventure, and that for its entire duration he had hardly left the bed of his beautiful singing star. Great joy broke out, and peals of laughter were heard from one end of the town to the other. There was not a single tavern where it was not the only subject of conversation, told and retold with gales of laughter, laughter that had its genesis in universal relief and joy. Thank God that even in this bleak world there was still some fun to be had! In a few days Prince René had become so popular that if he had been seen and recognized anywhere he would have been cheered to the echo.

***

The train stopped many times on that dark wintry night, even at small stations and sometimes at no station at all. The whistle seemed to blow continuously with long lamenting cries into the black night. We never knew where we were as none of the stations had any light.

Once again my thoughts took another direction.

In the second part of November, in an attempt to bring some sort of order to the people's lives, meetings were held to find a way to induce a feeling of unity, and this is when, in some secrecy, the organization called MOVE was founded. At the same time, those Transylvanians who happened to find themselves in Budapest, either for private reasons or official, formed the Szekler National Council.

Professor Benedek Jancsó was appointed chairman, but the real leader was Count István Bethlen. Men from all walks of life were to join the Council, and what bound them together was firstly that they were all Transylvanians and secondly their shared patriotic worries over the recent train of events. The radical wing of the government did not look upon the Szekler Council with favour but, since 'national councils' were then everywhere the rage, they felt unable to ban it. I had joined, since I knew I would be with many men of a similar mind to my own. And it was here that the idea started that we should send a delegate abroad representing only the Council, and who, being independent, could relate frankly what had really been happening in Hungary, who could tell the unvarnished truth to the victorious powers without being constrained by the official government line. Such a man's mission would be to explain why, from the people's growing desperation, the Communist movement was spreading, taking hold more and more every day, so much so that it was certain, if the victorious powers did not change the way they were treating our bankrupt country and give some help to those patriots of good faith, a Bolshevik triumph was inevitable. The immediate result of this would not only be a general breakdown that would make signing a peace treaty almost impossible but also that from our flames half the world would catch fire.

At that time we still believed that someone abroad would be interested in what we had to tell.

To realize such a project it would be necessary to obtain a passport and also sufficient money in foreign currency, which was not available to ordinary citizens. I was delegated to get this through Károlyi. If I remember rightly it was the afternoon of the military revolt that I went to see him. He was still shaken by that day's events and deeply shocked by them. It may be because of this that he received the Szekler National Council's plan sympathetically and agreed at once to provide that whoever was sent should travel as a private person. We talked for a long time of the dangers that threatened from all sides, dangers which would reduce him to being an empty puppet, deprived of all power, and how the whole political aesthetic of his plans for the nation, on which he had placed all his hopes, would be destroyed. It was with these fears in mind that he agreed to authorize the necessary foreign currency. I took this news back to the Council.

Now, however, an unexpected difficulty arose. None of the names we put to him proved to be to his liking, even though the first names we suggested had all been diplomats. He did not like any of them, saying that they would all make propaganda against him and he would be mad to send any of them abroad.

I went several times between the Minister-President's office and the Council, always proposing new names – but Károlyi would have none of them. His answer was always the same: he would not give passports to his enemies! This went on so long that I began to wonder if perhaps he had only pretended to agree to something that in reality he did not want. Therefore, only thinking to put him to the test, I asked, 'Well, would you give me a passport?'

He thought for a moment and then said, 'To you, yes! But I tell you, to no one else!'

That was when it was decided that if anyone was to go, it had to be me. And the decision had been taken because of a single, unpremeditated question.

For me this unforeseen turn of events was most disagreeable because, even though my friends urged me to accept the mission, I explained that I really wanted to go back to my home in Transylvania and had only remained in the capital to help settle this matter, as I knew that I was the only one who could handle Károlyi due to our connections in the past. And now it seemed that I had landed myself in it and would have to accept it. Nevertheless, I did make some conditions. One was that I should contribute from my own pocket one fifth of the money I was going to take with me – it would be in Swedish crowns – as I did not want the Szekler National Council to pay my personal expenses. The other was that before starting I should have time to go home to say goodbye to my father. Both conditions were accepted.

Since the negotiations with Károlyi had taken over ten days, my visit to Kolozsvár had to be very short. I was not able to leave until 23 December. The French Colonel Vix gave me permission to travel, provided I was escorted by one of his officers. I only had permission to remain there from morning to evening so, on Christmas Eve, I found myself on the night train to Kolozvár.

I only had a week before starting my journey to the west.

(This is the true story of how and why I went abroad on the last day of 1918. Count Tivadar Batthyány has written in his memoirs, which are suspiciously redolent of self-justification, that I left as Károlyi's envoy. That was a mistake. I was sent by the Szekler National Council and not by Károlyi from whom I did not accept any mission or any instructions. It is not surprising that Batthyány should be misinformed because by then he was no longer a member of Károlyi's cabinet. At the time of my departure Károlyi had no need of someone who was setting off into an unknown vacuum. A man such as myself, who had only the most uncertain connections with whom to negotiate, would hardly have been useful to him when Count Antal Sigray had been in Paris since 5 December. Sigray, whose son-in-law was the American ambassador in Paris, had far better connections than I did.)

***

As the train plodded slowly on through the night, my mind was filled with memories of all that had happened in the last few days, especially going back to Kolozsvár, my birthplace, and saying a painful farewell to my father. I was also filled with worry and distress not only for everything that had been destroyed but also for all the destruction still to come. My thoughts were like some devilish kaleidoscope, surfacing and resurfacing always in a different form, as visions changed and then vanished only to give way to others whose new form was as tormenting as the last.

As we travelled ever further from Hungary there was one overriding torment in the chaos of my thoughts: it was the feeling of homelessness. I felt torn from everything I held most dear. It was Fate that controlled my actions, not my own will. And so I, who from the beginning had wanted nothing but to go home, was now rolling further and further away from it.

Since then many years have passed, and in those years I have often thought how strange are the ways of Fate. Set on one's way by a single ill-considered spontaneous remark, one is led into a course of action that cannot be stopped whether one wants to or not. At the moment of departure we do not even dream of where our voyage will take us. Even when we have started we delude ourselves for an unconscionable time that in a short while it will soon be over, and we shall be free again to do as we please. Sometimes, in forests, one meets two such paths that, although divided perhaps by a stream or ditch, seem at first sight to run parallel to one another. One imagines that whichever one chooses will led us to the same place. However, slowly the paths diverge . . . and never meet again.

❧ Chapter Five ❧

During our long slow journey – I remember it was noon before we arrived in Vienna – I ran over in my mind the names of those acquaintances who might be able to help me in the adventurous enterprise upon which I had just started.

Our tiny compartment, piled high with luggage, was the ideal place for contemplation. Through the patched-up windowpanes and the slits between the wooden laths with which they had been fixed, I could get glimpses of the snowless land outside gleaming in the wintry sun.

Andorján and his wife, both tired out, were asleep. Even Lolotte was quiet and did not stir, no doubt sensing that the smallest movement could disturb her coverlet and let out some of the comfortable warmth created by her own body heat.

Once again, too, for the hundredth time, I rehearsed the arguments with which I would plead our cause.

Much care and attention is needed when negotiating with men we do not know. Not only do all men react differently in the way they take in what they hear, but there are also the very different national attitudes seemingly inbred, for example, in the French, the Germans, and the English, who will all find different aspects of an argument important or interesting. The matter under discussion may be the same, and so are the points one wants to make, but they have to be presented differently, with the tone, colour and emphasis all carefully tailored to the sensibilities of he to whom one is talking. Here it is vital to be able to sense the differences in human mentality and understand them; otherwise all presentation of one's argument will be fruitless. We ourselves must look at our case not with our own eyes but with those of the man we are trying to convince. As the French so aptly say '*entrer*

dans la peau du bonhomme' – to get in under his skin. Whatever
we have to say must be phrased according to his standpoint. Of
course, one must always keep to the truth not only for its own
sake but also because the smallest lie will sooner or later wreak
its vengeance upon us; but it is vitally important that the truth
must be expressed in terms of the other man's habit of thought.
The greatest mistake of German diplomacy, during and before
the war, was that it never ever took into consideration anyone's
way of thinking but their own.

Then I began to wonder if the first man I wanted to see would
be willing, solely on the basis of our old acquaintance, to discuss
affairs of state with someone who had no official status.

I was thinking of Esmé Howard, who is now British ambassador in Washington, and who was then *en poste* in Sweden. I had
thought of him firstly because he was within reach. Sweden had
remained neutral during the war and, among the neutral states,
had been the one that had shown most sympathy to the central
European powers (probably from fear of the Russians and
Bolshevism). I should be able fairly easily to obtain a visa for
Sweden and perhaps find there some measure of support.

My second reason for thinking of Howard was that when he
had been consul-general in Budapest some years before the war
we had begun to strike up a friendship, rare between men from
different countries, probably because we had many tastes in
common. He too loved classical music and had much appreciation for the fine arts. His wife was Italian, and that may have
accounted for that fact that he understood Europe and Euro-
peans better than many of his countrymen who (as he himself
wrote in *England and Europe*) can live for any length of time in
any part of the world and never understand anyone who was not
English.

Howard had another great advantage in being a cousin of the
Duke of Norfolk, head of one of England's oldest noble families
who ranked there almost as high as royalty. A man with such an
exalted background was not likely to be biased by current public
opinions, especially if these have been swayed by popular slogans of the moment and are infected by the shallow hatreds of
the mob. I clung to the hope that in him remained some vestiges

of that medieval chivalry which was based more on social sympathy than on geographical frontiers. With his privileged background he would surely, if he thought it right, be unafraid to
flout any diplomatic veto, if such existed, and listen to what I had
to say.

As soon as I arrived in Vienna I tried to get a visa for Sweden
but was unsuccessful as both the embassy and the consulate were
shut for the New Year. As I did not want to waste time in Vienna
I decided to try again in Berlin.

The former notary-public Charmant, who was Károlyi's
ambassador in Vienna, and Andorján took on the task of getting
our passports stamped at the German Embassy, and so I had
some time to see what the old imperial capital looked like after
the revolution.

***

For anyone who had not been there for some time the first shock
was the uncollected dirt and debris everywhere to be seen on the
streets and sidewalks. Vienna, which had formerly been one of
the cleanest of all big cities, was now a depressing sight. It looked
as if the streets had not been swept or watered for months. Most
of the shops were closed, there were hardly any cars to be seen,
and all those pretty women who used to throng the streets of the
capital had vanished into thin air.

I found myself in front of the Hofburg, and there another surprise awaited me. The great doors with the dome above, which
led from the Kohlmarkt to the Maria Theresia statue, were
closed. Only a tiny door at the side was left open, and in it stood
an armed soldier. Other armed guards were posted all round the
entire palace complex, including the two great museums. They
were all armed to the teeth, with hand grenades hanging from
their belts and guns on their shoulders as if they expected the
enemy at any moment.

I asked about this and was told that a few hundred officers, of
their own free will and dressed as common soldiers, had occupied the palace and the museums and in uninterrupted shifts,
guarded the place so strictly that no one was allowed in or out.

Deeply loyal, in spite of all that had been happening in the last weeks[33], they felt it their duty to guard what they considered imperial property. There, right in the centre of the city, the Hofburg was like a warship alone at sea, hopelessly battling against a raging storm and yet, manned by a loyal crew still faithful to their duty, still fighting on despite the fact that the leader to whom they owed that duty had abandoned them.

The sight of these men reminded me of the story of the faithful hound that guarded his master's grave until he died himself. But here in Vienna the tomb was empty for the master had long since fled to Eckartsau, no doubt he had been given no choice, and so the steadfastness of those guards was in vain. All the same it was beautiful to see and touching. It was the last time that there was to be seen the true spirit of *Mannestreue,* that ray of moral sunshine such as had been sung in the *Nibelugenlied*[34].

***

Knowing that assessment of the finances of the joint Austrian and Hungarian foreign offices had been given to a man I had known well ever since we had several times served together *en poste* in Germany and with whom I had remained good friends, I went to see him in the famous building on the Ballplatz. When the government had collapsed, my old friend had already reached the senior rank of councillor, perhaps even with the title of ambassador. Now he had been entrusted by the Austrian government – and also possibly by that of Hungary too – with the task of bringing order to the department's complicated financial and personnel problems.

The elderly porter on duty at the massive old doorway of the Ballplatz building seemed overjoyed to see me. This, I fancy, was not because he knew me but because he now had so few visitors and was longing to have someone to announce. He at once showed me up the huge staircase which had been mounted a hundred years before during the Congress of Vienna[35] by all those kings and princes big or small who were eager for Metternich to restore to them the lands they had once ruled. Upstairs I was greeted by an official with obsequious politeness and a moment or two later I found myself in that great writing-room from which the far-flung Habsburg Empire had been controlled for two centuries.

There was very little furniture and what there was had been arranged along the walls. At the far end of the room was a vast writing table of some highly polished dark wood on top of which gleamed some gilded Empire bronzes.

My friend got up from behind the table, obviously pleased to see me. Then he sat down again, and I seated myself in an armchair at the end of the table. After some little chat about the past we started to talk about the general breakdown of order and how it had come about. Somehow, in the voice of this man deputizing for a minister I detected no trace of that natural sorrow one might have expected from a high-ranking member of the empire's former diplomatic service. On the contrary, I sensed a sort of hidden joy as he expressed his regrets for what had occurred in the most banal terms, a joy that became less and less suppressed as he spoke. At first our talk was sluggish, but it was suddenly to change.

'Who would have thought,' he said, 'even a short time ago, that I would soon be sitting at this desk, the desk of the great Metternich? What a stupendous feeling! This is his inkstand that I use! This is his chair on which I sit! It is truly a stupendous feeling!'

It was obvious that he was very happy. In that room he saw only the furniture, the magnificent pictures and carpets of the palace of which he was now lord and master. He brushed aside the fact that in reality he was only an official brought in to list the assets of that once famous establishment prior to its liquidation. That the power had flown away and only the husk remained, like a gilded shell void of life, *that* he did not see. It was with pride and gracious condescension that he received me there.

And when I left he escorted me to the outer doors and shook my hand warmly as he said goodbye, saying that I must come again to see him next time I should be in Vienna.

'I am at your disposal in everything!' he said in the encouraging tones of one offering me the shining prospect of an embassy.

Then he returned proudly to his place of work, where Kaunitz and Metternich looked down upon him from the walls. The footman closed the great double doors behind him with much deference.

I went away feeling that, in spite of everything else I saw around me, I had at least found one happy man, reflecting what a treasure it must be when naïve joy in personal success can cloak reality with the thin pink vapour of content.

***

The next day we left for Germany.

It was the same crowd, the same broken windows with patchily mended glass and the same dirty seats. The train, crowded with dark-faced men and whining frightened women, dragged itself along just as slowly. After endless dawdling at a snail's pace we arrived at last at Salzburg.

During the long stretch that led to the Austrian border my anxiety had grown until I felt like a schoolboy who, after much special coaching, has to face new masters. What will they be like? Will they be over-demanding, or perhaps bad-tempered?

Just as when, for the last time before the examinations, I would revise algebraic formulae or Greek aorists, I asked myself for the hundredth time if I had properly hidden the considerable sum of money with which I had been entrusted.

It was well known that at the Austrian border there was a *Leibes-visitation* – a body-search – meaning that they would examine not only one's luggage but also the clothes one wore, all of them even down to one's shoes, to stop anyone carrying foreign currency, be it banknotes, gold or jewellery. The same occurs again on the German side to all travellers arriving in the country. Then everything had to be surrendered in exchange for local paper money and that, of course, at whatever rate they choose to apply.

I had already been warned of this in Budapest, and it caused me a lot of worry. Where should I put all those Swedish banknotes? In the soles of my shoes? But even during the war this had been a well-known subterfuge – and many people had lost everything by trying it. What about the lining of my jacket? But surely banknotes would crackle if the customs men ran their hand over me? In the seat of my trousers? There wasn't much room there, and it would surely look odd if it were too bulky?

Finally I discovered in a chest in which I used to store my old clothes, an ancient top hat, a real Methuselah of a hat. Some twenty years before it had been made for riding from an exceptionally hard felt and had a large brim. Inside there was a wide leather band to ensure that it sat well on the head, while at the back it had once had a ring to which a string could be tied so as to attach it to the lapel of one's coat. The ring had disappeared and in its place was a sizable hole.

I used to wear it when foxhunting at Zsuk and at least a couple of times it saved my life when I had a bad fall. It had braved thorny hedges and more than once had been severely damaged. Now it was purple with age, and its silk binding was in shreds. Not even a beggar would have touched it.

I took this weather-beaten old hat, which no one would suspect belonged to anyone with money, embedded my Swedish crown notes in the wide leather sweatband inside it and put my faith in its continuing to render me good service.

In Salzburg we were separated. Mrs Andorján, with the dog Lolotte, who counted as female, was ushered into the place for women, while Andorján and I took our places in a queue of male travellers.

One by one they let us through.

We then found ourselves in a strange corridor run up from wooden planking which changed direction every two or three metres and led finally to a box-like enclosure where each suspect traveller (and all travellers were suspect) was let in on his own. This was the place set aside for the *Leibes-visitation,* and here one had to undress, even to taking off one's shoes and socks. Everything was searched by hand, and they even felt under one's shirt.

I endured all this quite calmly. There are moments when one feels quite alone and needs a friend, but on that day I knew they would find nothing on me. My decrepit ancient hat was outside, hung on a carelessly protruding nail in the corridor. I had absolutely no fears that anybody would take it, for there was no one in the world who could possibly have wanted it.

I was twice searched in that labyrinth of odd twists and corners before we finally found ourselves safely outside on German soil, the Methuselah hat now proudly on my head. Throughout my travels it served me with honour, and with it I crossed the German border three more times before I finally reached The Hague.

There I bought myself a new hat, but I still mourned my old Methuselah, whose last office had been to serve me so well.

***

It was a long way from the border post at Salzburg to Berlin. Sometimes, for quite a stretch at a time, we would be ten people in a compartment meant for six – and then Lolotte had to be kept on someone's lap. All the same, we arrived in the afternoon of the following day and drove from the Leipziger Banhof to the Hotel Bristol in a heavily overloaded cab.

The streets were crowded. In double rows men in civilian clothes were marching, every tenth man or so carrying a placard saying NIEDER MIT EBERT – 'Down with Ebert' – or HOCH SPARTAKUS – 'Up with Spartacus', while on the other side of the street a similar procession carrying boards saying HOCH EBERT and NIEDER MIT SPARTAKUS, as well as others saying NIEDER MIT LIEBKNECHT, all very neatly written.

The two demonstrations passed each other peacefully and in good order on opposite sides of the street. Between them the cabbies drove their vehicles quite indifferent to what was going on. Occasionally one group would let out a cheer, and sometimes the other then did the same. Then, well drilled, one side would call out '*Hoch! Hoch! Hoch!*' before the other responded with '*Nieder! Nieder! Nieder!*' Then they would all fall silent and go on marching without any signs of emotion.

It all seemed a most peaceful demonstration, carried out with typical German discipline.

Only when we drove down the Wilhelmstrasse, past the Chancery and in front the Prussian Foreign Ministry, did we see anything to suggest that the situation was as serious as it was in reality. In all the doorways to those two buildings stood soldiers in steel helmets armed with machine guns.

And then, later in the tree-lined Unter den Linden, we met again only those apparently peaceful demonstrators with their banners.

We did not know it then, but we had arrived in Berlin on the first day of the Spartacist Rising.

❧ Chapter Six ❧

We managed to find rooms at the Hotel Bristol. Our windows were on the front side, and from time to time while we unpacked and made them tidy, we would glance out over the tree-lined Unter den Linden. We were on the third or fourth floor, and so one could see for quite a distance. Clearly in view were the Greek columns of the Brandenburg Gate, and at one side, further away in the grey distance, was the statue of Frederick the Great in the square in front of the imperial palace. The street was full of people strolling about, walking, talking, gazing around or just loitering on the sidewalk. There were hardly any cars to be seen and people crisscrossed the street, walking in all directions, only dispersing for a moment when one of the well-behaved groups of demonstrators marched by brandishing their party slogans. The demonstrators still occasionally let out a disciplined shout, but it seemed to raise no echo from the passers-by.

I do not remember having seen any armed civilians that afternoon. The crowd, gaping and staring, gave a somewhat merry impression as if the Berliners preferred to be amused by everything that was going on and, although from our windows above one could not hear what they were saying, I am sure they were making fun of it, thinking it all something of a lark – *ulkig*, as they would say in Berlin.

Towards evening it quietened down; at least we thought it did, and so we busied ourselves planning the next stage of our journey and decided to get our visas in the morning. There were no alarming signs in the hotel. Quite a number of foreigners were dining there, the hall-porter was saluting the guests with his habitual elegance, the waiters were serving dinner with their unusual false deference – although, no doubt, once back in the kitchen there was no more talk about veal chops or fried scabbard-fish. There they would surely be discussing the events of the last two days, how the Ebert government had dismissed Eichenau, the Chief of Police who had refused to give up his place in the Cabinet but who had gone so far as to arm the Spartacist revolutionaries. And maybe, too, they whispered among themselves that Radek, the envoy of Soviet Russia, had arrived in Berlin on the first of the month – and that if he were there it wasn't for nothing.

Foreigners just passing through knew nothing of all this, so we planned our trip in peace and went to bed. We awoke the following morning to the sound of gunfire. At first it was sporadic, and far away. The Unter den Linden was again crowded with people, but they were neither so quiet, nor so merry, as they had been on the previous day. Now they were curious . . . but frightened too. Some distance away a black mob was gathering, and later we heard that the offices of the Socialist newspaper *Vorwärts* had been attacked and burned down. Towards midday a wave of fear swept through the crowd, and everyone ran like madmen into the neighbouring side streets, or dived into doorways. In a few moments there was no one to be seen in the street. Then a few urchins raced by shouting '*Es wird geschossen!*' – 'They're shooting!' The strange thing was that these street-boys did not even try to hide but ran on screaming towards the imperial palace. Then there were a few moments of calm before machine-gun fire was heard from beside the Brandenburg Gate. We could hear well the sound of the bullets hitting some advertising placards and the metal reflectors of the streetlights, also the paving and kerbs of the sidewalks. All of this we could observe in comfort, and also in safety since the pillars beside our windows protected us. The shooting lasted only a few moments; then there was silence, and the public filtered slowly back into the street. In a short while everything was just the same as it had been; people stood about as before, gazed around and walked to and fro, every bit as if sudden death had not swept past them a moment before.

This happened more than once, including the urchins; and this same pattern was repeated many times during the first days of our stay. Shouts that there was shooting would start up somewhere, and everyone would run to take shelter; then they would all return with the unquenched curiosity and the indolence natural to the city-dweller. Slowly the crowd grew smaller, but the picture remained the same, that day and the next. These days were so similar that it is now difficult to recall the exact chronology of what happened. As foreigners we could not tell the reason for these sudden showers of bullets and did not really care, and so it was not long before we became as accustomed to them as we were to showers in April. We used to say, 'We'd better wait a bit, they're still shooting!' or, 'Now we can go, it's stopped', just as one might have said about rain. We lost half a day like this. By the time we had learned the pattern of shooting it was too late to go out and get our visas, and so we lost precious time when we should already have been on our way.

It was afternoon when I went first to the Swedish Embassy. Knowing Berlin well from the past I went on foot, not only because it was not far to go but also because I thought it would be interesting to see more than we could glean from the puppet-show we observed from the windows of the hotel. Only Unter den Linden, Wilhelmstrasse and Pariser-Platz had anything warlike about them. The park of the Tiergarten (which contained the Zoo) was as lovely and peaceful as on any other day. The beautifully tended lawns were as green as ever, and here and there were scattered some lemon-yellow leaves that had fallen from the lime trees. They were like golden coins. Blackbirds and titmice whirled playfully about, woodpeckers were tapping away, and sparrows settled impertinently on the marble statues and behaved in their usual disrespectful way.

I walked along Tiergartenstrasse and found it deserted. It was easy then to fancy myself back in the past – in 1900 and 1901 – when I had stayed there for some two years. Then I had lived not far from the park and in this very street I had often seen Emperor Wilhelm's carriage as he was driven swiftly from Potsdam to the capital, drawn by four magnificent Hungarian dapple-greys. They went like the wind. With heads held high, proudly, with a tremendous clatter of hoofs, they dashed by, appearing for a second at some turning and then, in the twinkling of an eye, disappearing at the next.

Even then I almost expected to see him racing by. Those wonderful dapple-greys! Where, I wondered, were they now?

Walking on, I arrived at the start of Siegesallee, and there I glanced at that row of marble statues of the Electors, which look as if they have been cast in molten wax, so repulsively smooth, shiny and greasy do they seem. Wilhelm II had thought to glorify himself by erecting them. There were about thirty, and the unveiling of each one had provided an unrivalled opportunity for delivering some *schneidisch* – spirited – oration with which the poor man had thought he would boost his popularity but which, on the contrary, by their unerring tactlessness, only served to dismay even his most fervent admirers. I was present on one of those occasions. The emperor's corrosive voice was unforgettable, as he declaimed his speech with disagreeable attempts at pathos and far too many words. Disagreeable, too, were all those run-of-the-mill Lohengrin costumes, silver armour, gilded helmet, box-leather thigh-boots, marshal's baton and, indeed, anything else which had a martial air. Standing there, with a belligerent expression on his face and festooned with the ribbons and chains of countless orders, he gave the impression of having borrowed it all to conceal the peace-loving middle-class soul he really was. At every parade I ever saw him attend I had the impression that, standing there in front of the soldiers of the most renowned and virile army and bodyguard in the world, he was the only one whose face did not fit.

I went on my way, filled with these and similar thoughts, until I reached the Swedish Embassy.

The ambassador, Baron Essen, received me warmly. He promised any help and support I might need but said I would have to return on the following day to collect my passport since the consulate office was closed for the afternoon, which meant that it could not be stamped before the morning.

I also heard from him that there was likely to be some difficulty about the trains because already on that day only one or two lines were expected to be functioning. It seemed that a good part of the suburbs had already been taken by the Spartacist rebels. 'We'll see what it's like tomorrow,' he said as we parted.

It was dark by the time I got back to the hotel, as I had to make a long detour to avoid the blocked streets. Still I managed it fairly easily. If I remember rightly it was then that I saw they were building barricades outside the Leipziger Bahnhof, but it is possible that that was on the following day.

On the morning of 7 January the gunfire started early. It sounded as if most it was coming from the city centre where, we heard at midday, the Communists had seized the town hall. From then on the awesome noise of firing came closer and closer.

The rear entrance to the hotel gave onto Behrenstrasse, which I had been planning to use on my way to the Swedish Embassy. Unfortunately there were guards there who would not let me go through to Wilhelmstrasse, which was on my route, because there was fierce fighting near the palace of the Chancellery just by the corner of Behrenstrasse. Machine guns were cracking away, and later that evening we learned why; the Spartacist men had taken the Hotel Kaiserhof and from its windows had been firing across the street at the Chancellery and at the Foreign Office next door. They met fierce opposition, and soon the Kaiserhof had been retaken by government troops.

Eventually I managed to reach Friedrichstrasse, where one could pass without any danger and where the solid blocks of the intervening buildings deadened the sound so effectively that one could almost believe that one was taking a walk in a quiet peaceful city. Most of the shops there were open.

After an extended detour I finally reached Baron Essen, who, as he handed me my passport, was able to tell me about the current state of affairs, which he saw as critical. No trains were leaving the city. The Görlitz Bahnhof and the Schlesischer had both been taken by the insurgents and reduced to ruins, and it could well be that this was true of the other stations too. The Ebert government were expecting guns from Spandau, but so far they had not arrived. The government's control of order in the city was uncertain since some of the police were already openly changing sides and joining up with Liebknecht's troops. By the following day it was quite likely that the Spartacist rebels would have become the masters, and from them it would only be a short step to the Soviet Russians.

We talked about all these agreeable possibilities sitting in deep armchairs in a wide window embrasure from which one could see the wonderful trees and lakes in the former deer park. What marvellous silence reigned there under those centuries-old oak trees! We could gaze along the wide avenues, now deep in shadow, where Frederick the Great had hunted the deer. And on the flat surfaces of the lakes we could just catch glimpses, in the fading light, of dark brown patches made by those flights of wild duck that still bred there.

From time to time, as we sat there talking, we would fall silent gazing over that wonderful landscape – but our hearts were still troubled by the worries of the day.

After one such pause Baron Essen had turned to me. Speaking without emphasis, as if it had been the most natural thing in the world, he had then said: 'If there should be trouble, I will take you with my embassy staff to Stockholm. I know that if the Communists come to power, I am certain to be recalled; but you, you could not get out on your own!'

I thanked him warmly for his generous offer, which was all the more touching as we had met for the first time only the day before.

Once again I had to make a wide detour to reach the hotel, and when I got there I found it ringed with gunfire, which had now moved up from the city centre to around the Brandenburg Gate and Pariser Platz.

That evening, when Mr and Mrs Andorján and I sat down to dinner, we found the hotel restaurant almost empty, while there also seemed to be fewer waiters about. The hotel's main entrance had been locked and barred far earlier than usual. We wondered then what we should do, finding it somewhat ironic that as foreigners in Berlin we should be trapped there by a revolution with which we had nothing to do.

Mrs Andorján was anxious to get to Paris by way of Copenhagen, and so her husband decided to accompany her as far as Holland before going on to Sweden in his capacity as correspondent of the Budapest evening paper *Az Est*. I also wanted to go to Sweden, but here we were, three of us – or rather four of us counting Lolotte – stuck in Berlin, unable to budge either forwards or backwards.

There was something ineffably comical about our situation, which that night proved to be noisier than ever before, with the sound of artillery fire from the direction of the imperial palace. We could see, too, flames that meant either a burning building or that the combatants were using flame-throwers.

The following morning it was impossible to leave the hotel since a battle was raging round the gates of the Tiergarten. We were then told that the Spartacists had occupied the park during the night and were now being besieged there by government troops. Sounds of fighting were also heard from behind the university and from one of the army barracks. Our hotel was strategically placed right at the epicentre of all this, and so on that day Berlin could not have offered us any place more interesting!

Andorján then went to see the Berlin correspondent of *Az Est* who lived somewhere near the Tempelhoferfeld[36], while his wife and I spent the day gazing out of our windows and, whenever there was a brief lull in the hail of bullets, taking Lolotte for a walk. At midday the hotel's manager told us that we could only stay until that evening or, at the latest, the next morning as the food supply depot had been taken by the Spartacists, which meant he would no longer be able to feed us. He had decided, in these circumstances, to shut up shop, and we could go wherever we chose!

When Andorján came back we discussed this new situation. A little later he went out again and by evening was back with the joyful news that he had managed to hire a private taxi whose driver was prepared to take us to Warnemünde, where one could take a ship to Copenhagen. The taxi driver had demanded a huge sum of money but as by then none of us was in a bargaining mood we at once agreed to split the fare and hop! Away we would go, whatever the cost!

As we had to quit the hotel the following morning we decided to send all our luggage as early as possible to the *Az Est* offices at the south end of Friedrichstrasse, while I would try to get Danish visas in the forenoon and rejoin the others as soon as possible at the newspaper office. From there we could set off unobtrusively.

The next day was 9 January. I entrusted my own small amount of luggage to the care of the Andorjáns and started off to find the Danish Embassy, which was somewhere behind the parliament building and between the river Spree and the Tiergarten.

First of all I had to head north because it was obvious that no one could go directly through Pariser Platz and the park gates as that was where two opposing forces were face to face. Accordingly I had somehow to get to the other side of the Spree and approach the embassy from behind.

After waiting for a moment of calm I managed to get across Unter den Linden, where all the shops were shut, and walked briskly along the almost deserted sidewalk. Just beyond the Friedrichstrasse station, in that already suburban district, the atmosphere changed dramatically.

Everywhere there was bustle and movement. Everyone seemed to be in the street. Butchers' shops, bakeries and other shops were all open. The bars were full of people, men, women and children, in groups, all talking away and eagerly discussing the news. Everybody seemed to be gazing to the east, in the direction of the Reichsrath, as if they were expecting something from there. Mingling with the crowd were some officers of the guard with great clanking swords (their barracks were not far off) and some other soldiers too, none too clean. I was surprised to note that they were not in battledress. They behaved in a friendly fashion with all the people they met, shaking hands and chatting; and although I was walking at some speed through the crowd, I had the impression that they were telling everyone that they would not fight either for the government or with the Spartacist rebels. Come what may, they did not care! Perhaps to underline their indifference some started flirting with some of the women in a most marked manner, so much so that the girls responded by tripping about, giggling and laughing.

Suddenly the crowd split apart to make way for a sombre group of workers to pass between them.

There were about two hundred of them, marching in rows of four, sombre of countenance and resolute, looking neither to the right nor to the left. They marched in total silence: not a cry, not a sound.

They were all dressed in shabby threadbare working clothes, but the rifles on their shoulders were brand new, their barrels as shiny as if they had just been polished. They looked as if they had been freshly issued from some arsenal that morning.

On they went, with heavy resounding steps, marching southwards in the direction of Unter den Linden and the Brandenburg Gate, marching towards their destiny, silent and serious.

And as they passed by, the gaping crowd fell silent too, as if even they could hear above their heads the rush of wings as the Angel of Death flew over them.

As I continued on my way I met two more such groups.

It was fascinating to be allowed this sight of a revolution in the making. I would have loved to have had more information and, with the writer's eternal curiosity, badly wanted to stop and ask questions as to what was happening. But I needed to hurry to finish my task. Still, I should mention that the people around me all seemed friendly.

In that part of Berlin there are many streets that spread out star-shaped from the Reichsrath, all starting from the axle of the windows of the palace. I had intended to use one of these on my way to the embassy, but as I reached the corner I was stopped and warned that it was impossible to pass that way because 'those scoundrels' were firing their machine-guns there. 'Don't go *that* way!' they said.

I thanked them for their kindness and then reflected that it was possibly my Methuselah hat, so old and battered that it had removed any suspicious hint of the prosperous middle class from my appearance.

Accordingly I made a wide detour by crossing the bridge over the Spree and plunging deep into the Moabit district before re-crossing the river by the other bridge at the Busch circus. And so I finally got behind the Reichsrath to the Danish Embassy.

Count Moltke, the ambassador, was at home and received me at once. I knew him well from the time, eighteen years before, when he had been one of the junior secretaries at the embassy, and we had spent many merry evenings together. Even though he was now an ambassador he had not changed at all. He came forward to greet me with just the same eager smile and simple kindly, gentlemanly manner.

He was much amused at the irony of my finding myself in Berlin and being obliged to make my way to Denmark by taxi, and immediately gave orders for my visa to be prepared. While the necessary formalities were being completed, we had a pleasant talk.

Outside the noise of gunfire grew louder, and now, from quite close by, there was shouting too. It sounded like a bayonet charge in the trenches.

In fact this was the day on which the Spartacists attacked the parliament building and, perhaps for the sake of variety, had chosen to do it from the Tiergarten side. And so, with my usual unfailing instinct, I had managed to drop myself right in the middle of it all – just where 'something was going on'!

Moltke most kindly made me stay with him until the fighting died down; and so we went on talking until some degree of peace seemed to have returned to the streets.

***

It was already one o'clock by the time I had reached the other side of Friedrichstrasse and out to the Tempelhofeld. I had managed to hobble there in a good old-fashioned Berlin *droschke,* which I had been lucky to catch. As the old nag trotted calmly through the city I could imagine him muttering to himself: '*I've* seen things much odder than this!' As it was, he never hurried nor seemed in the least unnerved.

The taxi, fully loaded, was already waiting, and so we set off at once.

We were filled with joy, not because of the seats, which were execrable, but simply because we were on our way at last.

The car was a small, old-fashioned, closed taxi. Our luggage was piled high on the roof and on the seat beside the driver. Inside there were two folding seats – one also piled high with luggage, while on the other perched Andorján. On the back seat I sat with Mrs Andorján. On my lap was a travelling bag and a rolled and strapped plaid rug. On Mrs Andorján's lap was a basket and, on top of that, the dog Lolotte. Until that moment I had not noticed how grossly fat the dog was; she was like a hippopotamus in that tightly packed space.

It was two o'clock in the afternoon when we finally took to the road.

When we first started I was disconcerted to see that we were not heading north, where our destination lay, but driving further and further towards the west. On and on we went, further and further from the road to Strelitz, where we would have been going, passing along little-used streets in the wrong direction!

As far as I could tell by peering round our mountains of baggage, we seemed to be somewhere in Charlottenburg, as indeed we were, for in a few moments we drove past the royal palace there. The suddenly we turned north, still by way of narrow deserted side streets.

At first I had wondered if our man was not just driving at random, but Andorján had assured me that he had already agreed to these detours, for otherwise we might not have been able to get out of the city.

Their strategy proved right and soon gave us proof of what an intelligent driver we had. Taking always deserted side-streets he would turn off the moment he saw three or four men standing about, turning left or right and doubling back to rejoin his route further on. He repeated this manoeuvre God knows how many times without a flicker of hesitation. In this way we zigzagged across the city suburbs for about two hours before we were able to join the highway north.

A couple of times some sinister-looking men tried to bar our way – on one occasion even grabbing at the car door – but our driver just cursed them in the best Treptow manner (Berlin's most colourful dialect!) and put his foot down, leaving them behind as we sped on.

This was when nemesis caught up with Lolotte. The moment those men came to the car window she started to bark – and what a slapping her fat back then got from her frightened mistress! This was no little satisfaction to me.

It was a great relief when we finally found ourselves out in the open country with fields and woodlands on either side of the road.

Finally night fell, the ink-black darkness of a January night, a darkness to cloak the fugitives' flight.

***

We motored on like this for a long time, sometimes managing to doze off in spite of the discomfort.

For a long time nothing untoward happened.

Then, suddenly, we stopped. We were surrounded by moving lights, some of which were directed at the inside of the car. All around were soldiers in battledress and tin helmets. An officer stepped up and asked for identification.

When our passports were returned to us he asked where we had come from.

'From Berlin,' we replied.

He then declared we could go no further, and when we asked why, since our visas were in order, he replied: 'The Berlin Police Department's certificate of residence is missing. This confirms the length of your stay. You should have reported your arrival and your departure. That is the law!'

We tried to explain that there was a revolution going on in Berlin and that even if police headquarters was still standing, the chief commissioner's office was under siege and no one not bent on suicide could have got anywhere near it.

None of this interested him. It was as if nothing we had said had even penetrated his head!

'*Laut Verordnung müssen Sie sich das Polizeiattest verschaffen!*' – 'It is clearly ordered that you must produce the Police certificate!' From this he would not budge and repeated his demand that we return at once Berlin to obtain the necessary certificate.

The obduracy of this officer in his determination to apply the letter of the law put us in a hellish position from which we were saved only by a tremendous bluff on the part of Andorján. He said he knew all about this *Verordnung* but that, according to its text, he had not been bound to declare his presence to the police since he was the new Hungarian government's ambassador to Copenhagen.

Upon this the officer stood back aghast, totally unable to remember what the *Verordnung* had said about diplomats, and began to falter. Andorján at once said menacingly that if we were not let through immediately he would at once send a dispatch to his government from where they stood!

The risk was too great for the German, who stood back and saluted.

All this took place at Neu-Strelitz. It was then about 8 p.m., and we were a hundred kilometres or so from Berlin.

Our original plan had been to have dinner there, but now we did not dare stop and give time for the officer to start thinking for himself. So we rushed on into the night.

***

Again it was a long, long road and it was about one o'clock when we finally arrived at Warnemünde.

It was pitch dark, and everything was closed. Hoping we might find somewhere to eat we drove straight to the harbour, but all we found here was a wooden hut that served as the port office. After much banging on the door some sort of night watchman stumbled out.

He ushered us into an ugly, freezing-cold room whose walls were of coarse planking, and after much discussion finally sold us some German sausage and some hardboiled eggs for an outrageous price and then left.

We lay down on some benches and very soon, despite nearly fifteen degrees of frost, fell into a deep sleep.

***

Now followed the most energetic morning of our journey.

Quite early we received the most dreadful news, really horrible news! Lolotte would not be allowed to enter Denmark, at least not until after forty days of quarantine. Not one moment less!

Our consternation can only be imagined, so much so that to this day my pen is unable to describe the happenings of that morning. The three of us – but not the dog, who remained calm: calmer and indeed friendlier than we had ever known her – became like the inhabitants of an anthill, swarming about in every direction.

Hither and thither we ran, holding discussions with the frontier police, customs officials and the port commander, all of them suspicious of these dangerous smugglers. It was all in vain. What we asked was impossible! Then we went to see the director of the Dog Pound, who turned out to be the same night watchman who had sold us two hardboiled eggs for such an exaggerated price the night before and who said that travellers to Copenhagen often left their dogs with him.

It was then that I noticed that he agreed to take care of Lolotte with oddly suspicious relish, and that when he stroked the animal's fat back it was with flashing eyes and much licking of lips. Clearly, he would cheerfully have eaten poor Lolotte the very next day. I had heard that in Germany fat dogs were considered a delicacy, and indeed I remembered having seen notices in butchers' shops which read MORGEN WIRD EIN FETTER HUND GESCHLACHTET! – 'Tomorrow we will be killing a well-fattened dog!'

Mrs Andorján was on the point of accepting this strange dog-lover's offer when I intervened. Even though I thought Lolotte a mannerless beast, I could not wish her a sad end in a hot oven, so I drew Mrs Adorján's attention to her pet's likely fate in the man's kitchen. So appalled was Mrs Andorján at this unhappy prospect that after an explosion of grief she decided she would rather poison poor old Lolotte on the spot and so save her from the roasting pan.

Her husband accepted this solution with no little joy and ran at once to find a veterinary. He came back later with the news that a veterinary was on his way equipped with a syringe and strychnine at the ready.

In the event his help was not needed. By the time Andorján came back I had found another solution. Moved by poor Mrs Andorján's tears and lamentations, I swore that somehow I would find a way to save Lolotte.

It was a bold plan, but it worked. We wrapped the animal in the English blanket that I always carried loose when travelling, strapped it well with a luggage strap until, as the blanket was fairly thin, it looked like any other rolled-up travelling rug. Luckily, the dog was so sausage-shaped and her legs so short that they did not protrude. Then I carried her onto the ship like that.

When we boarded no one bothered to have my rug unfastened and so I crept down at once to the lowest possible cabin, opened a small slit for her nose so that she would not suffocate, but kept her well strapped in until we were able to let her out in the Danish train.

Mercifully she did not bark, not even once. And this is the true story of how Lolotte was saved.

***

It seemed a long time before the ship started to shudder and then smoothly glided out of the German harbour. I went up on deck to find that the sea was calm, as smooth as oil, and from its silken surface came occasional flashes of silver.

On deck I found some twenty or thirty soldiers, dressed in dark-grey uniforms, standing or strolling about, some of them gazing eastwards towards the commercial docks. They were all French officers, and in their brand-new uniforms, there was nothing to show that they were newly-released prisoners of war. They looked well nourished, had a good healthy colour and talked loudly among themselves with shining eyes and a proud happy mien.

Seeing them there was completely unexpected and struck in me a most painful note. Until that moment I had only seen the men of a defeated nation, exhausted, strained to desperation by desperate struggles, whose manner and bearing reflected only the pain of their country's decay, no matter what their background or their loyalties. Now, for the first time, I met some of the victors.

The sheer toughness of the French, which in the past had been stupidly underrated by so many people, and especially by the Germans, had just been demonstrated in a world war. Personally I had always believed in it, but until this moment I had never seen so strikingly evident that Gallic self-esteem which not only characterized their disdain for everyone else but also strengthened the national characteristics of daredevilry and self-sacrifice which are one of the French nation's most marked qualities. It is not a particularly sympathetic quality, but it carries with it great force. As they stood there, so jaunty and defiant, with legs arrogantly thrust forward from the hip, all this passion radiated from them. Their very stance was witness to the flaming patriotism that had helped the nation to wait silently for nearly half a century so as to prepare themselves for the moment of *revanche* – revenge[37].

'*Y penser toujours, n'en parler jamais!*' had been the motto of the whole nation. It had been there deep inside men engaged in hand-to-hand fighting, and there whenever the common soldiers, the French *poilus*, perhaps subconsciously aware of their own weakness, felt the need of some extra boost to morale: some drug to give them endurance beyond their natural strength. This passion, too, would inflame their cruelty and the joy in wreaking pitiless vengeance, just as, after the chase, the dogs prepare to tear apart the prey they have just hunted to death.

And suddenly all these thoughts were made manifest in song. From far away came the sound of the 'Marseillaise'.

Two large troopships had just put to sea, and as they left the quayside, the singing started up. On board were two thousand French soldiers, also ex-prisoners of war, who had just started their journey home; and, as the sound of their voices reached us, the officers began to sing as well.

Never again have I heard that anthem sung as the soldiers sang it that day, singing triumphantly, with such boldness, defiance and so much joy in victory, that as the men, leaving the German sand-dunes behind them, were beginning their glorious and momentous journey homewards, their song took wings.

It sounded quite different from those occasions when we normally heard it – at concerts or other festive occasions. To begin with, it was far faster, with a quicker rhythm and with the words somehow broken up so that sometimes it seemed as if we were hearing two versions simultaneously: one drawn out and the other contracted. It was like a fanfare of trumpets: all embracing, merry, boastful and exaggerated. Here was the very essence of French *blague* mixed with what the Italians call the '*furia francese*'.

'. . . *le jour de gloire est . . . arrivé!*' – how true it was for them!

I went back inside the ship. It was better there, for no outside sound penetrated those portholes so firmly secured against the waves. All one could hear was the asthmatic breathing of the steam engines and the grinding of metal plates.

When we got further out to sea, the waves grew stronger, smashing themselves against the hull, and then one could hear the water on deck draining away with the rhythm of the waves.

The eternal indifference of nature to man throbbed relent-lessly against the ship's sides. Cut by the churning propeller, the water soon became smooth, clean and virginal once more, just as if that manmade monster had never sliced it apart – that element that could carry so much passion, so much joy . . . and so much sorrow.

ᑋ Chapter Seven ᑋ

A big disappointment awaited me in Copenhagen, for there I
learned that Esmé Howard was no longer in Stockholm. He had
left two days before for Paris to join the discussions of the
'*Grande Cinq*', that committee of the five principal victorious
allies at which President Wilson, Clemenceau and Lloyd George
were to redraw the map of Europe into that which we know
today.

With this news my whole plan went up in smoke.

I knew that Howard would have received me even though,
from the English point of view, I was still an enemy alien; and he
would have listened to what I had to tell him because he was an
intelligent and broad-minded man.

Now it had become impossible for me to reach him since he
was already in Paris, and I would never be allowed to get there.

I had no idea what to do.

Our ambassador in Copenhagen had left for home, leaving
Stanislaus Deym as chargé d'affaires at the embassy. I spent several afternoons in his company learning something of what was
happening in Hungary from those emigrants who had just got
out. Later I was to learn much more at The Hague.

In the elegant rooms of the Copenhagen embassy we would
drink tea in the company of Deym's Spanish wife, the lovely
Countess Claruchitta. The tea was excellent, and the furniture –
lit by beautiful, well-placed silk-shaded lamps – was superb.
Loveliest of all, however, was the hostess herself who, having
broken a leg a few weeks before, used to recline on a sofa,
dressed, in a lacy negligee, amidst a pile of brocade cushions and
shawls and was, I fancy, bored to death. Not many people called
to see them, and these were limited to a few neutral diplomats

and junior members of their own embassy. That was all. The Danes had always been friendly to the Allies, both because of traditional friendship and also from fear of the Germans. I saw none of them there.

In that scented drawing-room and in the presence of that beautiful lady, we all tried to appear light-hearted and merry, but the sense of the whole world turning topsy-turvy lay heavily upon us. The disastrous news arriving from central Europe grew daily more depressing and left us feeling lost and homeless like men in a lifeboat tossed about at the mercy of a great ocean.

Deym, whom I had known superficially since our days in Vienna, had at first received me coldly, but later, when I had convinced him that I was not travelling as Károlyi's envoy, his stiffness disappeared. Of Károlyi he had many hard things to say, and this was not only because of Deym's fierce sense of loyalty to the king but also because they had formerly been close friends. He had twice been asked to shoot at Karolyi's country place at Parád and had also been Károlyi's companion in that crazy adventure in the hot-air balloon of which I have already written.

There was no reason for me to stay on in Copenhagen, and in any case I found the atmosphere of that city intolerable. The streets were filled with all those French soldiers who had started on their journey home from Warnemünde at the same time as we did. The Danes gave them a tremendous welcome, and naturally their mutual celebrations largely took the form of drinking together; and the night was filled with sound of yodelling as, arm in arm, they staggered about the streets.

Mrs Andorján at first thought she might be able to go to France by ship, but this plan had to be changed, although she did not seem to mind, because the North Sea was still littered with mines, and almost every day we would read of boats and ships that had been sunk. So she then decided to try to get home by way of Holland. Andorján decided to go with her, and I joined them in the hope that somehow I could reach England from there.

For a long time we discussed which would be the best route. On paper the most direct way would have been through Berlin, but this was ruled out since we had been stuck in the German capital once already due to the Spartacist rising. Instead we chose a longer route by way of Hamburg, Bremen and Osnabrück, hoping that by so doing we could avoid any further adventures.

Off we set. Once again to Warnemünde, and from there due west.

The express was very crowded and very slow, but we were accustomed to both.

When we were already close to Hamburg the train suddenly stopped. We were in a small station, a very small station, and there we had to wait – and wait and wait without the train showing any signs of movement. The train attendants were busy discussing something with the stationmaster.

We asked ourselves what could have happened. What was going on?

Finally a train attendant walked the length of train. Everyone out! The train was going no further.

No further, at least not that day. No further? Because that very day the Spartacist rising had broken out there too, and the old Hanseatic city was already in their hands.

There was something fatalistic, and also comical, in the fact that we had all over again run straight into precisely what we had tried to avoid. It was just like Berlin. If we had gone by way of Hanover we would have had no trouble – and here we were!

I went to talk to '*Herr Stationschef*', who told me that Altona was still controlled by the central government, and that we could wait there to see what happened next.

'How far away are we?' I asked.

'About twenty kilometres, but you might have to go rather more as you'll have to keep away from the Hanseatic city limits.'

It was two or three hours before I could find some means of transportation. Finally I was able, with the help of the village innkeeper – with whom I adopted my best *Norddeutsch* accent to avoid arousing suspicion since foreigners were not much liked there – to get an ancient four-wheeler drawn by two sad-looking nags delivered to the station.

It was a dear old hackney cab, not unlike those old fiacres I remembered from my childhood, which used to ply the streets of

Buda when they still bore white number-plates. It was oddly constructed: half open carriage, half glazed-in coach. In the 1850s they were nicknamed *batár alahátt*, which was probably derived from *bâtard à la hâte* – a mongrel in a hurry. The rear part had a fixed roof with a perpendicular back to it, while the front seats only had glass windows at the sides and back. God knows how many hands this old rattletrap had passed through before landing up in a tiny village in North Germany.

Anyhow we piled in all our luggage – bags, baskets, strapped-up rugs and all that had now become so familiar – and then squeezed ourselves in: all three of us or rather four because Lolotte was still the Most Important Person among us.

Dusk was falling as we set off once again.

Where we went, through what villages we passed, I have no idea. Late that evening we arrived in Altona, where we found that order still reigned. There, too, was a hotel and, just as important, dinner as well.

The next day I managed somehow to telephone to Karl Mönkenberg, who lived in Hamburg and whom I had known from our days in the *Süd-Armée* – the army of the south. He was as astonished as I was that I had got through. At first his manner was coldly laconic, but this did not upset me, as I knew that since the Károlyi takeover in Budapest everyone had been ultra-careful about what they said on the telephone. I asked him if he could think of any solution to our problems. For example, were there any trains that could take us through to Holland? Could I see him somewhere? No, he knew of nothing; and as to meeting, no, not at present. However, as to trains he did not know for certain but believed that negotiations between representatives of the two cities were just then being held.

This, at least, seemed to hold some ray of hope. Then, around noon, came the news that the Spartacists would allow a single train to pass through Hamburg on the Bremen-Holland line provided that no one left the train while it was in transit – and that we had no intention of doing!

In less than fifteen minutes we were seated in our carriage. There were not many passengers, but not a few anxious faces since no one was sure that the Spartacists would keep their word and let us pass through all those many stations in the ancient city-state. No one knew, in that time of temporary and local changes of government, what strange decisions might still be taken.

Our train moved on slowly, with much clanking as it thundered over points, sometimes proceeding smoothly, sometimes in fits and starts, as we puffed and whistled our way through the many large covered stations and innumerable smaller stops in the Hamburg territory. Everyone sat close to the windows, hoping to catch a glimpse of what was going on; but no one liked to look straight out in case he was thought to be spying and got himself arrested. The picture was the same at every station we passed through: heavily-armed workers were standing at attention five paces apart beside the rails, all looking at the passing *bourgeoisie* with an expression of surly belligerence on their faces. There was something infinitely menacing about those lines of motionless men silently watching as our locked train passed slowly between them.

It took a long time for our train to get around the city and its great harbour. We could see nothing through the thick winter fog and so could not even guess where we were. Suddenly there was a tremendous clatter – we were on the bridge over the Elbe, the bridge that led to freedom. At once the train picked up speed, and the hazy vision of Hamburg faded in the distance.

Now the weather started to become clearer so that we could see how interesting was the countryside around us. We were crossing the northern end of Lüneberg Heath. It was wet and swampy, completely flat with seemingly endless meadowland and here and there groups of black pine-trees. Much of the ground was covered with some dark, faintly lilac-coloured scrub. It was a fascinating unusual landscape and made a strange picture – a lilac-coloured sea dotted with mournful groups of dark trees. It looked as if this land was almost uninhabited, for only occasionally did we catch a glimpse of one or two black-visaged men whose job was to dig for turf on the sides of the dyke along which ran the railway line. It was hard to believe that this deserted countryside lay between Germany's two greatest ports.

At Sägedorn, before Bremen, we stopped again . . . and just

stood there waiting. There seemed to be some more discussion
going on. What was the matter? Of course it was the Spartacists
again! That very day they had seized power in Bremen . . . that
very day!

We burst into peals of laughter; it was the only reaction possible. However, this time it did not matter since, after the urgent
sending and receiving of numerous messages by Morse telegraph, our train turned south and so we were able to reach the
frontier without any further mishap.

I have to admit that it was with great joy that we finally arrived
at The Hague, and especially for me to see again that sweet, old-
world perfect little capital with its apparently modest yet very
fine buildings. All the houses appear to have been constructed of
the finest bricks, their contours outlined with newly applied
whitewash, and the windows, framed in yellow stone the colour
of butter, shining and clean. The amazing cleanliness of the
houses comes from regular washing. This is not just an imagined
deduction; the Dutch really do wash the street façades of their
houses – and the inside courtyards too. People who do not clean
down the outside of their houses at least twice a year are considered dirty and neglectful. On that day, as we drove in from the
station, we saw an example of just that sort of beauty treatment
in progress. A man and a woman were at work in front of their
house. The woman was spraying the walls with a hose while the
man stood on a ladder wiping off the dirt with a special long-
handled broom shaped like a rake.

We stayed at the Oude Doelen Hotel. The name means 'the
Old Shooting Gallery', and I could imagine those hard tough
burghers of old exercising their skill there. What people they
were, those level-headed brave citizens, craftsmen, shopkeepers
and grocers who defended their little strip of land, most of
which had been recuperated from the sea, with the diligence of
ants, their religion and their freedom, never yielding to anyone,
neither to the fearsome Duke of Alba nor to the Sun King's
myriad armies! They even stood up to Napoleon. And they had
been able to keep their colonies, not by force but by good example and understanding and, in the last great conflict, were capable of accepting hordes of Belgian refugees without ever

becoming infected by the hatreds that war provoked. Only a few million souls, but what a nation!

Now, as the writing of these memoirs has brought me to that place where I was to spend so many months during which my home country was soaked by the blood-stained waves of political change, my memories of you, dear Holland, still touch my heart. You were then like a peaceful sunny harbour that gave shelter from those all-consuming hurricanes. You were like one of those happy Pacific islands that were never touched since no typhoon could breech its ring of rosy coral reefs.

❧ Chapter Eight ❧

It was at our charming old-fashioned hotel, the Oude Doelen, that I was to meet János Pelényi and his charming mother, who had come to The Hague on business concerning the Protestant Church. We soon became fast friends.

Not one of my old Dutch friends – and there had never been many – were living in The Hague.

On arriving my first action had been to visit the former Austro-Hungarian Embassy. I say 'former' because I found that big building now divided in two: to the left were the Hungarians, while the Austrians were to the right. The big central hall was a sort of no-man's-land where the carpet in the middle of the room served as a national frontier. I took it that the edge of the carpet was the real boundary, but I have no doubt that the carpet itself was considered to belong to Austria, since her citizens had usually been wily enough to secure the best part of communal property for themselves. '*Kleine Fische, gute Fische!*'[38]

A few weeks before my old friend, Lajos Széchenyi, who had been our ambassador, had died, so I found there only the chargé d'affaires, Count Calice, and Elek Nagy. They were both kindness itself; and Nagy, who had useful connections through his wife, proved helpful in many ways.

I find it hard now to recall exactly what I did in those first few weeks. I can still call to mind all sorts of faces, figures, situations and impressions but without any logical sequence so I cannot now put them in chronological order. Accordingly, I will recount them at random, just as one glances at odd snapshots as one lights upon them in an album of some long past journey.

***

My memories are of many different kinds, both good and bad. In The Hague at that time were gathered together many people who, like me, had been tossed this way and that by the storms of war until they found themselves on this narrow strip of land: just as floodwaters carry all kinds of flotsam along, only these are left, cast up on an alien shore.

So here are a few portraits. Let us start with Prince Blücher. Gebhardt Lebrecht, Fürst Blücher von Wahlstadt, was the grandson of the Blücher of Waterloo, that famous '*Marschall Vorwärts*' – 'Field Marshal Onwards'. He had a magnificent head and was the image of his great forebear, of whom I had seen several portraits in Berlin. On the day of those three battles at Quatre-Bras, Aliance and Waterloo, when already a 73-year old veteran, he had four horses shot from under him, had spent eighteen hours in the saddle until he was hurled into a ditch by the French attack and still, in spite of his great age, seemed the youngest of all those present on the battlefield.

From remarks he would drop from time to time I fancy that the grandson must have led an adventurous life. He was the heir to enormous estates in Silesia[39], yet he had lived for many years in South Africa on a remote plantation surrounded by blacks. He would speak about America and India as if he had spend a long time in both places and not just for pleasure but for business, and he would also speak with authority about breeding hunters and racehorses in Germany. With him one felt that he had lived through many vicissitudes and weathered many storms. His wife – Evelyn Stapleton-Bretherton – was a beautiful Englishwoman who had been thought by some Germans to be in the English intelligence service. Who knows? If so it might explain why they were then living in The Hague. It is equally possible that it was merely that she was anxious to get back to England and could make contact with her family more easily from Holland. After a while she was able to get home. When I knew her she was working on her memoirs, which were later to be published. I had a feeling that there had been some trouble with Emperor Wilhelm, although one day she showed me a photograph of herself launching a warship, which could hardly have been possible without the emperor's approval. They seem to have been great friends with Prince Heinrich of Prussia, who had served in the German navy, and always spoke warmly of him. It was, of course, true that the emperor was not on good terms with his younger brother, who had always been more popular in England than he was[40].

Blücher, always broadminded and objective, was blessed with boundless good will and sound judgement. It was out of sheer friendliness that he arranged for me to meet Colonel Oppenheimer, the British military attaché.

This proved to be quite an adventure, as much secrecy was involved. Blücher lived on the Vyverbergh in that street next to where the nobles used to have their fishponds. Sometimes I had to go there at night and was accustomed to taking different detours – going one way, returning another – so it was always a good half hour to get to or from my hotel, even though it was barely five minutes' walk away. The Hague was then thought to be a hive of spies and counter-spies (I never noticed any!). I then had to wait for a sign before I was allowed to ring the bell, and there were many other things I had to look out for before leaving the house.

Any respectable citizen, seeing me lurking there in the street until a streak of light from some window would send me hurrying to the door, must have thought either that I was bent on some lover's tryst or that I myself was the jealous Othello waiting for the seducer with a murder weapon concealed about my person.

Today I would have thought myself ridiculous and would have been inclined to laugh about it had not the root cause of all these precautions been so tragically serious.

I met Oppenheimer several times and so was able to discuss my information with him, always tailoring what I had to say to his English way of thinking. Finally I gave him a memorandum that differed in form only slightly from that I had presented to Treub, the Dutch minister of commerce. In this I described the real situation in Hungary, how the Bolshevik was rapidly spreading there and how this also exposed a dangerous threat to the rest of Europe.

Colonel Oppenheimer was a charming and highly intelligent man, and I was truly sorry to hear, some years later, that he had

had a fatal accident when climbing Mont Blanc. He was then working for the League of Nations at Geneva.

***

As well as Prince Blücher there were some other Germans at The Hague, a number of whom had their comic sides.

Among them were several titled ladies, most of whom – with the exception of one princess who was shortly to leave us – were real figures of fun. These were those poor millionaire American girls who, before the war, had been married for their money – not for anything else, I swear. These were the cotton, oil and sausage queens who had brought with them bulky fortunes that, as the war revealed, had been the only reason for such unselfish love-matches. From the outbreak of war not a cent had been received from America, and now they had come to The Hague, where they hoped they would be able to get money from overseas. However, nothing arrived and they suddenly found themselves poor and forced to live miserable lives, which surprised them no end. Of course they were outraged at their new lives, not the least because along with the money the husbands had disappeared too. Few people went to see them, and so, poor lambs, they were forced to make do with each other. And what did the poor abandoned ladies do all day? They played bridge hour-in and hour-out for quarters or tenths of a cent and that mainly on credit. I only went to see them once or twice as their company could only be enjoyed as a spectacle. They were rather like those big fat ducks that spend their days in plaintive quacking at the dried-up end of the pond.

***

I did not rely only on Oppenheimer in my efforts to find contacts in England. I had some other sources to tap as well. One of these led me to a man of somewhat dubious reputation but who was one of those interesting characters that come to the surface in wartime.

He was a Mr Leipnik, of Hungarian descent but long resident in England. As far as I could gather he was regarded everywhere, at home as well as abroad, as a most suspicious character. The intelligence bureaux of the central powers believed him to be an Allied spy, while our embassy at The Hague only communicated with him indirectly because they thought that, even if he were not a spy for the *Entente*, he must at least be an agent for the British. I needed someone like that, as I had to employ any means possible to get to our former enemies. Accordingly, I went to see him. As far as I could make out he had worked in England as a journalist and had earned himself something of a reputation, writing principally on sociological matters. He had prophesied the downfall of the central powers in the newspapers of several neutral countries and had suggested that salvation would only be found in the some system of universal brotherhood, such as a League of Nations. It is possible that someone had paid him to take this line, but it is equally possible that he did so from personal conviction. What, however, is certain is that in him there was an even stronger streak of personal ambition. This became clearer to me as I got to know him better.

Mr Leipnik lived at Scheveningen in one of those enormous fashionable hotels built along the seashore.

When I went to see him there it was February, and the six-storey hotel, the last before one reached the northern dunes, had a forlorn air since most of the hundreds of windows were closed and the portico boarded up. Everything that during the high season in summer would be bright with flowers and colour and new paint, was shabby, grey and battered. Everywhere, including the garden, seemed abandoned and strewn with rubbish. To reach his tiny room on God knows which upper floor I had to climb up a service stair. There, at last, I found the excellent Mr Leipnik.

He was a short man, thin and grey and wrinkled. His face was lined with deep furrows, and he was as yellow as a lemon. Also, alas, just as sour!

After a few polite preliminaries, I went straight to the point. How could I get to England?

'If I knew that I'd be there myself!' was the answer.

This was not a promising start, but as I persevered it soon became clear that my visit was for nothing.

He abused the English passionately – and every other *Entente* nation as well – complaining bitterly that during the war 'they' had all been only too happy to make use of him but now, now 'they' didn't care a hoot.

After hearing this I might just as well have gone straight back to The Hague, but now he started to interest me as an example of human oddity, and so I stayed, smoking innumerable cigarettes, and from time to time throwing in a word or two to keep him talking. This he did, airing countless grievances. He went on for a long time, talking without cease even when it started to get dark, walking up and down in that little room which was barely four metres from the door to the window over-looking the sea.

He abused everybody: he hated everybody. He declared that 'they' all owed everything to his noble ideas and generous spirit. Károlyi and Jászi had taken all their ideas from him but had no idea how to realize them – and not only that but they were stupid enough now not even to seek his advice.

It was the same with Lloyd George and Clemenceau – and Salandra – and everyone else too. They had without exception battened on him and stolen his ideas and were now merrily living it up in luxurious Parisian palaces, eating and drinking and toasting each other while he, the great Leipnik, was totally excluded. Even though their success was due to his wonderful ideas, they would not give him any credit. Of course they were full of envy and without talent, and so they saw to it that he was not only squeezed out and kept away from their counsels but also condemned to live here, in the misery of this shabby cold room, staring at the bleak ocean from the unheated squalor of this dreadful hole! This was their gratitude. This, their thanks, and this was how he was treated!

He went on for a long time, not exactly in these words, but endlessly repeating a theme that never changed.

There was something essentially dramatic in the way that, as the room grew darker, his shape became silhouetted against the big bay window with its greenish shimmering background of an ocean here and there covered with grey fog – that 'bitter sea' of Homer – an infinity of angry waves, their crests forever revealing that eternal, useless, restless wrath as it hammered itself against the hotel's sea walls with a rhythmic monotonous roar.

Whenever I think about Leipnik, this is how I still see him, pacing up and down, up and down, endlessly repeating his litany of disillusion to the accompaniment of the ocean's angry rhythm that seemed so symbolic of eternal hopelessness.

It was certainly an interesting experience!

***

There were other Hungarians at The Hague but none so tragic as Leipnik. For example there was Thyssen-Bornemissza and his wife. He had been one of the principal proprietors of factories in German heavy industry and during the war had already founded a firm in Rotterdam that had supplied the German war-machine from there. Also there was Miklós Vadász's younger brother (the one who can be seen drinking champagne in the Törley posters). If I remember rightly, he had got there by way of Switzerland. This Vadász spent his time in inventing all sorts of useless devices and liked to explain them at length to anyone who would listen. Later on he was to make a lot of money with his 'Mikiphone'.

However, I will end my brief list of exiles, not with him but with a young man from Budapest who called himself 'Monsieur de Solmont'.

He was what one would call a 'pretty boy', with wavy brown hair, smooth rosy face, and not tall but well-proportioned body. He was always elegantly dressed, with a flower in his buttonhole and a scented pocket-handkerchief in his breast pocket, the tip of which hung out like a dog's tongue in summer. He would appear in a different suit every day – in most colours of the rainbow – and either beige or two-toned shoes. He trod so lightly, his shoes might have been fitted with springs.

The Andorjáns had known him in Paris, and so he was often with us.

I must say I envied him; not for his beautiful shoes, nor for his well-rounded muscles, but rather because he always seemed so satisfied with his lot. For instance, his real name was

Sonnenberg, and he was the son of respectable shopkeepers who lived somewhere in the Erzsébet district of Budapest. At some point he had changed his name to 'de Solmont' ('Sonne' becoming 'Sol' – 'Berg' becoming 'Mont'). This sounded well and vaguely aristocratic, and he was very pleased with it. Some French people – whose name really was de Solmont – did not like it at all and denounced him as an impostor. He himself related all this to me, most indignantly as if it were most unreasonable of them. They should have been pleased instead of objecting, he said, and that with his looks, clever manner and ready wit, and as a newspaperman, he added lustre to their name! It was monstrous that they were so ungrateful!

He seemed to have enough money – or least credit – because he had hardly arrived in The Hague before he had already rented a fine flat in the centre of town which was furnished with large sofas and Persian carpets, and soon invited me, with the Andorjáns and one or two other ladies, to tea.

Everything he offered us was expensive and good: caviar and sardines as well as oranges and pineapples. Even more expensive-looking was the host himself, who wore a multicoloured silk dressing gown and who did his best to charm us with gracious gesture after gracious gesture. So as best to show off all nature's advantages to the ladies he tried to organize a boxing match for their delectation. He explained that he was a marvellous boxer and that they really must witness his prowess at this most virile and elegant of sports, whose movements were so beautiful they really must watch it. We all agreed. Very well! Show us, then! Let us see! Then a slight difficulty arose as there were only two other men in the room, Andorján and myself, and neither of us was willing to take part in an exhibition of that sort. 'No matter!' we said. 'Show us alone!' . . . and he did!

He took off his silk brocade coat and started to box in his pink tights. He did it very well, tiptoeing about with graceful steps that owed much to the dance. He turned this way and that, sometimes stealing forward with a cunning little feint, or jumped lightly sideways, or was suddenly brought up, jolted by the awesome blows of an invisible opponent then, with lightning speed, bringing down the non-existent enemy with such a fierce blow to the chin, nose or solar plexus that he was knocked out with dev-astating skill. With all this effort he became quite heated, as with teeth clenched, he pranced about the room wearing a triumphant smile and now and then shouting out some technical term so as to impress his spectators. Finally he got so short of breath – no wonder after such a fight – that he sank down on a sofa amongst all the ladies and demanded that they feel his biceps. See how strong they are! How hard! It was clear that anyone struck by him would swiftly be finished off, dead or maimed for life! Oh yes, he was that sort of man!

A truly wonderful fellow, that little de Solmont!

Later, and most unexpectedly, the perpetrator of this extraor-dinary performance was to get his comeuppance. Although at that time I did not know it, and was never to learn the reason, he had an enemy at The Hague who, anxious to teach him a lesson, who had been looking for him for some days. One evening on returning to the Hotel Oude Doelen I was told by the hall porter that there had been a fight in the entrance hall that afternoon. Well, I thought, so little de Solmont has had a chance to deal with his enemy!

Later that evening Andorján told me what had actually hap-pened.

The enemy was having tea in the hall with some ladies when de Solmont came up to him and said a few words. No one knew what was said. All that was certain was that the newcomer got up and dealt the great boxer two ordinary little slaps on the face which made de Solmont fall to the ground, breaking three chairs and some Delft vases in the process. This is all I know. We never discovered if de Solmont had been hurt by some piece of broken pottery, or whether he had fainted. All that was certain was that the poor fellow had to be dragged out by the waiters, while his enemy just returned to where he had been sitting. The affair had no other important consequences that I knew of except that our young friend was thenceforth forbidden to enter the Oule Doelen, and so I did not see him again. I was sorry because he might have taught me to box, which can be a wonderful thing, as this story shows.

***

At that time I only made the acquaintance of two Dutch politicians. One was Treub, of whom I have already written; the other was Jongheer van Karnebeek.

I met both through the good offices of Elek Nagy.

I do not have much to recount of Treub, who was most amiable when I gave him my memorandum and who seemed to appreciate the implications of the growing Bolshevik threat in Hungary and who had promised to get it laid before the *Grand Cinq* in Paris. However, a few days later the 'Republic of the People'⁴¹ took power in Budapest, so it was evidently too late for my memorandum to be of any use in Paris.

At much the same time I had for the same reasons visited Karnebeek on a couple of occasions, as I had hoped that perhaps he would be able to persuade Count Loudon, then Dutch ambassador in Paris, to raise the subject there. At our first meeting the minister had seemed disposed to do so, but soon this willingness disappeared, as it seemed that he was beset with many worries that required all his attention and all his energy. He told me what now follows, and I relate it here because I found it so interesting. The Belgians, as a fine return for Holland having accepted, fed and housed many thousands of Belgian refugees during the war, now charged the Dutch with having let the invading German army pass through the province of Limburg and demanded compensation for this in the form of handing over the province of Zeeland (Flanders) and the mouth of the Scheldt. In vain did the Dutch government argue that the Germans, if refused passage through that narrow strip of Dutch territory – which was only a few kilometres wide and impossible to defend – would have broken through by force, and that Queen Wilhelmina's government had given way only to save her peace-loving subjects from the devastation which resistance would inevitably have brought with it, and also that it had had no strategic effect since their army opposing the Germans had already been overwhelmed, the Belgians would not relent and so presented the government of Holland with a most awkward and perilous predicament. The dykes forming the banks of the Scheldt were higher than all the neighbouring towns and villages whose survival depended on their careful maintenance. This applied to the whole territory almost as far as The Hague. Karnebeek described it well when he asked: 'Do you know what this country is? It is very little land surrounded by a great deal of water!'

This was not generally known at the time.

The question of Zeeland became public knowledge a few days later.

I am glad that I happened to be there just at that moment and happy that I was privileged to see for myself the quiet, courageous, unified and dedicated patriotism with which this tough hard people faced a threat of force.

Everyone had their post and stood at it. Everybody did their duty naturally from their queen, who never ceased to go from house to house in the villages of Zeeland, to the dockworkers and organized socialists. Everywhere was one single cry: 'Resist!' Resist until the end, resist even the Great Powers, the millions of France's great army, the powerful fleet of England, always resist, never give in: it was better to die. It was the noble spirit of freedom inherited from their brave ancestors that had always preserved the Dutch people despite their paucity of numbers.

Holland did not have to mobilize; she chose another way. Anyone who volunteered was issued with a rifle and a beret; and almost everybody did volunteer, from boys who were hardly out of their teens to old men with grey hair. Everybody: men of all kinds and all professions.

I saw many such civilian volunteers – berets on heads and rifles on shoulders – as they bicycled by, every afternoon, on their way to some meadow where they drilled. In a few days, out of nothing, was created a huge army on wheels – two of each, as everyone in Holland owns a bicycle and all the roads are bordered by special tracks for them. And all this was done without advertising, speeches or posters, quietly and simply with all the calm of inner strength.

At that time I also saw an interesting march through the city centre of the Dutch capital.

It seems that a few days before I arrived in The Hague there had been some sort of attempted revolution. The would-be insurgents occupied the state library, which is situated between two streets near the royal palace. There the Dutch citizens cut them off, attacked the building and, not being like the milksops of other countries, fired steadily at it until the grey stone sculptured façade was dotted with bullet holes like a white shrub in full flower and soon forced the insurgents to surrender. The lion's share of this restoration of order had, in fact, fallen to the Catholic bodies who, since their co-religionists were in the minority, had all come together under one command. In this hour of need they marched out, led by the Abbé Nolens.

To prove their solidarity when it came to a threat to the whole nation, such as the Zeeland affair, and also to show publicly the part they had played at the time of the recent attempt at revolution, the Catholic organizations arranged this demonstration march through the streets of The Hague. Perhaps too, they thought it a good moment to show their strength.

This demonstration march was joined by many, many thousands of people. In front of each group was carried a placard bearing the name of the town, village or association which it represented, and at the head of the procession, as well as between the marchers, was carried the gold and silver Papal banner.

It was fascinating to see both the calm and the interest that was accorded to this massive demonstration, but it was even more fascinating to see, in the multitudes that thronged the sidewalks, a crowd largely made up of the Protestant majority, who watched the marchers with such patience and real sympathy and did not appear to mind that it was the papal yellow and white and not the *Vierkleur* – the blue, white, red and orange of the national flag – that was carried before them. It was particularly interesting that this should be so here, in Holland: that country which had once led the world, and fought so many terrible battles, in the Protestant struggle against Catholic oppression. Interesting too to note how the Dutch people still today will never fail to refer proudly to all the suffering they had had to endure in defending their Protestant faith at the siege of Haarlem and at the time of the Duke of Alba's cruel persecutions and the countless sacrifice of Protestant martyrs during that war.

These were indeed men of high quality.

***

Now came the end of March when news came from Budapest that the 'People's Republic' had been declared and that the Bolsheviks had come to power.

With this news the whole reason for my mission vanished.

Of course none of this was wholly unexpected, but the *fait accompli* meant that I had to make a momentous decision. Of the funds I had with me, enough of the modest sum of my own money I had brought to pay my personal expenses remained to cover my living costs for the next few months; but I had to face the fact that for a very long time ahead I would not be able to count on receiving any more, either from Transylvania or from Budapest. Who could guess for how long the Soviets would remain in power?

Pondering all this I decided to cast around for some occupation that would earn me a living. This was not easy in a foreign country. I could not do it with my pen as I could write acceptably only in German and French, neither of which were any use in Holland. I had never learned any craft, and I could hardly start now. I could think of only three sorts of work for which I was fitted.

The first was to seek employment in some riding school where I could be paid for breaking in young horses. Such jobs, however, were very uncertain as well as time-consuming and there were not likely to be many of them – and those were probably all filled or obtainable only through social introduction and patronage.

Another idea that would have been more fun was to capitalize on my skill at billiards, learned in the course of many otherwise wasted evenings in Berlin where I had taken part in many semi-professional tournaments. Perhaps someone would take me on as *marqueur* (billiard coach) in a coffee-house? Then I reflected that this was not really an attractive idea after all and would be a singularly dismal occupation.

The third seemed the most promising – to become a professional painter. I felt that maybe I could do small portraits that would be good enough for those with limited means. Before the war[42] I had often tried my hand at this for my own pleasure; and later, when I was ordered to the headquarters of the German Army of the South, more for political than military duties, I had done a number of smallish watercolour portraits. This, I decided, is what I would try now.

Two things would be necessary if I were to succeed in this venture. The first would be to drop my title, as such things inevitably give an impression of amateurishness and so people expect something for nothing; and the second that I should first get in some practice so that I would be able to accept commissions without hesitation.

Accordingly, I moved out of the Hotel Oule Doelen, which was now too expensive for me, and went to live in a little wooden hotel which stood at the edge of the Bosch, that large park which had once been a hunting preserve of the Dutch ruling family and which is situated between Scheveningen and the bathing beaches.

Luckily, on arrival at my new abode, I was able to write my name in the guest-book as plain Mr Bánffy as, not arriving directly from abroad, no one asked me for my passport.

Now started a new chapter in my wanderings. It was to prove a busy, amusing and relatively carefree time, to which I always look back with pleasure.

ꙮ Chapter Nine ꙮ

Soon after I had moved into the simple little wooden Hotel Bellevue, I went to see the Master-Painter Aarlof who ran a school of painting in his attic studio. He lived in a villa on the far side of the beautiful Scheveningen Bosch.

One could see from a distance that this was the home of no ordinary man. It was quite unlike the modest, typically Dutch homes, of Aarlof's neighbours, being a sort of exaggerated imitation of the English 'cottage' style, with steep roofs which occasionally reached almost to the ground, giant chimney-stacks which towered high above and everywhere windows which jutted out at unexpected places. There were odd protrusions here, as well as rounded bay windows at different heights. These all seemed to be fitted with blown glass panes which resembled giant monocles all clustered one on top of another and gave the impression that behind each one somebody was lying in wait.

The master of the house was also unlike all the others from those parts. He was like a Frenchman with a scrupulously polite manner rarely found in a Dutchman. Of course, if one has studied in Paris, then . . . well . . . of course one has to show it! One owes it to one's pupils to let them know at once that one is different from the others – you might say more elegant than those who have worked only in this benighted little country. One owes it to one's public, does one not? Paris, of course . . .

His appearance was also Frenchified. He was a thin, stringy, little brown man with bluish-grey hair and curly moustaches dyed as black as soot. Naturally, he wore a brown velvet jacket in the traditional *rapin*[43] style and a flowing silk necktie, loosely knotted in a bow. Oh yes! Everything was just as it should be.

His manner was kind, even endearing, and his fees were quite high for, as he explained to me when accepting me as a pupil, otherwise it was quite impossible. Not only that but live models were only available if the pupils paid for them, and so if not one had to be content with still life, which in itself he said was *educatif* (and in this he was right!). But if anyone wanted models, they were not expensive. The cheapest were old women; men were more expensive, and even more expensive still were nudes. He could provide, he said, whatever one wanted, and he was in contact with some of the best available. He then asked if I had any painting materials, and when I said I had not but would buy them that very day, he said: No! He would get them himself, everything of the best quality, canvas, paint, palette, easel, everything. He knew best how to get everything at the lowest possible price (this was not true) since he could get a discount from the shop (which was true).

All this cost me quite a lot of money, but this was unavoidable if I was to benefit from 'Master' Aarlof's teaching. If I wanted to get in some practice I had to do what I was told.

The following morning he took me up to the school studio, presented me to his other pupils, showed me my place and set up a still-life arrangement for me made up to two magnificent oranges and a lemon. Then he left.

Our schoolroom proved to be quite small, hardly more than five-metres square. In front of the inside wall was placed a heavy Neidlinger stove and in front of that was a screen used whenever they had a model. The remaining free space was barely three metres deep. All six of Mr Aarlof's pupils – there were four women and one man as well as myself – took our places on the shorter side.

The man was a gruff young fellow, completely devoid of talent. He soon left us after a violent disagreement with the 'Professor' conducted in a whisper. Among the women were three charming young girls; one of them, a snub-nosed dark girl, was Aarlof's daughter; the next, also pretty, was some sort of relation of theirs from Rotterdam; the third, whom Aarlof treated with marked respect, was the daughter of a distinguished man from The Hague, a *Jongheer*[44] no less, and was a real beauty always elegantly dressed; while the fourth was a sad timeworn widow with lank black hair who, industrious as an ant, worked diligently until nightfall. The first three spent their days giggling and eating sweets or disappearing into the other attic rooms nearby to have a whispered girlish gossip in secret and returning to their drawing boards only when the master's steps were heard on the stair. And, indeed, why not? I soon learned that both the *Jongheer*'s daughter and the girl from Rotterdam were engaged, while Aarlof's daughter seemed already to be in love. Why should they strain themselves to create the image of two oranges and a lemon? They surely had more enthralling things to think about!

At midday the 'Professor' returned. The girls tried to look as if they had been working, and he glanced cursorily at what they had done. Then he uttered a few words to the widow, condescending but polite . . . and then came to me. He looked at my painstaking but commonplace effort – it was many years since I had painted in oils – and then simulated some slight appreciation, saying that my technique was all wrong and that therefore, on the following day, I should go directly to his own studio downstairs where he would show me how to do it right.

The next day I was there. Aarlof's own studio was a splendid, richly furnished dark room with many carpets and voluptuous sofas.

In front of the window there was the portrait of a woman, nearly finished and pleasant if not very good. It was obviously flattering, elegant and attractive and belonged to the 'Oh, how lovely!' school of painting, with all the prettiness of an advertisement for Odol toothpaste or some cosmetic, the sort of picture of which the grandchildren to come would say: 'Look how beautiful Grandmother was when young!' No one would ever be disturbed by seeing it on the drawing-room wall: it would not clash with the good quality – if banal – furniture, but it would not interest anyone either.

However, I should not make fun of Master-Painter Aarlof, for would I not be producing just the same sort of work when I started painting portraits for a living? I must say too that his painting did not lack either skill or knowledge.

All the same, I have to admit that there was something in his work that I found disagreeable. The whole painted surface – faces, hands, clothes, everything – seemed to shimmer, which had a curious effect on the simple quality of his colours. It reminded me of the strange iridescence one sees on those 'Souvenirs of Sorrento' one finds painted on seashells in Naples. It was not long before I discovered how Aarlof achieved this odd effect. It came from his way of painting, and he did it like this: firstly, after establishing his design he would draw all its outlines in charcoal then all the important lines would be reinforced with black India ink; then, when all was ready, he would start to put many different coloured paints on the canvas, completely at random and regardless of the traced outlines of the design, so that they all spread and mingled. This was how he prepared his canvas. At this stage it seemed only like a dazzling display of colour – and it was only then that he began to paint the likeness of what he had before him.

It was this that gave the strange iridescent shine to the finished portrait; and it was obviously an effect of which Aarlof was very fond, for he had used it for the early pictures he had painted of his wife and young daughter as well as many others I saw in his apartment. I have no idea where he learned this technique for it certainly did not come from his teachers in Paris. It is possible that he got the idea from some of Rembrandt's greyish skies or perhaps from the warm tones that artist used for deep caves because they too occasionally have the same shimmering look to them. The most striking example I know is to be seen in a *Diana and Endymion* now in Vienna, where the moonlight seems uniformly grey when seen from close to but has a trembling sort of glitter from afar.

He showed me several of the pictures he had produced in this way and, since one can learn something from everything, I tried it out on the first studies I did for him. This was not a success. All the same, I did find one part of it useful: this was using India ink to fix the lines first laid with charcoal because, providing on does not let the paint dry (*'peindre dans la pâte'* – as the French say) the inked outlines of the drawing can always be seen even when one has strayed from them.

***

I suspect that Aarlof may not have been all that convinced of his own talent since in all other artistic matters he certainly had excellent judgement.

Later I was to become sure that this was so. It began when there was to be a masked ball in the town. Aarlof was very excited and induced the three pretty girls in our class to join with him in going as Bluebeard and three of his wives (I need hardly say that the sad-faced widow was not invited to join them). For days nothing else was talked about in the studio. The girls were always trying on caftans and giving each other brief glances at silk bloomers before snatching them away again and hiding them with much giggling, tickling and whispered naughtiness in each other's ears. Aarlof himself came in several times to show off his yellow brocade turban, which everyone duly admired, and also to offer much advice as to everyone's costumes.

The day after the ball no one turned up at the studio, but three days later they all returned and spoke of nothing but the ball. It was splendid, the girls said – 'Wonderful! Beautiful!' – and laughed and whispered in corners even more than usual. Aarlof then came up to us to bask in his own glory, and, since he wanted somehow to immortalize the lovely memory for posterity, he gave the order for all the pupils to have ready for the following Saturday – it was then Tuesday – a coloured drawing on the theme of Bluebeard.

As it happened this proved most opportune for me.

At home in my little hotel room I worked long into the after-noons, trying out different studies for my 'Bluebeard' in sepia, coloured India inks and watercolour.

By Saturday I was ready with a finished drawing of our Blue-beard, which I had completed with a watercolour wash. I even included a portrait of our Lolotte begging pillar-like on her large behind.

On Saturday we were all there to show off our efforts. The girls' work was feeble, although that of the *Jongheer*'s daughter did have some merit. The widow, offended, at once declared she had not even tried.

As a result my effort was like a Derby runner competing with Shetland ponies. Aarlof himself was taken by surprise because until then all he had seen of my work had been the painstaking studies I had produced according to his own system, while I had had the benefit of having originally being taught to draw by the great Bertalán Székely. Well! After much praise for my 'Bluebeard' he took it away with him.

At first I was not very happy about this because I thought he wanted to keep it for himself; but what happened next turned out to be most flattering.

After a few days he took me aside and told me that he had showed my drawing to a fellow-painter who, in his opinion, was one of the greatest living artists. I asked who that might be.

'Van Koneinenburgh. Isn't his name familiar to you?'

I had to admit that it was not, although I did manage not to show how funny I found the name since it meant 'rabbit-hutch' in Dutch. What a name for an artist! At home people would have died laughing.

'*Ça, c'est un peintre!*' said Aarlof, meaning that he was a real master of his art!

I mumbled some polite words about how happy I would be to meet yet another renowned painter, but Aarlof, to his credit, refused to accept the compliment to himself, making a resigned gesture – as much as to say 'I am far from being in his class!' – and going on to say that he had taken my drawing to Van Koneinenburgh, who had liked it and wanted to meet me. And not only that but, on that very day, he was expecting us both to take a cold supper with him.

So that evening we went to Van Koneinenburgh's house. He lived in a tiny studio apartment in one of those houses in the oldest part of The Hague. Everything there seemed to have a soft brownish hue as one sees in old Dutch paintings. Every corner was piled high with drawings and also paintings that had been started and then abandoned as well as giant portfolios hardly able to contain them all.

In this dark crabbed little space – such as Rembrandt may well have worked in – Van Koneinenburgh's wonderful Beethoven-like head seemed doubly impressive.

He spoke very simply, with no affectation, with the calm air of one whose work was inspired by a single refined spiritual ethic, for one could see that, for him, only art was important, and in life only art mattered. The picture was completed by his wife. She was a local girl, that same sort of housewife one sees skimming milk or mending clothes in seventeenth-century paintings. Broadly built and heavy, every time she looked at her husband one could see in her eyes a strange fanatic flame, a mixture of reverence and maternal love for that gentle husband for whom all struggles seemed vain, who never achieved success, was almost unknown and who only occasionally received some small municipal commission which just tided them over and enabled them to survive – and all this for a man she herself knew to be truly great, as great, in fact, as any in the history on the Netherlands.

And, indeed, he was a great artist. His style was an unexpected mixture of modern ideas and those of the early Flemish masters. His compositions resembled those of Memling and Jan van Eyk seen through modern eyes. His mastery of draughtsmanship was truly extraordinary, and his execution simple and severe, like that of Dürer. Sometimes a single line would be enough to express his intentions.

The walls were covered with large-gestured compositions, cartoons for mural competitions that had invariably been won by other painters whose clever facile work was more immediately pleasing but milder and less epoch-making and memorable than his.

We stayed with him for a long while. I spent most of the time poring over the drawings in the portfolios, refreshed by a glass of beer and some slices of cold meat which were brought in by the artist's wife. Each time she brought over a new drawing she glanced questioningly at her husband as if to ask if it were all right and not a profanation. Only when he nodded approval did she put the things down beside me. I understood that these studies were sacrosanct, only to be shown to those few who were considered worthy. This was confirmed as we walked home, for Aarlof then told me that it was an exceptional honour as Van Koneinenburgh only showed his work to those he decided were exceptionally deserving.

I returned there several times during my stay in The Hague.

Van Koneinenburgh had some interesting theories and liked to talk about them. How one related the placing of one's composition to the space it occupied, the distribution of colour and tone and the relationship to be established between each of the principal lines of the drawing were all matters for which he had developed his own system. He believed there were mathematical rules to be followed, for in his mind all those lines and apparently otherwise meaningless angles were filled with life and expressive force. In consequence, he fancied that he had discovered a universal law, although in fact, of course, it was only a natural rationalization of his own way of making a design and not a rule for anyone else.

***

Van Koneinenburgh's sympathetic appreciation of my work was very helpful to me because it boosted my self-confidence. It also reinforced my feeling that soon I ought to quit the eternal diet of the two-oranges-and-a-lemon still-lives. I didn't really mind that, but I did want to work from a live model and would soon have to insist that one was hired. It would be a big decision to take since the other pupils said that working from life was so difficult and anyway they were not at all happy about the extra expense. However, when we did get one they all worked from it, and the good Aarlof gave them life lessons too.

The life lessons produced no little trouble. One or two of the models just walked out, while one elderly woman invariably went to sleep in mid-session. At length Aarlof found a really good female nude who seemed to be a professional model and not a half-hearted amateur like the first ones. It was true that she was very expensive, but she held her pose and was beautiful with lovely colouring. She was a real Flemish woman, more a pink-fleshed heifer than a milk-cow, just as Rubens would have chosen, rather heavy but very young with a milk-white skin. I set to work eagerly and after a few preliminary outlines decided to try a life-size nude study. But trouble followed, and what a depressing story that turned out to be!

I had already worked for about four days on the painting, and it was going very well, when one morning Aarlof brought in a new pupil. This was a most elegant man, highly scented and sporting a monocle and gaiters. He was slightly balding but had a most distinguished air. Our professor introduced him to us – he had a German name which sounded vaguely aristocratic – sat him down facing the model (*my* model), pressed a minute drawing board into his hand, spend a little time whispering and laughing with him and then left us. During one of the model's rest periods I remember stepping over towards our new student. On his drawing board there were some shapeless doodling, more like smudges than actual drawing.

'I haven't done any drawing for a long time,' said the man with the monocle, as if to justify himself on seeing my surprise. Then, when the model resumed her pose, he picked up his diminutive 'drawing' and left without another word. He never returned, and neither did the model! The whole of the next day we waited in vain: she did not turn up that day, or the next, or even the day after that. Nevertheless, I was foolish enough to hope she would still come back. Then the sad-faced widow enlightened me. She waited until the others had already left and then told me what she knew. We need not delude ourselves: our model would not be coming back, for the man with a monocle had whisked her away. She herself had known this would happen as soon as Aarlof had brought him in; and since then she had even seen the two of them in a car with the girl all dressed in new clothes –she was no longer an artists' model! Seeing my dismay she started telling me all sorts of disagreeable things about our professor who, she said, was a dreadful man and that our monocled friend had probably bought a picture from him. 'For that,' she said, 'Aarlof would sell the whole world – he'd do anything for that! He's that sort of man!'

All that may have been true, but at any rate there was nothing I could do about it. I told Aarlof the widow's news, as ironically as possible, and he at once made out that he too was indignant (and even referred to the monocled man as 'a pig'). However, since it was clear that he had, under the surface jesting of my remarks, grasped the real significance of my sarcasm, he promised to find me a real model.

***

It took some time for my anger to evaporate. Then I decided I would myself start to search for a suitable model. I would find the right sort of model and engage her myself. Then I would not risk being tricked so easily. It occurred to me that, as there were always so many painters at Scheveningen in the summer and that there were also plenty of pretty girls there who often wore their enchanting national costume, I would go there to look around. With luck I might succeed in finding one willing to sit for me in costume; and so, on Sunday, I set out for the fishing village that lay close to the bathing resort.

There I beheld a sight worth seeing. All dressed in the traditional local fashion, the girls wore winged little lace bonnets and white blouses above which were collars of black cloth lined with some light material in vivid colours. These last were thrown back coquettishly to show off the linings. Their skirts were also embroidered with similar brightly coloured stripes, and, too, they wore multi-coloured stockings and highly-polished clogs.

So far so good! But I still had to capture one of those who were now strolling about. I would have to try to speak to her and convince her, not in a tearing hurry, as all those arm-in-arm strollers seemed to be. Along with one or two fishermen, they all seemed to be heading for the sand dunes just north of the village. I started off in the same direction, expecting to come across them spread out a little and sitting on the sand. Climbing to the top of the first dune, I sat down, and started drawing having cunningly worked it out that once they saw me sitting there, the natural curiosity of all Eve's daughters would sooner or later draw one or two to approach, and so we would start talking – for by then I had already a superficial knowledge of their language – and in this way, little by little, I would convince one of them to sit for me.

Well! I just went on drawing and drawing and drawing. Time passed, and no one came near me. In the course of half-an-hour, and then three quarters of an hour, I only caught an occasional glimpse of a coloured collar or a lacy bonnet, and these were all holding hands with some fisherman or other before they disappeared, and once again I found myself sitting all alone in the middle of this desert of sand. Perhaps, I thought, there was some dancing going on somewhere. That is where they must all have gone. But the only music to be heard was the sound of waves beating on the shore.

Quite some time was to pass like this; and there is no more dismal place to sit alone than on the top of a sand dune. I did not think that all those nymphs could have gone too far away, and so I started after them, trudging through the deep dry sand, than which nothing is more tiring. At every step one sinks in up to the ankles, and when one climbs up a slope one slides down just as far. Mercifully, I did not have far to go to discover the reason for my solitude.

Just where I was, the dunes had formed themselves into a quantity of little hillocks seven or eight yards apart with, between them, little valleys bordered by steep curved banks just as if nature had placed screens around them. I only discovered this then, but I fancy the youth of Scheveningen must known this all their lives, just as they also knew how resilient was the desert grass that grew there, how soft the sand beneath, how clean it all was so that nothing left marks or stains on elaborate collars or skirts, and that clogs never got lost there even when sometimes kicked off. Hidden away in each of these cushioned bowers of burnt golden sand and silver grey grass was a couple in sweet embrace reclining on their superb natural couch – and as for poor me, I felt like some foolish primeval mammoth, unconsciously trampling on the happiness of others.

I need hardly add that I quickly fled away!

***

It was about this time that, on his invitation, I went by way of Haarlem to Aardenhout to visit Oszkár Mendlik, who in my opinion was not only one of the best of contemporary painters of seascapes but who also ranked with the greatest of all time.

However, before I write about that visit, I must tell about an experience I had while on my way there, partly because I would like to evoke such a pleasing memory but partly also because, much as a travel agent will advertise some little-known but agreeable resort, it seems to me to be my duty to pass on to all lovers of beauty my total surrender to what happens in Holland in the middle of April. It was at this time that my trip coincided with the tulip harvest. This lasts for three days during which they cut all the flowers so as to encourage the bulbs to grow larger.

I travelled by train to Leiden and from there on by tram along the highroad. When we had left behind the walls of the old university city we passed by lengthy *polders*, those sea-water lakes which once served as protective moats to the ancient fortifications. After that came meadows full of cows and then, at the turn of the road, suddenly before us was laid out an astonishing picture. As far as the eye could see there stretched out a wide plain covered with the brightest of colours, all set out close to each other. There were long rectangles of which one would be red and the next yellow. Then would come pink or purple. The whole countryside was like a giant chessboard on which the God of Spring had magically changed every square to a different colour. On all sides the gardeners' entire families were at work cutting flowers – every man, woman and child of them. Near the road children were everywhere. The girls all wore garlands on their heads, those good black-and-white cows sported wreaths, as did the cart-horses, and even the telegraph poles were festooned with flowers which reached up as far as the wires overhead. All around there was this pageant, an orgy of brilliant colour helped by bushels of flower heads strewn all over the roads, the ditches, the tramlines: indeed everything that could be reached was covered by this limitless beauty. It was as if the very spirit of spring could not control its own abundance.

Tiny children were stumbling about weighed down by their flowery robes, pretty fair-haired girls were offering bouquets to all who passed and, if one laughed and joked with them, they threw more bouquets after us. Our journey to Haarlem covered at least twenty kilometres, and so dazzling was the entire trip that when we reached the city and saw its dull grey houses ahead it was almost as if one had suddenly been struck blind.

Everyone should see this who can: it is an unforgettable sight.

Haarlem, as the capital of the tulip-growing region, celebrates the flower harvest with a national exhibition at which all the growers compete with each for the annual gold medal awarded for the best new tulip.

The exhibitions are held in a series of vast glass houses surrounded by clumps of rhododendrons, hyacinths, azaleas and other flowering plants. In the centre there is a large dais, upon which are all the new varieties, some rigidly upright, others with their blooms at the end of more flexible stems, which are competing for the prize. Some of these do not even look like tulips, for their flower heads have the most bizarre forms as well as the most unexpected colours. When I was there the Gold Medal was awarded to a dark purple flower that was almost black, with long pointed petals, each like the blade of some murderous dagger, bordered with blood-red lines as if they had just been withdrawn from a mortal wound. It was a beautiful but wicked flower, scentless, which stood aloof on its stiff pale green stem.

Aardenhout is only a few kilometres from Haarlem.

The Mendlik villa stood in the middle of a park of fine oaks.

I was received so warmly with real Hungarian hospitality that I almost felt as if I were back in my own country in happier times.

My great tie with Mendlik was that he too had been a pupil of Bertalán Székely and shared with me a deep admiration for that great artist who, unhappily, had been misunderstood and little appreciated during his lifetime. His charming wife was a talented sculptor who did me the great honour of doing a small clay bust of my head and shoulders. I have this still, and it gives me great pleasure[45].

Mendlik's seascapes were sensational. The best were his sketches in oil, painted from nature, of which among the most impressive was a series he had recently painted on card while sailing from Rotterdam to New York and back. During this voyage Mendlik never set foot on land, since, as an 'enemy alien', he was not allowed to land in America. There was a terrible storm during the voyage, so fierce that in order to paint it he had to be tied down on the bridge so as not to be swept away by the waves. He was that sort of painter! The first of the series was done when first signs of the storm began to appear on the horizon. Then came the way the waves changed colour as the storm tossed them about, followed by the effect of the rising wind until the tempest was at its height, raging round the ship with the winds now so strong on the waves that all one could see were greyish-yellow mountains of water colliding into each other, bursting and shattering into watery fragments, although without leaving any foam; and finally an unbroken surface subdued by the hurricane's strong hands. I am sure that no one else ever painted like that!

It is terrible to think about what it can mean to be lashed to an iron railing during such a storm, when the crest of every wave sweeps over the deck. One is forced to admire the man, as well as his work, who will brave such conditions and endure such sacrifice.

৵ Chapter Ten ৵

I will now recount some of the main incidents of the rest of my stay at The Hague.

Between these milestones life trickled on in quiet monotony. The mornings were spent in the studio and most of the afternoons too either there or in my hotel room, drawing; except for those days on which I might go to see some famous collection, either public or private, of which there are so many in this rich little country. Then I spent an occasional evening with János Pelényi and his family or with Elek Nagy, who was then living in a villa where, sometime in March, the storks delivered a by then well-rounded baby son.

They were very proud of this uniformly pink and plump child 'whose like the world had never seen' and from whom even a few moments' separation was so unthinkable that, whenever I went to lunch at their home, there in the centre of the table, instead of a bouquet of flowers, the chubby baby himself would be placed, while throughout the meal the only subject of conversation would be his intelligence and beauty. It was most touching to see the Nagy's happiness . . . but for me, who for many long months had had no news either of my father or of my sister and her family, this only added to my sense of being uprooted and homeless.

⁂

With the coming of spring Aarlof would take his pupils out into the country so as to make landscape studies. On one of these excursions I was to have an experience that I found most interesting since it gave me a new insight into the high degree of culture to be found in every strata of Dutch society.

I had seated myself in a marvellously green meadow beside a canal. Behind me were some black-and-white cattle in a row, each one tethered to a stake by a long line. On the other side of the canal was a farmhouse with some fruit trees in the background, while in the foreground two boats were tied up. At one side there was a private bridge leading to the homestead.

I set to work to make a picture of this, and when I had been working at it for some time I saw the farmer crossing the bridge and coming towards me. He stepped up quietly and for a little while stood behind me.

For a while he just stood there looking at the drawing. Then he waited a moment and asked if I could possibly finish the boats first because he would soon be taking one of them to row into town. Not straightaway but in half-an-hour? He could wait until then. He added that he had come over to ask me this as he did not want to spoil the progress of the drawing, but as he would have to remove one of the two boats he had thought he would tell me in advance so that I could organize my work accordingly!

Wasn't that extraordinary? Where else would one find people with such real unaffected goodwill?

I had another experience somewhat similar to this. It occurred when I was doing studies in my hotel room. I had been working on an illustration of the classical tale of the nymph Daphne, who was transformed into a laurel-tree, and I needed to look at a free-growing laurel with naturally leafy branches because it would be ridiculous to show the beautiful nymph changing into a bush clipped like a pyramid.

I thought it would not be too difficult to find. Even though in other countries laurels are to be found trimmed into special shapes from the time they are quite small, in this country almost every tree – oaks, beeches, poplars, maples and others too – are carefully pruned right to their utmost tips. To find a laurel growing naturally I had to consult a local gardener.

Eventually I found a man who looked after the lawns and flowerbeds of the villas nearby and went to see him.

'Where,' I asked, 'can I find an unclipped laurel?'

'There are none in The Hague!' he answered, 'but if you go to Delft there is a gardener who has quite a large park and who, especially for painters, had grown all sorts of trees as they would be found in the wild. I should ask him, he is sure to have what you want.'

Once again I was to reflect that only in this perfect country could one now find such politeness and such good manners.

***

It was now the end of May, and I think it was just about then that Miklós Vadász arrived in The Hague. His brother had told us a long time before that he was coming, and so we had been eagerly awaiting him. We were all glad to see him not only because he was a man everyone liked but also because he brought us news from home, from which we had been completely deprived. Although he told us terrible things about the awful poverty that was everywhere evident, it was still good to get any news and to know what had been the most recent developments. I fancy that this was the time when General Smuts' mission to the Hungarian Soviet was the centre of interest.

Vadász was just as elegant and well turned-out as he always had been, but overlaying his habitual *Weltschmerz* – pessimism and world-weariness – there was a new sense of bitter disillusion. He had come a long way from that excited mood when I had last seen him at the time of the 'Aster Revolution'. Since then his illusions had proved baseless, and his disappointment was painful and hopeless. It was with deep sadness that he now told us: 'There is no longer anything to hope for there!'

He too needed to earn a living in The Hague, and so he asked me what might be possible there. I told him that things were very difficult; there were almost no high-class publishers of glossy magazines or elegant journals such as might be found in London or Paris, and what there were did not offer any opportunities for people like us, since all the available posts were already filled by local artists who, although they might not be his equal in skill and talent, were accepted and popular with the Dutch public. At first he did not believe me; but within a few days he was convinced I had been right. Then he decided to do portraits in oil.

This was a forlorn hope, since Holland boasted plenty of eminent portrait-painters who already had good connections and whose names were well known. To challenge such men one had to be world famous like Philip László. To me this plan seemed hopeless from the start, even if his talent had matched his ideas.

However, he started off in high spirits and, for the first time in his life, began to paint in oils.

Mrs Andorján sat for his first two attempts which, if I remember correctly, were for one large picture and one small.

They were terrible! Really terrible!

This proved how different is painting from drawing. Miklós Vadász, who was such a master draughtsman that even his monochrome drawings could give the effect of colour and whose handling of chalk or merely the 6B Castell Pencil when drawing the most amusing coloured posters or lithographs was so masterly, could only produce the oddest of strange effects when trying to paint realistically. In his drawings everything was placed just right, yet in his painting his colours had no depth or light or air but seemed as formless as would some dull-coloured pieces of paper placed haphazardly beside each other.

Not that he himself saw this. He showed me proudly his first efforts, and, although I did shake my head once or twice, I did not want to dampen his enthusiasm and so merely said they would do all right as first attempts but that he still needed more practice. As he thought these first canvasses were perfect he did not accept my opinion; and this, perhaps, is why he never improved. He was firmly convinced that every one of his paintings was a huge success to the point that he declared repeatedly that until now he had never realized how 'simple' it was to paint!

It was touching to see not only how Miklós Vadász, happily unconscious of the truth, thought his own smears wonderful but also to note his slightly patronizing sympathy not just for my own smears but also for those of all other painters too.

It was about this time that I was trying my hand at copying a Rubens portrait in the Mauritzhuis.

Vadász often came to visit me there and we would wander through one or two rooms in this most exquisite of picture galleries. Now the Mauritzhuis must certainly be one of the most perfect of the smaller museums. A small two-storey townhouse built of smoothly worked stone, it cannot have more than fifteen or twenty rooms but everything in it, without exception, is first class. All the most famous of Flemish painters are brilliantly represented, Vermeer, Ruysddael, the two Hals, the Bruegels, all of them, as well as many Rembrandts of his finest period when he rendered every canvas he painted transcendent and mysterious. Yet Vadász could not pass a single picture without finding some fault or other – only Vermeer escaped his disapproval. Despite all this, I was always pleased to be with him as he was an essentially good-natured and pleasant companion.

I also have him to thank for a most interesting encounter.

One day I was standing in front of my own canvas, while Vadász was sitting on a chair nearby and chatting away, when a new visitor entered the room. He was a tall thin but powerfully-built, man with a noble head and impressive bearing. Vadász got up and they greeted each other. Vadász then introduced us, and we exchanged a few polite phrases. Then the two of them talked together. It was Ramsay Macdonald, leader of the British Labour Party.

He had come to Amsterdam for a world Socialist conference, and he had come for just half a day to visit the Mauritzhuis, putting off all work just to see the collection. Even though he was the leading spirit, indeed the most important figure at the congress, he had taken this time off. It was a only a passing incident, but it seemed to me so typical of this Socialist leader of the working class whose epic life struggle was to make his life and love of his country so remarkable.

***

Aarlof, who had received something of a cold shoulder from me since the affair of the model, now somewhat belatedly decided to make amends for the past and surprised me by producing a really first-class nude female model. She was a most interesting girl, small and fine-boned, with flexible joints and a lovely skin the colour of old ivory. Her body was uniformly golden brown, so much so that at home I would have taken her for a gypsy. Perhaps she was, although she came from a village near Amsterdam where the whole population is said to be dark-skinned. Apparently, they had been settled there since the time of the Spaniards.

Her full, rather Negroid, mouth and bluish curly hair, along with long almond-shaped eyes made her head exceptionally interesting, enhanced as it was by a strange, somewhat melancholy expression. I was overjoyed to have her pose for me. She never let me down and remained as my model faithfully all the time I stayed in The Hague.

She was an extremely nice girl and engaged to be married. Her fiancé was an artist, and together they planned a career on the stage, but not until they had enough money to buy what they needed. They loved each other dearly but had decided none the less to wait until then – and everything cost so much! She was quite sad when I said I would only need her in the mornings because then it would take longer to save up what they needed. When she asked if she couldn't also sit for me in the afternoons and I had to reply that that would be too expensive for *me*, she at once offered to sit in the afternoons for less provided we could work at my hotel. Apparently, if she worked at the studio she had to pay out a part of her earnings (she did not say to whom!); but in my rooms, well, that would be different.

I agreed, not only because she asked me so charmingly but also because she had such an interesting head. I thought I would do one or two portraits of her in watercolour, just as if they had been commissioned. So I asked if she had any good clothes, and she announced proudly that she had *one* that was very beautiful. It was her gala dress, which she wore only on the greatest occasions. She said she would bring it for me to see.

The next day she arrived at the hotel in the same old dress she always wore to work, but on her arm, carefully wrapped in paper, she carried her silk dress. She blushed when she had put it on and indeed looked very pretty in it. She was not in the least flirtatious, and I am sure was utterly faithful to her beloved artist, but on this day at least she showed how pleased she was to show off her prettiness when dressed in her silken dress, which was so different from the worn shabby frock she usually wore.

In my little room I could only get a proper distance from her by seating her on the table and myself on the windowsill. In this way I did three small portraits of her. It took me three or four days.

This had an unexpected result.

One evening, as I was on my way down the dark corridor to tackle the set meal in the hotel dining room, I was addressed by a broad, heavy, elderly woman, who asked if I were the 'Monsieur Banfi' who lived on that floor. I bowed, and she went on to ask: 'How much would you charge to do a portrait of me, such as I saw in your room?'

'You see,' she explained, 'yesterday, when I went by, they were making up your room and the door was open . . . and I saw the ones you had been doing . . . '

I had to think quickly. I did not want to ask too much in case it discouraged her; but not too little either, or my work would be held of little value. So I asked for two hundred florins, which would be more than enough to keep me for the next two weeks. Of course she started to bargain, and we finally decided on one hundred and fifty. That was agreed. Tomorrow in her rooms at the hotel? That was agreed too, and I said I would be there at four o'clock.

She received me in her living room, dressed in her best clothes. She wore a dress of dark-blue silk brocade with a cascade of fine lace at the neck. I looked at her carefully. She was one those women from Java which Dutchmen living in the colonies often married and brought home, where they were at once accepted and received in Dutch society without a hint of discrimination. Once in Holland they often moved in the highest society, and there were not a few *Jongheers* with Javanese mothers or grandmothers. This is just another instance of the wisdom of the Dutch in not treating their colonial subjects as social pariahs but rather accepted them with the respect due to another human being. As a result they have kept their colonial possessions without the aid of large sea or land forces, and this despite the fact that Java and Borneo are rich and eminently desirable colonies.

We soon established the pose, which had to be both comfortable and also cast the least possible shadows on the face (this last so as to diminish the wrinkles – although I did not say that to her).

It proved to be a most interesting challenge. The broad face with its jutting cheekbones gave her an almost Chinese look, which was enhanced by her hooded oriental eyelids. Although she was no longer young, her hair was still as black as soot and as smooth and shining as if she were wearing a satin helmet.

She sat as calmly as an eastern idol and never uttered a word. As a result, I was able to make swift progress with her picture, even though I never made her sit more than an hour or so at a time so as not to tire her.

I had been at it for about three days when her husband came to see us. He was a thickset, fair-haired Dutchman who was already balding. He had all the corpulence of prosperous good living emphasized by a massive watch chain. Without any form of greeting he stepped behind me, looked at the half-finished painting, stared at it for a while and then walked over to his wife. They then spoke to each other briefly in some language I did not know but which sounded like the twitter of small birds interspersed by an occasional click. After a few words the lady turned to me and asked 'Do you usually stop at teatime? Because if you do I will order you a cup of chocolate.' Then added with emphatic generosity: 'Chocolate . . . with whipped cream!' The man then nodded to me significantly as if to say: 'You see, we don't begrudge such extravagance to a poor painter!'

Of course I accepted with pleasure not only because of the chocolate but also because I saw he liked my picture. (I have to admit that I had to some extent flattered my sitter, much as the good Aarlof used to do).

From then on I got my chocolate every afternoon and, five days later, the watercolour portrait of the lady was finished, and it only remained for me to fill in the background in my own room. When I delivered it there was a great family conference; they looked at it from every angle and in every light, and then they started off again in the bird-twitter language. Finally the man turned back to me and said: 'My wife has a lovely diamond brooch. Could it still be included in the portrait?'

'Of course,' I said. 'I just need to see it pinned on.' So she went to fetch her 'broosh'. It turned out to be a tiny diamond surrounded by arabesque scrolls; pinned into the loose folds of lace it almost disappeared. I knew at once that if painted as it was this little drop of a 'broosh' wouldn't have the effect they so clearly wanted. At once I said I would paint it back in my room because only there did I have the right sort of paint.

'You don't have to take the "broosh" with you, do you?' asked the lady with barely concealed anxiety. 'Oh, no! I can do it from memory,' I reassured her and returned to my room.

I painted in the brooch twice as large as it was, and the diamond four times its real size. After a quarter of an hour I returned to the couple, and they were overjoyed. Again they looked at it from every angle and in every light. Finally the husband patted my shoulder in the most cordial manner and said: 'Don't you think . . . ' By now he had already called me his dear friend and went on: 'don't you think that the diamond is really a little bigger? Not much, but just a little bit?'

He looked at me so beseechingly that, even though I knew he knew very well that it was not bigger at all but actually much smaller, I realized his words really meant 'Please. For my sake, make it bigger!'

Naturally I did what he asked. After admitting I had got it wrong I went back to my room and painted in a stone on the lady's bosom that looked as if the Kohinoor had whelped. When they saw it they were enchanted. The next day I handed over the picture, framed and mounted and was immediately and gratefully paid. Furthermore, the husband lost no time in commissioning a portrait of himself and another of his mother; and this time he did not quibble at two hundred florins . . . which just goes to show how true is the saying, 'One good deed deserves another'!

This little tale is one of my favourite memories from that time, which is why I have related it at such length. Later it was to have rather an amusing sequel.

Two years later the artist Ede Telcs, who had been unable to find work in Budapest, accepted a post at Begheer's silver shop in Amsterdam as a sculptor of small objects. Before the war I had a seen lot of Telcs and his family when I had designed the pediment for the statue of Queen Elisabeth he had made for the commemorative exhibition. One day, on returning to Budapest after representing Hungary at some conference abroad, I was telling him about my adventures in Holland, and he at once told me that his daughter had met the Javanese lady and seen the portrait in her apartment. By chance the lady asked her if she knew the Hungarian painter 'Mr Banfi'. 'Of course,' the girl had replied. 'He is Count Bánffy, our present foreign minister!'

'Oh, no! That's not him!' replied the lady. '*Our* painter was a *very modest unpretentious sort of man!*'

In vain did Telcs' daughter explain that she knew it for sure, and even recognized my signature. Then I had been a refugee, now I was a minister. But the old lady would not be convinced. It was impossible: *her* poor painter was someone quite different!

***

As it happened, those commissioned portraits were never to be painted, for on the very same evening I received a telegram from István Bethlen. There were just three words: RETURN AT ONCE!

I knew immediately what this meant: it meant the Soviet regime in Budapest was collapsing, it meant returning home, it meant the end of exile and of homelessness; and it might even mean a return to Transylvania, my native land.

Even so, when, after hurriedly packing, getting visas and saying goodbyes, the train steamed out of the station in The Hague, and that enchanting city faded from view beyond the wide green meadows, the joy and hope engendered by my going home was tempered with sorrow: sorrow that I was leaving this place where I had lived for many months comparatively free of care, sheltered from the storms of the great world and engaged in simple honest work. As the train clattered through the growing darkness, racing towards the east along the endless straight railway track, I was subconsciously aware that it was taking me to new responsibilities, to trials and disappointments, to live surrounded by passion and hatred, to the acceptance of heavy duties, and maybe also to joyless and possibly fruitless struggles.

∽ Chapter Eleven ∽

Vienna had changed a great deal since I had spent a few days there the previous January. The volunteer officers' guard that had closed the Hofburg and transformed it into an impregnable citadel in the centre of the city had dispersed as soon as the monarch and his family, under the protection of an English military escort, had left for Switzerland. Perhaps this had been a wise move, since the emperor's continued presence in an increasingly Red Vienna might have put their lives in danger, and it may well have been this thought that persuaded him not to follow the example of Prince Ruprecht, heir to the throne of Bavaria, who sat out the short-lived Soviet rule there, and that of the Bulgarian King Boris, who never left home either. I do not know enough about the reasons that persuaded King Karl to leave, and I have had no means of checking the contradictory explanations I have heard from other people[46].

What, however, is certain is that after the king's departure those who had remained loyal to the dynasty, along with many other conservatives, were seen no more. Whether they had retired to their country properties or gone to live in small provincial towns, they had somehow vanished from sight – disappeared! Simultaneously the government of *Deutsch-Oesterreich* leaned ever more to the left.

The Communist government in Budapest had been making as much propaganda as possible in Vienna, and if they had succeeded in gaining power there, as they might well have at the time of the Bolshevik uprising in Bavaria, they might easily have soon held sway over the whole of Middle Europe.

As it was, the Communists had made two attempts to seize power in Austria, and could well have gained the upper hand if

Schober, then head of the police and later chancellor of the republic, had not acted with speed, energy and good sense to frustrate their repeated efforts. Schober's position with regard to the weak and vacillating Renner-Bauer administration was never easy because most of the so-called political 'leaders' at that time never for a moment forgot the possibility that Bolshevism might win the day, and so, to save their own skins no matter what transpired, they took care to keep good on terms with both sides. It was a form of life insurance. Perhaps they were merely obeying the adage *'Nichts Gewisses weiss man nicht'* – 'Nothing is certain you don't know for sure', as my poor grandmother used to say in intentionally bad German.

Then, in the first days of May, Schober managed to lay his hands on some documents which contained proof of Béla Kun's subversive activities in the Austrian capital, and these he laid before the government in Vienna to show the extent to which its own power, together with their own persons, was in danger. It was from this moment that Schober was given a free hand in combating the Bolshevik propaganda with proper energy . . . and also treating the plight of the Hungarian refugees with more sympathy than they had hitherto received.

This welcome development came about as a result of an unpremeditated and risky enterprise.

At that time there was a whole cohort of refugee Hungarian army officers in Vienna under the leadership of Colonel Count Takács-Tholvay, who headed the military committee which had taken over after Austria had been separated from Hungary. A group of these officers somehow discovered that a Hungarian Soviet commissar called Fenyö, was coming to Vienna and bringing with him a huge sum of money – many millions, it seemed – destined to finance a Communist uprising in Vienna. They had also learned that this Fenyö was bringing with him the holy crown of Hungary which, it was rumoured, the Communists were anxious to smuggle abroad to sell. (This last rumour had even reached us in Holland, where, with the help of Elek Nagy and Thyssen-Bornemissza, we had formed a committee to buy up St Stephen's Crown, should it turn up for sale somewhere, so as to make sure it did not fall into the wrong hands and forever become irrecoverable. Alberge, the famous Amsterdam antique dealer, had promised me to keep an eye on the world antiquarian market for us.)

The officers in exile contacted some Hungarian politicians then living in the Hotel Bristol (this was the most prestigious and adventurous group of exiles to whom I shall return later) and these enlisted the help of an English journalist who, although not only as a favour, agreed to act as if he were an English diplomat[47].

On 2 May the officers broke into the Soviet Hungarian Embassy, locked up a few employees they found there and waited until midnight, when Commissar Fenyö arrived and was caught by them. He had not brought St Stephen's Crown, but he did have the money, amounting to some 135 million in various foreign currencies and 'blue money'[48].

They then locked up the commissar and found a safe place for the money (which was later used to finance counter-revolutionary activities in Austria and Hungary). Finally they took a look at all the documents they could find; and here they were in luck. On the next day when, after a complaint from Béla Kun, the Austrians came to arrest them, they were able to furnish the chief of police with written proof of the subversive plots which had been hatched in the Soviet Hungarian Embassy. These not only included their detailed plans for overthrowing the Austrian government by force but also for robbing a bank next to the Bankgasse offices by means of an underground tunnel. A few days later the Viennese police released the Hungarian officers on bail.

It was directly after this that Schober turned his full offensive against the Communist propaganda and started treating the Hungarian exiles with benevolent neutrality.

***

At that time there were many Hungarian refugees in Vienna. As well as hundreds of army officers and a quantity of eminent politicians, there were also members of parliament, dismissed government officials and civil service employees, and many others who, although they had never been concerned with politics, were in danger of imprisonment because of their social position or wealth.

Those eminent exiled politicians who had grouped themselves under the leadership of István Bethlen were in regular touch with the 'national' government in Szeged[49], sending officers and information there.

At the time of my arrival their headquarters in Vienna were in a narrow little office in one of the houses in Lugeck Square, next to busy Roteturmstrasse. However, it was possible to get there by way of the many small streets and passages that are to be found everywhere in Vienna, and this meant that one could arrive by at least ten different ways and leave by ten others. This office had to be manned at all hours, for, although the police closed their eyes to the activities of the Hungarian counter-revolutionaries, they did nothing to protect them. And the Reds, fully aware that serious work was being done there against them, had already tried several times to force their way in.

It was a strange time then in Vienna. While the Austrian authorities took no notice, a serious battle was being waged between the civilian Hungarian refugees and the subversive Communist agents from Budapest. Everyone carried a gun, for, although the dimly-lit streets of Vienna seemed peaceful enough, we still had to take evasive action if we sensed that we were being followed, turning to face whomever it was and waiting until he had passed by. In one or two restaurants we would find some Reds dining at another table, and so we would have to keep a wary eye on those who were watching us while seeming to sip our beer light-heartedly with some of those Hungarian ladies who had followed their husbands to Vienna.

These last were mostly young and pretty, for it was only the young who were prepared to risk this often-perilous exile. There was an amusing tale about how one of them got to Vienna, a tale that shows how enterprising a clever woman can be.

Together with her husband, she had been in hiding in a country house near Győr. They decided they would try to escape across the border to Austria, and so her husband, who was wise in the ways of the world, at once started to investigate all possible means of escape. He pored over innumerable train timetables, taking many notes, and, after much thought, decided that it would be best if they took separate trains to Bruck and met there at the bridge which formed the frontier. He declared that all would go well provided she learned his lessons well. This she did, to the point of getting bored with her husband's endless repetition of his instructions. On the following day he left to take the train from Györ, while the wife took another to Óvár. She arrived at Bruck according to plan, but her husband did not, despite the fact that it had been he who for several days had been telling her what to do. It had been he who had gone on repeating 'Now don't miss the train! What on earth will I do if you don't turn up? I'll die of worry. For Heaven's sake, use your head for once!' and many other remarks even less flattering. And then it was he who failed to turn up. The clever intelligent man had boarded the wrong train and was taken to Sopron instead.

In the meantime the wife had to wait. She was dressed as a peasant woman, and very pretty she looked with a kerchief on her head and ample skirts. On her back was a bundle, and hidden inside her clothing were her jewels. She had no documents of any kind on her since, although her husband had spent a large sum of money in obtaining false identity papers, he had not given them – or any money – to her because everyone knew you should never entrust anything important to a woman as it was sure to be mislaid as soon as it was most needed!

What was she to do? Her husband had ordered her not to leave the station. 'Don't go straying off somewhere!' he had said; and so she just had to stay . . . and wait.

She waited all day.

Then, seeing that her husband still had not turned up, she went over to talk with the frontier guards on the bridge. She sat down on a bench with them and started to chat and joke with them. Then she began to tell them of her awful predicament: her aunt had gone back into the town and didn't seem to be coming back, but she couldn't get across the frontier without her. What was she to do? She had to return to Austria where she had work, and her employer would be sure to beat her if she was late and didn't show up on time. And so she prattled on with her tale of woe while, I am sure, smiling sweetly at those indomitable military men until they melted and not only let her cross the border but went so far as to escort her as far as the Austrian guard post so as to ensure she came to no harm!

A week passed before the husband managed to reach Vienna; and I am sure he was not allowed to forget his tardiness for many a day, and no doubt found himself well and truly punished in more ways than one!

***

With the money they had 'acquired' in the Bankgasse raid, the refugees were able to put in hand some of the plans they had been making. One of these was to recruit bands of patriotic troops to go to the Vas and Zala districts next to the Austrian province of Styria and take control of these normally quiet border counties[50].

At this time there were plenty of available officers among the exiles, but very few ordinary soldiers. It was therefore decided to recruit men from those elements of the unemployed Viennese who were honest, determined and well meaning. Small advertisements were put in a number of daily papers offering good pay to strong and courageous young men. Those interested were requested to report to certain 'X, Y and Z' offices between specified hours in the morning and late afternoon. I only know the story of one of these recruiting posts because I had it direct from a friend who was the treasurer there. However, I believe it was much the same in the others.

This particular post was opened at a restaurant in Landstrasse called the *Rother Hahn* – the Red Rooster. The recruiting committee consisted of five officers. On arrival there in the morning they were surprised to see many eager young men waiting for them on the pavement outside; and, as the day went by, their numbers continually increased. Inside the recruiting went slowly because each candidate had to be carefully checked to be sure of his nationality, his political views and his personal history. Also it had to be just as carefully explained to him what he was being hired to do. The restaurant's main room was full to overflowing, while outside many hundreds were waiting to be let in, so much so that traffic in Landstrasse was brought to a stand-still. Of course this was not really surprising since there were then so many unemployed in Vienna.

The policeman posted in Landstrasse was astonished by the crowd gathering there and at once assumed that if young working-class men were being recruited there it could only be the work of Bolshevik agents and so telephoned the police station for orders. He was at once told that everyone there, recruiters and recruited alike, should be arrested without delay.

Towards noon a band of policemen, led by a detective, entered the *Rother Hahn*.

'*Hände hoch!*' – 'Hands Up!' cried the detective, gun in hand.

The result was panic. Those recruits who had already been signed up disappeared in seconds, while two of the five recruiting officers escaped in the general confusion. Only my friend and two others stood their ground. The detective asked them for their identity papers. He was already somewhat taken aback to discover that of the first two he spoke to one was a major of hus-sars and the other a captain, but when he heard who my friend was – he bore a noble name well known in Vienna – his astonish-ment was such that he was only convinced of the truth of it on examining all the papers.

'*Jésu Maria!*' he cried in his Viennese dialect. '*San's denn a Verwandter vom lieben Grafen Anton? Und von der Gráfin Sarolta? Und wie san's denn a Bolschewik worden?*' – 'Are you a relation of dear Count Anton? And of the Countess Sarolta? How did you become a Bolshevik then?'

It turned out that in his youth the detective had been a forest guard on their estate and knew and loved the whole family who had always been so kind to him that he remembered them with great devotion.

After that it was not difficult to convince him that men were being recruited to fight the Communists, not to aid them. The detective would then have been happy to let everybody go free but had been ordered to round up all those involved and escort them to the local police station. He was very loath to do this. It was unthinkable that such important, nobly born gentlemen should be marched through the streets in broad daylight with a police escort! He hit upon a neat solution. It was simply that the 'prisoners' should walk ahead, just as if they had been taking a stroll, while the police, carrying their piles of confiscated documents, should follow ten paces behind. The detective himself would be on the sidewalk, from time to time waving a hand to indicate when they had to turn left or right until they all arrived at the police station.

The police commissioner was a neat little official smelling of ink. With scrupulous courtesy he carried out his duties to the letter of the law. He retained only the papers relating to the case while my friend's personal belongings, including his chequebook, were at once returned to him. 'I will telephone immediately to headquarters for further instructions,' the commissioner said. 'In the meantime, gentlemen, please make yourselves at home!'

By then it was already midday and, as the reply did not come at once, the policemen sent round to the nearest good restaurant for some lunch for the detainees, while the detective did his best to entertain them. A few hours went by like this until finally the order came for them to be set free. Towards evening those members of the recruiting committee who had not tried to evade arrest were allowed to depart in peace.

Not so those who fled. With the usual Hungarian conspirator's disdain for taking precautions, the other two went out for a pleasant stroll that same afternoon. As they walked down Kärtnerstrasse they were recognized by one of the would-be recruits. This goody-goody busybody rushed off to tell a policeman, who blew his whistle for help, and soon the two officers were arrested and sent under guard to the chief of police's offices on the Ring. There they were to left to pine in solitary confinement for several days. At length the Refugee Committee learned what had happened to them and applied officially for their release, which, at long last, was granted.

As I only returned to Vienna at the end of July, my personal knowledge of events dates from then. Otherwise, I have to depend on what I was told by friends who had been living there. So I have decided only to recount here what has not been published elsewhere but which seems to me to characterize the atmosphere we lived in those days.

In the Vienna of those days I knew only of two bright oases where the gaiety of the old imperial city was kept alive.

One was the Zichy villa in Hietzing, where many of the refugee ladies would meet in the afternoons to play bridge for some imaginary currency since no one had any real money. There was plenty of light-hearted flirting and, as there were plenty of men and very few women, the so-called weaker sex had a very good time.

Many months later, back in Budapest, I met one of these beauties again.

'We haven't seen each other since the days of the Bolshevik threat,' I said.

'Oh! Whatever became of that dear old Bolshevism?' she replied, smiling.

***

The other oasis was Frau Sacher's shop. Old Frau Sacher, who owned the famous hotel that bore her name, was the last truly activist believer in Legitimacy in Austria. She even managed to resist the determined and persistent pressure of the Renner-Bauer government.

This government tried its best to break her. They had her electricity cut off, they withdrew her license to sell alcoholic drinks, and they even provoked her staff to strike. They fined her and did many other things to bring her to heel, but she never yielded. She closed her restaurant, keeping only the shop open, and there she sat, enthroned on an armchair placed near the cash register, for all the world as if she were an empress herself. Here she would receive all her old loyal customers, who would drop in from time to time, ostensibly only to buy a tin of sardines or a small jar of 'Mixed Pickles'[51] but really just to kiss her hand and gossip about those wonderful days of old now only a memory. She was indeed the last ruler of the old *Kaiserstadt* – the imperial city.

***

I saw only two of those left-wing actors in the tragicomedy of Budapest[52]. These were Baron Lajos Hatvany and Vilmos Böhm.

Here in Vienna Hatvany was just the same sort of '*kibitz*' to the refugee committee as he had been to the revolutionary 'statesmen' back in Budapest.

The nature of the *kibitz* is that he always attaches himself to the winning side. If a player holds a 'full house, aces high' a *kibitz* would behave as if he had personally arranged it, and if the lucky player fails to double, the *kibitz* would then shake his head vehemently to show that that is not what *he* would have done if it had been *his* hand in another game. A *kibitz* would make out that, of course, 'X' should not have played trumps but something quite different, as he had suggested, but then no one listened to him, oh no, not to him!

At one time he had basked in the reflected glory of Ady. Ady, who resented Hatvany's bragging about his share in the poet's glory, took his revenge in some of his poems. Károlyi did it differently.

Hatvany's book *The Story of a Month* was his way of '*kibitzing*' the October Revolution. In this work he attributed any success to his influence; he had advised this, he had pointed out that; and it had only been his foresight that had prevented any number of possible mistakes.

In reality he never had any influence even though he had usually been on the spot. It is true he was at the Astoria and also in Belgrade, but in his book, which was written that same December to blow his own trumpet as soon as the revolution had apparently achieved its aims, Hatvany took all the credit to himself, so much so that anyone who read it was apt to believe everything he wrote, and this was the basis for much of the hatred he was to inspire later, poor man, when all he had done was to stand behind the real leaders with his fingers crossed!

It was the same in Vienna. Despite the fact that Communism, as the logical outcome of the Károlyi regime, had ignored his radical opinions and landed him, that great industrial millionaire, in penurious exile far from home, he now adopted an Olympian pose and issued his approval or his objections as from a great height of empirical wisdom. Alas, it was only the waiters in restaurants who bowed deeply when they caught sight of that thin face whose carefully composed expression seemed to resemble that of Lucifer.

One of the results of the great hostility his absurd vanity had provoked was that, one evening, while walking down the Ring, he was attacked and beaten up.

At dinnertime one day he left the Imperial Hotel and was walking to the Grand Hotel, with a lady on each side of him and an Italian journalist – could this have been a precaution against an expected ambush? When they were halfway along this wide boulevard a dwarfish but muscularly built man tapped him on the shoulder from behind and said, 'If it please your Lordship?' Hatvany turned, thus letting his two female protectors get a step or two ahead, and was given two hefty blows to the face so noisily that they could be heard, it was said, from the Opera to Schwarzenburg Square. The Italian newsman jumped to his aid, but the attacker was not alone, and his companion at once landed him a heavy blow too. The Italian screamed out '*Soccorso! Soccorso!*' – 'Help! Help!' which brought other members of the Italian Mission running from the Imperial Hotel to the aid of their compatriot. Unfortunately only one man was caught, the one who had struck Hatvany, while the other, he who had hit the Italian, escaped. By then, hearing all the noise, a crowd had gathered in the street, and so back into the hotel went the officers, together with their squat prisoner and the offended journalist. There followed a long discussion, but when they confronted the prisoner with the man who had been hit, the latter declared that that was not the man who had hit him; *his* attacker had been a tall skinny man. Excuses were made all round, and as the dwarfish muscular man spoke Italian there followed a general scene of reconciliation, with much hugging and toasts in champagne, to celebrate the renewal of peace. No one bothered any more about poor Hatvany who, as always, had stayed outside the hotel and so had taken no part in the discussion! He had been propped up on a bench between his two lady friends, bent double because it seemed that to defend himself he had flung himself down on his back, and someone had stamped on his stomach in the general confusion.

No one bothered about him or his complaining. Neither friend nor foe seemed in the least interested, and indeed he could have been knocked silly a hundred times and nobody would have

taken any notice. It would have been of no consequence compared with the real course of events. Once again he had merely
been there, and this of itself was of no importance.

***

While I was in Vienna the head of the English mission, Sir
Thomas Cunningham, invited István Bethlen to a discussion
with Vilmos Böhm, the communist Hungarian Soviet envoy. I
encountered Böhm's car just as he was arriving and recognized
him immediately even though I had only seen him once before
when he had been Secretary of State for War in the Károlyi government. He had somehow managed to obtain this post even
though he had no precise position in the Socialist Party. Being a
typewriter mechanic by profession, he had been employed for
many years in the War Ministry to maintain all the typewriting
machines in good order. Seeing him now, I was reminded of an
amusing anecdote about him.

The day after his appointment as minister he was mounting
the stairs to his new office when a band of young female typists
came down on their way to lunch. One of them gave the new
minister of state a little tap on the shoulder and said 'Böhm, old
thing . . . nice to see you . . . Do take a look at my Remington,
there's something wrong with it!' and ran down the stairs without waiting for an answer.

Böhm was later to move on to greater things. After becoming
army commissar he was appointed commander-in-chief of the
Red Army, and in this position one must admit that he was sensible enough to let his Chief of General Staff, Stromfeld, act
without referring matters to him. At the same time, he would
defend him against those whom Stromfeld had antagonized.

So it turned out that perhaps his years in the War Ministry
had been useful experience for him, after all!

It seems to be axiomatic that in revolutionary circumstances a
big role often has to be played by a man who would in peaceful
times be quite differently occupied and who would never, as they
say in the theatre, be cast for anything more important than a
member of a crowd or a soldier. A junior secretary becomes an

ambassador and, for a few hours, a young lieutenant has to play the general. It is all luck. One is on the spot; there are no other candidates. If a man is there just when an emergency occurs and decisions have to be taken in the absence of any higher authority, then he may find himself filling a post he either never dreamed of or for which he would normally be fitted only after a lifetime of service. It might happen, from time to time, that a man of real talent will emerge and, with a tremendous leap upwards, gain a position that would normally have taken years to aspire to . . . and this is admirable. Most are not like that. Many of such upstarts will think of the part they have been called upon to play by so many extraneous influences as gained only because of their own exceptional merits. Often such men later find themselves, perhaps for the rest of their lives, disillusioned, bitter and ripe for intrigue. This is inevitable. Once order has been re-established such men are soon cast aside, but will they ever recognize that this is due to their lack of ability? Oh no! It is rather that they are victims of other people's malignance. Nothing is more difficult to forget than political responsibility, especially when it has come unexpectedly. In times of revolution there is not a man who does not feel himself capable of anything. He seizes the moment. He starts with great vigour, but how often are his actions foolhardy or ill considered . . . and how often are they unscrupulous?

***

As an example of this, let us consider the extraordinary tale of the so-called '*brucki-puccs*' – the unsuccessful coup at Bruck. I tell it exactly as it was recounted to me by several men who took part in it. What led up to it is obscure enough, but the *putsch* itself happened like this: At the beginning of June news arrived that the counter-revolutionary government of Julius Károlyi[53] had been formed at Szeged. The Allies did not then recognize it, as the victorious powers, according to Colonel Cunningham, would only accept a government formed on unoccupied territory – and Szeged was then still occupied by the French. This did not worry Bethlen, who at once entered into regular communication with Károlyi's group in Szeged and sent there most of the exiled officers in Vienna so as to form the nucleus of a re-formed national army. He also sent money from the millions obtained from the Bankgasse raid.

The exiles who gathered at the Hotel Bristol took a different line. All right, they said, if a new National government has to be declared on unoccupied Hungarian soil, so be it! Here they were close enough to Bruck-Királyhida. They would surprise the place, occupy it themselves and declare a new government there!

They went at it without further delay.

The following plan was quickly formed. Secret envoys would contact a group of suitable men of good will, who would hide near the station on the Hungarian side of the river Laitha. There they would wait for a group of officers from Vienna to arrive on the Austrian side.

First of all they had to be sure of who and how many men would be able to be collected in secret beside the bridge over the Laitha. It seems that the numbers were mustered with not a little commotion, rather like bidding for the bank at baccarat. Some of the conspirators seem to have been carried away by typical Hungarian overconfidence, while others, more realistically minded, started thinking in terms of twenty or thirty. The more dashing thought of hundreds, and there were those who guaranteed that at least two thousand would rally to the call. Next the groups began to enlist the help of some of the officers who were gathering at one of the small hotels in Josefstadt. Many of those then waiting in Vienna were eager to join the venture, all the more so because the leaders firmly declared that everything was in readiness. The recruits were assured that many thousands were only waiting to join them on the Hungarian side and that even machine guns would be available. It was wonderful how every detail had been worked out so brilliantly. On the night chosen they would be transported by taxis to Bruck, and there they would hide close to the bridge which formed the frontier. A locomotive would be reversed across the bridge, pushing empty wagons into which they would climb and so would be whisked into the station under the noses of the Communist guards. Once there – hee! hee! – they would be joined by the waiting recruits, disarm the Red guards . . . and Lo! They would declare a national Hungarian government on unoccupied Hungarian soil, which the Allies would naturally recognize!

One thing remained: a government had to be formed before the raid, and this had to be done in secret so that no one on the other side should start talking about it. This was done; and at once they all began to talk about its members as if they were already ministers.

Like all good Hungarian secret conspiracies – and Hungarians are unsurpassed at keeping secrets! – they all talked about it far too much, so much, indeed, that it was said the Vienna cabbies knew about it days in advance, and in their thick Viennese dialect, took much pleasure in saying to everyone: '*Ti Kraffen kehn nach Pruck*' – 'So the counts are all off to Bruck!'

At last the long-awaited night arrived.

Some forty officers gathered in front of the hotel in Josefstadt, where ten taxis stood ready to transport them to the field of battle. All of them had a little money, a travelling bag, soldiers' caps and army belts; some even had a revolver. Then they asked where were the guns and ammunition that had been promised. These, they were told, were still hidden and would be supplied separately. Each officer would receive a weapon on arrival at Bruck because in Vienna it would cause something of a stir if a lot of gentlemen carrying arms were seen getting into taxis. They all congratulated each other – it had been well done, very cleverly done, they said!

Off they went, into the wild summer night. In the first car was the leader of this military expedition and behind him, in proper military order, were the other taxis filled with helmeted, leather-belted but civilian-clad braves.

A single car separated itself from the others. This took a roundabout route as it had to pick up the Mannlichers and the ammunition.

After quite a while it arrived at the doors of an old monastery in a lonely street. This is it, they said. This is where the monks will hand out the weapons they have hidden for us.

An officer got out and looked around. The street was empty. This was the moment. Now he could safely ring the bell, and when the doorkeeper looked out, the password 'Jerusalem' could be whispered in his ear.

One of them rang the bell. Then they heard steps approaching, and finally a tiny window was opened in the massive oak door.

'*Was wollens?*' – 'What do you want?' said an unfriendly voice from the darkness inside.

'Jerusalem!' whispered the officer into the tiny opening.

'*Wa-as?*' – 'Whaat?' came from the darkness.

'Jerusalem!' repeated the officer, this time more loudly.

The little window was slammed shut, and footsteps died away on the other side. Outside they waited, imagining someone had gone to fetch the arms and ammunition, although still thinking it odd the man had gone away without a single word of reply . . .

And there they went on waiting . . . for a very long time. Nothing! Not a word, not a sound. Nothing to suggest that anything was happening inside, either to bring out the weapons or the ammunition that had been so carefully arranged by the new 'minister'. An hour went by, and then an hour-and-a-half, and still nothing, nothing, nothing. And time was rushing by.

Anxiously they were thinking that the others would already be at Bruck, waiting for their weapons; and that the attack was planned for that very night. It was impossible to wait any longer, and so they decided to ring again.

Ring again they did, several times. Finally, after a long wait, the same heavy footsteps were heard from inside the door. Once again the tiny slit was opened.

'*Was is?*' the voice asked again.

'Jerusalem!' repeated the officer and then again, very distinctly, 'Je-ru-sa-lem!'

'Go . . . !' bellowed the unseen voice, using a vulgar command no one would want to obey and in a rage again slammed shut the tiny window.

As this was obviously the only reply they were likely to get, it was now clear there was no more business to do there, and so the only thing to do was to follow the others as swiftly as possible and report that the excellent password had not worked. Otherwise the others might start something while still unarmed.

Off they raced in their taxi and at last arrived in Bruck, where, on the Austrian side, they found some of their companions who had been posted there on guard, while the others had repaired to a neighbouring hostelry which was called, as if to emphasize that everywhere thy were pursued by the colour red, the *Rother Ochs* – the Red Ox. There they found the whole band, together with the 'general staff' and the 'ministers'.

The new arrivals then told of the failure of the password, but no one admitted responsibility, indeed they all accused each other before finally agreeing that the blame must lie with some of those who had stayed in Vienna instead of coming with the main group. The matter of 'Jerusalem' was never cleared up, not even years later.

Neither did I ever get to know why they stayed at Bruck at all and, having stayed, why they did not attack that same night. This was because I heard the tale not from the leaders but from their soldier followers. Be that as it may, they did stay and decided to launch the attack on the following evening.

What does one do if forced to spend the day waiting at an inn? What else but quaff a *spritzer* or a beer or some other heart-warming drink? And since they were so many, what more natural than that someone should start singing – many lovely songs, nostalgic sad Hungarian songs, interspersed with some crackling csárdás? Never mind if they could be heard on the sidewalks outside: there weren't many people about and, anyway, the Lord loveth men who make music!

Not only that, but as it is irksome to sit still all day long, some of them ventured out for a stroll or to the local tobacconist for cigarettes or picture postcards. After all, perhaps the sight of strangers in that little-frequented border town, gentlemen in civilian clothes wearing army caps and tight leather belts, would not really attract any attention. There was nothing special about them; it wasn't as if they were in full uniform!

And so the day passed.

In the afternoon two workmen crossed the bridge and came into the inn. When they sat down at a neighbouring table, some of the officers thought they might have brought over a message – but no! It turned out they were Reds sent over to spy! So they found themselves arrested instead, dragged upstairs to a vaulted passage where they were interrogated and finally locked in one of the guest rooms with a guard at the door so that they should not escape and carry back the news of what was being so secretly prepared.

At last the evening came, and the company moved off towards the bridge over the Laitha. There they lay down by the rails on the edge of the embankment. Again they waited for a long time.

Night fell. Somewhere out of sight a locomotive's whistle sounded. Perhaps that was the signal that it was coming? Then a red lamp was seen several times, swung to and fro and then extinguished.

Finally there was complete silence: perhaps nothing was coming!

General argument followed. It was clear that someone should go on ahead, but who?

Only one man had a proper gun. It was one of my friends who had brought his own sporting rifle: a Mannlicher-Schönauer. The others said that he, the one with the gun, should be the one to go. He demurred.

'Why me?' he argued, forcefully pointing out: 'with this weapon I can shoot accurately more than a hundred metres. The men with revolvers should go first. They can only shoot at close range.'

And so this is what they did. Some five of them set off, one of the 'ministers' being among them.

Then, forty or so paces behind, followed the main body, led by the only man with a rifle; and then, according to the accepted rules of strategy, came the recruits.

The advance party set off. When they set foot on the bridge shots were heard and also what sounded like machine-gun fire. They stopped and conferred with each other: could it be that the Reds had noticed something and were aiming at the bridge? And if this were so, would it not be foolish to try to cross to the other side? So they returned to the main body of men most of whom, hearing the shots, had lain down between or beside the rails, while some sought refuge in empty trucks. (Eyewitnesses tell how one of the leaders, a large plump man, had flung himself down between the rails where, so the legend goes, he lay so flat that the others lost sight of him). There were still occasional bursts of fire from the other side, so they again consulted one another as to what they should do and how to do it. Again it seemed difficult to decide.

In the end, fate took a hand. Those in the rear announced that the *Heimwehr*[54] were marching up from Bruck, and soon their steps could be heard.

'Run for your lives! Scram! Hide in the empty wagons!' someone shouted. Once inside, in the pitch dark, they started sharing out the money they had brought with them – apparently about six or seven million from the Bankgasse raid – so as to save as much as possible. In a wild hurry they were saying, still in total darkness, 'Here! Take this million!' Others would call out: 'I don't want it. I've got two already!' So they hid it, stuffing money into each other's pockets or boots or wherever else they could find.

But the *Heimwehr* did find them, which they might not have done in the dark had not one of the ministers, a great hulking fellow, left a leg sticking out of a wagon he was too tall to climb in it.

'Where there's a leg, there's a man,' guessed one of the Austrian policemen, and promptly pulled out the would-be minister. Then they arrested the whole band and took them back to their barracks, where they were treated with much cordiality and provided with food and drink.

At first it was planned to intern them in one of the border towns, which potentially could have proved fatal for them, but they were eventually shipped back to Vienna and confined in the Schottenring whence they were finally released through Bethlen's intervention.

None of these men came to any harm; and only my friend who took his sporting rifle to Bruck was a loser. The *Heimwehr* confiscated his magnificent Mannlicher-Schönauer, and he never saw it again.

They were still laughing about the *brucki-puccs* when I arrived back in Vienna. Here I have told the story for its humorous elements, but when I reflect on how much danger so many trusting young men were placed in by the thoughtlessness and sheer superficiality of the organizers of the *putsch*, I am appalled. Nobody ever admitted being responsible.

***

A few days after the Böhm-Bethlen meeting came the news that the Soviet government in Budapest had resigned[55] and that Peidl had taken over and formed a new cabinet.

At this point, Colonel Cunningham, Borghese, the Italian chargé d'affaires[56] and, I understand, the French appealed to the Hungarian politicians in exile to put together a real national government to include members of all parties and which could succeed Peidl. They assured them that such an administration would be recognized by the Allies, and that its representatives would be invited to the Paris peace conference. Discussions about the formation of such a coalition led to endless wrangling, as it always does when disparate groups whose following is uncertain vie for position and power while contending with the internal stresses caused by personal ambition. Several days passed in this way.

In Vienna they were still arguing – and bargaining over which posts would fall to whose lot – when more news arrived from Budapest.

The Peidl government, after finding itself powerless because of the occupation by the Romanian army, had suddenly been swept away by István Friedrich, who had seized power himself. This created an entirely new situation and made nonsense of the idea that the Allies should confer with Hungarian political exiles in Vienna when there were now two governments in Hungary, one in Budapest and another at Szeged.

Although no one had much confidence in Friedrich, for his extreme leftwing actions in support of the October Revolution were still too recent to be forgotten, we decided all the same to return at once to Budapest and to start trying to bring about some sort of political unity without bothering too much about personalities.

***

If I remember rightly, the train that brought back the Hungarian exiles from Vienna left about 10 or 12 August.

It comprised a long line of shabby coaches. Of the politicians I recall only Bethlen and Lovászy, but there were also many private citizens coming home from Austria. I sat in a compartment with old Gerbeaud, a most sympathetic and intelligent man whom I had known for many years. During our long trip he first of all told me how he had been ruined by the Communists and then proceeded to explain to me all the tricks of the trade in the making of chocolates. It was fascinating, for he was a first-rate specialist in his own line. It was doubly entertaining since it was an age since I had conducted any conversation that did not concern politics.

Our journey was a series of fits and start, a slow jolting progress, without incident, passing through one lonely deserted station after another. Finally we arrived at Györ[57].

The station was hung all over with bunting and flags of the national tricolour.

There was a throng of people on the platform and also in the town, where all the municipal functionaries dressed in their old Franz Joseph uniforms were gathered to greet us. I think it was the mayor who welcomed us, first greeting István Bethlen.

I am cursed by always being fearfully bored by all speeches on festive occasions, for no matter how good they are one always knows, even before the speaker opens his mouth, what he feels and what he will say. So rather than listen I spent the time scanning the crowd. Behind the local officials, and quite close to them, stood a half-circle composed of several rows of large women with generous figures, all broad-cheeked and with double chins, richly dressed in silk skirts and tight bodices. Seeing them reminded me of the rich fertility of the Hungarian soil. They were the fishwives of Györ!

These ladies were wreathed in proud, charming welcoming smiles; they had not come only to bid us welcome but also to receive our congratulations, for it was they who had finally brought the Communist sway in Györ to an end, several days before it collapsed elsewhere. It seems that the leading Red commissar had so maddened them by some confiscation order or other that they had stormed the town hall, pushed aside the guards, forced their way up the stairs to the principal floor, seized the unfortunate commissar and flung him out of the window. Judging from their strong arms and their huge brawny hands, the commissar must have had a bad time of it! One had to admit that all this must have taken much courage for if they had not succeeded, bloody retribution would surely have followed. It was lucky for them that the Communist regime was then in its last days and had no time to order punishments. Hearing this tale from the welcoming committee, we went straight over to join the band of heroic fishwives, who seemed overjoyed to receive our praise and grateful handshakes.

Then the train's whistle blew. It was time to be on our way.

***

Then came the evening, followed by the night; but the train kept slowly rolling on its way. It seemed a long, long time.

We passed dark, unlit stations, rumbling over screeching points and rails that seemed to cry out. It was as if we only went forward to the sobs and complaints of this lost and ruined land that seemed to have been left behind, just part of the debris of war and revolution . . .

The night became ever darker, ever more disconsolate until that little joy that had awoken in our hearts because our exile was at last at an end, slowly died away, leaving behind only deep anxiety for an unknown future.

The stormy years were over, but those that followed held no pity for our homeland.

Twenty-Five Years
(1945)

Translators' Note

Most of the Bánffy papers and archives were destroyed when the retreating German army set fire to the castle of Bonczhida at the end of the Second World War. In June 1945 after the horrors of the Battle of Budapest, Miklós Bánffy, with Countess Bánffy and their daughter Katalin, returned to Kolozsvár to see if any of their possessions could be saved. In November of that year news came that their Budapest townhouse had been occupied by Russian troops and their possessions there thrown out into the street whence a kind relative had salvaged what she could. Countess Bánffy and her daughter rushed back to the Hungarian capital leaving Miklós Bánffy at Kolozsvár (Cluj) as he was still hoping then to recuperate what was left of the family forests. Soon after this the frontier between Romania and Hungary was closed by the military, which meant that the family was separated. This lasted until 1949 when Count Bánffy finally obtained permission to rejoin his wife and daughter; he died in Budapest in the following year. These memoirs were started in 1945, when he found himself on his own in Kolozsvár.

The reference to Fortéjos Deák Boldizsár (the Crafty Deak Boldizsár) in Bánffy's Introduction is to the eponymous author of the fictional *The Memories of the Crafty Deak Boldizsár*, which Bánffy wrote and published in Kolozsvár in 1930 in his ancestral home. He wrote it in archaic Hungarian, and used the literary device of stating that it was edited from an ancient manuscript he had discovered in the Bonczhida archives. This was believed by a number of literary historians at the time until Bánffy, who loved to tease, revealed the joke. Soon after this he started work on the trilogy *Erdélyi Történet* – *The Writing on the Wall*, of which the first volume, *Megszámláltattál* – *They Were Counted* was published in 1934.

Patrick Thursfield and *Katalin Bánffy-Jelen*

Introduction
by Miklós Bánffy

It is just twenty years since Hungary was forced to sign the Treaty of Trianon. In this treaty the Hungarians had been branded as war criminals even though none of us had wanted war until we were dragged into it by foreign powers who forced us into battle and the death and annihilation of our country. It was to be the same twenty years later.

Today we are once more surrounded by ruins, worse ruins now than before because the land in which we lived has been laid waste by war as if trampled over by the Four Horsemen of the Apocalypse. Our cities and villages are all in ruins; our economy and our agriculture are destroyed. Hundreds of thousands have been made homeless.

Everything that we worked so hard to achieve after Trianon and which we had built up over the first ten years of struggle; all the fruits of our self-sacrifice, care and dogged determination, have now been taken from us.

The annihilation that the second catastrophe Fate has brought down upon us is infinitely worse than the first.

Even to think about it is beyond bearing: terrible to contemplate what led up to it all, terrible to know that all our efforts to rebuild were for nothing.

For someone like myself, who was one of those who worked so hard for the rehabilitation of our country after the First World War, all that is now left is to ponder on the past and recall something of what actually happened. After a long life this is the only treasure I still possess. And yet, in a way, I do have another treasure in the experience of politics, which I acquired – sometimes as an active participant although mostly as a passive one – over the last fifty years. Although much still remains, even this will die with me. I have made no notes and have never kept a diary. Countless documents, letters and *memoranda* which I did keep have now been either burnt or dispersed. I only have what is in my mind, and that only until I cross the river of life. Once the crossing has been made, even that will vanish as well. It is uncertain how long I have, but the end cannot be far away.

It was these thoughts that have made me start these memoirs. I want to describe what I know of those events, both at home and abroad, which led the Hungarians from Trianon firstly to the Vienna decisions of 2 September 1938, and 30 August 1940, and finally to that fatal road to ultimate disaster. I wish to tell what I myself did, because only he who has really achieved something has the right to judge. I want to explain the reasons why and also to describe some of the people who have played a decisive part in the shaping of our history. I want too to look critically at the conduct of our affairs and to look at it particularly from a foreign point of view because since 1900, when I had a diplomatic post in Berlin, although I have (twice) been both a member of parliament and a prefect, this has also been my own.

Of course everything I put down today will be somewhat sketchy, partly because to go into full detail would require many volumes and also because it would take years to write. And at my age, although I now have plenty of free time, I cannot see myself undertaking such a task.

All the same, I can still put down some of the essentials as well as some of the conclusions that, by learning from the past, we should now be drawing from it all. Perhaps in some way this work of mine may prove useful to my countrymen even though I have always been all too aware of the truth I once put into the mouth of one Fortéjes Deák Boldizsár, a character in one of my books, where I made him say: 'Perhaps this story can bear witness, if not for the many then for a few, that it is with sorrow that I have experienced with my own writings that it is rare indeed for a man to take the written word to heart and become any the wiser for it'. Yet I feel impelled to set down what I remember, if not to help others then at least to serve as proof of our feelings at the time and the zeal with which we tried to rebuild our country. Perhaps also my tale of one man's experiences will serve as a useful source to someone in the future wishing to study what happened to Hungary twenty-five years ago.

⚭ Chapter One ⚭

The Treaty of Trianon was signed on 4 June 1920, and, as I recall, was ratified by the National Assembly in Budapest toward the end of August.

In his heart no Hungarian ever really accepted the terms that had been forced upon us.

From a political point of view Hungary had been obliged to choose between two opposing attitudes. The first was that of acceptance, both officially and publicly, of the treaty's terms: the second, which is what soon became generally adopted, was to look upon the document as something only signed under duress, to deny its validity and to demand its revision. This amounted to a hard-line 'No! No! Never!'

Faced with the terms of the Treaty of Frankfurt, which brought to an end the Franco-Prussian War, the French had adopted the first course even though they thought in 1871 just as we did in 1920. In his heart no Frenchman was ever resigned to peace terms that tore the provinces of Alsace and Lorraine from the heartland of France. Nevertheless, when the treaty had been signed, the order had been given: '*Y penser toujours, en parler jamais*' – 'Think of it always, speak of it never!' Everyone, not only the officers of state but the entire press and the public, every last man, in groups or individually, upheld this principle for forty-three years. And what an admirable principle it proved to be, giving to all an inner strength and discipline, keeping alive a profound patriotism in everyone's hearts, existing in the blood as true and natural as mother's milk. There was no need to feed this patriotic feeling with slogans, for these would have been superfluous. Such a feeling is not eroded by silence for without words it still works in the heart towards that never-spoken but never-changing goal. Truly great is the nation that can do this.

By adopting this policy the France of the Third Republic was enabled not only to avoid any friction with her immediate neighbours to the east but also to acquire Tunis and Morocco and peacefully build a colonial empire in Africa reaching almost as far as the Equator. This could never have been achieved in the face of English disapproval if Germany had not remained passively helpful. It is possible that Wilhelmstrasse fully believed that the lesson of Sedan[58] ruled out any possible future retaliation by France. And they certainly felt that allowing France to occupy herself in grabbing new colonial territories in Africa would tie down her armies and provide a useful new object for any chauvinistic ambitions she might still have.

No doubt, the open defiance shown by what was left of Hungarian people after the partition enforced by the Treaty of Trianon told the world of our unrelenting opposition. However, it would have been better for our country if we could have followed the example of France.

It was obvious that in the foreseeable future nothing would change what had been decided at Trianon, and that many years would pass before some radical changes in Europe would make it possible for a revision of terms even to be mentioned. Until such time came, obdurate refusal to accept the situation would mean isolation for Hungary and with it much harm and little possibility of progress. The treaty terms had left many questions unresolved. The letter written by Millerand, the French prime minister, to the Hungarian delegate at the conference left the consideration of revising the frontiers dependent upon unspecified future conditions; thus leaving the door open to later discussion. Furthermore, although the terms affecting the status of ethnic minorities were sketchy and unclear, they nevertheless gave Hungary a moral right to try to alleviate the social conditions of Hungarians now living outside the country's new borders. If a favourable atmosphere could be induced this would entail negotiations with Hungary's new neighbours and, from an economic point of view, could bring great advantages.

In the first year after the treaty's ratification all political life in Hungary was devoted to creating order at home and bringing an end to the White Terror[59] that had threatened to destabilize the newborn state.

The administration destroyed by the revolution had first to be reconstituted for better or worse, as circumstances permitted. The state finances had to be put in order so that the machinery of government could function. There were also many problems concerning the membership of parliament, which now consisted for the most part of men with no political schooling or experience and delegates of the National Smallholders' Party led by Nagyatádi-Szabó. These were divided into small cliques who voted either from sheer well-meaning ignorance or for personal gain, or even from emotion aroused by political slogans. Most of the ministers' time was taken up in coping with unnecessary bickering in parliamentary debates, leaving them little opportunity for serious planning. As a result, for a whole year no decision was taken regarding what should be the country's official foreign policy. Although on the very day the treaty was signed the president of the National Assembly declared that it 'contained moral and material impossibilities and that no one can be bound by impossibilities', and although delegates from the newly separated provinces produced a petition addressed to 'all the countries of the world' in which they swore to work to rejoin the mother country, these were all only individual opinions and protests and were never official decisions of policy by the government of Hungary; nor did they influence the future behaviour of the majority.

That this was so was proved by Prime Minister Pál Teleki when he contacted Benes, the prime minister of Czechoslovakia, with whom he initiated the first discussions with representatives of one of the newly-created neighbouring states. These were held at Bruck, where Hungary was represented by Teleki and his foreign minister, Gustáv Gratz, and although no tangible decisions were taken at least the meeting was held in a friendly atmosphere and ended with a promise to meet again.

Such was the political state of Hungary as regards both internal and external affairs. What was to come was still uncertain.

Then came King Karl's first *putsch*, which turned out to be an adventure fit only as a subject for operetta.

The king travelled through Austria in disguise and entered Hungary with a false passport, arriving at Szombathely, where he drove to the archbishop's palace. As it happened, József Vass, the minister of education, chanced to be there while Teleki was not far away, staying at Antal Sigray's house at Ivánc where he had gone for a brief Easter holiday. He was at once informed by telephone.

Poor King Karl had arrived full of hope. For months he had been visited at the small castle of Prangins on Lake Geneva (offered to him as a refuge by the Swiss government) by a band of eager adventurers representing all sorts of diverse interests, business and political. Many of these had hopes of arranging the sale of the Habsburg jewels, an enterprise that promised great rewards as they were known to include the 'Florentiner Ei', the huge egg-shaped diamond of the Medicis. This band of opportunists brought with them hopeful and wonderful news, mainly from Paris, for at Prangins nothing else would bring the promise of money.

Furthermore, it seems probable that a few well-meaning and loyal Habsburg supporters also sent encouraging reports from Vienna, Budapest, Bratislava, Brünn and Prague – perhaps also from Zagreb – all of which King Karl believed to be true. He really did believe that everywhere hearts were throbbing with loyal eagerness and that he had only to appear to be instantly reinstated upon the throne he had abandoned. This would be the Hungarian throne and, once restored there, the Dual Monarchy would again be his, and he would return to Vienna as emperor on the shoulders of the Hungarians. And if not actually on their shoulders, at least at the head of a Hungarian army; for even he knew well enough that Renner's Austria was hardly aching for his return.

For King Karl himself it was self-evident and completely natural to assume that, once restored, not Budapest but Vienna would be the Imperial capital once again, and that he would return to the Hofburg and Schönbrunn, the ancient seats of the Habsburg-Lorraine family. This, at least, was his goal and the ultimate object of his dreams.

Naturally, Vienna was not mentioned by him at Szombathely. There he spoke only of his 'beloved Hungarians', and it was evident that he first wanted to secure a foothold in little Hungary. To this end, his hopes were centred on Admiral Horthy for the simple reason that just before he became Regent, Horthy had sent a letter to him at Prangins. Although when abdicating the king had absolved everyone from their oaths of allegiance to him, Horthy had written that he considered his assumption of the position as Regent as a necessary but essentially temporary arrangement, and that as soon as circumstances permitted and he could do it without endangering the welfare of the nation, he himself would resign and return the supreme power to the rightful sovereign.

It was this confidence that had prompted his return. He understood, he said, that everything had been arranged and that one of his agents – probably the man who called himself Belmonte and who had been awarded a title of by the king – had brought him the encouraging news that his restoration would be favourably regarded by the victorious powers, and so all was well, was it not?

He paced up and down the room and, although he could speak excellent Hungarian, he was now so excited and in such good humour that he spoke only in German.

All he seemed to want now was advice on how best to reward Horthy in a manner worthy of him. 'Shall I give him a dukedom? Yes, that would do admirably. *Glauben die Herren* – do you think, my lords, he would like that? Or should I give him the Grand Cross of the Order of Maria-Theresia? Yes! That would be even better. I brought it with me. You all agree he'll be overjoyed? *Nicht war das wird ihn freuen, dass muss ihn freuen* – He'll be overjoyed, won't he? He must be overjoyed.'

And he went on like this for some time, speaking of nothing else. Teleki, József Vass, and Mikes, Bishop of Szombathely, listened to him in amazement. He never once asked how he was regarded by public opinion, nor what was the view of the majority of the people, or even that of the parliament of long-suffering Hungary. Clearly none of this seemed important to him, so convinced was he that his arrival was joyfully awaited.

The next day the party set off for Budapest in two cars, Karl in the first and Teleki in the second. Because of some mechanical trouble the second car was left behind on the way, and so King Karl arrived in the capital alone. It was about noon.

First he stopped at the prime minister's office in the fortress of Buda and there hurriedly washed his hands at the fountain in the courtyard before crossing to the Royal Palace. Horthy had just sat down to lunch when he was called from the table by an aide-de-camp who announced that the king had arrived and was waiting for him in the study. Horthy, of course, rushed there at once.

Their talk lasted some two hours, and it seems that Karl repeated all the things he had been saying to the ministers at Szombathely about the news he had heard from Paris and how everything was ready for his return. He then put the insignia of the Grand Cross of the Order of Maria Theresia on the table in front of Horthy, presumably as a gesture of encouragement. The Regent, however, pushed it to one side and started to explain the realities of the situation. What his actual words were I do not know, but it is certain that he made it clear that to attempt a restoration would be an insane adventure. The Great Powers were sure to object, while the newly independent states would mobilize immediately and threaten armed intervention. Invasion would follow with the inevitable risk of a further division of the country, this time even worse than the first. He probably also went so far as to say that public opinion did not look kindly on the idea of welcoming as their ruler a sovereign who had abandoned his post barely a year and a half before. Horthy must have spoken wisely and well, for the result was that Karl got back into his car and returned to Szombathely. It had been agreed that he would return at once to Switzerland and that every effort would be made to keep the whole excursion a secret.

Of course the secret was not kept. By the afternoon of the same day all Budapest knew it and, as was their habit, the good people of Budapest at once made a joke of it. They said that one of the Regent's aides-de-camps with the unusual name of Magosházi[60], was heard to say in a thick Hungarian accent as he escorted the king down the palace staircase: '*Majestät, das war überflüssig*' – 'This was unnecessary, your Majesty!'

The remaining details of the intended *putsch* were not in the least humorous.

Karl stubbornly refused to go further than Szombathely. He had promised to leave Hungary, but now he did not want to go, no doubt fearful of the scene his wife would make if he returned empty-handed, for it was well-known that Queen Zita could be a dragon when roused. Karl therefore had to invent excuses for his departure, excuses that would account for his lack of success. Accordingly, he announced that he had caught cold in the open car and was now forced to keep his bed. The principal ministers – Teleki, Bethlen, and Apponyi – rushed to Szombathely to reason with him, as the situation was becoming dangerous.

Already on the afternoon of his arrival the Great Powers had sent a protest to Budapest and, while Karl lingered at Szombathely, increasingly menacing messages arrived daily demanding that the ex-king should leave Hungary at once. But when he finally agreed to leave further difficulties arose. The Swiss government refused to accept him. They were angry that Karl had broken his imperial word, for when that hospitable country had given him a warm welcome in 1918 it had made only one condition, which was that if the king wished to leave Switzerland he must first notify the government in Bern. Karl had made light of this and furthermore the 'court' at Prangins, explaining why he had not been seen on his customary walk, had lied and said that he was ill in bed. And this was not all. The Socialists in Austria declared that they would not permit their former emperor to pass through Austrian territory, while the railways threatened to go on strike if this was allowed. Eventually, after much pressure from the Great Powers all was settled and Karl, under the auspices of the western allies, was escorted out of Szombathely, and Hungary was rid of the dangers this childish prank might have provoked.

As it was, the Teleki government was forced to resign.

On the afternoon this happened I heard the news that Horthy had asked István Bethlen to form a new cabinet. Bethlen had been head of the Refugee Bureau since its creation a year before. This had been the first official position he had ever accepted even though from the first years of the century until 1918 he had been a member of parliament, belonging to the Apponyi Party. His word carried a certain weight, although he had always remained a backbencher. Although he spoke in the House only rarely he was known for the seriousness and objectivity of what he had to say; and because he scrupulously avoided rant and bombast he was fundamentally different from the demagogues by which he was surrounded. Tisza, at the end of his term as prime minister, had wanted to strengthen his government by the inclusion of some opposition members and offered him a portfolio – and later, if I remember correctly, so had Esterházy – but Bethlen would never accept. The same thing happened again when Horthy wanted him to be prime minister: firstly when the Károlyi-Huszar and later the Simonyi-Semadám governments resigned. On both these occasions Bethlen replied that the time was not yet ripe.

I once wrote a short character sketch of István Bethlen for the *Nouvelle Revue Française* in which I compared his political career to the evolution of life on our planet from amphibian creatures of the sea to four-limbed mammals on dry land. Bethlen managed not to be conspicuous at either stage. As an amphibious lizard he neither grew to monstrous proportions like the dinosaurs, nor did he develop protective armour plating or rows of needle-sharp spines; he did not grow enormous hind-legs like the Brontosaurus nor anticipate the dachshund-like ichthyosaurus. As a mammal he neither grew short horns nor spreading antlers; he did not elongate his nose to a trunk nor reduce his toes to hooves like the gazelles or to shovel-shaped extremities like the primitive sloths. His teeth never became fearsome fangs. Bethlen's evolution was never confined to any one special direction. He kept five fingers on his hands and five toes on his feet, and his teeth remained even; and so, having no special distinguishing marks, he remained, among the mammoths, cave-bears and sabre-toothed tigers, a small defenceless but highly intelligent if modest member of the animal kingdom. He merely awaited his destiny wishing neither to be classed as a wanderer on the prairies nor one dwelling in swamps. And so, when the third era dawned, and his time had come, he was able to become the lord of all creatures because he owed allegiance to none.

For István Bethlen this time came in the spring of 1921.

It was a well-chosen moment, and for the next ten years he controlled the destiny of Hungary until, by his own choice, he relinquished power much to the disappointment of the majority and the chagrin of parliament. During those ten years he found himself having to cope with many a dire crisis that would have taxed the powers of lesser men. A month after accepting office he was faced with the dispute over the rape of the Burgenland, and then came King Karl's second *putsch*. This was a far cry from the light-opera farce of the first, for it was aggravated not only by dissention in the army and a revolt by the gendarmerie but also by the threat of armed intervention from abroad. Then came the affair of the forged French francs[61] to be followed by scarcity of jobs and the steep rise in wheat prices. All of these problems would have defeated a man of lesser calibre. In the world crisis of 1931 he resigned, too tired to fight yet another battle.

Bethlen and I were linked by a long-standing personal friendship that had originated in our childhood. Later he married a close relative of mine. From the autumn of 1919 he had lived close to us, and I often used to lunch or dine at his house. Our opinions were the same on most matters and so, when faced with any special political problem, he would usually discuss it with me. Because of this, I found it quite natural that he should telephone me in the afternoon he accepted office, assuming that he wanted to discuss some aspects of his new responsibilities. So when it appeared that he was asking me to be his minister for foreign affairs it came as a complete surprise.

Unexpected though this was, it came as a logical consequence of the work I had been doing in the previous two years. As I have written elsewhere I went abroad in December 1918, with the full knowledge of Mihály Károlyi, on a mission for István Bethlen, then head of the Szekler National Council, to try to work towards obtaining for Hungary a more favourable and just peace treaty than seemed likely to be our lot at the time. I spent some six months at The Hague, and when I returned I was sent off again, this time as an official representative of the Hungarian government. In January 1920 I found myself sent to London at

the same time as Apponyi and Bethlen were despatched to Paris
as the Hungarian representatives at the peace conference.

Once in London I was able to make a number of useful contacts within influential political circles and managed to win some
of them over to our view that a punitive and unfair treaty with
Hungary was in no one's interests. Among these men was Lord
Asquith, the former prime minister, and I look back with gratitude to the goodwill and understanding of Lord Bryce, Robert
Cecil, Lord Newton and Montague, to the help of Mr Bowie,
chief secretary of the Unitarian and Presbyterian churches,
and to Webster McDonald, one of the leaders of the Scottish
Presbyterian church. I also made contact with the Socialist Party.
I received energetic support from the Unitarian and Presbyterian leaders and also from Sir Lucian Wolf, principal secretary of
World Jewry, who himself wrote proposals for settling the problem of the ethnic minorities and which were entirely his own
idea. Despite the fact I was still technically an 'enemy alien', I
was received by the recently appointed foreign minister, Lord
Hardinge, who accepted from me various memoranda concerning these and other problems.

I was able also to gather some support in the City, the centre
of all business in the British Empire, as a result of my bringing
from Hungary the power to negotiate concessions to drill for oil
on Hungarian soil. My talks in the City were mainly with the
chairman of Anglo-Persian Oil, Lord Snowden, and his agency.
For me, this entailed much hard study for I had no business
experience and knew nothing about the exploitation of oil
deposits. Somehow I managed to master enough of the subject
to be able to discuss the matter with some degree of sense.
Frederick Picker, who came with me as an oil expert, was my
mentor and as a result we became great friends. In the autumn of
1920 we were able to settle the details of an oil-drilling contract
with Anglo-Persian, and on my second visit an agreement was
signed with the Hungarian government.

The contract was for drilling in the district of Somogy-Zala
where, oil actually was discovered later at Lispe. Unfortunately,
the Anglo-Persian exploratory drills found nothing, and the contract was allowed to lapse. I write 'unfortunately' because had

English capital remained invested in Hungary it might well have been of much help in our handling of foreign affairs.

This was a very exhausting time for me especially, as János Pelényi, later our ambassador in Washington and for many years a most helpful colleague who had come to London with me from Holland, was sent shortly afterwards to America. I then found that everything had fallen on my shoulders.

Only those who have tried it will know what it is like to find oneself alone, the unofficial envoy of a small country that has just lost a war, in the still hostile capital of the victor. To get anyone even to speak to me entailed endless hard work, attention to detail and, above all, tact.

Here I must pay a tribute to a most gracious lady who really deserves to have been mentioned before all others. From the day I arrived in England I never met a cleverer nor a more enthusiastic supporter of all things Hungarian than Rose Wertheimstein, the Hungarian-born wife of Charles Rothschild. Her help was invaluable as for many years she had held a unique position in London. This was doubly true at the time of my visit since, as a result of her husband's illness, she was running the affairs of the Rothschild Bank herself. Then, and later, we could always depend on her help in any matter concerning Hungary.

In her house I almost felt I was breathing the air of my own home; and the lion's share in any success I may have achieved in my mission was thanks to her advice and help and to her mediation on my behalf. She died just as the clouds of war were once more gathering over Europe, and so these few words of mine must be my epitaph for her. The tears form in my eyes every time I think of her.

As a result of my time in London, and of the firsthand knowledge of English foreign policy I was then able to obtain, I found nothing but cordiality in Anglo-Hungarian relations; and this feeling endured all the time I was foreign minister. Nothing, however, could change the harsh conditions that had been written into the peace treaty. Even so the propaganda we were able to make seems to have filled our enemies with some apprehension. Tilea, the last envoy sent by King Carol of Romania to London, wrote in his recent autobiography that it was my propaganda which had made necessary the visit to London at that time by the Romanian prime minister, Vajda-Vojvod. To read this many years later gave me great pleasure, for the most flattering appreciation can be gleaned from what our enemies write about us. While in London I was unable to get in touch with our delegates to the peace conference in Paris. They were kept in strict seclusion at Neuilly, and communication with them was only possible on the few occasions when I found some trustworthy traveller who would take my reports to Budapest, whence they were forwarded to Neuilly. In fact, I was only able to do this twice, for confidential reports could not be entrusted to amateurs because of the great risk of their going astray. Also I was able only to summarize my discussions with the politicians in England without mentioning their names, since if ever these were indiscreetly leaked I would find every door closed against me. Because of this, it was only my discussions with the church leaders that could be reported in full, and so it soon became vitally important that I should go to Paris myself.

The French authorities treated me with far more rigour than their English counterparts. I was able only to get permission for a few hours' stopover between the arrival of the Calais express in Paris and the departure of the Trans-European the same evening. That I was able to get in touch with Bethlen during this brief time I had to thank my good friend Andor Adorján, who was then living in Paris with his French wife and editing, I seem to recall, some works of lithography. Even though it is hardly pertinent to the tale I have to tell, I feel impelled to describe this meeting in some detail because its circumstances turned out to be so hilarious. It was the most absurd anecdote of my entire diplomatic life.

I arrived in Paris about noon and found Adorján waiting to meet me on the platform. As we drove to the Hotel Continental he outlined his plan.

All the delegates to the peace conference were forbidden to come into the centre of Paris and were not allowed to contact anyone apart from their own colleagues[62]. They were, however, allowed to walk in the Bois de Boulogne. And so it was arranged that Bethlen and I should meet there, at three in the afternoon, on a prearranged bench half-hidden in a thicket. It was easy to keep watch on the paths leading to this bench, so if any unknown person was seen approaching, someone would whistle a warning and we would have time to separate. Adorján and Pál Teleki agreed to be our watchdogs; and all seemed fine and dandy. It was now that a malicious Fate intervened. Adorján and his wife gave me a sumptuous lunch in the hotel. They knew from the time we had spent together at The Hague in 1919 that I was very fond of oysters and, to my great joy, had ordered a couple of dozen. Stupidly I forgot that oysters should really only be eaten in the cold weather of winter and not in a warm April. The pink-coloured *Marennes* looked a little suspicious, but I ate a few so as not to offend my host. Afterwards we went to the Adorján's flat, and we had barely arrived when I began to feel so sick I nearly fainted. Even a small volcano was nothing compared to me at that moment and, as it seemed impossible for me to go on to the Bois de Boulogne, Adorján drove off by himself to warn Bethlen that I would not be coming. Hardly had he left than I began to feel better, so I decided to follow him. Luckily his wife knew where we were to meet, and so we boarded a taxi and set off. Perhaps it was the jolting of the taxicab that started me off again, but whatever it was we had to stop twice to obey the commands of my internal volcano. Somehow, thank God, we arrived in time.

Teleki and Adorján took up their sentry-posts and, sitting on the bench, I began my report. It was like a theatrical farce. 'Robert Cecil thinks . . . ' I would start and then, 'Sorry!' as I jumped up to embrace the nearest tree. Then I would start again, 'Mr Bowie, chief secretary of the Unitarian Church, promised that . . . Sorry!' and off to the tree again. This went on for an hour and a half until, in spite of it all I managed to relate everything I had to say and also receive Bethlen's messages for Budapest.

That evening I was well enough to board the train and by the time I arrived home I was quite fit again. It seemed that having to deliver this fatal report had saved me from the worst effects of oyster poisoning from which people have been known to die.

When I accepted the portfolio of foreign minister I had no detailed programme ready, for, as I have already mentioned, the offer came as a complete surprise. As it happened, this was no great matter at a time when little Hungary was like an orphan standing forlornly in a corner of Europe, friendless and surrounded by enemies. It was then an open question as to which great power might be won over, and indeed, whether anyone could be won over at all. All we could do was to wait until matters settled down, for at that time the conquering nations formed a united front antagonistic to Hungary. That this was so was clear enough at the meetings of the Council of Ambassadors in Paris. Much time would have to pass before any of them could be induced to act without consulting the others.

All the same, there were signs that some countries might be prepared to act independently where their own commercial interests were concerned. For example, it was certain that the signing of the contract with Anglo-Persian Oil was effected with the knowledge of the British Foreign Office; and this had been brought about by Hungarian initiative. Some months after I had returned to England an important commercial proposition was received from France. It was linked to some political proposals and was brought to us by Dr Halmos, a businessman prominent in French commercial circles who had delivered the Millerand letter and who was therefore already known to us. Dr 'Almosz', as the French pronounced his name[63] was a friend of Loucheur. His proposition was that the Hungarian State Railways should be leased to a French commercial company that would undertake to repair and put them in good working order if the Hungarian government would grant a long enough lease. The political quid pro quo was that, in return for this concession, France would take Hungary's side in all international disputes and would support her interests.

The offer was put forward by Gyula Andrássy, and our discussions, if I remember correctly after all these years, were attended by Pál Teleki, Bethlen, Nagyatádi-Szabó and, I fancy, Apponyi. At that time France, under the premiership of Poincaré, was the Allied power most interested in Europe. Italy's attention was concentrated on her newly acquired foreign possessions and her uneasy relations with Yugoslavia, and so any question unrelated to these two preoccupations held little interest for her. It was also significant that foreign business in France had always been dictated by her foreign policy, far more than was the case in England. It had always been so. French investment in the Suez Canal, the Panama Canal, and more recently in the Russian loans, had all been financed at the demand of the Quai d'Orsay, sometimes involving great losses. It was therefore clear that the proposed contract with the Hungarian State Railways (Magyar Allami Vasutak – MAV) was not only a business proposition but also had a political purpose.

It was a difficult question. For the Hungarian government to allow the direction of the national transport system to be handed over to the representatives of a foreign power required very serious consideration. It had not to be forgotten that when a state as small and weak as Hungary made a deal with a powerful foreign power then the agreement would always be one-sided no matter what the terms of the contract might specify. In the event of disagreement the stronger party would always get its own way. Nevertheless I was personally in favour of the idea as I believed that the commercial enterprise would find itself obliged to work to the advantage of Hungary if only to safeguard its profits. Furthermore, knowing the French and their many great qualities – mainly courage and a sense of honour – as well as their faults – vanity and greed – I felt that if they were treated rightly they could be guided to follow a correct path. Later on the Hungarians did lease not only the state railways but also the entire State economy so as to obtain a loan from the League of Nations and, as far as I know, no harm came of it. So, provided the text of the agreement was unexceptional, I proposed that we accept the proposition. I am sure that it would have given us a great advantage in our handling of foreign affairs and, at the very least, would have meant an early end to the desolate state of the Hungarian economy.

However the meeting decided the other way.

There was a long discussion, dominated by the most legalistic of our politicians who argued that a sovereign power could not abrogate, even temporarily, control over the running of its trains. They based their opposition almost entirely upon this one point.

It may be that they were right. It is certain that such a contract could only be successful if handled with great tact and if the lesser power understood and was able to take advantage of the psychology of the greater. If not, only trouble would ensue. With my upbringing largely influenced by French culture I was hopeful then; but today I cannot tell if I was right in that assumption. There is no way of telling and, in any case, no reason to waste words on what never happened. To speculate on what might have been is a futile exercise if the ultimate results of commission or omission are not later made clear. As it was, the Hungarian railways were soon enough running as before; and so all one can say today is that, if we had had the protection of France, our relations with our new neighbours would probably have been different from what they subsequently were without it.

৵ Chapter Two ৵

On the afternoon I accepted the post of foreign minister only one decision was made: that we must at once make contact with the newly-created states and try to establish friendly relations. My guiding principle was that even though the Great Powers would decide the all-important terms of the peace treaty, our problems with our neighbours would only be resolved by agreement between ourselves. This would still be true even if we succeeded in getting into closer touch with one or more of those Great Powers. Such contact would only have its effect on major issues, and it would be unthinkable even to try and involve their interest in run-of-the-mill petty grievances. Our daily existence required that we made common cause with at least one of our new neighbours in a way agreeable to both parties. At that time it was clear that, with some obvious exceptions, this should not prove too difficult. No matter what border changes might be effected, our peoples would always have to live next to each other and, apart from being linked by the geology of the former Hungary and its existing water-power system, all these peoples were still economically independent.

Our relations with Austria were straightforward enough, although it was true that the question of the Burgenland would soon have to be discussed. The Treaty of St Germain had shaved off a narrow strip of land on the borders of the Sopron-Zala and Vas counties and handed it over to Austria. This decision was quite meaningless, for it affected only 4,020 square kilometres of land, just a few miles wide and a hundred kilometres long. It was an absurdity, as there was no railway line and no main road crossing the area: one could only travel there on foot, stepping out of it every now and then, since every stream and every mountain ridge traversed it crosswise. It had no name, but like a foundling had to have one invented for it, so the good Austrians called it the 'Burgenland' after the string of border fortresses constructed along its length by successive Hungarian kings during the Middle Ages as a defence against marauding Germans. Its cession to Austria was perhaps one of the silliest decisions to be incorporated in the various Versailles treaties, but, like all the rest, it had to be signed without demur at Trianon.

It was due to be handed over to Austria at the end of August 1921. At this time it seemed no more than a distant storm cloud on the western horizon, and we still hoped that it might be avoided, perhaps in return for some economic concessions. After all, it consisted of little more than forestland, of which Austria already had plenty. This was not a mere pipedream, for many highly-placed Austrians felt the same way, realizing that it would be senseless to antagonize their former comrades-in-arms for the sake of such a small piece of territory which, in any case, would still be dependent on Hungary for its food supplies.

Relations with Yugoslavia were tense. The Serbs were still in occupation of the whole of the county of Baranya, although, as they were entitled only to that part south of Mohács between the Danube and the Drava, the rest would have to be returned to us. This they were reluctant to do, mainly because of the coalmines around Pécs. As a result, they tried to influence the local inhabitants to proclaim a 'Republic of Baranya' with the intention of then getting this new 'republic' to write to the Council of Ambassadors demanding to be incorporated in the new Yugoslavia. Unfortunately for them, the good people of Baranya refused to cooperate, and the plan failed.

Our relations with Yugoslavia were also poisoned by the expulsion of many thousands of Hungarian families and the rough treatment meted out to them.

With Romania, matters were even worse. Painful memories of the occupation of Budapest were still fresh in the memory. When they withdrew, and even before this occurred, the Romanian troops removed almost the entire rolling stock of the railways, factories were dismantled and their machinery looted, as well as thousands of telephones and all of the farm animals from the

Great Plain. And it was not only from the State lands and those of the great landowners that everything was stolen, but they also removed every last calf, indeed every animal they could find, from thousands of small farmers. Only south of Gyoma were the peasants able to save some part of their stock.

This was not generally known at the time, and I have never since seen it written about. This is why I now tell the story of what I saw with my own eyes.

At the beginning of November 1919, just after the Romanian armies had withdrawn, I had occasion to visit Nagykigyos[64]. There were no trains – since the wagons and locomotives had all been looted – but I managed to get there by a contraption known as a railcar, which was simply an old taxi fitted with iron wheels to fit the track. Until I reached Gyoma I did not see a single animal, not even poultry. In some places I saw farming folk – men and women – doing their best to hoe fields that had been left fallow: at others they were standing forlornly about, helpless beside the unploughed fields. Beyond Gyoma everything was different. They were ploughing away with horses, and even oxen; and here and there one could see a few hens clustered around the farmhouses. I asked in Nagykigyos why this was, and they told me that, south of the desolate area I had noticed, the Romanian general Mosoiu had been in command and that he had not only forbidden all looting but had also punished it severely.

This proved a most interesting truth: namely how decisive can be the will of a strong commander, and that, given goodwill and energetic leadership, the mob can just as easily be led to good as to evil.

From the Romanian point of view, the looting of the Hungarian countryside in 1919 was a significant political error. This was the one moment in history when a true cornerstone for peace could have been laid between the peoples of Hungary and Romania. Hungary had joyfully welcomed the invading Romanian armies as liberators and, if the Romanians had accepted that role and refrained from looting and destruction, their behaviour would have gone so far towards healing the centuries-old rift between the two nations that mutual goodwill and brotherly understanding might in time have finally been achieved.

In the first days of the occupation, and as soon as I heard about the looting, I went to see Dr János Erdélyi, who had just been appointed governor of Budapest and who was living in the Hungaria Hotel. I also called upon Mr Diamandi, at the Gellert Hotel I fancy, who was the Romanian diplomat appointed as liaison officer with the army, told him what I felt and asked him to telegraph my views to Bucharest. I also wanted to reach Gödöllo, where Crown Prince Carol of Romania was rumoured to be staying, but failed to obtain the necessary permission. The wire was sent, but a few days later a negative answer was received from Prime Minister Bratianu. This was shown to me by Erdélyi. It declared that 'Romania cannot be built otherwise, only in this way', which was their way of saying: 'only with loot from Hungary'.

And so the systematic looting grew worse and ever more all embracing. The museums and the Royal Palace were protected by the American Colonel Bandholtz, but he could not defend the factories or the country's agricultural heritage. The mood of the Hungarians turned swiftly to hatred; and so the psychological moment passed and was irretrievably lost. This was a terrible pity, for in many ways a country's foreign policy will depend on the mood of its people, while material considerations are dwarfed in comparison. This has been especially true in modern times when international relations are no longer arranged by the cool objectivity of diplomats but rather the passions and hatreds of the crowd. These events were clear proof of that.

It was at this time, when the deep resentment of the Hungarians over the Romanian occupation had reduced relations between the two countries to their most explosive, that the situation was made even wore by the expulsion of more than a hundred thousand Hungarians from Transylvania. In their fool-hardy ignorance of local facts, the authors of the peace treaty had linked automatic citizenship of the newly created or newly enlarged neighbouring states with a notion of 'residency' as opposed to domicile. The result, in Transylvania at least, was that countless clerks, teachers, professors, shopkeepers and craftsmen who for decades had lived and worked and acquired property in the towns or districts that been transferred to

Romania now found themselves deprived of civil rights and destitute. Under the pre-war Hungarian administration, no such notion of 'residency' had existed except for those who wanted to play some part in the local administration and who needed to prove their eligibility. In addition, many people found themselves deprived of their heritage because, although born in Transylvania, they had spent much of their lives elsewhere and so did not figure on the residence lists. These were all expelled from the land of their birth and pushed across the border.

There was something else that added to the numbers of those expelled. In the early summer of 1919, apparently because Budapest was then under Communist rule, Maniu decreed that all salaried officials in Transylvania, which everyone knew was soon to be ceded to Romania under the forthcoming peace treaty, must swear allegiance to their new state. At this time there was still no treaty concerning these former Hungarian territories, and even though the so-called 'London Protocol' had promised Transylvania to Romania, there was as yet no legal document establishing the change of sovereignty. If the Romanians had wished to provoke non-cooperation they could not, knowing the Hungarians' inbred respect for legality, have found a better way of doing it. Unanimously, all those affected by the new ruling declared they would swear nothing until the peace treaty had itself been signed and ratified. And so it happened that university and high school professors, teachers, and civil servants at all levels suddenly found themselves ordered to leave the country, sometimes with barely twenty-four hours' notice. In this way, countless men and women born in Transylvania were forced to flee with their families, leaving behind their homes and all they possessed. Only if they had complied with Maniu's technically illegal decree would they have kept the right to stay in their native land.

In their hundreds they arrived at the frontiers; and there the Hungarian government denied them entry because the now bankrupt country could neither find a place for them nor provide for their keep. Their fate was terrible. Sometimes they were forced to stay for weeks camping at the frontier until the Hungarian state took pity on them and let them in, whereupon they became squatters on the outskirts of Budapest, living in abandoned railway wagons which had been left in disused sidings, or in now empty barracks. Many spent years in these appalling conditions until the Refugee Bureau, which had been formed to solve this problem, was finally able to restore to them the dignity of somewhere decent to live.

Of all the state employees, only the railway workers were spared this fate, for they were better organized than the others and were also realists who did not bother with legalistic quibbles, like those of the educated middle-class. Sensibly, they took their new oath of allegiance and so were able to stay in their homes and continue to earn their daily bread and provide for their families.

This awareness of the sufferings of all those Hungarians expelled from their homes poisoned Hungarian public opinion. Almost every refugee had relatives or friends in what still remained of Hungary after Trianon. Everywhere one heard tales of atrocities, some no doubt exaggerated; but they all added to a climate of opinion that made it impossible for Hungarian politicians to make any approach to the Romanians.

Feeling towards Czechoslovakia was less strong than it was towards the other two countries that were later to form the 'Little Entente'.

It was true that refugees also came from there, but in much smaller numbers; Czech troops had not ravaged Hungarian farmland, and memories were still fresh of the days when the Red Army under Stromfeld and Julier swept the Czechs from Northern Hungary. Although it was not much spoken of, this did much to restore the diminished self-esteem of the Hungarians. In addition the Czech administration, most of whose officials had been trained under the admirable Austrian system, handled the situation according to the accepted European principles. The new head of state, Professor Masaryk, wanted to respect not only the letter but also the spirit behind the terms governing the treatment of the ethnic minorities. In this he was not universally successful and indeed found himself occasionally frustrated by various statistical or administrative stratagems beyond his control. Nevertheless, it was certain that far fewer complaints came from the Hungarian minorities in Slovensko than did from those in our eastern and southern neighbours.

It was the realities of this situation which had made it possible, when the Teleki government took office at the beginning of 1921, for approaches to be made to Benes – although, as it turned out, without any positive result.

It was this experience that prompted me, as soon as I took office as foreign minister, to resume the interrupted negotiations with Prague. Since it was I who had initiated this approach, and as the more recently appointed foreign minister of our two countries, it was natural that I should be the one who made the first move. After an exchange of telegrams it was agreed that we should meet at Marienbad in the first days of May.

My first action was to study the records of the Bruck talks, which cleared up two issues for me.

The first was the revision of the new borders: the second, the question of the Burgenland. These negotiations had not arrived at any final decision, and so one could only deduce that not only was revision of the new borders still possible but also the price Hungary would have to pay would be a political contract by which Hungary 'voluntarily' agreed to renounce some 26,600 square kilometres of her former territory.

As regards the Burgenland, it seemed that Prague had quite different ideas from those incorporated within the draft of the peace treaty. To begin with, she was not at all pleased that Germanic Austria should increase her territory in this way, and secondly it seemed likely that the new Czechoslovakia had the notion of creating some kind of corridor between the northern and the southern Slavs. This had not taken the form of any concrete proposition, but the intention was there.

As I recall, I started out on 6 May. It was interesting but painful to travel along the river Vag, through the Kisalföld. I had often visited this part of the country in my youth, as many of my relations and a lot of friends lived in the region. So many old memories came to me then. At Galanta[65], at the parliamentary elections in 1902, I had gone with Mihály Esterházy to support him as he canvassed the electors. We travelled from village to village in a long cavalcade of cars. János Hock came with us, having agreed to speak in the districts where there were Hungarian villages. He was paid a substantial fee and, as he was an

accomplished speaker – a star performer, as they would say today
– he was extremely useful and earned every penny he was paid.
About one third of the electorate in this district was made up of
Hungarians and these were all staunch supporters of the 1848
Party[66]. There were some villages where it seemed likely we
would be welcomed only with cudgels, and others, quiet and
sleepy, where it was difficult even to start addressing the people.
We would be greeted with catcalls as soon as we ascended the
wooden plank-stands that were to serve as platforms for the
speakers. Then some local bigwig would stand up and declare
that here they were all true-blue supporters of the Independence
Party and away with us as no one wanted to hear what we had to
say. Then came the miracle. Hock would utter a few words about
Hungarian hospitality and mutual understanding: he argued
with nobody, but whenever he was able to get out these few
words everyone started to listen. During his speech he would
often single out some member of the audience that, with his
remarkable perception, he had realized was not very popular in
that locality, make a joke or two at his expense, and soon had the
entire audience in splits. After that his oratory took wings, and
when he had come to an end all the villagers would cheer, and our
departure would be like a triumphal march. We only failed in
those villages where Hock could not get out those few magic
words. There were only one or two, for as a speaker he was a real
artist. The opposing candidate was called Kormos[67], and Hock
would make amusing jokes about this in each village with unfailing dexterity and wit. And the proof of his skill was that he
would invent different jokes for each village so that we, his companions, should not get bored by repetition of the same speeches.

This memory in particular tied me to Galanta, but there was
no corner of the Kisalföld plain which did not hold its special
souvenirs for me.

Surány[68] – where surely there used to be the best partridge-
shooting in the world, and where the carriages which were used
by the guns carried watermelons to quench their thirst. Diószeg
– where I once had to get out of the train at 20 degrees below zero
and hire a sled to reach my cousins' house at Ciffer[69]. On the way
the snowdrifts were so deep that we had to get out more than ten

times to shovel away the snow. The driver had a sensible sheep-skin cap, but I had only brought a light hat suitable for shooting and nearly lost my ears from frostbite. Cseklész, Vedröd, Galgóc, Vörösvár and Szomolány – there were sweet memories buried everywhere around me that came to life only when we passed by or I sensed their nearness, as the express train rushed on its way across the fertile plain.

Now everything seemed incandescent. I was surrounded by the lavishness of spring, the cornfields, smooth and rich; the great spreads of sugar beet planted in long, moss-coloured rows; the alfalfa fields already richly burgeoning into leaf. Apple trees in bloom. It was a bitter feeling, for we had lost it all. Then we arrived at Zsolna. It was here that six years before I had seen those long lines of military trains, where they had waited, often for days, filled with strapping young Hungarian soldiers until they were carried off to battle and death. This place too had its memories, and most painful they were[70].

In Marienbad we stayed in a luxury hotel, and I recall wondering if it was the one to which King Edward VII would come every year at the beginning of the century when he was spinning the webs of the *entente cordiale* with Clemenceau and Isvolski, the then foreign minister of Russia, and where he smoothed over the differences between England and Russia and he planned, no doubt along with others, the encirclement of the central powers.

Of course, King Edward had been there in the high season, in August when swarms of elegantly-clad guests came to the spa to bathe away their accumulated fat. Now, in May, the resort was almost empty. The countryside is lovely, hilly and covered with pine forests, all well cared for and in that impeccable order imposed by the Austrian system of forestry management: a system taken over by the Czechs and impeccably maintained. There were no fallen trees to be seen, no dried-up or dead trees, crooked and hollow. Every pine was healthy and towered straight as an arrow. The forest started where the hotel garden ended, and we could walk in it for hours, as in a park.

Benes arrived on his special train. He was a small and insignificant-looking man. His whey-coloured eyes had an unusual sheen and were always watchful, like those of a fox. He spoke pleasantly enough but patronizingly, with more than a touch of condescension, as people who have more than their fair share of good luck so often do. Although Benes must have spoken German, for his country was still part of Austria when he went to school, our discussions were held in French. He was possessed of a highly accomplished political vocabulary since he had, on Masaryk's recommendation, been accepted as a student at the Académie des Sciences Politiques in Paris, where he had obtained his diploma. In spite of his perfect mastery of the French language he was sometimes difficult to understand because at that time, and indeed all the years I was in contact with him, he had a very strong Czech accent. I never heard if this disappeared later.

We discussed by what means we could reduce the tension between our two countries and whether we could find a common platform that would enable us to act together in all the questions concerning the Danube Basin.

I outlined a plan that involved cooperation by the three countries of Czechoslovakia, Austria and Hungary, which in central Europe still formed a bastion of the western way of life: a link which, in my opinion, was a good enough reason for all three to understand each other. Knowing how vain Benes was, I made it clear that in this triumvirate the leading role would be his.

As to the Burgenland, it seemed to me that Hungary could settle this directly with Austria, and so that question could come later. Firstly, I suggested that we should get things clear between ourselves. I said that as far as Czechoslovakia and Hungary were concerned there seemed to be two highly important unsolved issues and that, if these were not first settled, Hungarian public opinion would not accept any further *rapprochement* between our two countries . . . and the government would fall. The first was the future of Hungarian minority groups in Slovensko: the second, the modification of the new Czech-Hungarian border as redrawn by the Treaty of Trianon. It would be vital in this context not only to wipe out the most unjust and unacceptable aspects of the proposed borderlines – such as those at Balassagyarmat, where the Hungarian town's vineyards now found themselves in Czechoslovakia, and

Sátoraljaújhely, where the border ran between the town and its railway station – but also to take into consideration which districts spoke what language.

As it happened, Hungarian public opinion had not been as outraged by the Hungarian minority's loss of civil rights in the new Czechoslovakia as it had been by what had been perpetrated by the governments of Yugoslavia and Romania. It was for this reason that I based the need for revision of the frontiers on ethnic grounds alone.

I did not emphasize this, not only because the frontier questions had first come up at Bruck but also because I had some good reasons of my own for hoping that we might obtain some profit from reopening the question of the Czechoslovak border.

While in London in January 1920 I had seen hung in the window of the Geographical Society in the Strand a large map bearing the title 'The Eastern Europe of the Future', and on it the Czech-Hungarian border clearly showed the foothills of the Carpathian Mountains in Hungarian hands. It seemed certain that what this map showed had come from official sources in Paris, all the more so since Constantinople and the surrounding country on the Bosphorus was shown as belonging to the League of Nations, which the newspapers of the day had reported as being the official Allied proposal and which indeed had been incorporated in the first draft of the Treaty of St Germain. This, however, when presented to the Turks for their signature, met with such a blank refusal from Kemal Ataturk that the matter had to be held over for the Treaty of Lausanne, when the territory was left in Turkish hands.

I wanted to buy this map as proof of official intentions, but the shop had been closed and when, after a few days, I was able to return, I was told that that map had been withdrawn and its sale forbidden! An English friend gave me the explanation. The map had originally been drawn in the spring of 1919; when, a little later, the short-lived Communist regime took power in Budapest the highest councils of the Big Five decided that the foothills of the Carpathians could not be left in Hungarian hands lest they offer a route to Western Europe for the Soviets. Accordingly they should be re-awarded to Czechoslovakia.

My other private reason was based on some information that I had from a man in contact with the English delegation to the commission charged with preparing the terms of the various treaties. This was particularly relevant to my present talks with Benes. I had been told that before the committee started work on defining the borders of the new Czechoslovakia, the French foreign minister Berthelot had said to Benes: '*Demandez beaucoup!*' – 'Ask a lot!' Berthelot and Benes had been fellow students at the Académie des Sciences Politiques and had always been good friends. As a result, Benes asked for as much as possible, basing his policy on the idea that whatever he asked for was likely to be reduced and because his old friend had said '*Demandez beaucoup!*' so as to give him room to manoeuvre. Accordingly, he had drawn a line from which he could easily withdraw without giving away anything of true value to his country. This is how so many districts with a preponderant Hungarian population had found themselves on the Czech side of the frontier, for which the Big Five had given their unquestioning approval. And so Masaryk and Benes had obtained far more than they had originally hoped for.

Knowing all this, I hoped for an important revision of the border, not quite as much as Hungary was to receive from the first Vienna Award of 1939 but close to it.

Benes did not go quite so far as to envisage the return to Hungary of Losonc or Komárom, but it was made clear that a prerequisite to revision was that Hungary should sign a mutually agreed document accepting the award to Czechoslovakia of those other parts of the Slovensko that were not now under discussion.

This, of course, was self-evident, for it was on this assumption that our talks were based; and if we wanted to maintain normal, indeed friendly, relations with any neighbour it could never be on the basis of an intransigent refusal on our part to accept established fact.

Accordingly, my position was simply that we Hungarians would accept the major distribution of territory and renounce our claims, provided always that in return we would receive back enough of our former lands that Hungarian public opinion would consider the talks to have been a success. Without this we would have achieved nothing; and the essential truth of this statement was at once accepted by Benes.

We also spoke of the region's economy, but this was of minor importance compared with the revision of the frontier.

All of these discussions were held in a most friendly atmosphere, and when we parted I felt that we had at least come closer to solving the major problems. This was confirmed to me by Tahy, our ambassador in Prague, who assured us, after being in contact with Masaryk, that the president was prepared to go even further than his more cautious foreign minister.

I therefore went home satisfied, not bothered by the fact that we were still a long way from actually revising the frontier. It was always so, at the beginning of any diplomatic discussions, for one must not imagine that the practice of diplomacy in any way resembled working in some mysterious Devil's Kitchen. In fact, it is far more like the cattle market: the seller demands a high price, the buyer offers something lower: the seller praises his livestock, and the buyer makes unflattering comments on its quality. After much discussion and argument both sides agree to a price midway between their first positions. That Benes had accepted the principle of frontier revision was, in the circumstances, a decisive step towards solving the problem.

We had to change trains in Prague, and before the evening express left I had time to buy a most beautiful ham in one of the fine butcher's shops. It was good Bohemian ham – real ham at last – and I was so happy because such a thing had long been unobtainable in Budapest. I wrapped it carefully and pondered with whom I would share this delicacy.

Alas, it was very warm in the sleeper and it was not long before the ham began to smell. It had to be thrown out as soon as I reached home.

It was like an omen, prophesying that everything I thought I had achieved in Marienbad was to suffer the same fate as my cherished ham.

And so it turned out: although not at once.

ꙮ Chapter Three ꙮ

As soon as I returned I made my report to the prime minister. We had not taken any minutes of the Marienbad meetings as this was only done when some tangible results might be expected, which was not the case with preliminary talks. However, as is the usual diplomatic practice, after each phase of the discussions I would immediately dictate to my *chef de cabinet*, Lajos Rudnay, a word-by-word account of what had just been said between myself and Benes; and this account was used to give a clear picture of our talks in my report.

I also gave my account to Admiral Horthy even though at that time he did not intervene in the handling of foreign affairs in the way he was to do in later years. He trusted our judgement, particularly that of Bethlen.

Bethlen heard my report with pleasure. It was, he said, an encouraging start and we should carry on in the same fashion. However, we would have to proceed with great caution and take trouble to prepare Hungarian public opinion slowly. It was certain that Hungarian political circles would not take kindly to the realization that the country should give up of its own free will as much of her ancient possessions as the Treaty of Trianon would wrest from us, even if we were to receive in return some territory populated by Hungarians. So legalistic was Hungarian thinking that few people would give any thought to practical gain but would blame us instead for failing to press for our just rights. Such a reaction could bring down the government, although this would not be the worst result for our country, which would in fact be the stopping of that political process we believed to be the best for the nation's future.

He was quite right, and indeed when I talked to various political leaders, for the first time in my experience of foreign affairs, I found myself faced with that legalistic approach and that unreal and impractical way of thinking that I had only known previously from the debates in parliament under the Dual Monarchy. Even at that time, as I have written elsewhere, this attitude had poisoned public opinion and caused much trouble for us.

Then, of course, we had still been an integral part of a great power, and most people believed – myself included – that, even if the peace of Europe were to be threatened by such issues as difficulties in the Balkans or the French desire for revenge, the world would be saved from war by the careful balance preserved by the Great Powers and by the wisdom of their cabinets. This is what had happened at the time of the Agadir crisis, of the annexation of Bosnia, and when the Balkan war broke out. Hungarians always imagined themselves to be in this reassuring position and so were never really interested in foreign affairs. As regards military matters, only those that affected our relations with Austria and with the ruler were real to them. No one stopped to think of our army as a defensive wall against countries beyond our borders, or that the Dual Monarchy's surest power lay in the strength and readiness of its forces in Europe and that it was because of this power that Hungarians remained masters in their own country. Again no one remembered that, numerically speaking, Hungary was a small nation and that, since the understanding with Austria brought about in 1867, Hungary's ancient liberties had only been maintained in so far as she remained a part of the greater Austro-Hungarian empire. Were this bastion to fall then it was inevitable that Hungary would stand defenceless in the event of world conflict.

Hungarian public opinion never thought about such matters and certainly did not trouble itself to try to understand them. The only 'foreign' country for most people was Austria, but even here no one was much interested in what was going on or what political factions were at war with one another. No one considered the real power structure in Austrian society, for the only matters considered worthy of interest were legalistic aspects of relations with, and opposition to, the King-Emperor. This was the Hungarians' supreme preoccupation.

It was a strange way of thinking. For the entire middle classes the only real problems were those of internal politics. Only these would rouse them, and these alone could provoke riots. In the coffee-houses perhaps some sales clerks or junior tax-collectors would sit discussing the finer points of international law and commerce, and would quarrel bitterly, as in other countries, about abstruse issues of interest only to legal specialists, but no one else bothered with such matters.

All this was characteristic of the years before the war, and I only mention it now because this legal hair-splitting found its way into the public's conception of foreign politics and was to bedevil the handling of our foreign affairs.

This attitude must be discussed, because it is central to understanding how such a feeling was born and therefore why the Hungarians chose a road that would lead to their country's undoing.

I shall have to approach the subject in a wide circle, even if it seems to lead me somewhat to stray from the main purpose of this book. I feel, however, that it were best to do it here because in what follows we shall meet this strange legalistic approach again and again; and I shall start by tracing first its historical origins and then its later development.

I am convinced that, just as Freud has attributed many of our adult emotions and actions to some long-forgotten happenings in our childhood, so the reactions and passions of nations today have their origins in their history. The manner in which nations react to world movements is determined by the historic past which long ago established their ruling habits of thought. The childhood of nations lies in the experiences of previous generations, and it is these experiences that have gradually and slowly over many years, shaped and formed the national spirit. Great men of their day – Gábor Bethlen, Ferenc Rákóczi, Lajos Kossuth[71] – had a profound influence on the development of national ways of thinking, and our attitudes today would be incomprehensible if we did not take this into consideration, just as Napoleon, Bismarck and Lenin have left their indelible stamp on the characters and attitudes of the Frenchmen, Germans and Russians who have come after them.

These influences work both ways. The leader is never quite immune from the attitudes of his day even though it is his personality that leaves a stamp upon his times and those that follow and which defines the direction and ideals which, for many years to come will guide the aspirations, the emotions and, if you will, the spirit of the people. This is so important that it should only be with the deepest sense of responsibility that anyone should venture upon trying to be a nation's leader. Such a man's virtues and faults can have their effects for centuries to come.

I believe that the tragedy of Hungary's present situation cannot be understood if we do not look carefully at our history. The key to today lies in the struggles and torments, battles, sins and omissions of the past.

I would like to present a short survey of the last few centuries of Hungarian history to show how the political attitudes of today have developed.

Mohács

The story of Hungary's troubles really began at Mohács[72]. This disaster and the following Turkish conquest divided the country into three parts. In the conquered territory all Hungarian political life came to a stop and the land was ruled by pashas, *begues* and *spahoglans*. The nobles fled to the north, to the west or eastwards to Transylvania. The country people and the serfs mostly stayed where they were, for they had no part to play and nothing to do except try to stay alive.

The western and northern parts of the country came under Habsburg rule, and this part of the land kept the name and constitution of the kingdom of Hungary. On paper, it still figured as a country independent in its own right and owing allegiance only to its king. In reality, Hungary was little different from the other provinces owned by the Austrian monarchy. These too had their own constitutions from the beginning of the seventeenth century. The rights and powers of the Czech, Austrian, and the Tyrolean peoples differed only slightly from those of the Hungarians. Each had the power to raise taxes and make laws, and the Czechs even had their own king[73]. Nevertheless, they had in reality only the character of provinces under a common ruler, since the direction of nearly all affairs remained in the hands of that ruler and all important decisions regarding the economy or the army were made by him.

In those days the relationship between king and country was much the same in many other countries of Europe. The difference was that in countries like France and Spain the ruling monarch identified himself only with the interests of his own country, whereas the Habsburg emperor, having so many diverse countries under his sway, was bound to have as many diverse interests. The Habsburg hegemony had largely been acquired through inheritance and was only held together by the dynasty to which these multifarious territories owed their allegiance.

In countries where there was a national monarch, the fact that the subjects' powers were limited to a having a hand in law-making and tax-raising was not necessarily a disadvantage, since a national monarch, like a benevolent father providing for his family, would work to make his country prosper and so deepen the nation's pride in itself. It was also in the monarch's own interest to do so, since his power and prestige depended on that of the country he ruled. With it he rose or sank. The unity of the French and Spanish kingdoms was cemented because their ruling monarchs were truly national, whereas parliamentary government had been known to be the opponent rather than the promoter of such unity.

But the sway of the Austrian Habsburgs was very different. Since the thirteenth century the rulers of Austria had also been emperors of the Holy Roman Empire. This title had been invented so as to postulate a single ruler of the whole world, as it was then known, and its holder was the greatest feudal lord in Europe and also the worldly leader of the Roman Catholic Church, just as the pope was its spiritual leader. It was the Habsburgs' ambition truly to realize this intention, although only the Ottos and, for a short time, Charles V, attained it.

Nevertheless, the dream floated continually before the eyes of successive Habsburg monarchs; and the many different countries over which they ruled were expected to serve the same goal, each according to its geographical position and capacity to contribute to the common ideal. Moravia, the Czech people and the two Austrias – Styria and Carinthia – furnished recruits to the army, silver and iron. The Tyrol was the gateway to Italy, while the lands in Alsace and Flanders formed a defensive rampart against the French, much as the narrow strip of the kingdom of Hungary did against the Turks. Although gold from Hungarian mines was an important asset, the real value of Hungary to the emperor was that the country was like the outworks of a castle stronghold from which the main walls and the gates could be defended, where the enemy could be held at bay, where forces gathered before a sortie and where they re-grouped after a defeat. It was where defensive skirmishes took place, and if men were killed there it did not greatly matter, for it was more important to hold the inner castle. For the Habsburgs the inner castle was Vienna and the hereditary lands. Hungary was used by the emperor to defend this stronghold and, from the beginning of the sixteenth century until well into the eighteenth century, this was Hungary's only value for the dynasty.

It was for this reason that the growth, development and well-being of little Hungary was of small interest to the man who was Hungary's king; for between the ruler and the ruled there did not, and could not, exist that paternal relationship which tied a native monarch to his people. The Hungarian gentry felt this strongly when, after Mohács, they chose a Hungarian king, and unfortunately it was with him that Hungary's tragic future was to start; for King John I (János Szápolyai) was too weak in every respect to achieve what was expected of him.

And then there was Transylvania. To contemporary eyes the peculiar situation of that province was not yet clear, except that in the fifteen years of ineffective struggle against the Turks that followed the defeat of Mohács it was accepted that for the time being Transylvania could not be rescued from the Turks.

The reality of the situation was finally expressed by Friar George in 1542 in the Agreement of Gyalu which postulated, in effect, that direct rule by the king of Hungary would only be accorded when that king should prove stronger than the Turks, but not before.

This decision showed sound political judgment. The Turkish Empire was all-powerful to the east and south, in the Havasaföld and Moldavia, while to the west were the newly conquered lands. Transylvania was thus poised as if between the jaws of a giant pair of pincers, ready to be crushed. Between the kingdom of Hungary and the province there was only a narrow strip of unconquered land along the Erdös Kárpátok (the Carpathian forests), and the only road followed the Upper Tisza and the Lower Szamos rivers. Therefore there was no alternative to autonomy for the province, both for political and geographic reasons. The fact that, despite geographical position and political necessity, it was still possible to build up, however modestly, a flourishing Hungarian way of life, was due to other and deeper reasons.

At the time of the Arpád kings[74] Transylvania had been a separately governed province. More important, however, was the fact that in the hundred years after 1437 a spiritual fusion between the three ethnic groups that constituted the people had grown and developed into a real sense of mutual dependence and self-protection. That this sense of mutual interest and help for each other was only rarely manifested in the first fifty years of Transylvania's autonomy – and even on occasion briefly deteriorated into mutual hostility – proved nothing, for brothers often have their disagreements. What was important was that the feeling of solidarity – the *Zeitgeist*, in Freudian terms – was at the very core of Transylvania's survival as an entity of its own. At this time that part of Hungary under Habsburg rule had no national cohesion at all. The part beyond the Danube was merely a string of border fortresses. In the north it was much the same, while other parts of the country remained under Turkish domination. Only in Transylvania did a living form of national consciousness develop under the sway of a truly national ruler.

Contact was retained with the kingdom of Hungary and at the same time Turkish suzerainty was acknowledged, with the result that Transylvania obtained from the Porte far greater autonomy than was experienced by Moldavia or the Havasaföld, where the rulers had been nominated by Istanbul.

In Europe a new era of absolutism dawned after the Peace of Westphalia[75]. Constitutional government ceased to exist and was replaced by the absolute power of the ruler, and this brought with it a pronounced improvement in statesmanship, a new respect for the national interest, a keener appreciation of the need for sound economic policy, the development of industry and the exploitation of customs levies. Commerce was developed and experiments made with taxation policies. At this time countries where the national monarch had absolute power achieved real progress from the stagnation of the past.

The Habsburgs also tried the absolutist approach, and this worked well in their hereditary lands. Now was the beginning of the industrial prosperity of the Czechs, for there the tax burden was extended to include the nobility and the clergy. The dynasty here achieved its undoubted autocracy without difficulty, since Bohemia had no constitution since the Battle of the White Mountain (1620)[76]. Here, as in the hereditary lands, the Habsburgs imposed direct rule from Vienna, and so effective was the wide influence and power of the court that the transition to absolutism was achieved without opposition, since popular opinion saw nothing but advantages to be gained from the victory of state power over the diverse interests of class and race. Clearly this meant the simplification of government, the unification of the laws and increased security for all. The imperial government was Germanic, and most of the territories, or at least their governing classes, were Germanic too. In this way every vital force was on the side of the court. Members of the nobility were drawn to leading posts in the national administration, the clergy were united by the re-imposition of Catholicism, while the petty nobility, the middle classes and the leaders of industry found themselves united by a common interest in supporting the system. Harmony was thus achieved between the policies of the ruler and the interests of the ruled.

But in Hungary this harmony could never be realized, for the simple reason that harmony between the monarch and people

could only be built upon mutual confidence, and here confidence
was lacking on both sides.

The emperor was unable to forget that while he was engaged
in the fierce battles of the Thirty Years' War, and even before
this when he was defending his power in western Europe, his
Hungarian subjects had not only failed to come to his aid but had
also on numerous occasions sided with his enemies, be they
Turks, Swedes, the French, or even Transylvanians. The insurrections led by Bocskai, Bethlen and Rákóczi[77] were supported
by the whole kingdom to the point that few Hungarians stood by
the legal ruler.

On their side, the Hungarians could not forget that their own
king seemed to hold them in small consideration, neither hon-
ouring his promises nor providing for their defence – or only
doing so in a derisory fashion – and that consequently between
the capture of Budapest by the Turks (1541) and its liberation
(1686) their country had declined into a state of decay. The
imperial government seemed not only incompetent but also
unscrupulous in everything that concerned the well being of
Hungary, and this was compounded by the undoubted fact
that in this government the last word came always from
foreigners.

After the defeat of the Turks at the battle of St Gothard
(1686)[78] a twenty-year peace treaty was signed with the Ottoman
empire but, instead of profiting by this success, the Hungarian
king left the Turks in control of a large part of Hungarian territory so as to have a free hand in his western wars, thereby once
again breaking the promise to which he owed his throne, namely
to defend the country.

Not only did he fail to exploit this victory over the Turks but
also he used it to abolish Hungary's constitution. Gathering a
parliament together was a slow and complicated business: how
much quicker and more modern was a system of absolutism by
which government was effected by decree. So this is what Vienna
did. The last vestige of parliamentary control, the voting of the
taxes, was also bypassed by placing the maintenance of the
armed forces stationed in the country on the shoulders of each
territory. Parliament did not have to meet for that: a simple

decree sufficed – this city or country, had to pay this or that sum. Who needed parliament for that?

Cities became poorer. Entire villages faced destitution, and their populations moved to the Turkish-occupied territories to escape the blackmail imposed by Flemish, Serb or German mercenaries. The re-imposition of Roman Catholicism was also achieved by force, especially where the majority had long been Protestant.

The castles of the nobility were garrisoned by foreign troops. There was no place for Hungarians in the central government, where everything was decided by Czechs and Germans. Sometimes it would happen that the voices of the native palatine, chief justice or treasurer would be heard, but they had no authority in the Council. Every decision taken was based upon whether or not it was to the advantage of the hereditary Habsburg lands and whether their defence or economy would benefit.

As more and more conspiracies provoked more and more unrest, so this was punished in the courts, usually by confiscation of property. Many of those who suffered in this way took refuge in Poland, Transylvania or with the Turks; and when war was declared between the empire and France, there was open rebellion in Hungary led by Thököly.

This was the state of relations between the king and his Hungarian people when, after a few years, the war of liberation from the Turks was started with the formation of a new Holy league by the Pope, the emperor, the king of Poland and the Venetian Republic[79].

Liberation and its Consequences

Liberation from Turkish domination proved to be a new turning point in Hungarian history, for it had a decisive effect upon the development of the role of Hungary in relation to the Habsburg monarchy.

It was here that the standpoint of the leading Hungarians proved crucial, for they found themselves not on the side of the liberators but on that of the Turks; and in this their example was freely followed by the mass of the people.

Why Thököly remained in hiding with his Turkish allies was understandable, for the position and power he had gained had been through insurrection against Vienna. Although many of the grievances which had led to his uprising had been settled by the meeting of parliament in 1681 – a moment when he could have made his peace with Vienna – one can sympathize with his reluctance to abandon a patron to whom he had owed his previous success. He was not a man to change allegiance from one day to the next.

Less understandable was the attitude then adopted by the men of Transylvania. Mihály Apaffy and his all-powerful chancellor Teleki had no such moral obligations, and both hated Thököly; yet they adopted a similar attitude to his. It was possible they were inspired by a spirit of rivalry, for the last thing they wanted was that a '*kuruc*' king should be on better terms with the Porte than they. So they remained on the Turkish side even though they had witnessed the terrible defeat of the grand vizier before the walls of Vienna and the humiliation inflicted upon his army. They even persevered in this when Buda had already been liberated and Thököly had fled. It was almost as if they had been hypnotized by the power of the Turkish hegemony.

Teleki, however, to save his own skin, secretly made his own peace with Vienna; although he still reiterated his allegiance to the Porte in council and in parliament. Worse than this, he then proved sufficiently two-faced publicly to denounce Miklós Bethlen, who had proposed that Transylvania should now join the liberating power.

That this would not have been easily achieved is clear, for the oppression of the previous decades, the inquisition and religious persecutions were still fresh in everyone's memories. The Austrian armies, composed of Flemings, Germans and Prussians, tormented the people no less than had the Turks. Yet if on the king's side there had been a commander like the soldier and poet Zrínyi, or like the great Palatine, Miklós Esterházy[80], or even better if at the head of Transylvanian affairs had stood statesmen of the quality of Gábor Bethlen or of the much earlier Friar George, things would have taken a different turn. These men, with their highly developed political sense, would have grasped that the western coalition represented a far more powerful force than had ever previously been brought to combat the power of the Ottomans, and they would have seen that this was the moment when they could – and indeed should – have broken with the Porte and so put Transylvania at the head of the Hungarian offensive against the Turkish Empire. There is little doubt that Apaffy and Teleki could then have achieved this, just as Zsigmond Báthory, facing far stronger opposition, had done a century before.

But this historical opportunity was missed, and in the event the majority of the Hungarian people – some still in the Turkish camp and not many more on the side of the liberators – as well as the Transylvanians, remained passive spectators while their Habsburg king with his foreign mercenaries liberated the country. Hungarian help was largely limited to furnishing some light cavalry patrols and some auxiliary troops.

These circumstances had a fatal effect on later developments.

The government in Vienna – not without reason – decided that as it was their troops that had brought about the liberation of Hungary, so the country was theirs to dispose of as they wished.

The constitution was maintained, but for form's sake alone, only to be invoked if necessary, and everything was decided by the central government in Vienna without any reference to Hungarian opinion. Even so, the Palatine, Pál Esterházy, did his best to establish a government with jurisdiction only within the borders of Hungary (including the re-conquered territories), but which would have control over the two most important national responsibilities: defence and economic development.

He had no chance of succeeding, since the government in Vienna held a very different view of how things should be done in Hungary. In no way would it consider relinquishing control of the armed forces, nor was it prepared to give any power to the Hungarians, whom it had never trusted before and now, after the proof of Apaffy's and Thököly's allegiance to the Turks, trusted even less. This was retaliation for Apaffy's sin of omission. If a sizable Hungarian force with a Transylvanian leader had helped in chasing out the Ottomans, Transylvania and the Hungarians

might have had their say in establishing a new order in the kingdom. As it was, they were excluded, and direct rule from Vienna
was immediately imposed.

In these circumstances it was natural that the country felt it
could defend itself only by strict insistence on the rule of law.
The Hungarians' sole shields against the forces of absolutism
were found to reside in the ancient laws of the country and in the
king's coronation oath. These were the only defences left to
them. In this they were not mistaken. The central government
was to find itself in need of help from the Hungarian people, as,
for example, when scared by the widespread growth of unrest in
1681, or when their cooperation was essential, as in matters of
succession to the throne. It was such occasions as these, when a
new oath or proclamation was to be made – even if it was not to
last for long – that proved to the nation the strength and importance of adherence to its constitution and how important it was
that they should not allow it to be changed in any way. It became
deeply ingrained in the national conscience that if they should
permit any modification, any alloy to be inserted – even were
it only in respect of some ancient patriotic feeling – then the
Tripartitum, that tightly stretched chain, would fall to pieces the
day even one small link was allowed to fall from it. It stood as
read that one of the most important factors in this defensive
battle with Vienna was the understanding that, as both Emperor
Leopold and his sons were deeply religious men, so they could
be trusted not to break their oath.

The conviction that the written word always triumphed in the
end became the cornerstone of Hungarian political thinking.

During the eighteenth century this feeling became ever
stronger, while other political realities paled beside it. The
earlier insurrections led by Bocskai, Bethlen and György
Rákóczi had been started in defence of the national constitution,
and they had resulted in the re-establishment of the ancient
Hungarian laws. It was the same with Thököly and Ferenc
Rákóczi. That those first successes in re-establishing the
common law of the land were in great measure due to the Thirty
Years War and later to the war between Austria and France – and
that these victories were brought about by the political

realities following the peace treaty of Szatmár and the assembly of the parliament at Sopron – may have been grasped by the leaders of the day but was never understood by the Hungarian people.

The same could be said of the parliamentary successes in 1790 even though Emperor Joseph II had already found himself obliged to withdraw many of his decrees. At this time, although the stubborn resistance of the counties had carried some weight, the deciding factors had been economic chaos and the problems of foreign policy. The loss of the Belgian provinces, the unsuccessful war with Turkey and the growing tension with Prussia broke the will of the dying emperor. His successor, Leopold II, found it necessary to re-establish national government in Hungary but only so as to have a free hand to make order in the growing confusion of the empire. The revolutionary ideas percolating from France posed little threaten to Hungary but were spreading their poison in the Belgian and Italian provinces as well as those that bordered the Rhine. This threat of revolution and its possible effects were clear enough to Leopold who, as grand duke of Tuscany, had ruled as an enlightened reformer with methods very different from those of his older brother. But now, although as king of Hungary he might formerly have followed his brother's less enlightened example, he promptly offered plans of reform to the Hungarian parliament and allowed the old popular constitution to be restored without demanding any changes at all.

In this way the great things that were happening in Europe played a decisive part in the development of Hungary's political destiny. The country's subsequent successes, disasters, movements and sins of omission cannot be understood unless this is fully understood too.

This was hardly noticed either by the average Hungarian or by the national historians. They saw only that the written law was ultimately successful, and the lesson they learned from this was that nothing was stronger than the law.

The 1848 crisis and its solution in 1867 seemed to prove the same argument, and even Ferenc Deák[81] constantly referred to the law as existing in 1848 in his 1867 negotiations. For him this was the most sensible tactic, as he was dealing with an emperor anxious to secure his throne by winning the sympathy of the Hungarian people. The signatories to the 1867 agreement knew this well, even if the Hungarian public neither grasped this nor the fact that there would have been no negotiations if Austria had not just lost two wars, one in 1859 and the other in 1866, both of which had gravely shaken her economy as well as diminishing her standing with the other Great Powers.

Hungarians still saw only the triumph of law over violence, and this is the origin of all dependence on legalistic thought in Hungary.

And national historians continued to interpret the story of Hungary from 1867 to the end of the century from the same point of view.

In human terms it is not difficult to sympathize with those historians who had themselves lived through the era of absolute despotism and witnessed the never-ending executions and imprisonments of the oppressive Bach regime[82]. Their entire lives had been lived with these memories, as had those whose only experiences of being harassed by the Austrian police had taken place in their childhood. Here is an example. It happened to my father in 1850.

My grandparents had a house in Budapest in what was later called Széchenyi Square. There was a narrow strip of garden by the house where my father, then aged seven, often played. He wore a grey linen suit with braids instead of buttons, and he was extremely proud of it thinking it very Hungarian indeed. A passing policeman caught sight of the boy and as he too thought the suit Hungarian, took out a pair of scissors and threatened to cut off the offending braids. My father ran away, the policeman ran after him. Luckily the door of the house was not far away, and my father was nimble enough to dash up the stairs before the officer of the law could catch him. All the same the catchpoll yelled after him: '*Rebellhund! Sau-magyar!*' – 'Rebel dog! Hungarian swine!' Even in old age my father would swell up with anger as he told the tale.

Other children must have had similar experiences, and so it is natural that the generation of historians who had seen what had happened in Hungary after 1867 would tend to write in extreme terms, praising anyone who opposed the rule of Vienna and casting the blame for the failures of patriotic heroes not on the shifting balance of European power but rather on intrigue and treason. Eminent and sensible men, good Hungarians all of them, such as Palatine Miklós Esterházy, Pázmány, General János Pálffy, Ferenc Széchenyi, and György Festetics – realists who understood when it was fruitless to fight the decrees of Vienna – were either ignored or vilified. Those of them who, after the failure of a struggle against the government in Vienna found themselves obliged to accept the situation and do what they could to salvage what still remained to them, were branded as traitors. This is why Sándor Károlyi was called a traitor: he who had come to such an agreement with Pálffy in the peace of Szatmár that not only was there no possibility of retaliation but also that Rákóczi, had he so wished, could have remained in the country and retained all his possessions. This is why Görgey was also called a traitor even though it was obvious that Kossuth, while himself fleeing abroad, had appointed him governor at a time when the military situation was hopeless. Surrounded and with his army cut to shreds, Görgey had no alternative but to surrender. His decision to give himself up to the Russians and not to the Austrians showed that he hoped the Russians would treat as prisoners of war the Hungarian soldiers who had been fighting for their freedom. In this he was not mistaken, and it was not his fault that they were later handed over to Haynau by order of the tsar. Nevertheless, history has branded Görgey a traitor and so he has remained to this day.

It was this sort of biased history that was taught to two generations of Hungarian youth: to teachers, professors and country schoolmasters. In this way Hungarian thought was saturated with a historic creed that was both false and incomplete and reinforced the popular conviction that reliance could only be placed in the law.

All this had a further deleterious effect on Hungarian political thought.

Without exception, every leader of popular protest failed in his mission. These men were tragic heroes, but they achieved nothing: and so for us they had something akin to the Jewish ideal of the Messiah who would suffer for the sins of others. This may seem beautiful in religious terms, but it can be unrewarding when it comes to politics because the role models are not men who have achieved anything for their country but rather those who have become martyrs in the attempt. In the public eye the glory lay in their misfortunes. Bocskai, Gábor Bethlen, and György Rákóczi were not popular figures even though they stood for freedom of religion as the very foundation of Hungary's constitutional life and spent their lives defending it. Even István Széchenyi has never been loved – however much may be written about him, and despite the fact that in Budapest he built the Chain Bridge and the Academy; tamed the Vaskapu (the Iron Gates); brought under control the flow of the rivers and revitalized navigation on the Danube; that it was he who so reorganized the breeding of horses as to be the real creator of the Hungarian bloodstock industry; he who was the first to abolish noble privileges and liberate the serfs; and who was sufficiently farsighted to predict the adversities that, within a few months, would bring ruin to the country. What Ferenc Deák actually did is now often forgotten even though it was he who, in 1867, obtained for Hungary more independence that it had known since the Habsburgs had inherited the throne. The popular names are Thököly, and even more so Ferenc Rákóczi and Kossuth, whose policies led only to disaster: the first on the plains of Majtény and the second at Világos. Although it is beautiful and praiseworthy for a nation to remember and revere its heroes, from the point of view of political understanding it can only do harm to forget that the real basis of national prosperity lies in realistic and creative work that is successful.

A further disservice to the nation was inflicted by the lopsided rendering of our history as taught by those historians of the past century who followed the lead of Thaly, the self-appointed court chronicler to Rákóczi.

According to them, the downfall of their heroes was not brought about by the military might of the Habsburg army – previously occupied elsewhere but now free to bring its full force against the Hungarian uprising due to the improved situation in other parts of Europe – but was really caused by either a lack of conviction and confidence on the part of their followers or by treason. This argument took it as self-evident that in reality the Hungarian people were naturally so strong that their victory in war was certain unless they were betrayed. The historic truth that, despite its courage, Hungary was such a small country numerically that it could never ultimately prevail against the strength of the Germanic Austrian Empire escaped their notice. Led by Jenö Rákosi, a whole school of Hungarian sages taught and thought in terms of twenty million Hungarians and a realm that stretched 'from the Carpathians to the Adriatic'.

It is easy to comprehend how this view became so popular, for it fed the national vanity and that tendency to exaggeration to which Hungarians have always been so inclined.

The generation before World War I grew up with this teaching, and because it was taught in all the schools it soon became accepted as patriotic dogma. Those who praised it were patriotic; those who dared express doubts were not. Public opinion degenerated to the point where no one would accept the smallest criticism of the idealized popular heroes and became incensed if anyone spoke of them realistically. Typical of this attitude is what happened when an eminent historian of the new school wrote truthfully about the flight of Rákóczi. Such a storm broke out that the students broke into the bookshops, seized all copies of the offending works, made a bonfire of them in the marketplace and burned the lot. This occurred everywhere, not just in one or two cities.

I have described this particular aspect of Hungarian public opinion in such detail because without having fully grasped what people thought it is almost impossible to understand later events. The Hungarian conviction that the law is stronger than anything else and will always ultimately be victorious will be with us throughout everything I have to tell.

This sympathy for the theory of martyrdom, which is so flattering to the national consciousness, and the fact that unsuccessful venture, rather than political success, will always win the heart of the people – who, as they say in England, always loves the underdog – had some surprising effects. King Karl's return at Easter, which to every thinking mind only proved his childish thoughtlessness, had its partisans. 'Look!' they said. 'Our king loves Hungary! How wonderful! How nice he is!' That Hungary would only have meant for him a springboard from which he would leap towards Vienna, that his restoration in Budapest would have brought about a new invasion and the destruction of what remained of our small country, was never even considered by those who now discovered their royalist sympathies. Before King Karl's first *putsch* most of these people had never given a thought to him or supported the Habsburgs. Until then most people who still wanted a monarchy only thought in terms of the policy of Admiral Horthy, although there were others who dabbled in the idea of selecting some member of the Italian royal family or even Prince Teck, the queen of England's brother and a descendant, on the female line, of a Rhédey prince of Transylvania[83].

There was, perhaps, slightly more reason to think of this last personage than of any member of the House of Savoy. While in London I met a man called Felbermann, who busied himself promoting the cause of Prince Teck. He was a pleasant well-meaning little man who hailed originally from the Erzsébet quarter of Budapest. He had lived for many years in London and there acquired a fortune and taken British citizenship. He had also become friendly with the Teck family and written a book about them and their connections with Hungary. He gave me a finely bound copy of this[84].

I believe that it was due to his influence that Prince Teck visited Hungary with his wife some time at the end of 1920 or the beginning of 1921. It seems likely that Felbermann had suggested to Teck that he should show himself there and that, if the Hungarians – whose enthusiasms were lightly given – should take to him then would it not be better to sit on the throne of a small country than to live in London on an empty purse? Naturally he was made much of in Budapest, for even a semi-royal prince was a rare bird for us in those days. We gave him an excellent supper in the ground-floor hall of the National Kaszino Club, with many flowers, gleaming silver, fine food and fine wines – very fine wines and plenty of them.

After the supper several of us, all men, sat round the prince. He was a tall handsome man, florid of complexion, with a small fair moustache: the type they call in England a 'military man' – which always means good-looking but does not necessarily suggest the possession of brains. The conversation turned to the guest's Hungarian forebears, and one of us asked the prince if he possessed any work of art or weapon that had belonged to his ancestor, Prince Rédey. 'Oh yes I have,' he replied. 'I inherited his sword.' Someone must have whispered in his ear that I collected old Hungarian weapons, for he then said, not to me but to the general company: 'I wonder what it can be worth? I have no use for it and would gladly sell it.[85]' Poor prince! He was always short of money. His debts had more than once been paid by his sister, the queen, and so it was understandable that, after drinking a substantial quantity of heavy wine, he might think of peddling his great-grandfather's sword in Hungary. However, it hardly sounded encouraging from the lips of one who might become a candidate for the throne. He was promptly nicknamed 'Prince Tök' – 'Prince Pumpkin' – and this was the sole result of his visit to Hungary.

After King Karl's escapade to Szombathely no other pretender to the throne of Hungary was ever considered or even mentioned. This was when the legitimist movement had its beginnings, even if only with a number of aristocrats, some leaders of the Catholic church, a few Jewish bankers and those officers of the old combined Austro-Hungarian army whose most cherished memories were of their youth in the Imperial capital.

But for those events now about to confront us in the summer of 1921 this sudden recrudescence of legitimist feeling did fatal and irreparable damage, for this was the moment when we had to face the cruellest condition imposed upon us by the Treaty of Trianon: namely the surrender to Austria, our former ally and comrade in arms, of part of our sovereign territory.

The question of the Burgenland was upon us; and that is what will be the subject of the next chapter.

❧ Chapter Four ❧

The peace treaty had specified that the new borders should come into effect the moment the treaty was ratified. The Serbs would have to evacuate that part of Baranya left to Hungary, while simultaneously we had to surrender the Burgenland to Austria.

This was very painful for us.

The other former Hungarian territories which Trianon had awarded to our neighbours had been occupied by them since the end of hostilities, and all Hungarian officials had been expelled by the occupying powers. It had not been so in the Burgenland, for there the Hungarian government still ruled and the order to evacuate would have to come from us. It would be we ourselves who had to order Hungarian officials to leave their posts; and it was like being told not only to chop off one's hand but also to serve it up on a silver platter.

The worst of it was that Sopron and its surrounding territory had to be handed over not to one of the victorious powers but to Austria. Not only was this deeply humiliating but in it there was also a diabolical irony. For centuries Hungarians had fought successfully to defend Hungarian land from Austria; but now, when the Allies had broken up the Austrian Empire, it was demanded of us that we should surrender to Austria land that had always been ours.

This was exacted from us at a time when Austria was as much a vanquished nation as we were and, what is more, vanquished in a war into which we had been drawn only because of our connection with Austria, a war that was wanted by no one in Hungary and which had started because an Austrian archduke had been murdered. The ultimatum to Serbia had come from Vienna, and in the royal council that had ordered it the only dissenting voice had been that of István Tisza, prime minister of Hungary.

It now was demanded of Hungary that she should hand over to Austria land that had been Hungarian since the days of the Arpád kings.

This was a most perverse idea. It seems to have originated in the desire of the victorious powers to drive a wedge between Hungary and Austria and to create such hatred and distrust between our two peoples that we should never again become allies. It was a measure conceived in hatred, just as were all the other vindictive conditions imposed on the defeated by the conquering powers at Versailles.

Already in June I had been discussing with Bethlen whether there was anything that could be done, for to the Hungarians the enforced surrender of the Burgenland was the deepest humiliation of all. He and I both saw the problem in the same light, and so we decided that we must do something about it.

The first and biggest obstacle was that the decision of the Council of Ambassadors had decreed that the handing over of Baranya and the Burgenland must take place simultaneously. Both had to start, if I recall the date accurately, on 23 June. This would mean that if we attempted in any way to delay matters on our western frontier the Serb evacuation of Baranya would stop at once, and we would ourselves have created an impediment to the recuperation of territory to which we had full rights under the terms of the peace agreement. It was clear to us that while this condition was insisted upon there was nothing we could do about the Burgenland.

Accordingly, my first task would be somehow to have this obstacle removed. It would be difficult, but I had to try. Luckily I was on good terms with the ambassadors of the Great Powers.

The British ambassador was called Hohler. In his diplomatic career he had been in many stormy posts. Before being sent to Budapest he had been in Mexico, where he had lived through several revolutions, and before that, I fancy, was in Japan, where there had been a military revolt. He had hardly been in any post where there had not been some unrest. He seems to have been something of a stormy petrel. He was highly intelligent, shrewd, with a great knowledge of the ways of men, and basically a good man. I was on intimate terms with him.

The French ambassador was Foucher. I was on even closer terms with him, perhaps because he too was a writer, and I had read one of his novels. This had not been world shattering, but it had shown he had a poetic instinct. He was not as sharp-witted as his English colleague, but he was as wholesome as a loaf of bread.

The third was Prince Castagnetto. He was a real charmer, an enchanting Neapolitan: witty and clever as only Italians manage to be. He had a sharp and cynical sense of humour and the social grace of a real cosmopolitan, as is well demonstrated in the following anecdote.

Castagnetto was the title he bore, but his family name was Caracciolo. It was one of the most distinguished names in the kingdom of Naples, and for centuries his family had played an important part in the history of southern Italy. It happened that about this time I had read a book about the battle of Lepanto, which in 1571 had brought an end to the supremacy of the Turks in the Mediterranean. The Christian fleet had been divided into three parts, one of them commanded by a Caracciolo. I thought it would flatter Castagnetto if I mentioned this, because his ancestor's fellow commanders had been none other than Don John of Austria, the son of Charles V, and Admiral Doria, the famous Doge of Genoa. Such little remarks often give as much pleasure to the recipient as would a small gift; and there is a saying in French: '*les petits cadeaux entretiennent l'amitié*' – 'small presents keep friendship alive'. And so I threw this ancestor into the conversation.

Castagnetto's eyes glinted, and I could see at once that he knew very well that I had mentioned this so as to flatter the vanity of his family. Then he laughed.

'Oh yes, it is true,' he said. 'But my family has a memory even more illustrious than that. Another of my forebears was raped by Cesare Borgia!'

And in this way he showed me that he was not to be influenced by an appeal to family pride. In the matter of the date for evacuating the Burgenland I turned first to Hohler. Even if he had not then been the ambassador with most influence and if I had not been so impressed by his strength of character, I would still have turned first to the English.

Italy did not normally have much to say in the Council of the Ambassadors, while France usually took the side of Yugoslavia. Not, however, the English who had never had much sympathy for the Serbs.

The only argument I could use in trying to prevent the simultaneous evacuation of the Burgenland and the handing back of Baranya was what I knew about the way the Serbs had already made use of their occupation of our territory. As I have previously mentioned, the Serbs had done everything they could to have the whole of Baranya proclaimed an independent republic. Lindner, who had been Károlyi's defence minister, was then in Pécs for this very reason, doing his best to stir up support for this project principally among the miners of the region. Whether he would have any success we did not at this time have any idea, because who can tell what effect propaganda posters will have? One can find desperate men who can be persuaded to treason everywhere. Another important factor was that all around Szabadka had been stationed an entire Serb battalion, thus giving rise to the suspicion that the Serbs were again planning to use the army to gain their ends, and that Lindner's republic would be proclaimed and then defended by force of arms. This idea was strengthened by confidential reports from the region telling us that some Serbian officials had let it be known that they did not intend to move from where they were.

This all added up to a most convincing picture; and this is what I used in my approach to Hohler.

I explained what dangers lay in simultaneous evacuation: namely that if, when we had evacuated the first or even the second zone of the Burgenland, the Serbs raised some objections and did not quit our part of Baranya, we would be faced by a *fait accompli,* for by the time telegrams could arrive it would be too late to do anything about it. Hungarian public opinion would never stand for our having given away the Burgenland and gained nothing in return. This would be a national catastrophe, and the government would inevitably fall. There would then be endless diplomatic protests and, taking into account the warlike disposition of the Serbs, it was likely that they would resort to arms before giving up Baranya. And as they were already be in possession of that southern province, who would come forward to drive them out by force? The Great Powers? Could one really imagine that any one of the Great Powers would mobilize against Serbia when peace had only so recently been restored, especially on such a trivial matter as who controlled tiny Baranya?

As I am sure my readers will understand, everything I said was true and in no way exaggerated. It is always a mistake to think one must lie in diplomacy. It is one of the diplomat's fundamental rules that, although there may be things than can remain unsaid, what is said must be the truth. Always tell the truth. Lies are stupid and often harmful, for sooner or later one is found out and then one has lost all credibility forever. Lying is also bad because it can only be convincing if he who does it is himself convinced he is telling the truth. That we also had other reasons for wishing to do away with the simultaneous evacuations I did not say; but what I did say was utterly truthful and backed up by fact.

After presenting my point of view I asked the British ambassador if he would be able to get the Council of Ambassadors to arrange that the Serbian withdrawal would start at least one day earlier than ours. This would mean that we would already be in possession of the first zone in the south when we handed over the first zone in the west. In this way we would be sure, when we left the second zone of the Burgenland that we would also get the second zone of Baranya.

I shall never know if Hohler read carefully through the whole bundle of data which I had had translated into French for him, but I am sure that he had also had similar information from British Intelligence which was always remarkably well-informed and seemed to have observers everywhere.

At any rate he promised to put forward what we asked.

If I remember correctly, it was at the end of July that we heard from Paris that the Council of Ambassadors had accepted our point of view. This gladdened my heart, and I thanked Hohler most warmly. This at least saved us from the worst we might have feared if the Serbs were to prove unreliable, while it left the way open for the Hungarian government perhaps to rescue something of the Burgenland.

It had been arranged that the Burgenland was to be evacuated in three phases, while Baranya was to be completed only in two, so that if the Serbs started to move out a day earlier than we did, we should be in full possession of our part of Baranya when we had only just started our first phase of withdrawal. This decision gave us the opportunity to plan how we might be able to save Sopron at least and with it the old natural Austro-Hungarian border, which the Trianon terms had so cruelly and senselessly wrenched from us.

In the succeeding weeks it gradually became clear that there would not after all be any difficulty in the return of Baranya. The Serbian army was still armed to the teeth in the country round Pécs and Szabadka; but Lindner's propaganda had failed, and the inhabitants of Baranya awaited their return to Hungarian jurisdiction with such evident joy that we no longer had any qualms about the matter.

This meant that we could concentrate all our efforts on the Burgenland.

We had several different ideas as how best to proceed. The most realistic seemed to be that we should take up one of the other points of the Trianon agreement, namely that as a consequence of the dissolution of the monarchy Austria and Hungary should divide the Habsburg properties between the two states. Amongst other things this meant that Vienna should send back to us that part of the imperial collection of art treasures that had originally come from Hungary. We had already asked the Austrian government to honour these treaty terms, but had met only with delays and evasions, both as regards the general property and also the imperial art treasures. One possibility therefore was to declare that the second and third zones of the Burgenland would be retained by us until such times as we received a satisfactory answer to our just demands concerning the Habsburg properties.

Of course, this was merely a matter of form to justify our delaying the evacuation. But for a small and unarmed country such as ours, form was highly important if we were to be able to justify opposing the will not of just one but of three Great Powers.

However, it was even more important to our plans that the inhabitants of the territories to be handed over should be provided with an opportunity to demonstrate their patriotic feelings towards Hungary. We were fairly sure that not only Sopro, which was mainly German-speaking, but also those other parts of traditionally Hungarian territory – with their Hungarian, Croatian and even Austrian peoples – really wanted to remain with us. Only the Germanic folk from the Pinka Valley and along the river Lafnitz were drawn to Vienna; and that was because it was there and at Graz that they found a market for their vegetable produce.

The marshalling of the inhabitants was not my responsibility, and so I know little about how it was organized. I believe that much use was made of the youth organizations and of the younger government officials who came originally from those regions. Some of these had already returned to their homelands, and many others were also hoping to go. It was soon clear that it was no secret that an important demonstration of public feeling was being planned, and that all Hungarians were waiting with baited breath to see what would happen in the Burgenland. No one, however, knew exactly what it was that the government was going to do. Ráday, the minister of the interior at the time, most ably shrouded his plans with secrecy so that all that was known for certain was that something was in the wind.

The only real evidence was that István Friedrich went to Sopron before the date set for the evacuation and settled himself in one of the spa hotels.

Friedrich had had a colourful past. He had been a member of Károlyi's party at the time of the October Revolution. He had led the mob to confront the armed police on the Chain Bridge, when the police had fired into the crowd.

Friedrich had not been harmed, but three people had died – some said seven – and many more had been wounded. In 1919 he had led a band of desperate men against the Peidl government and had himself briefly held the reins of power. Having thus made himself prime minister, he had then started the 'White Terror' as a means of staying in office. Later he was removed by Sir George Clark, the envoy of the League of Nations[86].

Friedrich evidently had no idea that the government was behind the Burgenland plan. He had obviously worked it out that if he himself were to lead a popular demonstration there, this would do much to restore his tarnished reputation. So he decided to play the people's leader. He travelled all over the territory and held meetings in Szombathely, where he imagined, as did others who were not in the secret, that he would appear as a leader of the resistance. However, the government would never tolerate interference by anyone thinking only of their own personal interest. The venture was risky enough and would succeed only if the game was played with one man holding all the cards; and that man had to be the prime minister, whose responsibility was to the country as a whole. As a consequence, Mr Friedrich was given a 'friendly' warning to make himself scarce without delay. He did so, but he ever afterwards harboured a deadly hatred for Bethlen, joining forces with all the prime minister's political enemies, even with the Legitimist Party that, from someone who had been a leader of the October Revolution and one of those who proclaimed Hungary to be a republic, represented an astonishing switch of allegiances.

And so we come to the return of Baranya. To supervise the reoccupation by Hungary we appointed Field Marshal Soós as governor of the province.

Soós rode into the territory at the head of his troops in a veritable storm of flowers. It was lucky that he had a calm mount who did not bolt when surrounded by bevies of young girls all dressed in their brightest colours clustering around him and accompanying him all the way – and who remained unaffected by the thunderous cheers ringing in its ears, by the garlands of flowers which the girls threw and which soon covered Soós, as well as his horse, from head to tail. Soon so little could be seen of the field marshal that from a distance it seemed that a gigantic bouquet of flowers was moving slowly through a crowd of thousands.

The reintegration of Baranya as part of Hungary was achieved everywhere with the same festivities and left little for me to do except compose the government's official declaration, which task fell to me because on such occasions every word carries an important political message.

What I had to do as regards the Burgenland was much more difficult.

To be sure that we remained in full control, the government ordered in every available gendarme and reinforced them with extra volunteers, mostly members of the Special Forces, which were later disbanded. These were largely made up of veterans of the war who were therefore well used to discipline. That we needed so large and experienced a force was due to the extreme length of the Burgenland strip. Any disturbances or signs of unrest would have been fatal to our hopes, and discipline had to be strictly maintained. The gendarmerie numbered between two and three thousand men, and they were commanded by Colonel Lehár, the composer's younger brother. The governor, Antal Sigray[87], knew and understood the local people well, as he owned land near Sopron. The Great Powers' military observers were already in Sopron, although I personally only had dealings with one of them. This was Colonel Ferrario, who seemed most sympathetic to us.

The handing over of the second zone of Baranya and the evacuation of the first zone of the Burgenland went smoothly enough.

That afternoon we held a cabinet meeting the only subject of which was the text of the Hungarian government's message to Austria, which I have already outlined. All the other members of the government agreed the motion; I was the only minister to vote against it. It was clear to me that as the minister who had originally agreed to the simultaneous exchange of the two southern and western provinces, it was morally impossible for me now to vote for a motion I had not previously discussed with Hohler, who would have been justified in considering such an action as perfidious. As the Chinese say, I would 'lose face'. I therefore had no alternative but to offer my resignation.

In doing so I explained that Hungary would be at a great disadvantage in the crisis that was bound to follow our action if we were to be represented by a foreign minister in whom the representatives of the Great Powers no longer had any confidence.

This came as a surprise to the other members of the cabinet, all of them, that is, except Bethlen, whom I had told in advance and who, after some demur, had accepted my point of view. He and I had already agreed that after my resignation, and until my successor should be appointed, I would continue to be in charge of the daily conduct of foreign affairs, but that Bethlen should sign all documents presented to him on my advice.

It was important that the foreign ambassadors should hear about all this firstly from myself, and at once. Therefore as soon as our meeting had ended I went straight over to the Ritz, where Foucher was then living. I had thought it best to tell him first and to test his reactions. He was very surprised and, as regards my departure at least, sincerely distressed. He at once called up Hohler and asked him to come round and did the same with Vinci, who was acting as Italian chargé d'affaires while Castagnetto was on leave.

It seemed to me that there was a strange gleam in Hohler's eyes as he came in. I then again recounted everything that had taken place at the cabinet meeting and explained that, in consequence, I had resigned my office and would be leaving the government. As I announced this, Hohler said that what I had done was right and I saw the glitter of suspicion fade from his eyes. He, as I saw at once, was not surprised by the government's attitude and seemed to take the whole matter quite calmly. It was not the first storm he had weathered in his diplomatic career, and it is possible that he had always had some notion that the Burgenland problem would not be settled smoothly. I am not sure of this, for we never afterwards discussed the matter, but it has always seemed probable to me.

In the days following I went to my office as usual and, as they always had, the ambassadors would come in to consult me. In vain I would tell them that I was not really there, but no matter what my excuses they would still insist upon telling me what they wanted the Hungarian government to know. I accepted these messages *ad referendum*; and this went on for a week. Finally, Hohler said that it was time to end this playacting and that I should withdraw my resignation as they would rather have to deal with me, in whom they had confidence, than with someone new to them: 'We prefer to have here a gentleman like you.[88]' I replied that I was flattered by such a request coming from him as a friend, but that I would only be able to accept the foreign minister's portfolio again if I was called upon officially to do so by all three ambassadors. They did this the following day.

This was a great satisfaction for me as it only proved how right I had been to resign and risk leaving the Foreign Ministry just when I was about to be faced with an interesting problem. If I had not acted in this way, Hohler and his two colleagues would have believed me to be a most unreliable person whose word could not be believed. It is true that I would have remained foreign minister for some time, but it would have been in the most disagreeable circumstances, which in turn would have made it impossible for me to cope with the weighty task of finding a solution to the Burgenland situation. As it was my own position was now stronger than ever, which proved of immense value to the country, since throughout the trials to come I could always remind these colleagues that I had remained in office at their request and that consequently I had the right to appeal to their goodwill. This proved its value in all those many petty details whose solution ultimately depended on the ambassadors' approval. Moreover, I very much doubt if otherwise we could have arrived at the agreement over the Burgenland, which was afterwards to be signed at Venice.

I do not intend to write here a full chronicle of the Burgenland negotiations, merely to put down enough so that what happened can be fully understood.

Along the line of evacuation a band of armed freedom fighters stepped in. Today we would call them partisans. On the evening of the first day they attacked the Austrians already established in the first zone. These Hungarian partisans were all tough young men. There were not many of them. One group numbered about a hundred, another only some thirty or forty. The entire force did not exceed two to three thousand; and yet, as I recall it, within a week all the territory already handed over was back in their hands.

The Austrians never took the offensive. It seems that they believed that we had a formidable army in readiness to back up the irregulars. I do not know this for certain, but it is what I have been led to believe; and it was confirmed by what I was told by an English journalist who had at that time visited first the General Staff in Vienna and afterwards came on to Budapest. The Austrian Chief of General Staff had shown him a map of their military dispositions. All along the Austrian side of the border there were small and large circles and squares marked in red, and it had been explained that here was a division of twelve thousand men, here a brigade numbering six thousand and so on and so on. This one represented infantry, and so did this. All along the line of the Danube to the new Yugoslav frontier the map blossomed with red marks. The journalist then asked where were the enemy. 'The enemy? They are circled in blue. We don't know exactly, but we guess that on the river Lafnitz there are some three or four hundred men. These dots represent groups of perhaps thirty-five or forty, while this larger dot denotes about six hundred.'

'Why do you not attack if you have such an overpowering force?' asked the Englishman. The Chief of Staff just shrugged 'We couldn't do that,' he said. 'It would be too risky!'

Coming straight from Vienna, my English journalist friend told his story in high good humour.

It was also possible that the government in Vienna was afraid that their entire army might refuse orders and just go home, for it was quite certain that the Austrians had no warlike spirit left in them at that time. This was, of course, one of the reasons why there were so few casualties on either side. It was at this time that we began to hear all sorts of humorous anecdotes about the guerrillas on the border, like the '*kuruc*' stories of long ago. Here are three of those that we heard then.

A group of partisans, said to be about eight or ten men, encircled about thirty Austrian soldiers and disarmed them. No harm was done to the prisoners, but they did not only have their weapons removed but also their warm army trousers. The weather turned cooler so the lightly clad partisans pulled on the thick Austrian breeches and turned the Austrian soldiers loose to find their way home clad only in their dark-green army tunics with the gold braid that none of them liked. And so the Austrians went free, with helmets on their heads and their upper parts glorious in the *Waffenrock*[89] but otherwise only their underpants.

Here is another story, this time from a little further south.

In spite of being strictly forbidden to cross the border into Austria proper, an overeager partisan leader, with a band of some fifty men, attacked a Styrian village where a battalion of Austrians had been stationed. He was a shrewd man and led his little attacking force down the valley that led to the village. On both sides the hills were covered in forest, and only a narrow strip of meadow on each side of the stream was open country. He ordered some forty of his soldiers to advance along the meadow, keeping up heavy fire. The rest of his men he sent through the forest, blowing trumpets and making as much noise as possible. Indeed they made so much noise that the Austrian battalion commander assumed some immense force was approaching. He thought it prudent to evacuate the village and retreat, whereupon the villagers lost heart and fled. That is, all the men fled, but the women and girls refused to budge, saying that *they* were not afraid of the Hungarians; and indeed they were not. By the time news of this reached us and the group were ordered to withdraw, our soldiers had spent three days riding on the crest of the wave, and the band of partisans marched away to the Hungarian border escorted by weeping women.

My third tale is about a Viennese millionaire, an industrial baron who had rented a shoot near Pápa in the Bakony Mountains. The season for deerstalking started in September, and so the baron set out in his magnificent Mercedes, his mistress beside him, along with her lover, an Austrian count. The car was laden with hams, *foie gras*, preserved fruit, champagne and other wines. They headed for Bruck-Hegyeshalom on the Hungarian border. He had been warned in advance that this was not the moment to travel in that part of the country, but the baron knew better, saying that he did not give a fig for the partisans and would have four good sporting rifles with him anyway. The party had barely crossed the river Lafnitz when it was stopped by a band of partisans who surrounded the car and insisted that they go, car and all its occupants, with them some six or seven kilometres to the military headquarters of Iván Héjjas, who was in control of the territory between the Danube and Lake Fertö. Héjjas spoke only two languages, Hungarian and Albanian, having learned the latter in 1913 when Prince Wied[90]had been put forward by us as candidate for the Albanian throne. As it turned out, Prince Wied never reached Albania, but Héjjas had gone ahead of him and learned there this universal language. Through an interpreter he informed the millionaire that his car and his weapons would be impounded for the duration of hostilities, but that as soon as the fighting was over they would be returned to him. He would not, however, allow the party to continue their present journey, although they would be permitted to return home unharmed . . . and on foot. It was not far to the Austrian border.

Baron Habig and the Austrian count started off to find the frontier; but not the lady. It seemed that she had the eye for Héjjas, having not failed to notice how good-looking he was. So she said: '*Schöner Bandenführer, ich bleibe mit Dir!*' – 'Oh, handsome leader, I will stay with you!' But, despite the fact that the girl was very pretty, all the handsome captain replied was: '*Jetzt Krieg . . . nix Frau . . . Marsch weg!* – 'There's a war on . . . no women . . . on your way!' Later she went to London, where she was kept by a press baron.

Here I will jump a little so as not to finish the tale later. When the partisan bands dissolved a month later Héjjas came to see me in my office. This is when I first saw him, and it was true that he was a fine-looking man, rather like a Spanish toreador. He came to ask if the Foreign Office would accept the Austrian millionaire's car and guns and restore them to their rightful owner.

I told him that I did not want to become involved in this and suggested that he should go to the Austrian Embassy and hand over the car and guns himself. And so he did. When he arrived and told the doorman his name the door was at once slammed in his face. The terrified doorman ran up to the office and announced that the terrible Héjjas was demanding to come in with four guns on his shoulder. Indescribable panic broke out until some employee bolder than the others decided to risk his life, opened the door a slit and asked what this ferocious visitor wanted. Only when he had been convinced that the guns were not loaded, and that it was only a question of handing them over, did the panic subside and Héjjas was let in.

I heard all this from Héjjas himself when he came back to show us the official receipt. He was still laughing when he left the ministry.

By the middle of September the hostilities had ended, but the problem had yet to be settled. There was a further complication in the first zone, for after it had been reoccupied by the partisans it proclaimed itself as the independent republic of 'Lajtabánság' with Pál Prónay as head of state. This seemed to me not only somewhat childish but also nonsense, but his new self-appointed status had clearly gone to Prónay's head if he was trying to form a government and was behaving as if he were a legitimate ruler. Unfortunately, this affair dragged on so long that government control of the territory was lost, and complaints soon started coming in from the southern part. None of this would have been of any importance but it was enough to spoil the mood of the inhabitants who had until then all been pro-Hungary. One serious complaint was that the partisans had bought the whole local production of cereals but paid for it only with fine words.

In foreign affairs the situation was more serious, for what had just happened at home proved again how easy it was to start a fight and how difficult to restore peace.

We had received several demands from the Council of Ambassadors to recall the partisans and proceed with handing over the Burgenland. We replied that these rebellious armed bands were independent of the government and would not obey our orders. If we were now to withdraw the government troops from the second and third zones, this would immediately lead to uprisings there too, followed by complete anarchy. We were able to gain time by the exchange of documents, and, for my sake, the ambassadors did everything in their power to help our cause, although they were not able to do more than delay action on the treaty terms since they were only the mouthpieces of the Council of Ambassadors. It was clear that a solution had to be found and that what was needed was someone who would act as intermediary before the situation became so aggravated that the Great Powers felt obliged to force Hungary to comply, not merely by written demands but perhaps also by economic sanction or by stopping all shipping on the Danube, which was, in any case, due to be controlled at the end of September.

In this critical situation I tried first to find a solution through Castagnetto, who had been on leave in Italy but who, when the first news broke of the Austro-Hungarian hostilities, raced back to his post, travelling from Vienna via Sopron, through the thick of the fighting. The armed bands not only let him pass with no delay or difficulty but were also wily enough to show how much they loved Italy. They feasted him in Sopron, where he made a brief stop and then, wherever he went and wherever he paused on his way, they cheered the Italian flag on his car. So he returned to Budapest in high good humour, and I felt that he had a real understanding of our cause. We soon became firm friends, and I often used to go to his house. His wife, too, was a charming woman.

At the end of September, in the course of one of our talks, I asked if it would not be possible for him to suggest to the Italian government that they did something to help. He said he would do his best but that I must understand that whatever he did would merely be his own personal action, for he had had no official instructions to intervene. In the next few weeks I would repeatedly ask him if he had had any reaction from Rome, but the answer was always negative. October arrived: still nothing.

As the matter was now so pressing I decided to reopen the discussions I had had at Marienbad and remind Benes of those talks in which we had referred, albeit only briefly, to the Burgenland, and mentioned that cooperation between Hungary, Austria and Czechoslovakia would be much easier if this problem could first be solved.

Question and answer passed rapidly between us, and since I could not leave Budapest for more than a day, Benes came to meet me at Brünn. Before I left I let the Italian ambassador know that, since it seemed that his government was reluctant to mediate, I felt obliged to try something else. Castagnetto agreed that I had no alternative and so, on the morning of either 4 or 5 October, I am not now sure which, I left for the Moravian capital.

The immediate result of our discussion was that Benes without hesitation officially accepted for his country the role of mediator between Hungary and Austria. He was most sympathetic and asked for nothing in return. He did not even mention the Czech-Yugoslav corridor, and I took this as a most hopeful sign. There was more news waiting for me at home.

Now followed the most dramatic day of my ministerial career.

In the morning Castagnetto came to see me with advance notice, although he could not yet say anything definite, that he believed his representations at Rome had succeeded. This was in confidence, from one good friend to another, and must remain a dead secret. It was very good news indeed.

I was still feeling somewhat dazed when late the same afternoon, I was told that the three ambassadors wanted to see me urgently. I imagined that it was because of what I had been told that morning and so awaited them with joy.

You can imagine my consternation when Hohler, speaking for all of them, announced that the Great Powers would no longer tolerate our remaining in the Burgenland. He then handed over an ultimatum, stating that we had three days to withdraw our forces and disarm the partisans, and, in the most menacing terms, said that should we fail to carry out this demand, the Great Powers would use every means, including force, to make us do so.

My heart constricted as I read this. I answered that I could not make any answer until I had consulted the prime minister.

Now the ambassadors started to leave the room. I found myself unable to keep from turning to the Italian and saying 'This is not what I expected from you!' in a voice full of anger.

Castagnetto gestured me to say no more and, as the others were already at the door, said hurriedly that a long coded message had arrived from Rome half an hour before and that it was now being decoded. Perhaps . . . ? Then he quickly joined his colleagues lest they should notice that he had stayed behind.

At that moment I thought this was said only to forestall my reproaches.

I rushed over to see Bethlen, and we discussed the matter at length. It seemed that Benes's mediation had come too late and that we could not resist any longer. If we were to do so, then the Great Powers would almost certainly set the Serbs on us as their army was stationed in full force at Szabadka, barely eighty kilometres from Budapest. The Serbs would like this. They were already angry with us over Baranya and no doubt reckoned that by spilling a little blood they might get it all back. We could not defend ourselves in the field because by the terms of the Trianon treaty we had been obliged to disband our standing army and operate only with young recruits. At that moment we did not have more than six or seven thousand men, and even if we had possessed more, of what use would that have been? Inevitably, there would be a new war, and this would be followed by the occupation of our country and more looting and plunder just as there had been three and half years before. Not only that: one needed more than an army to wage war, one needed economic strength too, and where was that to be found in our ruined impoverished land? Nearly everybody had already been ruined by the state loans raised to pay for the war we had just lost.

This was a bitter moment. We now had to face the fact that all our work to save Sopron had been in vain and that our country faced a new humiliation. Even to think about it was almost unbearable. Beset by these sad thoughts we talked for a long time.

Then they announced that supper was ready and, as we walked to the dining room, I was called to the telephone.

It was Castagnetto. He said that he had something of the utmost importance to tell me, and asked me to come at once to see him. He would, he said, willingly have come to see me but he was shortly expected at a formal banquet at the Hotel Bristol and that if I would come there he would immediately join me in the foyer even if they were already at table. He would leave orders for them to call him as soon as I arrived.

I raced down from the Fortress and within ten minutes I was there in the foyer but did not have to wait as Castagnetto came straight out to join me.

'*On a déchiffré le télégramme. L'Italie a offert sa médiation et le Conseil des Ambassadeurs l'a approuvé*' – 'They have decoded the telegram. Italy has offered to mediate, and the Council of Ambassadors has accepted the offer.' Wonderful news, indeed, and completely unexpected. Only fifteen minutes before we had been in despair, and now we could glimpse salvation. Such sudden twists of fortune normally occur only in romantic drama.

The ambassador handed me a tightly written page. It said that we and the Austrians were called to attend a conference in Venice on 11 October, which was to be presided over by Toretta, the Italian foreign minister. Castagnetto and General Ferrario, the head of the Allied Control Commission in the Burgenland, were to accompany me. The Hungarian delegation would be housed at the Grand Hotel.

I felt such joy that I almost hugged the plump little Italian. The good fellow was obviously as pleased as I was, for even his monocle seemed to sparkle with pleasure, and I realized what a fine man he was.

'I wanted you to know at once . . . that's why I asked you come,' he said as we shook hands warmly on parting. He then went in to his dinner, while I rushed back to Buda.

The supper was not even cold when I got there, but what a different mood we were in from half an hour before. Then we faced ruin, humiliation and failure; now suddenly our prospects were rosy and brilliant, and we were filled with hope.

I could not stay long, as Castagnetto had agreed that I should at once release this great news to the press. It was already nearly ten o'clock, so I would have to move swiftly if it were to be in the morning papers. Later I went happily home to bed.

It seemed to me a good omen that it was to Venice that we should have been called because that city of lagoons had been my first sight of Italy when, in my teens, I had gone to stay with my good aunt Elise, my father's elder sister, who had married a Count Berchtold, and took her family there every spring to stay with her mother-in-law, the old countess[91]. We came every year with my father to visit them, and it was then that I first met the real Venetians. I recall that one year it was so snowy that the statue of Colleone seemed to be wearing a white sheepskin hat.

Later I went back so often that Venice became a passion for me. It was there that I paid court, and homage, to the world-famous beauty, Annina Morosini, called by the Italians 'La Divina'. I went often to La Fenice opera house, and to many balls and soirées attended by the descendants of those famous doges whose portraits had been painted by Titian, Bellini and Tintoretto. I loved that mysterious city, with its secret palaces, the faint sound of water from its canals, its kind, friendly people, its excellent small eating-places, even the slight smell of decay rising from the lagoons. I knew all its treasures, all its delights, and I had always been happy there – sometimes very happy indeed.

So now we were to go there for final decisive talks. It was a good omen.

We knew that we would never be able to retain the entire Burgenland, but at least mediation meant there was a chance of a compromise, a middle way by which perhaps we would be able at least to keep Sopron and its immediate surroundings, maybe even more. This would mean a great deal to Hungary. What was even more important was the exhilarating hope that at Venice we might finally achieve peace and at the same time, although now a small and impoverished country, inflict just the smallest of dents in the unjust Treaty of Trianon.

ᐒ Chapter Five ᐓ

The Hungarian delegation consisted of István Bethlen, myself, Sándor Khuen-Héderváry (head of the political section at the foreign office), Lajos Valko as economic expert, two or three secretaries and old Fabro, the great master of Hungarian stenography. We travelled in a private railway car, as we needed space to study the texts in detail and decide every small aspect of them. We had not had time for this in Budapest since we had had to leave in such a hurry.

We all lunched and dined together, surrounded by files and documents, on meals brought in from the dining car. Only Fabro stayed away, eating in his own compartment the food he had brought with him for the journey: bacon or salami. I forget now whether he told us he was on a diet or whether he preferred his own food, but the real reason was that he found the restaurant car food too expensive. He was known to be careful with his money. However he paid for his stinginess while we were in Venice.

When we arrived at the Grand Hotel, Fabro took one look at the splendour of this luxury hotel and declared that he would not stay there but would install himself at the Bauer-Grünwald, which was known to be cheaper. It was close enough for us to call for him whenever we needed him. And so it was. For the entire three days of the conference he remained stuck there in his room, as he dared not go out in case we should send for him. When we were leaving to return home and asked for our bills the manager of the Grand Hotel told us that we had been the guests of the Italian government, and that he had been forbidden to accept any money from us. So it turned out that we had lived there completely free, eating the most wonderful *branzino* (sea-bass), scampi and other seafood, as well as delicious beef and venison –

we, the semi-starved citizens of Budapest – while poor Fabro, having refused the room reserved for him, was obliged to pay the bill. His entire expense account (which was fairly meagre) was swallowed up even though he had been careful to eat most frugally; and all the time he might have been feasting with us for nothing, and living in a style to which he had never been accustomed, poor man. He only heard this unhappy news in the railcar on the way home, when the young secretaries made fun of him thus adding aggravation to the understandable chagrin of this good-hearted old scientist.

The conference was held in the Venice Town Hall. General Ferrario took us in gondolas, and we found ourselves delivered to a fine early baroque palace on the Grand Canal that had once been the home, I fancy, of the Venier family[92]. Inside there was an immense hall stretching the full width of the building with, on one side, a magnificent ornate staircase, very steep, as staircases are apt to be in Venice.

On arrival we went first to a room next to the conference hall to pay our respects to Foreign Minister Toretta. He was a short small-boned man with greying hair. His face was also grey, and, what is rare in Italians, he seemed insignificant and reserved. What is also rare in Italy is that his manner was laconic. I do not intend these remarks to be taken as criticism because he not only appeared to be full of goodwill but later proved to be so during our official discussions. There we also met the Austrian delegation headed by Schober, now chancellor, and the head of the political section of the Austrian Foreign Ministry. This last was present because in Austria the head of government is also the minister for foreign affairs. As I write I cannot recall his name so I shall refer to him as 'Mr S'[93].

The discussions took place in the big hall. Toretta sat at the head of the table, and next to him were two Italians who wrote the minutes and Castagnetto. Bethlen and I sat in front of the windows, while opposite us were Schober and his right-hand man, the foreign office official. Because they faced the light I was able to observe them well.

Chancellor Schober was a sympathetic type: chubby, of average height. His hair was cut short, his beard was white, but his face was young looking. He looked clean and well groomed, and one could see that his clothes came from an excellent tailor. Wherever I might have encountered him I would have known, even from twenty paces away, that he was Viennese. He was intelligent and well intentioned, and this had been put to the proof for the Hungarians when he had been chief of police in Vienna in 1919. Bethlen had known him from that time. He seemed to me to be a wise and peace-loving character who would probably have been far more at ease sitting in Grinzing with a glass of *Heuriger* wine and listening to the music than here at the green table discussing complicated issues in a language that was not his own, in this case French.

His right-hand man from the Austrian foreign office was quite different. He might have come from anywhere: from Portugal or even Miskolc. He was thin, balding, with a sharp somewhat bent nose, and was clean-shaven. He may have had a bad liver, for his skin was yellowish green. He was very eager and fidgety and passionately argumentative. His French was quite good and, although Schober may have understood everything, he was not so fluent so the aide did all the talking for the chancellor. He would start every sentence with: '*Monsieur le chancellier m'ordonne de dire . . .*' – 'The Chancellor orders me to say . . .' He even said this when the Chancellor had not opened his mouth.

Sympathetic though the Austrian head of government appeared to be, his foreign office sidekick made himself objectionable by constant quibbling. We were able to take advantage of this.

The talks went slowly. Toretta opened the discussions with a lengthy speech then documents were read. All of this was necessary, but it took time. Finally we arrived at the crux of the matter.

We asked for a plebiscite to be held in Sopron and the surrounding area, which we defined exactly upon the map.

Our demands were limited to that, just that. We had decided on this after much thought and reflection, and although it was a pity that we could not ask for a much wider area, reason told us that it would be wiser to limit the plebiscite to such territory that we knew would vote for Hungary with a large and decisive majority. We did not wish to risk winning only by a few hundred votes. The feeling in other parts of the Burgenland was no longer unanimously in our favour, as it had been when this affair started. The partisans had kept order, but the fact that armed strangers had billeted themselves in the villages had caused much friction – a natural result of any lengthy occupation. And in the south, that part where Prónay had appropriated all the cereals and livestock and only paid with promises, the mood of the locals was definitely against us. We could count on no support there.

Our demand started a violent argument, the Austrians fiercely opposing us. They gave no sign that they were at all interested in what the people living in and around Sopron might want; indeed, their only argument was that Trianon must be observed to the letter. Again and again there sounded the '*Monsieur le chancellier m'ordonne de dire* . . . ', as the Austrian Number Two grew angrier and angrier. Finally Toretta cut off the discussion by declaring that there should be a plebiscite in the disputed territory.

This was our first real achievement.

I cannot now describe the progress of the conference step by step: in any case, there would be no point. That afternoon the report of the Economic Commission was received, and although this also caused a lot of bickering, a just solution was found. Much time was consumed before a new subject could be broached, as we had to wait for the minutes of the previous discussion to be prepared and agreed. This provided me with a free hour and a half in which I was able to revisit some of my favourite spots in Venice. I went to the Church of S Maria dei Miracoli; I looked at Sansovino's little angel in the basilica, and I wandered along some of the little alleys that held for me memories of some fifteen to twenty years back.

Castagnetto invited me to dine with him at one of the most exquisite and typically Italian restaurants on the Merceria. His other guest was the once famous beauty, Princess Giustiniani. Their love affair had been known to everyone about twenty years previously, for they never tried to hide the attachment between them. On the contrary, so the story ran, they had gone out of their way to present themselves as living reincarnations of the story of Venus and Cupid as painted by some great artist of the past. It was said that they followed the original in every detail, which – as Venus was always scantily clad and Cupid never sported evening dress and a starched shirt – caused no little comment, even from the freethinking Italians. The three of us supped together and, as I sat at the table, I had the feeling that some sparks of romance still irradiated the otherwise mundane conversation of the heavily made-up old lady and our balding but still handsome host. As a writer, I stored up this fact in my mind, thinking how I might one day use it in a novel.

I also learned a most important fact at that supper. While we waited for the lady, I mentioned how well intentioned I had found Toretta, 'I see your influence there,' I said to Castagnetto. 'Well,' said the ambassador, laughing, 'not entirely. He has his own reasons.' Then he said something that took me completely by surprise. 'Toretta was our ambassador in Vienna at the time the peace treaties were being drawn up, and it was he, probably from fear of the Czech-Yugoslav corridor, who invented the Burgenland. Yes it was he: Toretta! He went specially to Paris just for that!' Castagnetto went on to tell me that it appeared that, as a result of the local uprising, he had been somewhat ashamed that his suggestion had brought about such fatal results and that, in consequence, he was now trying to undo some of the damage he had caused. 'He hesitated when I advised him to take this course two weeks ago. What decided him was your turning to Benes, thereby raising once more the spectre of the Czech-Serb corridor.'

The next day the conference reconvened.

This was the stormiest day of all. The row started with the discussions about how to revise the frontier. Bethlen and I at once made reference to the *Lettre d'Envoi* the French prime minister, Millerand, had sent to the Hungarian government with the terms of the proposed treaty in which we were assured that the border commissions would take into consideration our views and the wishes of the local inhabitants. According to this letter, the border committee would be authorized to propose substantial changes. We insisted that this document should be mentioned in whatever text was finally agreed.

This provoked a furious argument, with the Austrians protesting fiercely against any inclusion of this letter.

There now occurred a somewhat comic misunderstanding. Khuen-Héderváry, who sat behind us, was suddenly heard to whisper: 'They don't believe it either!'

'What?' we thought, 'Bethlen and Bánffy? *They* don't believe it either. *They* don't accept what the Great Powers promised us officially, the only promise we ever had which softened Trianon's harsh terms? Well!' we thought, 'Let's get on with it!' And we fought all the harder.

Schober's aide raged on, and even Schober himself grew red in the face; but we did not relent, so much the more when Khuen-Héderváry whispered to us once more, this time saying: 'They don't recognize it.' We both took this to mean we should persevere, but we were wrong. What Khuen-Héderváry had been trying to point out, so that we should not use the point against Austria, was that the *Lettre d'Envoi* had been addressed only to Hungary, and that its validity existed only between us and the Great Powers. Of course I had known this, but I had forgotten it in the heat of argument. We did not grasp this until there was a pause when the president stopped the discussions because of the Austrian's violent reactions.

Then Khuen-Héderváry was able at last to clarify what he had meant.

All the same, this misunderstanding on our part acted to our advantage because it gave us something on which we could yield, which is often desirable if one does not want to seem over-obstinate. So we dropped the question of including the *Lettre d'Envoi* in the agreed document, but its exact meaning got in anyway, although in different words, and we would never have achieved this if we had not argued so fiercely for the letter itself.

So this misunderstanding became an amusing example of how, even in the most serious moments of international negotiations, chance can play an important part.

The task of finding a settlement to the border dispute was given to the military observers of the Great Powers. We agreed to this since General Ferrario (his two colleagues were a lieutenant-colonel and captain) was a good friend of ours. It had been agreed that, pending the Sopron plebiscite and the report of the border commission, the area would continue to be policed by the Hungarian gendarmes. We had suggested this initially, but the official proposal had come from the Italians for the reason that it would be much more costly if English, Italian or French troops were to be stationed there. Much to my astonishment this went through quite smoothly.

Somehow we got towards the end of the conference.

Then the Austrians put forward a new demand: it was that Hungary should clear the area of the irregular guerrillas.

Of course, we could not openly accept this responsibility since to do so would have been tantamount to acknowledging that the partisans had been supported by the Hungarian government. We therefore replied that we would do everything in our power to make the partisans lay down their arms, and that we had reason to believe they would listen to us, but that as they were not government troops but were recruited mainly from the local citizenry, we could not order them to leave the territory.

Now Austria demanded that, in the circumstances, Hungary must suppress the guerrilla bands by force if necessary. Failing our government's readiness to do this, they would consider the whole agreement null and void, refuse to sign any document and leave the conference table without delay. At this they started to rise from their seats.

It was a horrible moment.

We were asked either to abandon all our efforts for peace or to agree to take up arms against all those honest young Hungarians who had fought so valiantly for their country's cause.

It was true that we were confident that the partisans would obey our instructions; but to give a written undertaking to take up arms against our own flesh and blood was unthinkable: to that we could never consent.

A solution had to be found, and in such a tight spot one's mind can work at the speed of lightning.

I got up and asked the chairman Toretta for a brief recess.

Bethlen and I then retired for moment to one of the window embrasures and then went together to Toretta.

I then put to him the solution I proposed. Explaining that Hungarian public opinion would never accept either the Austrian proposal or that we should agree to act as a police force for Austria, but recognizing that the conference would end in failure unless we could persuade Schober and his delegation that the terms of the agreement would be carried out smoothly, we suggested that we would acknowledge our responsibility to evacuate the territory if we could do so privately to the Italian mediators and not publicly to Austria. No one else should know of this commitment, but we would give him our personal word of honour that our promise would be kept. Based on this, Italy should be able to declare that she would guarantee the peaceful handing over of the Burgenland and, hopefully, this would satisfy the Austrians.

Toretta was delighted, for if the conference were to break up without agreement, the fiasco would not only affect Italy's international standing but also his own position as the minister responsible.

We returned to the conference hall, where Toretta announced that Italy would guarantee that the terms of the agreement were carried out. He said this in an authoritative tone, admitting no contradiction. The Austrians were appeased, for any cavilling on their part would now would suggest a lack of confidence in the Great Powers.

This is the true story of the Venice conference. It was a real success for us, as we had achieved everything we wanted.

It was certain that Sopron and its surrounding country would stay Hungarian; and indeed when the plebiscite was held at the end of December, sixty-three per cent voted in our favour.

We also obtained an agreement that the border commission would take into account not only the economic and geological report of the Hungarian government but also the views and needs of the local inhabitants as expressed by all the villages along the frontier.

Not only this, we also succeeded in our demand that the Hungarian gendarmes should remain in place during the plebiscite. This was in the interest of public confidence and not because we had any intention of using force to obtain the results we hoped for. This would not only have been immoral but also, according to what Machiavelli laid down as worse in politics, stupid at a time when international observers would be everywhere and we needed the goodwill of the people. Our continued presence would also be decisive since many of the individuals composing the mass of voters had no firm opinions of their own. Such is the psychology of crowds that the majority will follow whoever appeared to be in power, and so to many the presence of our gendarmes would signify that power still remained with the Hungarian government. Those friendly to Hungary would have the courage to speak up, and the more cautious would follow their example. This would be particularly important for a whole string of villages, including all the Croatians (who had always been pro-Hungarian) and not a few Germanic ones too – in effect, all those on the eastern bank of the river Lafnitz – would probably vote to remain Hungarian.

The dividing up of the Habsburg possessions and the return of the art treasures that had come originally from Hungary were also settled satisfactorily at this time.

Another somewhat comic incident occurred when we came to sign the documents. Under the old rules for international agreements, the signatories had not only to sign their names but also affix their seals. This seems to have been a legacy of the Middle Ages when not everyone could write properly. Neither Bethlen nor I knew about this, and only Khuen-Héderváry wore a signet ring, which he would need for himself. The matter was solved when our ambassador to the Quirinal, Count Albert Nemes, lent us the two seals he had on his watch-chain, one of which he had inherited from his mother, who had been born Baroness Wodianer. So Bethlen used the arms of the Nemes family, while I employed the time-honoured crest of the Wodianers. I mention this for future students of heraldry lest they should imagine that, sometime in the first part of the twentieth century, the Bánffys had exchanged their old griffon for the Wodianers' red-wrapped tobacco leaf and sailboat! We left Venice full of hope.

As our train crossed the dike to Mestre I leant out of the window to wave goodbye to the city of lagoons where once again

I had found myself filled with joy and where I had had such good luck.

We were all in a good mood, except for Khuen-Héderváry who seemed full of gloom. It turned out he was highly superstitious and that he thought it a bad omen that the agreement had not only been signed on 13 October but that the day had also been a Friday. He had done everything he could to have the agreements drawn up by 12 October, but there had not been time even though the drafting commission had worked without stop right up to midnight.

The rest of us just laughed; but Khuen-Héderváry was soon proved right.

A week later King Karl arrived at Sopron; and this second *putsch* nearly destroyed everything we had just achieved.

ᴥ Chapter Six ᴥ

We did not arrive back in Budapest until after ten o'clock in the evening of that Saturday because we had to return by way of the Tyrol, Vienna and Bratislava.

Even though it was so late there was a huge crowd waiting for us at the Western railway station. The platforms were jammed with people, and we were greeted with a speech by Ferenc Herczeg. There was such a multitude of people that our car was hardly able to move because of all those waving their hats and handkerchiefs in the air and trying to touch our hands. The next day the capital was filled with joy, as everyone understood that the Venice Agreement had been a great victory for us. On Monday Government-Commissioner Antal Sigray, Colonel Lehár, Ostenburg, Ranzenberger[94] and Prónay, the commanding officer of the gendarmes, were summoned to the prime minister's office to make preparations for the plebiscite and arrange for our gendarmerie to be under the authority of General Ferrario. We also had to discuss the most important question of the disbanding of the partisans without delay.

We outlined what would be needed and established every detail of the actual deployment of our forces. There would be no need of so many gendarmes: at least four-fifths of their number could be recalled at once.

It was mainly Bethlen who did the talking, because these matters came under his authority. As he went into all the details, I was looking at the others. Ranzenberger and Prónay listened in silence. Both of these were big strong men, Prónay with fists as large as horse' hooves, while Ranzenberger was built like a prize-fighter. Both were clearly proud of their physiques, and I noticed that, as they sat there listening but not speaking, again and again they would flex their muscles as if somehow they were both trying to impress upon the other how terrible each could be. It was difficult not to smile.

I could not say the same of Ostenburg. His name had originally been Moravec but apparently he could not use this because of some ancient feud, and he had therefore chosen the better-sounding Ostenburg. He, like Prónay before he had become a gendarme, had once been notorious as the leader of one of those irregular bands that had wreaked so much havoc at the time of the White Terror. Moravec/Ostenburg just sat there lazily, occasionally nodding his head when Colonel Lehár said something.

Lehár himself was very different from the others. He was a good-looking military type, intelligent, reserved: a man of few words.

I had known Sigray for a long time. He was an old friend with whom I had often played polo. He was bold and witty, with a quick brain. As I silently watched these last two I had the impression, from what they said and asked, that they shared some secret idea, something that qualified their reactions. Although they agreed with everything, and accepted all the arrangements, they seemed to speak with some hesitation. They would say things like: 'All right, if it turns out like that . . . ' or 'Yes, that *could* be done.' rather than 'It will be done.' or 'We'll do that.'

Accordingly, when the discussions were over I sat down next to Sigray and asked for an unequivocal promise from him, as the man responsible for carrying out the government's decisions, that I had his word of honour that he would faithfully execute the programme we had just agreed.

For a moment Sigray seemed to hesitate. Then he said: 'All right. I give my word of honour,' and we shook hands.

After the meeting the two of us shared a car back into town. We were both in a good humour and discussed the tasks ahead of us like friends not simply as official colleagues. Then Sigray suddenly threw in the remark: 'If King Karl should happen to be there, I'll put him on a train and send him to you.' Astonished I then asked: 'There's no question of that, I hope?' 'No! No! But one never knows with him. I just meant that I wouldn't bother with him myself but let you sort it out back here.'[95]

Unfortunately, I did not take this casual remark seriously at the time. I just replied: 'God forbid! But if he does turn up, it would be best for him not to stay there.' If I had then thought to ask Sigray why he had mentioned this I might have then discovered, and thereby have better understood, what later occurred, but we let the subject drop, as he then started to talk about something to do with the conference, and the king was not mentioned again. It was as friends that we parted in front of the Ritz.

It was either the same day or the next when Gustáv Gratz, our ambassador in Vienna, came to see me at my request. I had asked him to call because we had chosen him to represent Hungary at the economic conference due to be held at Portorosa on 21 October.

When I entrusted him with this task he at first hesitated and then tried to get out of it, although without giving me any reasons for his reluctance. Finally he accepted.

This also did not arouse my suspicions, because I imagined that as my predecessor as foreign minister, he might now resent taking orders from me. However, he did take the dossier from me before returning at once to Vienna since he would have to leave on 19 October.

Some little time before, the prime minister had held some confidential talks with the Legitimists. As I have already written, these people had grown in strength ever since the king's attempted *putsch* at Easter, and so Bethlen had thought it best, at least for the time being, to keep the matter in the air by arriving at some sort of compromise. He had therefore, with the agreement of Andrássy and his friends, worked out a declaration of which the substance was that in the present situation, and for some time to come, the government would be unable to consider the question of the ruler, but that he was convinced that the matter could not be resolved without involving the king[96].

Bethlen had agreed with the Andrássy Party that he would include this in the speech he was to give at Pécs on 20 October, when an important meeting had been planned to celebrate the return to Hungary of Baranya. As well as the head of government, several ministers and many members of parliament would also be there.

I believe that these discussions had been held before we went to Venice, but I did not take part in them and only heard later about the agreement.

I was not present either at Pécs, but stayed in Budapest.

Apart from myself and Belitska, the defence minister, all the other members of the cabinet had accompanied Bethlen to the meeting.

The twentieth of October was a Friday, just a week after the Venice conference. On that day I needed to telephone Sopron about some minor matter. In the late afternoon I called long distance and, after a long wait, our exchange told me that it was impossible to get through and that there must be some fault on the line.

I then went to the prime minister's residence to have dinner with my cousin, Margit Bethlen. From there, both before and after our meal, I tried again to call Sopron and, later, Szombathely. There was no reply from either.

Now I began to be puzzled, so I asked Belitska to come over, and together we sat by the telephone from nine o'clock until eleven. Still no answer. Belitska grew tired of waiting and went home, but I began to be worried and felt that something must be wrong. Finally it occurred to me that perhaps the superintendent's department at the post office could get through on their own line.

So I asked for their help.

Finally, at half past eleven I received an answer. They told me that they had got through, but only to Szombathely. A post office employee had answered the call. She had said just a few words before hanging up, just enough to pass on a rumour that King Karl had arrived in Sopron and that the Government-Commissioner had forbidden any communication with Budapest!

The omen had been proved true.

Bethlen returned early on Saturday morning. I had sent word to the station of the news from Sopron. Soon afterwards there was a conference of the government ministers and talks with Horthy. By noon reports had started coming in, not from Sopron itself but from Óvár and Győr, where there were those conscientious enough to send us what information they could. So as to give a coherent account of King Karl's arrival I will tell what happened in chronological order even though it was only later that we learned some of the details.

On 19 October King Karl presented himself at József Cziráky's house at Dénesfa[97]. He arrived with Zita and Borovicsényi. Borovicsényi was a secretary at the embassy who, on his own request, had been granted leave from the foreign office to attend King Karl. The intention had been that he should send back regular reports as to what was happening in the exiled court. His duties should have included his trying to dissuade King Karl from attempting a second *putsch* and also letting us know of the King's intentions. It was some time before we had realized that he was unsuitable for that post, as he had been seduced by the glamour of the 'court'. It was probably clumsy of us to have sent him there. Borovicsényi had been Bethlen's secretary in Vienna in the spring of 1919 and it had been part of his duties then to liase with the representatives of the Great Powers, which sometimes involved him in fairly important matters. As so often happens in revolutionary times, some quite mediocre characters find themselves in positions way beyond their real capacities simply because they happen at that time to be the only people available. Such persons are apt to fancy themselves geniuses, and this is what had happened to Borovicsényi. When normal times returned he had gone back to the foreign office in the same, or maybe only slightly higher, grade to which he would have been entitled by his years of service. Unfortunately, after his time in Vienna, he had thought himself worthy of better things and decided this was a backward step.

In Budapest he was always discontented and always criticizing whatever was done, which is probably why Kálmán Kánya, the foreign minister's deputy who dealt with staff matters, gave him leave.

King Karl's other companion was Queen Zita herself. It must have been a hard decision to leave her many children – for she gave birth nearly every year – in order to be at her husband's side, but she did it even though she was once again pregnant. She was, of course, a strong-willed woman. When her husband had still been heir to the throne she had come to Kolozsvár; and as I had been assigned to her service I had several days in which to observe her at leisure. This little anecdote may help illuminate her character.

One day it had been arranged that she should visit various places in the town including the Transylvanian Museum and several churches and convents. Archduke Friedrich, then commander-in-chief of the army, arrived on the same day and also wanted to see the sites of Kolozsvár. This immediately created difficulties because the Archduchess Zita declared she did not want to meet Archduke Friedrich anywhere. Accordingly, the day's programme had entirely to be rescheduled, which was not easy in such a small place. The cars would have to make all sorts of detours so as not to meet on the road. It was a real headache, but in the end I thought I had worked it all out. If everyone kept strictly to the times allotted for each visit, then the two would not meet. But it was not to be. No matter how often I would say, with watch in hand, that it was time to go, we always stayed too long wherever we went. And so it happened that, although we managed to avoid an actual meeting, their cars did pass each other while going through the park. Zita was furious, and when angry she could be terrifying. She went very pale and her tongue darted in and out of her thin lips like a snake's. *'Ich hab 'doch gesagt, dass ich ihn nicht sehen will!'* – 'I have already said I will not meet him,' she said over and over again, and her whole body trembled with hate.

How this fierce hatred began, I am not sure but I suspect that it started when Queen Zita's family, the Bourbon-Parmas, lived in Pozsony (now Bratislava) in somewhat less affluent circumstances than the immensely wealthy Archduke Friedrich nearby. Furthermore, it is possible that, as the Bourbon-Parmas did not rank very high on the royalty scale, they may at that time have been treated by Friedrich in a manner they found humiliating.

One might also add that, just like Friedrich, the Bourbon-Parmas had a number of pretty daughters, and that when Archduke Karl first came to Pozsony (Bratislava) it was to woo one of the archduke's daughters, but he fell in love with young Zita instead[98].

All this may have provided her with reasons for disliking Friedrich, but her furious rage must have been an inherited family characteristic. Her mother had been a Braganza princess, grandchild of that King Manuel of Portugal who, it is said, chased his own father from the throne after killing the king's favourite minister with his own hands. Queen Zita, with her dark hair and olive skin, had inherited the Braganza looks; and it may be that on the Parma side there were some worrying hereditary traits, for among her half-brothers and sisters not a few had been either mad or dim-witted.

However, when she wanted she could be most charming even though echoes of her iron will could be heard in every word she spoke. It seems likely that she came with her husband this time because, knowing his indecisive character and general softness, she was determined he should not again return to her unsuccessful and shamefaced.

They arrived at Dénesfa by aeroplane, where many people just happened to be collected together, ostensibly for the christening of one of Count Cziráky's children, a function which would provide an excellent reason for their presence there that day. Gyula Andrássy was stepfather to Cziráky's wife, and György Pallavicini was his son-in-law. Countess Cziráky's sister, the beautiful divorced Princess Kája Odescalchi, was there too, having only just returned from Lucerne, where King Karl and his family had been staying ever since the first *putsch*. She had been there several times before, presumably acting as messenger for the Legitimist Party. All the noble aristocrats taking part in the new *putsch* were either close relations of Andrássy or part of his intimate circle of friends. Sigray was the only exception. Analysing all these facts, and knowing all the relationships, it is not difficult to unravel the conspiracy. It was clear that everything had been planned in advance, and Andrássy's later statement – that they had known nothing beforehand and that King Karl's arrival had taken them all by surprise – was clearly untrue.

Andrássy had previously discussed the statement that Bethlen was to make in Pécs and knew well in advance that this would be done on 20 October. Accordingly, King Karl's arrival was planned so that he should already be in Sopron by the time

Bethlen was due to speak. This is why it was forbidden for every telephone and telegraphic line to be used so that the prime minister could not be informed before he uttered those phrases concerning the king. The conspirators must have thought that by doing this they would so tie Bethlen's hands that he would be prevented from ever afterwards acting against the king's return.

All the armed gendarmes in the Burgenland were under the command of Colonel Lehár, and as Lehár was their man it meant that his entire troop of some three to four hundred men[99] was at their disposal. This would be enough to quell any resistance, and that is why the Burgenland had been chosen for launching the *putsch*.

This is also why the christening of the Cziráky child had been postponed for months – a thing almost unheard-of in Catholic families – so as to have the excuse of the 'chance' gathering at Dénesfa; this is why as early as mid-September they had sent Countess Aimée Pálffy, who had previously been lady-in-waiting to Queen Zita, to Pinkafö to win over Prónay, who until then had always been in favour of a free election to settle the question of the monarchy. Indeed, Prónay fell in love and married the beautiful Countess Aimée, but beautiful though she was, she could never persuade him be anything but neutral. It is true that he did not side with Horthy, but he did not side with the Legitimists either. It is possible that his appointment as Lajtabán (governor) of Lafnitz, which had made him almost an independent ruler there, had gone to his head, and that he too had appreciated, as England had done during the Boer War, the 'splendid isolation[100]' of his position.

Further proof that all this had been planned in advance was the so-called 'chance' presence in the neighbourhood of István Rakovszky, who had been the most turbulent member of the former coalition government and was now Speaker of the House. I do not know if he had been in Györ or Magyarovár, but by Friday 20 October he was in Sopron and had already appointed Karl's new prime minister.

Gustáv Gratz also arrived from Vienna at this time, having abandoned his official assignment, and was at once given a ministerial appointment. Because of Gratz's absence from Portorosa

Hungary was left without a representative at a conference when matters of great importance to us were to be decided. It was also odd that Prince Louis Windischgrätz, King Karl's intimate friend, an adventurer who was later to be so involved in the forged francs scandal, had left Switzerland at just this moment on his way to Slovensko by way of Prague. He too must have been on some Legitimist mission, for it seems likely, as this was afterwards much talked about, that he had convinced the unhappy king that the Czechoslovak army would rise and declare itself for the Habsburgs. However, Windischgrätz was detained in Prague and was allowed to go no farther. I later had a great deal of trouble to get him released, which did not prove easy[101].

It was also obvious that Sigray and Lehár knew all about the king's plans from the start, which is why they had spoken in so equivocal a manner on 16 October, when we had been discussing the Venice agreement. This would explain why Sigray had been so reluctant to give his word to carry out what he had just accepted to do.

This also explained why Gustáv Gratz had tried to get out of representing Hungary at Portorosa, and why he had lingered in Vienna for no apparent reason.

It was therefore futile for them to argue that everything that had happened was mere chance. Such perfect collusion and coordination are never by chance. These men all acted to a preconceived plan in which their roles had already been determined. The only thing they never considered was that this plan could be the ruin of their country.

That this did not happen was no thanks to them.

On Saturday morning we held a council meeting at Horthy's residence. We decided we must resist. At midday the ambassadors of the Great Powers came to see me and handed over an ultimatum that declared they would never tolerate the return of King Karl and that, if we allowed him to remain on Hungarian soil, this would mean armed intervention and the occupation of our country.

I told them at once of our government's determination to stand firm and let them know that we would do everything in our power to make the king leave. I told them all that we then knew about the situation.

We had learned that Karl had left Sopron bound for Budapest that morning. He was accompanied not only by his new ministers and his court, but also by an armed force of two to three thousand and some artillerymen. This therefore became a case of open armed revolt on the part of the newly recruited troops who had given their oath of allegiance to the new constitution, and we had decided to treat it as such. If necessary, we would meet force with force, but first we had decided to try to ward off the danger by persuasion. Accordingly, we despatched József Vass, the minister of education, to meet the advancing king. He seemed an appropriate choice since, as he was a Catholic priest, we hoped he would have some influence upon Karl, and especially upon Queen Zita. According to the news we had received, the railway trains carrying the rebellion towards Budapest were travelling remarkably slowly. We hoped, therefore, that Vass would meet them somewhere near Győr. We did not then know that we had sent our envoy in vain, for Karl refused to receive him, and instead Vass found himself locked into a small compartment on the train.

Soon after midday consuls of the three neighbouring states – Czechoslovakia, Serbia and Romania – arrived. This was their first collective action, the first symptom of what, after the king's *putsch* and because of it, came to be called the 'Little Entente'.

They were also full of menaces and gave us an ultimatum to get rid of the king. I told them that I had already given our reply to the representatives of the Great Powers – which pleased them – but that we considered the problem of the king to be an internal affair which we were disinclined to discuss with anyone except the Council of the Great Powers which, as guarantors of the peace treaty, was the only body qualified to deal with the matter.

I do not want to go into the details of everything that passed that day – indeed, I don't think I could – but I will try to convey its essence and that of which I still have vivid recollection.

That afternoon I went to see the prime minister and asked what he had heard, where were the insurgents, and was there any news of Vass?

Bethlen replied that the king had left Sopron in three trains, in the front two of which were the armed troops and in the last he himself and the entourage. They were still somewhere between Györ and Komárom, travelling very slowly because they stopped at every station and made addresses to the people. They had started late from Sopron because the king had attended an open-air mass on the platform and had then inspected a guard of honour and went through every little trick of royal protocol due to a Habsburg. This delay was obviously to our advantage as it gave us more time to organize our resistance. General Koós[102] was called back from Pécs by Horthy because there were hardly any troops in Budapest itself. Pál Nagy, the army chief, had collected every soldier he could find, but they were very few. There was talk of enlisting the university students, and it was possible that by the following day we might have enough men to offer some resistance but certainly not before then. Consequently, we sent Siménfalvy with a team of railway workers to take up the line at several places so as to slow the insurgents' advance. 'I do not want to agree to any further damage to the railway system, any blasting of tunnels or blowing up of bridges, as that would do enormous harm and would be far too expensive to repair later,' said Bethlen. Now it was already getting dark. The direct line on his desk started to ring, and Bethlen walked over and picked up the receiver. He only spoke for a minute or two, and all I heard were the words 'I will do whatever is my duty to the country!' Then the caller evidently said something more, and Bethlen replaced the receiver. He was smiling.

'Do you know who that was? Rakovszky. And do you know what he said? He said that he will not negotiate with us, and that if we do not resign at once he'll hang the lot of us!'

We did not, of course, take much notice of the hanging threat, although knowing him we knew he was quite capable of stringing us all up. Still the threat was timely, for it reminded us of what would happen to us if our resistance failed. We two, the head of the government and his minister for foreign affairs, would most surely be arrested and flung into prison: Bethlen because he had ordered the resistance and myself because I had agreed to the ultimatum of the Great Powers. Bethlen said he would remain in the prime minister's office, and we agreed that I should go over to the French Embassy, which was just across the road from my apartment, as it was vital that at least one of us should stay free so as to be able to act if confusion were to overcome the country. It seemed that this should be me who might be most effective since I was on good terms with the Allied ambassadors.

This is how we parted that evening.

I called upon Ambassador Foucher, who declared himself most flattered and said that he would cover me with the Tricolour to make sure I was well protected. He at once gave the necessary orders, and that evening I brought over a change of clothes and linen, some few personal objects . . . and, of course, quantities of cigarettes.

Early the next morning I was woken by my old valet, András Szabó, with the news that the people in the market were saying that there had been some fighting at Budaörs[103]. I dressed hurriedly and went at once up to the Royal Palace.

The prime minister was with Horthy, so I went to join them. I found them in one of the halls on the first floor sitting at a long table was covered with maps. Pál Nagy, who commanded the army, was with them, as were one or two officers of the General Staff. Near the entrance on the other side of the hall stood Horthy's *chef de cabinet*, Albert Bartha, leaning against the wall. He was a pitiful sight, very pale with eyes almost closed, and his expression was one not of fear but of bottomless misery and despair.

I stepped up to the table. Pál Nagy was making his report. He said that we now had enough troops at Budaörs, but that the soldiers were reluctant to use their weapons. The infantry had fired a few shots, but our defence would crumble at once if the other side opened fire. Having said this, he left to return to the silent firing line.

Horthy was very calm and resolute. I never saw him as calm as he was then. He was a good soldier: there was no doubt about it. This is how he must have been at the battle of Otranto when, already wounded, he drew the fire of the entire Italian and English fleets on his flagship, the *Navarra*, so as to give time for his own weaker fleet to get away. Bethlen was the same as he always was: cool and matter-of-fact. They were now discussing which general to send over to talk to the rebellious troops and explain to them that by acting as they did they were forswearing their given oaths. They were all volunteers, recently recruited, and they had made their oath of allegiance to Horthy. The officer to be chosen should also try to contact the king and offer him a ceasefire so as to put a stop to this fratricidal struggle while negotiations took place.

It took a long time to decide upon a name, a long time even to think of someone suitable. What was his name? I can no longer remember, but it does not matter. Considering the wretched part he played it is better it should not be remembered. He was a strutting military type, with tremendous moustaches and swelling chest, who stamped his feet and walked about with much sword clattering, as if he thought this necessary in a soldier. He agreed to everything, everything! Many times he swore eternal fidelity to Horthy, and then he left, stamping his feet as before. For continuity's sake, I must mention here that he betrayed everyone. What happened to him on the other side I do not know, neither am I sure that he was not all the time secretly in touch with the royalist group.

All I know for certain is that he came back that afternoon to report that his mission had been a failure and that he was now a captive, a prisoner of war, and that he had been allowed to return on his word of honour merely give us King Karl's message that anyone who took up arms against him would be executed. This message he delivered and then drove away, with the lie upon his lips that he was returning to captivity. However, not only was he not a prisoner but, as the highest ranking officer present, had been put in command of the rebellious troops, and it was he who ordered them to scale the heights of the Budaörs Hills where our defences had been posted.

We only learned about this man's falsity sometime that evening, and the details on the following day. About noon I went over to the British Embassy in Tárnok utca. Loud cannon fire could be heard. Hohler received me in his bedroom, I do not now remember why: perhaps he had a cold. As a dressing gown, he wore a long brown kimono he had brought from Japan. We sat in the corner near the window in two small armchairs, a coffee table between us. I told him all I knew about this deeply worrying situation, and how we had tried to bring about a ceasefire. Hohler offered the protection of England, and suggested I should move in with him, but of course I could not accept this as I had already had the same offer from Foucher. We talked for a long time about what promised to be a most dismal future.

Then a most strange thing happened. In the middle of the rather dark room I saw a grey cat. It looked at us. 'Is that your cat?' I asked Hohler. 'I don't have a cat. No one in this house has a cat. I can't understand how it got here,' he said; for he too had seen it when I had. We both got up. The cat had disappeared the moment we started talking about it. I had seen it dart under the bed, so we looked there for it. It was not there. Hohler, like many Englishmen, was superstitious and was determined that it should be found at once. I too became caught up in the excitement of the search. Passionately we looked everywhere, behind sofas and chests of drawers; we crouched down and even lay on the floor; we pulled the bed from the wall and soon the room was in chaos; but the cat was nowhere to be seen. The door had been closed, and so had the windows. It could not have left the room, and yet it was not there: just not there. We had to abandon the search.

If I had been superstitious I might have taken this for a fatal omen, coming just after I had just been threatened with hanging. As it was, although I did not believe in such things, all sorts of similar stories came to mind. It is true that in these cases the cats are usually black, as messengers of death should be, whereas ours had been grey. I could see that Hohler was thinking the same thing and was convinced it was for me. The shade of the ghostly cat hung over us, as we parted for, when Hohler pressed my hand with unusual vigour, it was as if he never again expected to see me alive.

Luckily, I was never harmed: then or later. If I had been the story of the cat would have been repeated everywhere, and a superstitious world would have discussed it for decades to come; all the more so as Hohler, as soon as I had left, called his staff together and searched the whole place in vain. The grey cat was never seen again, just as it had never been seen before.

That afternoon there were renewed sounds of artillery fire – and then silence. At any moment we expected Lehár's attacking troops to appear from somewhere by the Farkasrét[104] or from under the Gellert Hill and – behind them, of course – King Karl, wreathed as always in smiles.

So, obviously, did others, as was proved by the presence along the Hunyadi János Road and at the corner of Disz Square of numerous small groups of giggling girls and swaggering young men, all dressed in their best. They were hoping to see King Karl's victorious soldiers marching into the city, and they wanted to be the first to do so, as if to symbolize the cheering crowds to come. There were two or three more little groups at the turn in the road and higher up at the Lonyai Villa and at the beginning of Várszinház Street (named after the Palace Theatre). In fact, they were everywhere, which we took as a sign that everything would be settled quickly and not in our favour.

However, nothing happened until nightfall.

When I had finished my work at the Foreign Ministry I went home. I was just about to go to bed when, at eleven o'clock, the telephone rang and I was summoned to go immediately to see the Regent. I had already sent away my official car and so had to find a taxi, which took some time, before I could hurry away up to the Royal Palace.

Horthy and Bethlen were there, waiting for me. They quickly told me what had happened.

During the afternoon Lehár's troops had started their attack. Ours, mostly newly recruited young university students, faced them boldly. Some were in uniform but the majority, poor fellows, were still in civilian clothes with tricolour armbands on their sleeves. Unfortunately eleven of them were killed. Then a most unexpected thing happened. From the armbands, and from what several of our boys had said, Lehár's gendarmes discovered that they had been ordered to fight with a lie. Their superiors had told them that a Bolshevist revolution had broken out in Budapest, and that it was this they had to fight. When they learned from their prisoners that this was not true and that they had been used without their knowledge to attack Horthy, they were dismayed, refused all further obedience to Lehár and melted away.

The result was that King Karl sent us a message saying that he was ready to surrender and asking that we should send envoys to him with our conditions and inform him what we would do to ensure his safety.

This was one of those extraordinary turnarounds, of which those stormy days were to prove so rich.

And here too, as so often in life, the drama had its comic moments.

At the palace we decided to send Kálmán Kánya as our principal envoy, accompanied, as we might well need a legal specialist, by Térfy[105] who was not only our minister of food but also a most eminent jurist.

Khuen-Héderváry and I went to rouse Kánya from his bed. This was a not unamusing incident, although it went off smoothly enough. We took him up to the palace and went in search of Térfy. He lived in a little two-storey house in Kaszino Street between Uri Street and the Bastion. A small door leading to the courtyard was open, so without more ado we went in and up to the flat where Térfy lived. We rang the bell. After ringing several times, which did not surprise us, as by now it was after midnight and everybody was no doubt already asleep, a maidservant came to the door. Then she opened a barred window just a crack and asked what we wanted. We told her we were looking for her master, that we wanted him to come with us at once and that it was urgent. We also gave her our names, but by this time she had slammed the window shut and run away, leaving us outside in the dark.

In a few moments we could see through the bars of the window that a light had gone on inside. With faint rays of light streaming towards us through the keyhole and under the door we imagined it would not now be long before they let us in. But no! No one came, and we had to go on waiting. Inside there seemed to be much activity. Sometimes the wench would race across the room and then disappear through some internal door before again coming into view, carrying some sort of small trunk or large parcel. She came and she went, and now there was more light – still not in the entrance hall but elsewhere in the apartment. We could see more activity through the open doors of adjoining rooms – but still no one came to the door even though we rang and rang with increasing energy.

Finally, after about twenty minutes' wait the entrance hall light went on again and Térfy himself opened the door.

'What?' he cried out in astonishment, as we went in. 'You? What a surprise! What a wonderful surprise!' Then we learned why he had kept us waiting so long. He had been arrested twice before, once at the time of the Communists and then again by the Romanians in Debrecen. Both times it had been at night, and both times he had been caught unprepared and so could take nothing with him to the prison. He had then decided that from that time on he would never go without a bag containing a change of clothes, food and some books to read; also that before leaving he would have a wash and a shave. Accordingly, as it seemed all too probable that he would again be arrested, he had instructed the maid that she was not to open the door if someone came for him in the night. The girl had received a nasty fright when we appeared but had not heard our names as she had rushed off to her master crying: 'They're here! They're here!'

We all laughed heartily at the misunderstanding. I have been mistaken for many things in my life – a poverty-stricken artist, a commercial traveller, the conductor on a ferryboat and a house painter – but never before a potential gaoler.

Next came the news that the royal couple, together with their entourage and Ostenburg's little troop of armed men, had left for Tata and were to stay in the Esterházy palace there[106]. They took Siménfalvy with them as a prisoner.

Here follows what he himself told of this experience.

He had been captured by Lehár's men between Györ and Komárom and locked in a cattle-wagon connected to the rear of the king's train. They warned him not to look out, or he would be shot. Nevertheless, whenever the train stopped, he did look out, either peeping through a slit in the door or the corner of a window. At nearly every halt, were it a station or signal box, he would see a well-dressed young man who boarded the royal train.

Then they had stopped for a long time at Biatorbágy, where there had been an open-air mass, an inspection of a guard of honour who had presented arms, and had gone through other court ceremonies. Later he had heard distant cannon fire. Sometimes he had caught a glimpse either of the king or Queen Zita taking a walk or chatting with the officers. Of course, he had not been able to hear any news and knew nothing of what was happening.

Towards evening he felt the train start again, this time moving backwards. It moved along in the same sluggish way as before, and again there were frequent stops, where the same young man he had seen jumping onto the train would jump off again and disappear.

It was already dark when they arrived at Tata. Suddenly the wagon door was wrenched open, and the same men who had imprisoned him now told him to take command of the guard and be responsible for the safety of the royal couple.

He looked after everything. Outside the king's rooms he placed armed guards chosen from among the officers who had remained faithful to the king and, when everything had been arranged to his satisfaction, he too went to his bed. He was aroused at about two in the morning. What had happened was that one of the partisan leaders, Rákosi by name, had decided to march to Budapest to offer his services to Horthy. On the way he arrived at Tata and there he found all the loyal guard asleep not only at the castle gate but also outside the king's door. Even Ostenburg was down in the basement with some woman. So he disarmed them all and placed his own guards in their place. General havoc everywhere! The partisan guards were filthy dirty from sleeping in the fields and dusty after their long march. Their clothes, civilian not uniform, were in tatters, and it was hardly surprising that everyone in the house imagined they had been attacked by bandits. It took some time for Siménfalvy to restore order and send Rákosi on his way. Finally silence again reigned in the castle at Tata[107].

So ended the first phase of King Karl's attempt to overthrow the government.

There can be no doubt that if Karl and Zita had not allowed themselves to be wined and dined in Sopron, had not wasted time attending military parades, *Te Deums*, open-air masses and formal reception of envoys and had had no more than two trains hitched together as one, then they could have reached Budapest either Friday evening or early Saturday morning, when they would have met almost no resistance. We had no resources, and we would have either been chased out or arrested. Then they would have been able to play monarchs for a few days at least. But for their awkwardness, and the childish conceit that allowed them to waste time on trivialities, that vital day and a half would not have been lost.

There can also be no doubt that their glory would have been brief. The Czech army had been mobilized and was being rushed to our border; while the Serbs had despatched yet another battalion to Bácksa to reinforce their forces already in Baranya. If a Habsburg king had seized power in Budapest, then there would have been an immediate Serb attack followed by a Czech invasion. The country would have been overrun. The resolute resistance of the Hungarian government averted this danger, at least for the time being.

Later the Legitimists were to say that had Karl been accepted by us, the Czechoslovak army would never have marched into Hungary because all those Slovaks still loyal to the king would have changed sides. There is no need for me to deny that, for it has been authoritatively refuted by one of the most reliable of King Karl's supporters, Tamás Erdödy, who had been a childhood playmate of the king's and perhaps his only true friend. Erdödy tells in his memoirs how the unhappy royal couple had been led astray and repeatedly fed with encouraging but false information by a group of desperate political exiles whose only hopes lay in the restoration of the monarchy. And it was these people who played up to the poor king, a man weak in every respect, who was not fitted to rule and who could not even have managed a medium-sized farm.

Some Hungarians who had taken part in the *putsch* later claimed that King Karl's return had been approved by the Great Powers. To refute this, I will again quote Erdödy. According to him Queen Zita's Bourbon-Parma brothers had brought the news that Briand, and not only him, had said that should Karl succeed and his restoration as king of Hungary become a *fait accompli*, then he, Briand, would be content to make only a formal protest and would try to win over the newly created states on our borders. This was said to have been stated by the French prime minister before the first *putsch* at Easter[108]. How much of this was true is anybody's guess. And even if it were true it would have been a weak enough basis for such an important enterprise, even putting on one side Briand's well-known unreliability. It was said of him, when he was still France's foreign minister, that if, in the middle of explaining his policy in the Assembly, he sensed that he was being received coldly, he was capable to saying the opposite before he sat down. He was an orator and a parliamentarian who was determined, above all, to remain popular. He had good manners and a most winning way of saying anything that would please, provided only that it cost him nothing. The message to King Karl, even if meant seriously, should only have been a very slight encouragement. It was always clear that the main obstacle was the attitude of Prague and Belgrade. It is impossible to understand how the royal party could possibly imagine that the Czechs and the Serbs would not intervene with force, regardless of any formal protest from the Great Powers, who would be obliged to validate such a protest. And France, once the Allied protest had become official, could take no other course but to follow suit. Briand's 'promise', dating as it did from before the first *putsch*, had become immeasurably less likely by the time of the second. And, even if it had ever been made, it was always possible that Briand had changed his mind after the failure of the first attempt.

I was at that time on such close terms with Foucher that, had he heard any whisper of all this, it was certain he would have whispered it to me too. I never then saw any change in his attitude to me, or in that of the other ambassadors, who remained as well disposed to us as they always had been, while insisting with continued firmness that we faithfully carry out every demand made upon us by the Council of Ambassadors – and the Council of Ambassadors was completely under the thumb of Benes.

This was perhaps the most important aspect of the situation during the second phase of the king's attempt to regain power.

In this crisis, where only a little provocation was needed, a renewed invasion of our territory would have been certain; and with it a further dismemberment of the country.

Karl and his accompanying party were then removed to Tihany[109] under the surveillance of the Allied powers. Karl and Zita were lodged in a Benedictine convent, the 'ministers' and others who had taken part in the plot being in a well-guarded villa nearby. There they were visited by, among others, Csernoch, the prince primate of Hungary, General Soós and by various politicians who, with the authority of the government, tried to persuade the king to abdicate his own rights, perhaps in favour of his young son, Otto. At this time, right at the beginning of the crisis, there was hope that this would satisfy Benes. However, influenced it seems by his wife, Karl was not willing to do this.

I had very little personal knowledge of these details at the time because I was then very much occupied with the daily worsening situation with respect to our foreign relations.

The first sign of things to come was that the Czechoslovak chargé d'affaires came to see me on behalf of Benes. He said that Benes still had friendly feelings towards me but that 'circumstances are stronger than friendship'.

I replied that the government had done everything in its power to foil the king's attempt at restoration and that therefore Hungary could not be held accountable for Karl's mad adventure. We sent the same message more than once to the Council of Ambassadors, stressing that the *putsch* had been foiled by our strength of purpose and resistance and that therefore we had the right to expect that the Council should recognize our good faith and energetic action by protecting us from the demands of the newly-created states.

I should mention here that a few days later the removal of the royal party from Hungary was finally completed, thereby satisfying the wish of the Parisian Council[110]. The English steamer, the *Glow-worm* and her sister ship, came up the Danube to fetch them, and as it was important that their journey should not be used as the occasion for a demonstration by supporters of the king, which would certainly have been used against us by Prague and Belgrade, I devised a plan with the director of MAV (*Magyar Allami Vasutak* – the Hungarian State Railways) and with the British ambassador, Hohler, that the train carrying the royal party should be officially scheduled to run from Tihany to Dunaföldvár, where they would board the steamer. However, a reliable chief controller was to travel with the engine driver and, just before the train arrived at the branch-line, would order him to go straight to Baja and not, after all, to Földvár. It was the same with the steamers. These were to dock the previous evening at Földvár but later to set sail under cover of night and tie up under the bridge at Baja. And so it happened. Only the four of us were in the know; and nothing untoward occurred. It was just as well. Indeed, at Földvár a number of local landowners had gathered to make a big demonstration, while the occasion had brought a large crowd to the station and the quayside who, even if they were not exactly supporters of the Habsburgs, would surely have cheered and waved, as mobs so often do if the occasion offers.

A tragic incident was linked to these events. József Hunyadi, the chief court steward, was not able to make the journey with the royal couple, and a replacement had had to be found in case they had needed something on the way. I had asked my old friend Miksa Hadik to go with them to Madeira[111] and stay there until Hunyadi arrived. The poor man accepted gladly, but when the car went at dawn to pick him up, they found that he had died in the night of a cerebral palsy. I mourned him greatly and still think of him today. He was a fine man.

In about a week the Czech mobilization was completed, and the army posted in readiness on our borders.

In the meantime, on the first day of the week, we had held an important cabinet meeting so as to hear what General Röder, Chief of the Hungarian General Staff, had to tell us and then to decide whether or not we too should mobilize.

Röder informed us that we had already arrived at the last moment when such a decision could be taken; otherwise it would be too late. However, the decision was not only a military one. There were also political considerations. If we were to mobilize then this would entail our releasing a supply of arms that had previously been hidden from the watchful eyes of the

Disarmament Committee and so reveal the continued existence of arms we had denied we still possessed. We would have no other way of defending ourselves. When he told us this I at once asked what were our military chances if we were fully armed and mobilized. Röder did not beat about the bush but told us frankly.

'We can resist for ten days, perhaps two weeks.'

'No longer?' I asked.

'No! No longer. The other side is four or five times stronger than we are; and besides we shall have to fight on two fronts: north and south.'

It was a dreadful situation and I was faced with a terrible responsibility. It was up to me to decide whether we should leave the country defenceless or take up the challenge when we were at such a disadvantage.

I decided that I would vote against mobilization and I am sure, even today, that I was right. Mobilization would have meant immediate war, for the Czechs and Serbs would hardly have waited until we were ready for them. They would have struck at once, albeit without their full resources. Therefore for us to mobilize would have been futile. And not only that but we would also have diminished our standing with the Great Powers by revealing our illegal cache of arms. If we had had any military prospect of defending ourselves and holding out for longer then, perhaps, the risk might have been justified, for while we held out there might have been time to find a solution, as in the case of the Burgenland. But to risk the country's safety when we could only fight for ten days or a fortnight, and then, after a disastrous struggle, to have to capitulate? No! That we could never accept. I repeated all my arguments, and the cabinet finally agreed with me. Röder then said that it was his duty to ask for an immediate decision, and so the responsibility fell once more on me, and I had no other course but to accept it. I stipulated, however, that our frontier guards should be withdrawn to half a kilometre behind the border so as to diminish the possibility of frontier incidents that might be used as a pretext for action against us. Röder promised this and was as good as his word.

One can imagine the sleepless nights I passed during the whole of that fortnight until the many problems provoked by the king's actions had finally been resolved. I had resolved that I would not live to witness a renewed invasion of my country as a result of any decision I might have taken and for which I would be blamed by everyone. My conscience was quiet, but one cannot live without honour.

These two weeks were the worst of my time as foreign minister.

Hardly a day passed without Benes coming up with new demands, at first directly to me and later through the Council of Ambassadors and always, contrary to all logic, accusing Hungary of wanting the Habsburgs back. His demands grew steadily. At first he only exacted the dethronement of the king, but he was not satisfied when, because of the pressure of the Great Powers, we accepted this, and went on to demand that this should be extended to cover all members of the Habsburg-Lorraine family. This was all done by ultimatum after threatening ultimatum. It was clear that he wanted war or at least a further dismembering of Hungary; and it was at this time that more than once I heard tell of an old plan that was being disinterred by which Budapest and its surrounding lands should be reconstituted as a small republican city-state, with the rest of historic Hungary to be divided between its three neighbours. It is possible that in this way Benes thought he could at last realize that project for a Czech/Serb corridor at which he had hinted during our talks at Bruck.

Finally we brought forward the legislation necessary for dethroning the king. I found it infinitely humiliating that we should be forced to this by foreign pressure, and began to think of resigning my office.

It was not that I wanted in any way to facilitate the possible return of the Habsburgs, but according to law the hereditary kingdom of the Habsburg-Lorraine house rested on the Pragmatic Sanction: that is to say, on the mutual defence needs of the hereditary lands. The final break-up of these had made it worthless – indeed, damaging – for Hungary. Restoration would have been a disaster for us, especially with a ruler who would always have been looking over his shoulder at the Austrian border and, regardless of whether it would ever be possible, wondering when he could make the leap towards Vienna. Restoration would also have brought with it a built-in obstacle to achieving those good relations with our neighbours, which I knew to be not only essential, but also sensible, practical politics. I could therefore hardly bear, as a result of my office, having to be the mouthpiece by which Benes's constantly blackmailing tactics were conveyed to our government.

On the very day that parliament passed the dethronement law, Hohler came to see me and told me, in the name of the Council of Ambassadors, that this was not enough and that Benes would not withdraw his troops until the day we passed further legislation declaring the permanent exclusion from the throne of any Habsburg.

I told Hohler that this message came too late, as on that very day we had already satisfied the requirements of the Great Powers. If I had known only twenty-four hours before the text of the proposed new law could have been modified, but now that the law had been passed it would be impossible to reintroduce it into parliament, and too humiliating for the nation. The demand was also nonsense, for diplomatic promises, and even laws, were not for all time but could always be changed according to the pressures of the day.

I explained that for these reasons I had to reject this new and wholly unjustified demand, and that it was now the Council of Ambassadors' turn to deal with Benes.

At this Hohler seemed somewhat uncomfortable. He told me in confidence that I could not count on this, and that the Great Powers would not intervene even if Benes were to attack us. The best they could offer would be *'leurs bons offices'*, by which he meant their moral support. More than this they would not do, and I should know what this was worth.

So it seemed that we were now faced with the threat of another war, a war that our own chief of staff had declared we could not win. Terrible is the situation of a small country that stands alone. Somehow I had to find a solution that would avoid war and with it the ruin of my country.

Nevertheless, for the reasons outlined above I was not prepared to agree to further legislation. I therefore said that I would personally send a declaration to the Council of the Great Powers stating that Hungary would not come to any decision as regards the monarchy without previously obtaining the consent of the Great Powers who were represented by the Council – not, that is, of the Council itself but of each national Cabinet. This was, of course, little more than pointing out the reality of the situation, for without the consent of the Great Powers no Hungarian king would be able to keep his throne. It was to our advantage that, although the Great Powers were still bound to each other by the need to keep watch over the distribution of war loot, it was certain that sooner or later their interests would diverge and then all would depend on the views of the strongest. It would also mean, and this would be to our advantage, that Benes would not obtain all he wanted.

Hohler accepted my proposed solution, and so I, having obtained my government's approval, gave it to him in writing.

This document put an end to all the unholy complications brought about by the king's *putsch*. It is true that Benes's attempts at blackmail had not wholly come to an end, for he now claimed that we pay the cost of the Czechoslovak mobilization. This was going too far, even for the Council of Ambassadors, and was sternly rejected.

One evening during that awful time I received a strange communication.

It was very late. I had stayed all day at my desk in the Foreign Ministry; had I been anywhere else, anxiety would have been the end of me. I needed to be there so as to be at hand if any news came in on which I would have to take immediate action. I was there each day from morning until late at night, remaining long after my secretary and cabinet chief had gone home. It was sheer worry that kept me there, for it was always possible that one of our neighbours might have provoked a border incident and used this as a pretext to invade us. I had withdrawn the border guards from the frontier to lessen this danger. I had prevented our mobilization, as I have already mentioned; but the consequence was that had Benes or the Yugoslavs attempted a strike, I alone would have been responsible for our defenceless state, and I could never have borne to have had that on my conscience.

Those were terrible nerve-shattering hours.

It was one of those awful evenings – I fancy it was during the first week of the Czech mobilization that someone knocked at my door and entered. It was one of the older clerks who was doing duty on the switchboard. I asked what he wanted, and he told me that a highly confidential communication had come in from Vienna and that it was something he could tell only to me and face-to-face. I replied that we could not be more alone as we were the only two people in the building.

So he read me what had arrived.

Our chargé d'affaires in Vienna reported that he had received a visit from an individual who had declared his intention of killing Benes and had come to the Hungarian representative simply because he had no money with which to make his escape and so was asking us for a million crowns (due to inflation this was not a large sum in those days). The chargé d'affaires asked what he should do.

I shuddered as I heard this. All the same, I asked a few questions. Who was this man? Where did he come from? Did they know him?

My clerk was unable to give me a proper answer. The message had been very cryptic. The name of the man had not been disclosed, which was not surprising; and all they had said was that he was a German-Moravian and a passionate supporter of the emperor, which is why he had decided to do this. He only needed the money to escape afterwards. Vienna asked only for one word: yes or no. Nothing else: but they wanted it at once. There was to be nothing in writing and so no trace of our complicity. But they wanted an immediate reply.

I made my decision at once. I said 'No!' and this was wired to Vienna that evening.

I tell this now not to represent myself as a Cato-like hero or as deserving a halo like the early Christians who, if struck on the right cheek, promptly proffered the left. Neither do I maintain that Benes owed his life to me. Few assassinations succeed where the assassin is not ready to lose his own life. And when they do succeed, like Caserio Princip and other fanatics, it is when they have no care for their own safety. We have seen recently that none of the attempts at killing Hitler have been successful because in each case the assassins tried to save their own skins, not that I thought of this at the time.

Although I at once rejected the proposal, it did flash through my mind how advantageous it would be for us if Almighty God, in his infinite mercy, were to remove Benes from this Vale of Tears. But somehow assassination is alien to the Hungarian character. In our entire history there has only been one instance of it, in the fourteenth century, when Kis-Károly, Carol the Small, of Naples had been crowned king by a group of hereditary magnates in the aftermath of the long-drawn-out disputes over the succession following the death of Lajos I and was killed by followers of the Queen Mother Erzsébet in February 1386. In other countries there have been countless instances, but not in Hungary. Maybe it is a sign of weakness, or a lack of fiery temper, or even an incapacity for hypocrisy. It is also possible that if one Hungarian becomes enraged with another for some political reason and rants about it loudly and without restraint, someone will get to hear about it – even if he imagines he has spoken out only in secret, and he will find himself arrested before further trouble can be made.

I repeat that I do not recount this so as to blow my own trumpet. I write it because it is true, and because it forms part of the picture of these troublesome times.

Later I found out who this mysterious would-be assassin was. He was a junior clerk who had tried to be many things in his life, including a private tutor and a dockworker, and who was an excitable and ambitious man. Restless and fanatic he seems to have ended his days in a lunatic asylum. I was told his name, but I have now forgotten it.

In drawing up the balance sheet of King Karl's mad adventure we must not lose sight of all the damage it did.

In foreign affairs it spoilt forever our relationship with the new states and put an end to any possibility of later understanding. It was due to the king's *putsch* that the 'Little *Entente*' was formed. Before that happened we had been on fairly good terms even though we had not signed treaties to prove it and we all still had complete freedom to act as we might wish. This had been clearly shown by our discussions in Marienbad. From then on, instead of having a friendly alliance with Austria and Czechoslovakia, we had to contend with the anti-Hungarian 'Little *Entente*' under the leadership of Benes. It was no longer possible for us to discuss mutual problems with each state individually, because all issues had to be submitted to all three, with the result that nothing ever got decided.

The *putsch* also caused great damage to the Hungarian army, which was then in the process of being reorganized. Many of our best and most experienced officers left the service because of their divided loyalties between the new oath to Horthy and their former oath to the king. Instead we found ourselves with a much less effective cadre, for very few of the new officers had had any wartime experience.

There were also divisions in all ranks of society. The Catholic lesser clergy and most of the great landowners, and those with average sized estates, became Legitimists. This was especially true in western Hungary. The clergy hoped, through the influence of Queen Zita, to obtain important places in the hierarchy of the Church, while the aristocrats, with only a few exceptions, refused to accept any public duties, thus aping the example of the French Legitimists, when Louis-Philippe, Napoleon III and the Third Republic came to power after the fall of the Bourbons. The young Hungarians of noble families went even further. The French at least were willing to serve in the army or as diplomats, because they believed that thereby they were serving their country rather than its present government. The young Hungarian aristocrats, on the other hand, stopped short of this and, because they were the most talented of their generation, had command of other languages, were in better financial circumstances and had more knowledge of the world, and were therefore at that time the most suited to a diplomatic career, their abstention had a most unhappy effect on our representation abroad. By taking this attitude they also did damage to themselves and, in their idleness, found little else to do but amuse themselves gambling and drinking – and not a few ruined themselves doing it.

Our immediate loss was the Burgenland. As I have already written, the Venice Agreement stipulated that, until the plebiscite that was finally to establish our new borders, our armed forces would remain there under the command of General Ferrario. But after Lehár had led them away to Budapest with his lies, they had all dispersed and had been replaced by foreign troops, mostly Italian *carabinieri*, and this had made the locals believe that Hungary had abandoned them. Although the plebiscite still went well in and around Sopron, the modifications of the proposed new frontier, according to the famous *Lettre d'Envoi* for which we had hoped after Venice, were now lost to us. Instead of a rational border which would have been much to our advantage, we found ourselves bound to accept the nonsensical rearrangement of the frontier lands as occupied two years later by Austria, which was to prove so much to the detriment of the local inhabitants.

I do not hold poor King Karl personally responsible for all this. He was a naïve man: weak as putty in the hands of those who wanted to obtain power through him. Truly responsible were those who turned his head with news which they knew not to be true; who were well aware of the realities of the situation in the country; and who, as experienced politicians, could not have failed to understood the ruin that restoration would have brought with it.

They were the real culprits, and no amount of justification can ever absolve them of their guilt.

↫ Chapter Seven ↬

The king's adventure was over, and less dramatic times followed. Nevertheless, I had plenty to do. There were so many documents I had to study and much I had to store in my memory that, for days at a time, I would be at my desk from morning to night, often until as late as ten or eleven o'clock. The Burgenland crisis and the king's *putsch* had meant that for over two months decisions on every essential measure had been postponed, and so speed was vital to clear up the backlog.

Our first task was to establish our embassies abroad. This had already been started before, but now we had to decide about two of the most important – London and Washington. There were also a number where our ambassadors had resigned after the king's *putsch* and where new men had to be found.

This was also the time for our first discussions with the Soviet Union over the release of 26,250 Hungarian prisoners of war. The other ranks had been sent home in 1919 and 1920, but the officers had not yet been released. An agreement in principle had been reached by the Teleki government, but no details had been decided. We had to make contact through the Soviet Embassy in Vienna. After much discussion we finally reached agreement in Riga. If I remember rightly it was on the basis of nine to one – nine of our officers for every one of those Soviet soldiers who had been thrown into prison after the fall of the Communist regime in Budapest. Although some of these – ten or twelve, I fancy – who had been given long or short prison terms, the majority had been condemned to death. I was much relieved that these men had been saved and would be able to take up a normal life again in Russia because I am, and always have been, opposed to the death penalty for political offences. Freedom of opinion is a basic human right, and although it may be justified to deprive a man of his liberty for the sake of public order, I consider it barbaric to deprive him of life. That can never be a matter of justice: only of political revenge.

It was at this time that we signed the peace treaty with America. This was done with much ceremony. We gathered at the American Embassy, which was then situated in the town house of the Széchenyi family on Andrássy Street. The treaty document had been prepared on a splendid sheet of parchment and was signed by the American ambassador and myself. The seals were applied, and it was this part of the ceremony that revealed how backward the old European countries could seem, compared with the technical advances of the New World.

First we had to melt the sealing wax, which was not easy as the seal itself was the size of a pocket-watch, and this meant that the wax had to be stirred while being heated so as to remain fluid. Khuen-Hédervary did the stirring with exemplary zeal, but even so the first two attempts were unsuccessful, and the wax had to be re-heated again and again until the deed was finally done. Not so the Americans who produced a clever little machine that was just placed on the document and, in one second, the Stars and Stripes and the American eagle were stamped on the page.

I was somewhat ashamed of our old European backwardness, all the more so as there were several American reporters there who took photographs throughout the ceremony and who seemed to find our archaic methods infinitely comical[112].

When the signing was over this important event was brought to an end with a number of impressive speeches declaring that from then on everlasting peace would reign between our two countries. These were not empty words, for we all believed it.

At that time nobody could imagine that the day would come when a Hungarian foreign minister would be mad enough to declare war on the most powerful country in the world[113].

Our most serious problem in appointing new ambassadors lay in deciding who should represent us in London and Washington.

I would have preferred to have György Festetics for London. His mother had been a daughter of the Duke of Hamilton, and so he had many relations in England. We had served together when I had been sent to England, and he was a highly experienced man with very sound judgment. Unfortunately, he would not accept the post. Despite this, I remained on good terms with his father who, even after the Legitimist *putsch*, continued to support my efforts. As it was, I found myself obliged, for want of a better man, to appoint László Szapáry, the former governor of Fiume, an ex-diplomat who was now quite elderly. At first he did his work well, but after a while declined into senility, fell in love with a young typist and started to neglect his work. He had to be recalled; but this happened after my time.

My choice for Washington was László Széchenyi. It was true that he had never held any official post but, as his father had been ambassador in Berlin for many years and his brother Dénes had been the last Austro-Hungarian ambassador in Denmark, he had grown up in an atmosphere of diplomacy. László was a realist and had a steady nerve. He had often been in the United States, which he knew well, and his wife was Gladys Vanderbilt, of the family of railway millionaires. For me this was a most important point in his favour since it would make a great deal of difference to the style of our embassy if it could rely on the support of her brothers' millions.

I could not admit this at the time, for Gladys was immediately suspicious that her husband had been chosen because of her. This, of course, was true; but it was not only because she was rich.

Gladys Vanderbilt was not only very beautiful she was also one of the most intelligent women I have ever met. She had a good heart, and in spirit she had become remarkably Hungarian. Even if she had not had a penny of her own she would still have been a wonderful support for her husband. After long correspondence the appointment was finally agreed; and in this László's elder brother Dénes was a great help, for together we explained to her that her husband would have been chosen even if she were not his wife. Her last worry was that her husband had no experience in office matters, but this was resolved when I assured her that the highly professional János Pelényi would remain with him in Washington until Széchenyi had fully learned his trade.

Pelényi was indeed a great help. He had gone to America at the beginning of 1920, officially as a delegate of the Protestant church, but with semi-official diplomatic status. He had an exceptional brain and a huge capacity for work. Before 1914 he had been consul in Cleveland. Just before war was declared he had become engaged to a charming but penniless American girl, and it was a measure of her sympathetic character that she waited for him until he was able to return after the war had ended.

When I first took office I had wanted to appoint him as counsellor at our Washington embassy, with the rank of head of mission. There was, however, just one serious obstacle: what would the man live on? America was a very expensive country, and the pay was not enough for a man with a family to support. As it stood, he could not possibly accept the appointment. I wanted to establish a special rate of pay for Pelényi and so discussed his promotion with Khuen-Héderváry before raising the matter with Nuber, whose job was to control all payments made by the foreign office.

I called him and told him what I proposed to do. Nuber demurred. I do not know if there may have been some old grudge between him and Pelényi dating back to the days when Nuber was consul-general in New York and Pelényi was his subordinate in Cleveland, but, whatever the reason, Nuber protested vehemently. He declared that it was impossible for anybody, no matter where he was posted, to get a higher salary than was due to his grade. I asked if he could get a supplement for the high cost of living? No, that was not possible. Nuber quoted all the official texts that prohibited such a proceeding. I retorted that is was his job to find a paragraph that would allow it, because such things can always be found if one really wants to do so. This only made Nuber even angrier.

The man's behaviour was quite improper and if I had not been restrained by my own sense of humour I would have become very angry too. As it was the scene was irresistibly comic: the little grey man jumping up and down with rage in the middle of the room and stamping on the floor with his tiny feet. He was like Chaplin doing a Red Indian war dance. He was throbbing with anger, huffing and puffing, sneezing and screaming, so much so that I almost burst out laughing. For a moment I left him to his stamping about and his rage and then said:

'Look, Mr Nuber, I must ask you a few questions. As a minister, do I have the right to give a man a special task and then remunerate him for his extra work and for the expenses entailed?'

'Why, of course ... yes ... but it isn't allowed ... it isn't allowed ... !' screeched the little man.

'Wait a moment, please. Do I have the right to establish a fixed expense allowance?'

'Why, yes, that too is possible ... but of course it isn't allowed!'

'All right. Look! I shall give Pelényi a special assignment. It will be to look after the well being of our immigrant workers in America, to help them maintain their Hungarian traditions and to visit them for this purpose whenever his other responsibilities permit. Therefore I authorize payment of the sum I have already mentioned, which will be paid from the secret fund and which will officially be granted for travel expenses.'

Little Nuber was so surprised he almost sat down on the parquet floor.

'You see? As I said before, one can find a legal way to do anything if one really wants to! And so now, Mr Consul-General, go back to your office, have the official documentation typed up so that I can sign the order in the morning.' When he was almost at the door, I called after him: 'Thank you very much for your excellent advice.'

It was a comic incident.

What was not so amusing was the silent resistance of the ministry's permanent staff who tried to sabotage everything that I proposed and every measure I put forward to modernize our methods and bring them into line with the spirit of the times. The administration as a whole was still rigidly following the methods of the Ballplatz[114] without having that ministry's ancient traditions. This was because most of the civil servants we employed now came from the lower grades of the old consular service or from other ministries.

The master spirit of the Ballplatz reactionaries was Kálmán Kánya, the minister's permanent adviser. He had also moved up from the consular corps having served in his youth in the Balkans – in Üsküb, if I remember rightly – and later in Mexico and other far distant posts. From here he managed to get transferred to the Foreign Ministry in Vienna, firstly in the personnel department and later was accepted into the diplomatic service itself. It is said that it was he who drafted the ultimatum to Serbia in 1914.

In the old civil service lists he appears as 'Herr von Kania'.

He was highly intelligent, with a vast knowledge of archives and historical events; but he was also spiteful and malicious, ambitious and vengeful. He loved to play at conspiracies. He financed confidential agents in Upper Hungary, in the lower Carpathians and in Yugoslavia, which would have been acceptable if he had not made the mistake of being personally in touch with them. He got himself into trouble over this more than once, for these informers were apt to turn to blackmail, and on one occasion his name was mentioned in a criminal trial in Bratislava. These activities he concealed from successive ministers because, in his view, such people were, like me, 'newcomers' who had not sprung from a lifetime in the Foreign Ministry and who were therefore categorized as dilettantes and interlopers here today and gone tomorrow. Such people should be told nothing. He, of course, would always be there and so everything must depend on him, and on him alone. Indeed, that is how it was; and he was feared by everyone.

As part of his Ballplatz luggage he brought with him all the old Great Power arrogance that had been such a feature of Austrian diplomacy. Such haughty self-sufficiency may have been justified in the time of the great Metternich but had later been no of help to the monarchy. This was now especially true for the small country Hungary had become. Kánya's hatred of the Serbs, his disdain for the Italians, and the superior attitude he adopted to all the newly formed central European states all stemmed from his time in Vienna. Nevertheless, he knew how to conceal his prejudices, at least in my time.

He was typical of the old-fashioned type of 'professional' diplomat in its most fossilized form. He was of the sort that thought of the conduct of foreign affairs as some sort of chess game. He brought all his skill and knowledge to bear on behalf of the white pieces, if he happened to be playing with them; but I am convinced he would have done just the same if he was playing instead with the black. He would regard his opponents' moves with complete detachment, just as if the matter in hand had no connection with flesh and blood but was merely an interesting variant of the skill of the game. In the past he had shown himself capable of being an excellent aide to a minister who was motivated by a strong patriotic feeling, for his knowledge and memory were invaluable. But these very qualities were a drawback in a position of power because his obsession with precedent and his eagerness to achieve little political successes obscured an understanding of our long-term interests and blotted out any clear sight of the greater national objectives, which should never be lost sight of when dealing with trivial day-to-day matters.

He would discuss every issue with the same detachment, whether it concerned the happiness or suffering of millions of his fellow men, as he would have approached an algebraic problem he had to solve to pass an examination.

Many years later, when Kánya had himself become foreign minister, someone asked my opinion of him. Half in jest I replied: 'Very able; but he would be just the same whether he did it in Japan or Hungary', which just about summed up both his qualities and his defects.

Kánya liked nobody, least of all Sándor Khuen. The problem was that, although Khuen-Héderváry was a loyal supporter of his, he had the disadvantage, in Kánya's eyes, not only of being a former member of the Ballplatz cadre but also in every respect a good man, well-meaning and devoid of ambition.

All the others in his immediate circle were treated as puppets whose every move was controlled by Kánya and who were scolded and tossed about as he saw fit. Sometimes he would reward one of his puppets with a sweetmeat and sometimes he would stamp on them; for he had the temperament of a sadistic slave driver.

Kánya's cautious reliance on precedent and tremendous capacity for hard work could have been of immense value to me, for his suspicious nature would have complemented my own great fault, of which I have never been able to rid myself, of being too trusting. Unfortunately, we never managed to come to a frank understanding and it was only at the end of my time in office that I discovered that he was my enemy.

Our first clash was characteristic of the relationship between us. This happened at the time the first representatives of the Nazi Party presented themselves in Hungary. They came in secret, and I was asked by the Archduke Albrecht to come to his house late one evening to meet them. It seems that they had been brought to the archduke by Gyula Gömbös.

Before deciding if I should go I asked Kánya for his opinion. He advised that I should. This turned out to be the first time that I discovered that Kánya was apt to have dubious acquaintances without telling me what he was up to. At that time, in 1921, Nazism was only just beginning to make itself felt and still seemed to be a relatively insignificant political party. Kánya told me that he had already been in contact with these two Germans, and that I should warn Gömbös not to negotiate with them himself because it was a foreign office affair in which he should not interfere. I hardly spoke to the Nazis at this meeting, but I did take Gömbös to one side and said what Kánya had asked me to say.

The next afternoon Sándor Khuen telephoned me and asked me to come to see him at the Kaszino Club on a matter of the utmost importance. I found Kánya with him, and although Kánya to a certain degree restrained himself, his voice trembled with rage as he accused me of having disclosed an official secret. It seemed that Gömbös had not heeded my instruction not to deal with the Germans himself but, perhaps out of wounded pride, had upbraided them, demanding an explanation as to why they had dealt with the Foreign Ministry and not solely with him. The Nazis, on their side, had reported all this to Kánya.

I was able to defend myself with a clear conscience for, as Gömbös had been sworn in as a Secretary of State, he too was bound by his oath of allegiance not to reveal state secrets. What I had told him was only what, as my official adviser, Kánya himself had asked me to say. After much argument Kánya calmed down and there crept into his voice a superior note of forgiveness tinged with a gracious and indulgent scorn such as one might use when telling a child who has been naughty to forget the matter.

It was just at this time that a political group calling itself the 'Awakening Hungarians' became active. Tibor Eckhardt, who was Secretary of State before Gömbös, now joined the opposition and headed the movement. The 'League of Revisions' also came into being then.

In my view both of these movements did considerable harm. We were still having quite enough trouble subduing the last vestiges of the 'White Terror', and I felt that the last thing we then needed was to have to cope with the harm that would be caused by a resurgence of racist theories. Personally I found it not unamusing that many of those who proclaimed the reawakening of the Hungarian race should themselves all seem to be of foreign descent: Swabians, Slovaks, or Serbs. There were certainly few real Hungarians in their ranks, apart from a few crackpots and some political scoundrels.

I felt especially strongly about the League of Revisions for which I could see no need and whose effect seemed likely to prove dangerously deleterious.

Something similar had been formed in France in the 1880s and had done much harm. There it had been called the 'League of Patriots' and its president had been a demagogue called Deroulède. One of its members had been that General Boulanger, who tried to make use of its declared aims for some ends of his own, although exactly what these were never became clear. The only certainty was that the League stood for *Revanche*.

The French government, however, did not stop at disapproval but after a few years took definitive action against it. Deroulède was arrested, and Boulanger killed himself as it was clear that he realized that he would find himself embroiled in a most serious international problem for the French government if he had been known to have fomented some kind of popular uprising which would inevitably have provoked German intervention. Both the government and the majority of the people desired nothing but peace, as they wisely knew that sooner or later *Revanche* would come, and all that was needed for it to be successful was the right political climate.

I had just the same feeling for the League of Revision. Firstly, I felt that agitation to revise the peace terms was superfluous. What need did we have to persuade ourselves, as choruses in opera are apt to do, that the mutilation to which our country had been subjected at Trianon had been both unjust and stupid? That was something no man in Hungary did not already know. To do this would have merely been to rub in our suffering and stir up unnecessary hatred. With human beings the urge to make peace takes some time to germinate, while *Homo sapiens* is always ready to hate. We saw this in 1914. Before the ultimatum to Serbia and the Russian declaration of war no one in Hungary hated either the Serbs or the Russians. On the contrary, after their gentlemanly conduct in 1849, the latter were if anything thought to be rather sympathetic. But in 1914, as a result of press propaganda, it took less than two weeks for an explosion of hatred, so much so that thousands rushed to enlist, even those who would not then have been called up. Such is the nature of the human animal. Find it in mobs, and the lust to kill is always there. Mankind seems to revel in killing.

Artificially to incite hatred is not only supererogatory in politics and foreign relations, it is also positively harmful.

Great nations, and even medium-sized ones, can always seek revision of frontiers by normal diplomatic means – if the political climate is favourable. No propaganda or previous jockeying for position is necessary, for if the right moment is chosen and there are good reasons for a change, then there is nothing to stop anyone from putting forward proposals for territorial adjustment. An example was furnished by Romania in 1912 during the second phase of the Balkan War. Before this no one had ever heard of Dobrudja, but when Russia lost patience with Bulgaria, Romania discovered that she had a claim to Dobrudja and, with a swift but bloodless attack, took it for herself. There have been other examples in more recent times. It is always possible to keep alive certain issues with propaganda abroad, but the acquisition of territory needs quiet patient work. No doubt it can be a help if the world gets to know about the existence of such a problem, but it is not until the world is convinced of injustice that redress can follow.

Propaganda, if too raucous, will always prove counterproductive.

The damage arises because in peacetime the nation that never stops menacing others and shouting about its grievances is at once labelled a disturber of the peace and blamed accordingly. Such behaviour is also stupid because it continually reminds others of the quarrel and strengthens their opposition. In the case of Hungary, it was especially senseless, for several million of our blood-brothers still lived in the neighbouring states, and it should have been obvious that their situation would become aggravated if there were too much noisy talk about revising the frontiers coming out of Budapest. I am convinced that we could have improved their situation if we had been able to suppress the irredentist clamour of the Hungarian people – not, perhaps, in my time but certainly later.

It was also counterproductive for the Hungarians still living outside our new borders because it strengthened them in the belief that very soon – tomorrow if not today and the day after tomorrow for sure – something would happen to change their situation. There developed among us an atmosphere of waiting for a miracle; and this made us neglect searching for a solution to problems which by their very nature could only be resolved in a time of peace that would favour the smooth running of our administrative machinery.

This noisy propaganda also did harm in a more general way. Success in foreign relations can only be achieved when the negotiator, be he the head of state or his foreign minister, has a complete knowledge of all the circumstances and can assess them coolly and objectively. The public can never know all the facts, and public opinion is always swayed by passion, never by reason and the best interests of the country.

It may sometimes be necessary to stir up passion, but only if action is to follow, as was the case with the Burgenland; but to go on doing so is a great mistake. If one particular hatred is allowed to become fixed in the public mind it can be like putting shackles on the politicians with the result that measures vital to the country's best interests cannot be passed since government is impossible without public support.

For Hungarians, the incessant poisoning of public opinion by irresponsible agitation can be especially dangerous. As I have already explained in some detail Hungarians, while always ignorant of foreign affairs and diplomatic strategy, are singularly receptive to martial slogans, revel in vociferous opposition and love to abuse those they believe to be their enemies. That old '*kuruc*' spirit that once cried out against the principle of Dualism[115] and manifested itself by always criticizing, always knowing better, and could earn popularity for anyone, providing he spouted enough nonsense, was now directed against our foreign policy. Just as during the first world war every small coffee-house had its 'Konrad' who knew best how every battle could have been won, now the times sprouted thousands more: Metternichs and Talleyrands of the coffee-houses, who, by alliances with Italy or England or even with Japan, won back all our lost provinces from the Carpathians to the Adriatic and fought bloody battles on the marble tables between the coffee and the cakes. All this, of course, without danger to themselves, for boasters are ever careful of their own skins.

Much of this came later, from the end of the 1920s to 1940, but this is when it all began. Although at the time I was not able to foresee clearly what was to come, I was already deeply worried and spoke to Bethlen about it.

He did not share my opinion, feeling that the Revisionist League would have little effect on foreign relations, as it was essentially only a social movement, far removed from government. In his view, it was vital that the nation should have its ideals, for without them it would become lazy and indifferent, and that therefore the revisionist movement would tend to keep patriotic feeling alive.

From Bethlen's point of view, this was all a matter of internal politics. I saw it differently, and this was the first time I found myself in disagreement with him. I let the matter drop, partly because of course it was still only an internal affair but also because the movement was still fairly insignificant then. In any case, for me there were other more important matters looming up. The international Conference of Genoa would soon be upon us, and I had to prepare for that.

This was to be the first international conference since the war at which all the countries of Europe would take part. As well as Hungary, there were the Turks, the Bulgarians, the Austrians and Germany; but, what was even more important, it was to be the first time that Soviet Russia had taken her place in the councils of Europe.

Facta, the prime minister of Italy, had been the moving spirit. The aims of the conference were somewhat vague. They included 'clarifying European questions' and, of course, 'peace'. These were mentioned in the official programme, and, as with such a generalized definition almost anything can be included, we had to prepare for every imaginable contingency. There was a great deal to learn, and a lot to discuss before the conference started.

Our delegation consisted of Bethlen and myself, with Khuen-Héderváry as foreign affairs expert; the economists Walko and Scitovszky; some secretaries and, of course, our master of shorthand, Fabro. I decided that we would need someone to handle the international press, so I took along György Ottlik, then *Times* correspondent in Budapest, and also invited Géza Herczeg. Both proved their worth to us.

We arrived sometime in March. We had reserved rooms in one of the luxury hotels in Nervi, just ten kilometres from Genoa. The garden was filled with marvellous palm trees and beyond them sparkled the dark-blue sea.

Our immediate task was to get to know everyone. At one of our first reunions we met the Marques Villa Uruttia, the Spanish ambassador in Rome. He was a most interesting-looking old gentleman who, with a long narrow face and long grey beard, could have been a portrait by El Greco come to life. Bethlen asked him how long he thought the conference would last, because he would have to go home in a week or ten days' time.

'Oh, dear!' laughed the Spanish marquis, his long yellow teeth glinting as he spoke. 'The general rule is that an international conference must last at least three weeks, otherwise the public would think we had nothing serious to talk about. And that is the worst that can be said of any diplomat!'

The old man proved right for, as I recall, it was not until the end of May that we returned home. Bethlen was unable to stay and went back after days, leaving me as head of our delegation.

My entire stay, as regards the conference discussions, was spent in hanging about. As we were such a small unimportant country, we were expected only to be part of some economic committee composed of specialist delegates – in our case Walko and Scitovszky – while my personal attendance was not required except at the infrequent meetings of the full conference.

However, it was extremely interesting to meet the various great men who represented the Great Powers, watch them at work and, if possible try to make use of them. It was also fascinating to watch what happened behind the scenes, especially when there was a clash of interests.

From this point of view, it was an extraordinary experience.

To start with our hosts: at that time the prime minister of Italy was Facta, an elderly but still strong man who was, of course, the conference's chairman. He wore his white hair cut short and, under his sharp eagle's nose, his long thick moustaches turned sharply up like the tusks of a wild boar. He would look around with a belligerent air and had a most military look. To me, he was the image of our own retired sergeants, all frightening moustaches and staring eyes. As it happened, he was of a singularly peaceable disposition. He came from a middle-class family in one of the small towns of the Romagna and had never in his life been in the army. He had a most merry disposition, was full of good humour, enjoyed excellent health and thought nothing was desperately important. I am sure he never hurt a fly.

The Italian foreign minister, *sua eccelenza il signore* Schanzer, was the exact opposite of Facta. He was always restless, nervous, running about full of worry. By origin, he was a Jew from Trieste who had escaped to Italy before the war. He was a slight skinny man, yellow-skinned and gaunt of face, which made me fancy he must suffer from some stomach disorder. He wore a long sparse brown beard, and above his forehead he had a shock of rebellious curly hair. This unusual mop of hair perhaps symbolized his irredentist past. He was always rushing about.

The other Italians were Visconti-Venosta, the elegant chief secretary of the conference who wore brightly-coloured waistcoats and was never seen without piles of documents under each arm; Romano Avezzano, a Sicilian who rarely spoke and who later became Italian ambassador in Washington; and another man whose name I have forgotten, who was then minister of agriculture, who was so immensely fat that he seemed wondrously suitable to represent that land of plenty and good husbandry. There was also another whom it gave me particular pleasure to see again. This was Prince Durazzo. We had been good friends in our youth. He had served in Vienna and later in the consulate in Budapest. It made us both happy to meet again. His beautiful old family palace stood on the Corso in Rome. I have heard to my regret that it was destroyed by bombing in the last war like so many other precious and irreplaceable things. He was a great help to me. For a short time he became minister of education but died soon after. We Hungarians lost much by his death.

None of these gentlemen, not even Facta and the excellent Signor Schanzer, was as important as Contarini, who had become as omnipotent in the conduct of Italian foreign affairs as had Holstein in Berlin after the departure of the Iron Chancellor, Bismarck. Like Holstein he had not started life as a diplomat but had been a civil servant, remaining always in the background. It was he who had masterminded the Italo-Yugoslav peace agreement, which was signed a few months after the Genoa conference.

At Genoa he was not part of the official Italian delegation and only came there every few days. Although his name might have suggested a Venetian origin, he came in fact from Sicily.

He was so busy that it was not easy to get in touch with him; yet, firmly fixed as he was at the centre of Italian politics, he was the one man I really needed to talk to. I wanted to raise with him the possibility of obtaining Italian help in improving relations between Hungary and Romania. Contarini was matter-of-fact and laconic. His appearance was insignificant, being short and dark and no different from hundreds of his compatriots. He might have been the pastry-cook at the corner shop or the mayor of a small town or merely a clerk. There was nothing remarkable about his appearance; and it was only when he opened his mouth that one could sense the tightly woven chain of logic that was so characteristic of him. He spoke only Italian, saying that he knew no other language. This was, of course of great advantage to him whenever he needed the services of an interpreter, since the latter could be held responsible for any misunderstandings that might occur. Luckily, I had enough Italian to discuss our problem – even if it was full of grammatical mistakes – and, as a result, Italy did try her best with Bucharest, although in the end it came to nothing.

And then there were the others. First of all the English – or rather just Lloyd George, for his colleagues did not greatly signify as far as we were concerned, and so I hardly remember them. I am sure they were all excellent men, but Lloyd George was such a dominant personality that all those around him were just pale shadows in comparison.

I have no need to describe what he looked like. Everyone knows his face from pictures and caricatures, with his long grey hair and short moustache. He was a Welshman, and it is in Wales that the blood of those original inhabitants of the British Isles flows at its purest. He was short and lively and a wonderful speaker, quite free of that sonorous spouting of slogans so typical of Hungarian orators. He spoke in short pithy sentences, at times sharp and cruel, at others full of humour and unexpected similes. He was like a conjurer who produces from his sleeves a myriad-coloured glass ball, live rabbits or a gold watch. He could do whatever he liked with his audience. At the first general meeting at Genoa he spoke with such optimism and so wittily that all his listeners came away happy and laughing and repeating his jokes. A few days later there was a press conference at which the principal item was to be a statement by Lloyd George. Everyone hurried to it, thinking what a joy it would be to hear him again. Lloyd George, however, perhaps regretting the optimistic impression he had given before, now painted such a tragic future for Europe that they all came away teeth chattering and deadly pale. He was indeed unsurpassed as a word-spinner.

He was not so very popular with his own countrymen, for the English regarded him as unreliable and secretive. With a knowing look they would say of him: 'Of course, he's Welsh!', meaning he was a 'rogue' or 'a sly customer' or both; and anyhow hadn't he managed to get rid of Asquith, who was not only prime minister but also head of his own party, and then put himself in his place? After the war he had called an immediate election and, by brandishing the slogan 'Hang the Kaiser', had himself elected with a huge majority. Once in office, however, the Kaiser was never mentioned again, and he even did his best to curb any feeling of hatred for the Germans. It was no wonder people were suspicious of him. They were also afraid of him, and the wonder really is that for many years he could do what he liked with the English.

In the general assembly hall our table was close to his. Since I had almost nothing to do I would draw caricatures, and it was from these sketches that I was able, a year and a half later, to work up the album of portraits from the conference that was to be published by Rózsavölgyi[116]. Lloyd George, of course, saw what I was doing when I was drawing him and winked at me with a wicked smile.

I very much wanted to meet him, and I think it was Count Mensdorff, the Austrian delegate, who introduced us. Mensdorff was an old acquaintance with whom I had many interests in common and who had been Austro-Hungarian ambassador in London for many years. I asked Lloyd George when he could receive me, and he replied: 'Anytime! Anytime! With great pleasure.' But nothing came of it, and it seemed that to obtain an audience with him was almost impossible. I even tried using the good offices of the sweet and pretty Mrs Snowden who, although no longer young, was still very attractive and good-hearted. Her husband later became minister for economic affairs in London and received a knighthood[117], so she became Lady Snowden. She often went round to see Lloyd George in the evenings to sing Gaelic songs to him, and it was she who persuaded him to promise to see me. All I had to do was to talk to his secretary immediately; but although I went several times to the villa where Lloyd George was staying, I only met with excuses. He was not there; he was busy just then; I should come back on the following day or, better, the day after. This went on for three weeks, until one day, when I was again sitting in front of the secretary's desk and he was again saying that no, his boss could not see me. As I was preparing to leave, a door opened behind me, and Lloyd George came in. He was wearing a dressing gown and slippers and, as soon as he saw me, started across the room to greet me.

'Oh, it's you,' he exclaimed, smiling. 'I'm so glad to see you at last! I've been anxious to meet you!' He then took me into the neighbouring drawing-room and started at once, with great charm, to talk as if we had been close friends. He agreed with everything I said, approved everything I suggested. Of course, I realized that it did not matter to him whether or not we obtained the Declaration we wanted promulgated at the conference[118], but it did matter to him that he should know all about it. He escorted me to the door when I left, and I seem to remember him patting me on the shoulder. He had a fascinating and altogether delightful way with him.

The story of this Declaration also had its comic side. We prepared the text while Bethlen was still with us and took it at once to show to the French delegate, Barthou.

The essence of our proposed document was that the Conference should declare the vital importance of the newly-formed states, not only keeping to the letter of their signed agreements as to the treatment of their ethnic minorities but also acting at all times in the spirit in which they had been written.

Barthou was a small man, very swarthy of countenance, and wore a beard and moustaches. He received us with marked coldness.

Bethlen started by explaining our proposed declaration. He spoke matter-of-factly and without artifice or embellishment. Barthou roundly rejected it. Then it was my turn to speak. Knowing something of the French mentality and also of their political vocabulary, I began by saying that we were turning first to France as the glorious home of Liberty. I spoke of the French devotion to Reason and Justice and how the small nations of Europe would always turn to France as the traditional Guardian

of Justice; and when I used the words '*La France*' or '*La gloire*',
I would pronounce them with the same enthusiastic inflection as
would any Frenchman.

Little by little Barthou came round completely. He now
answered that yes, that was something quite different; yes, that
would be possible even though I had only repeated exactly what
Bethlen had already said, although spiced with a French-tasting
sauce.

'Now,' he said finally, 'Let us draw up the text!'

I sat down at the desk, and he dictated. And what he dictated
was a much better and more resolute Declaration than ours had
been. When we parted he promised that he would ensure that the
Conference accepted it.

Well, the lesson, I suppose, is that if one is to confer successfully with foreigners, it is essential to know their way of thinking
and be able to put oneself in their place.

Our Declaration would have been made if the conference
had not broken up. The French always keep their word in such
matters, and at that time they were the arbiters in any question
concerning Europe.

There was no doubt, too, that the French delegation was by far
the strongest intellectually at the conference. There was the
famous Barrère, who had been ambassador in Rome for many
years, had a profound knowledge of Italy and whose influence
had been decisive when Italy had abandoned her alliance with us
in 1915 and joined the Allies. He was like one of those French
knights who used to roam the world in search of adventure. He
had the head for it too. With his boldly jutting aquiline nose and
cold grey eyes, I could well imagine him, strong and broad-
chested in breastplate and helmet, as one of those bold sons of
France who once carved out principalities in the Near East and
eloped with queens.

There was also Hanotaux, several times a minister and one of
the most eminent members of the Académie Française. He was
very well-meaning, clever and intelligent. It was always a pleasure to talk with him, for he radiated ancient French culture. I
became good friends with Hanotaux, who was my sincere

champion throughout my tenure of office, and I always think of him with much tenderness.

The German delegates I only met on an official level.

One was Herr Wirth, the chancellor, an insignificant philistine who counted for little even in his own country; and the other was the then foreign minister, Rathenau. Most of the latter's life had been spent in big business, and he had acquired an immense fortune. He had a good knowledge of art and was a noted collector. The Kaiser had often used him on missions abroad. Rathenau's appearance was striking. The elegance of his tall figure was accentuated by clothes of such high quality as to give him an almost exaggerated distinction. His face was remarkable, with rather thick lips that gave him a Negroid look. He was bald, with a pointed skull, and his skin had a darkish-green tinge. With his small tapering beard, he was like a half-Mongol, half-Jewish Mephistopheles. He seemed to be able to speak all languages, although every one with some sort of foreign inflection, and his manner of speaking was so modulated and honeyed, so sad and nostalgic, that he might have been a reformed devil.

At the opening session Rathenau made a most moving speech, describing Germany's poverty in the darkest terms. It was indeed a beautiful and affecting oration, but I must confess to have been somewhat surprised that the man who described all this misery in such heart-rending terms, did so wearing a pearl the size of a hazelnut in his tie, diamond cufflinks and a quantity of rings set with precious stones.

The real sensation of the Genoa Conference, however, was the Russian delegation. This was so not only so for the general public but also for the participating Great Powers, all of whom secretly hoped that the Russian presence at the conference would result in untold economic benefits for themselves.

Even today in 1945 I remember their first appearance as clearly as if it had been yesterday.

We had all been invited to meet the Russians at a soirée at the palace that housed the town hall. Everyone, even the most important, was there – including all the big stars of the conference, Lloyd George, Barthou, Wirth and Rathenau, as well as the lesser planets and their moons, although to these the multitude of guests in that huge palace paid little attention. That evening everyone was waiting for the Russians to appear. By ten in the evening the crowd was immense, and everybody was competing for the best places to watch the arrival. We all knew that the Russians had arrived that evening, were already installed at Santa Margherita and would soon appear.

The palace of the Municipio, like all the palaces of Genoa, was built on the hillside. Its courtyard was a closed square, surrounded by galleries on several floors, and here were crowded, head to head, thousands of guests, mainly women, very much like an evening at La Scala, Milan, with all the boxes filled for a gala opening. Everyone waited tense and determined, wondering what on earth the Russians would be like. How would they be dressed? Many fancied they would be wearing Russian tunics, workman's clothes or striped *kozak* shirts such as Tolstoy had donned in old age. All this eager speculation just added spice to the waiting.

I was on the first floor. Even though I was flattened against a pillar it was an excellent place for from there I had a direct view of the main door, the marble-floored courtyard and beyond it, facing the entrance, the monumental double stairway leading up to the staterooms. The marble court was empty as everyone was in the galleries.

By now it was almost midnight, and people were beginning to think the Russians would not come after all.

Suddenly they appeared, and a murmur of astonishment ran through the crowd. Each and every one of the Russians wore well-cut tails, white waistcoat and a wonderfully starched boiled shirt. They wore top hats and looked like fashion plates.

And yet they did not in any way give a bourgeois impression. They looked merry and proud and full of self-confidence. They marched in quickly, as if about to lay siege to the capitalist world that was awaiting them so eagerly upstairs. At their head was Chicherin, silk hat tilted slightly over one eye, who from time to time seemed to be exchanging jokes over his shoulder with the others as they moved swiftly without pausing for an instant, feet stamping defiantly, before passing out of sight behind the columns of the staircase. It all lasted only for a few seconds, yet it was unforgettable.

Two or three days after this, the first general assembly of the conference was held in the great hall of the Genoa Stock Exchange.

Hanging in a frame on one of the walls was a money-draft of Christopher Columbus. It may be that it is still there, because good old Columbus never repaid it; if so, it was a lucky chance since it gave a most particular spice to this, the world's oldest money market. The chairman welcomed the Russian delegation, and Chicherin replied.

He spoke in excellent French and with much wit. He praised Russia and her riches. With a finely ironic smile he started to list what treasures she possessed, what petrol, coal, vast forests, huge quantities of iron ore, copper, platinum, malachite, cotton and the best wheat in Europe. All these, he said, existed in vast quantities in Russia, and all were available to any country who would agree to buy them. He knew well that the capitalist world of business was practically drooling at the mouth to hear what he had to say.

After this, or maybe at the next session, followed discussion of the conference's organization, the language to be used for the minutes and the seating of the various delegations. Chicherin spoke on every subject. On the question of languages he insisted that Russian must always be included. As regards the delegations, he objected to the Poles, the Romanians or any delegates from the Baltic States being admitted to the same sessions as the Russians since, in his view, they represented territories stolen from Russia, and it was therefore offensive to him to be obliged to sit down with them. He even objected to Japan.

And, whatever he said, he said with the same ironic smile, partly to vex the assembly and partly to underline the Russian position. He knew perfectly well that the conference would not defer to him, but in his view this was not important provided he could cause the maximum amount of confusion and irritation to the so-called victorious powers.

Chicherin was always so surrounded by others at the meetings that I could never get near him. However, some three days later the king of Italy invited all the heads of the various missions to lunch on one of his battleships, and on this occasion I did finally get to meet him. Several small tables had been set up on the deck and by luck I found myself seated at the same one as Chicherin. He was seated one place away from me. I had good reason to want to talk to him as I needed to discuss the matter of the exchange of Russian and Hungarian prisoners of war, which had once again reached a deadlock.

He gave me a visiting card on, upon which he had scribbled a few words, and told me to present it whenever I could come to the Hotel Ferrari, which the Russians used as a base during the day as Santa Margherita was too far away.

Of course I went as soon as possible.

At the entrance there were three or four robust, thickset men, obviously bodyguards, broad-shouldered, strong, and well built. I gave them the card, but they did not let me in straight away. One of them disappeared up the steps of the hotel, while I walked up and down on the pavement outside. After a few minutes the man came back and gestured to me to follow him. When I arrived at the first floor someone again looked at Chicherin's card. The same person now conducted me to another room where a very old woman was sitting at the window. She too studied what was written on the card and then looked me over carefully. After apparently inspecting me for some seconds she waved me to a door at the back of the room. I went in. Chicherin was sitting alone beside a long table. He gave me a perfunctory handshake and then walked straight to the door by which I had come in and turned the key in the lock. Then he did the same at another door leading out from the back of the room. It was only after having shut us both in that he made me sit down and we began to talk.

He had very winning, almost hearty, manners. Quickly, and in a very few words, we agreed everything to do with the exchange of our prisoners and how the process should be restarted without further hindrance. When this had been settled he asked: 'Is it true the Hungarians hate the Russians?' and when I said it was not, he went on to say it would have been quite natural if we did since it had been the Russian army which had finally brought to an end the Hungarian fight for freedom[119]. I replied that this had left no resentment in Hungary, for Paskievich, after our surrender at Világos, had treated the defeated Hungarians with great fairness, and that everyone had known that it was not he but Austrian absolutism that had been responsible for the tragedy that ensued. In contrast to this, the Russian army had behaved correctly and even, in some places, left kindly memories behind them. To illustrate this, I told him an anecdote of those days.

In 1849 a Russian officer had arrived with a detachment of soldiers at a property belonging to my grandmother at Száss Bányica. Strict discipline was maintained all the time the Russians were billeted there, and cash was paid for everything they consumed.

When they left a few days later, the officer was standing with the overseer beside some rose bushes in front of the house. He asked who owned the property and, being told it was my grandmother, said:

'So it belongs to a woman?' Then he picked a rose, placed it in the lapel of his tunic and mounted his horse. As he rode away he called back: 'Tell your mistress that a Russian officer steals nothing from a woman except flowers!'

Chicherin was much pleased by this story, every word of which was true.

After that, we turned to more general questions, especially that of Bessarabia, where there were a number of special problems, some of which affected Transylvania. Chicherin spoke with much impartiality and understanding, and we parted in full agreement: so much so that I was left with the feeling that much good would come from it if we could have established full diplomatic relations with Soviet Russia. For many reasons this was then impossible.

During my first days in Genoa I had naturally paid visits to the delegations of the 'Little *Entente*' countries. Only Ionel Bratianu had come personally to see me at Nervi to return my visit: the others just left visiting cards. I did not have anything to discuss with Bratianu, for the relations between Hungary and Romania were then so strained that it would have been pointless to raise any specific question on the spur of the moment. We exchanged polite generalities only. Bratianu was very different from Benes. I at once felt him to be both calm and sincere, without a hint of deviousness. One felt in him the character of an autocrat whose will was law. This was the only occasion when we had the opportunity to talk until, five years later, in Bucharest when I went to arrange my Romanian citizenship[120]. Then his behaviour was such as to confirm the good opinion of him I had formed at Genoa.

I also made some other contacts with some of the Swedes, Austrians and Turks. The Turkish ambassador knew all about the cultural and economic agreement I had made in 1916 in Istambul and so had confidence in me. We agreed to share any useful information that might come our way. The Turk was especially interested in the English for it was suspected in Ankara that England might encourage Greece to attack Turkey. Several times during the conference I was able to tell him things he wanted to know, and he did the same for me. It was only the small change of diplomacy but useful all the same.

Although it is not really relevant to my story, I feel I must relate a ludicrous incident concerning Fabro. He came to Genoa not as the official stenographer of our Foreign Ministry but as the correspondent of *Pester Lloyd*. In this capacity he was also present at the king of Italy's lunch and afterwards sent off an account of it to his newspaper. The cost of any telegrams he might send had been included in his fixed expense allowance, and so he was anxious to keep the text to the minimum. He wanted to indicate that there had been no speeches at the lunch and so, in an odd mixture of German [sic] and Hungarian, he wrote the laconic message '*Déjeuner tost'os*': i.e., a lunch with formal toasts. Unfortunately, it was written incorrectly and arrived as '*trost'os*', which the editor took as German for 'inconsolable'. They wired back: 'Why inconsolable?' 'Why did he say that?' 'What had happened?' And so once again poor Fabro found himself forced to pay for an expensive telegram of explanation which would not have been necessary if he could have brought himself to send a few more words in his first message.

I did not meet any Italians who were not present officially at the conference because of the long-established diplomatic etiquette that such meetings do not take place while in foreign countries on this sort of mission. The rule is, of course, made to be broken but only in private.

An acquaintance of Hungarian origin, Stefánia Türr, offered to invite Mussolini to Genoa if I wanted to meet him. I did not accept, although I have often regretted it, as it would have been a most interesting experience, especially for me as a writer. However, I already held in such detestation the movement for 'racial purity' in Hungary – and, indeed, abhorred the thought of any organization that inspired hate – that I did not then feel any inclination to meet a leader who professed principles of that sort.

Despite diplomatic etiquette, I did make one exception in getting to know an Italian politician unconnected with the conference. This was Nitti, the former prime minister who had written a book entitled *Europa senza pace – Europe Without Peace –* in which he had been frankly critical of the peace terms that were imposed at Versailles and had shown much sympathy for the Hungarian people. I wanted to thank him for this; and I also thought it would prove useful to my country if I were to be in touch with him since there were many signs that the weak Facta government would soon fall and that, when it did, Nitti would be recalled to office.

I used the Easter holiday for this. Through our embassy in Rome I received a message from Nitti asking me to visit him at his flat in Naples on – if I am not mistaken – Easter Saturday. I told the secretary of the conference that I would be leaving for Rome that weekend. Luckily, the wedding of our ambassador's daughter to a Prince Antei-Maffei had been arranged to take place just after the holiday.

On Good Friday I boarded the evening express, and even though it went straight through to Naples, I left the train at Rome, thinking that if my movements were being watched by the police this is what they would put in their report. After a swift breakfast at the embassy I then left again, without any luggage, and took a taxi back to the station. Early in the afternoon I was in Naples.

Nitti lived up a very steep street on a hill in the centre of the city.

His looks took me by surprise. I had expected a typical Neapolitan of the Mediterranean type, black-haired, olive-skinned and the face of an eagle. Instead I found a rather small man, fair-haired, with a red face and a flat nose. His eyes, sunken deep in fat, radiated goodwill and great intelligence. He welcomed me heartily.

We talked for a long time. He assured me that he would help us as soon as he once again found himself at the head of affairs, which he was certain would be in a few weeks' time. I returned to Rome in the early evening. Unfortunately, those two hours are the only memories I have of him since when the Facta government did fall it was not Nitti who succeeded him in office but the March on Rome . . . and Mussolini.

The wedding of Count Nemes's daughter was held on the Monday or Tuesday after Easter in the church of Santa Maria della Victoria which since the war had become Rome's most fashionable place of worship. The ceremony was attended by hosts of princes and princesses all bearing names famous in history – such as Doria, Colonna, Aldobrandini and Borghese – and among them I found one or two acquaintances from my previous visit. Since I was neither a relation nor a close friend, and a heretic to boot, I placed myself discreetly near a side altar, where I was in no one's way and unlikely to cause a scandal by not taking part in all the genuflexion and crossings of oneself going on around me.

I have no idea whether all the wedding guests were devout churchgoers, for they gave the impression of merely attending a social gathering as secular as a charity concert. It may have been a fashionable church, but I personally did not find it conducive to worship. Above the altar there were no pictures but only reliefs in white marble by Bernini with various saints receiving their stigmata. Bernini may have been a wonderful artist, but his work here approaches the rococo, with its pretty female angels gracefully inflicting the five wounds with needle-sharp marble arrows and sadistic little smiles. All the while the saints swoon in ecstasy. The whole object makes a most perverse impression[121].

Afterwards I returned to Genoa, where the waiting in the wings went on for me as before. Discussions behind the scenes there were, for the most part with the Russians, as the English, French and, I assume, even the Americans hunted for their own economic advantage: all matters which did not concern me. If I had not had to stay for our Declaration I would have left long before the end.

I used to spend much of my time enjoying the art treasures in which Genoa is so rich. I saw the Holy Grail in the cathedral of San Lorenzo – the thick green glass chalice sanctified by the blood of our Saviour – and the onyx dish upon which Salome received the head of John the Baptist. Both of these dated from the early Renaissance and were set in gold and enamel, and whether or not we believe the legends, the objects themselves are so beautiful that discussion of their origin is beside the point. I also went to many privately owned palaces where I saw countless Van Dyk portraits made during that artist's protracted stay in the city. The acme of perfection was a Cellini amphora that I saw in the Doria palace, to which I had been taken by Prince Durazzo. Only the podium of the Esztergom Calvary comes anywhere near this unique masterpiece.

I also saw a living and walking masterpiece. This was the widow of the world-famous tenor Enrico Caruso, who had died only a few months before. She was then living at the Excelsior Hotel in Genoa. Every day, dressed in the deepest mourning – white, like the queens of France – the widow would take a walk along the terrace that stretched the full length of the hotel façade and from which there was an unsurpassed view of the city and the harbour far below. Her wonderful figure, enhanced by the soft folds of her dress, and her brown hair garlanded with a laurel wreath of white velvet, reminded me of a Greek statue, although none of the marble women on the Parthenon were more stunningly beautiful than she. She made a lovely sight as she walked up and down before the backdrop of the blue sea and the blue sky, with all the majesty appropriate to the wife of the king of all artists. Many people would climb up to this mountain terrace just to watch her and admire; and this was made all the easier since it was known that the sorrowing widow of Caruso was a very punctual lady, and that it was always at the same hour and for the same time – between midday and one o'clock – that she would appear in front of the drawing-room window and walk up and down. If it rained she would take her walk inside the great hall of the hotel; and never, in her great sadness, would she look at another person or talk to anyone. But anybody who turned up a little early for lunch at the Excelsior could see and admire her; and so many did this that it made good publicity for the hotel and perhaps was good too for the lovely widow herself.

And so the days passed.

At last, I think it was towards the end of May, Facta asked me to lunch. He lived to the west of the city at San Pier d'Arena in a villa built into the side of a cliff that jutted out onto the sea.

There were quite a number of guests at the luncheon, mostly Italian politicians as well as a few diplomats. We had been invited for half-past one; but we waited and waited and still did not get to table because *il signore* Schanzer, the foreign minister, had not turned up. They telephoned. Secretaries bustled in and whispered things in Facta's ear. Then they bustled out again. Something had gone wrong – and everyone felt it.

Finally, at half-past two, we sat down to eat – without the minister. His place, next to me, remained empty. It was on the hostess's left. Just across the table sat Signora Schanzer. She was a plump good-natured woman, the image of old Mrs Adler who had an antique shop in Kolozsvár when I was a law student. The poor lady looked very worried.

We finished the soup, and also a most delicious fish.

Then the door opened, and in came Schanzer: he was deathly pale. Uncertainly he stumbled to his chair and sank down as if he had just marched fifty miles on heavy flat feet. Facta and all the other Italians plied him with questions, but the only reply they got was a few broken words: '*Tutto e perdutto . . . una catastrofa . . . la conferenza si rotta . . .*' – 'all is lost . . . it's a catastrophe . . . the conference will break up . . .'

From all these questions I managed to glean that what I had already heard that morning as rumour was now confirmed as true. The Russians had made a commercial agreement with Germany.

Facta and the other Italians did not appear to regard this news in the same tragic light as their foreign minister; but Schanzer was a broken man. In vain did they ply him with champagne and the finest red wine. In vain did his nice wife smile at him and send encouraging signals telling him with her eyes and with waving hands that he should not worry, for this was nothing to fret about! Poor Schanzer just sat in his chair, hair and beard all in disarray, staring in front of him and touching nothing, while his pince-nez kept falling off his nose. He was a pitiful sight. I have never seen a man as broken as he.

By the time we returned the whole of Genoa was ringing with the news of the Russo-German agreement. Everyone knew it. The agreement had been made with great cunning. While everyone knew that the English, the French and the Americans were all competing for an economic agreement with the Soviets, no one, despite the presence in Genoa of some two thousand eager reporters who watched every move made by all those delegates, had the slightest idea of any discussions between the Russians and the Germans. Neither Wirth nor Rathenau were involved in the negotiations but a certain Baron Maltzan, whom no one had ever seen. The agreement was signed at Santa Margherita; and the reason the Russians rented the Hotel Ferrari in the centre of Genoa may well have been so as to divert everyone's attention there. According to this agreement, Germany would supply Russia not only with quantities of agricultural and industrial machinery but would also send her engineers and supervisors to build the factories and modernize the mines. It was a tremendous undertaking for Germany, since it was tantamount to taking in hand Russia's entire economy. It would help to end unemployment in Germany and bring infinite opportunities for German industry. The Soviets would pay in cereals, manufactured goods and raw materials. All the advantages that the English and American capitalists had hoped for now fell into the lap of the Germans with one stroke of a pen.

The Victorious Powers were deeply shocked.

Schanzer had been right. The conference broke up.

Now at last it became clear to everyone that all those slogans about bringing us together to work for peace were little more than a smokescreen to cover the Great Powers' desire to meet the Russians and find a new market for their wares. And now all that treasure Chicherin had dangled so temptingly was to go towards rebuilding defeated Germany's industry! The disappointment was shattering.

It was the end of the conference: and the end too of the Declaration we wanted so much but which was now just another piece of unfinished business. There was no longer any reason to stay on; and everyone left soon after the departure of the Great Powers.

Almost the only tangible legacy of this first pan-European conference was the album of caricatures I was to publish a year and a half later: nothing else remained.

When we left Italy every delegate to the conference was accompanied to the frontier by a detective – for our security, they said!

Mine was a most sympathetic little Italian who hailed from somewhere in the Veneto. When he first presented himself to me he asked how I was going to travel, when, and where? I told him I would stop in Milan so as to go to a performance at La Scala. The following day I would go over to Novara to call on my old friend the Marchese Ferrario. From there I would travel to Venice and so would find myself at the frontier in three days' time. My detective was filled with joy when he heard my plan, for this meant five days' special pay for him. He asked if I would expect him to act as my guard all the time. 'Of course not!' I replied. Then he revealed what he would like to do. He proposed something beloved of all Italians – '*Una piccola combinazione*' – 'a little conspiracy', by which instead of keeping me under surveillance he would go back to his own part of the country and spend those few free days with his fiancée. '*Una bella ragazza*' – 'a beautiful girl' he said as he produced her photograph. At the frontier he would be there well on time to sign the certificate swearing he had never left my side for an instant.

And so it was.

We said our farewells at the frontier. I pressed a generous tip into his palm as we shook hands, and I stepped into my compartment. As the train started my little Italian friend cheered me on my way with a hearty cry of '*Evviva!*' He was a very nice young man.

⁓ Chapter Eight ⁓

It was the beginning of summer when I returned home from Genoa.

As soon as I was back in the office Kánya, who had deputized for me while I was away, made his reports of what had happened during my absence and what decisions had been taken. I was not able to take charge immediately as I had to spend a week at the Városmajor sanatorium for an urgent but minor operation, and then Professor Manninger only let me go home on condition I did not go out for five or six days afterwards.

On the morning of my return to my own house there occurred the incident that spoilt forever my relationship with Kánya.

It was the day when the Serbian ambassador was to have his first audience with Horthy. This was due to take place at eleven o'clock in the morning with all traditional pomp and ceremony. Kánya mentioned this, along with a number of other matters, but failed even to hint that he had decided to waive some of the traditional customs that had always been observed on such occasions. The accepted order of ceremony was that the newly appointed ambassador, in the presence of the foreign minister or his representative, hands over his Letters of Credence to the head of state and pays his respects with a suitable speech to which the head of state replies. After this the ambassador, now fully accredited, presents his suite. According to centuries-old custom, the foreign minister of the host country provides the transport to and from the ambassador's residence and the palace, and etiquette prescribes that as many cars or carriages needed to seat the entire ambassadorial party comfortably and in a manner suitable to their number and rank will be available. The embassy will previously have let the ministry know what will be needed.

The procession takes place with much festivity and ceremony. At one time gilded carriages would have been used, but now cars were sent with a high state dignitary called the '*Introducteur des Ambassadeurs*' whose presence symbolized the invitation of the ruler and whose duty it also was to escort the ambassador and his suite on the return trip after the audience. We used to entrust this office to István Bárczy, secretary of the prime minister's office.

All this would be preceded by an exchange of letters between the two countries' foreign ministries in which the name of the new ambassador was submitted for approval by the host government. This is called the '*Agrément*' – whether it is asking or receiving approval. The government to which the ambassador is being sent has the right to object when the name is submitted, and, if one is not accepted, another name must be put forward. *Agrément* is not required for any other members of the embassy staff, such as attachés or secretaries. It is neither expected nor requested; and foreign ministries are expected to send whom they wish without limitation. All junior members of an embassy staff can be changed whenever the ambassador wishes without any formalities. On the other hand, when the ambassador is changed the whole process has to be gone through all over again in all its stages. This is the unwritten rule of diplomatic practice.

In the case of Yugoslavia, Belgrade acted strictly according to the rules. The name of Mihailovic, who had been Serbian chargé d'affaires in Budapest before the ratification of the peace treaty, was put forward. We gave him the *Agrément*. They also told us all the names of the junior members of the embassy staff, most of whom had already been some time at their posts.

In this case, the situation was somewhat unusual in that neither the ambassador nor his staff arrived after the *Agrément* for the simple reason that they were all there already. This was, of course, one of the effects of our having lost the war, for the Victorious Powers had sent in commissioners without asking for our approval. In this capacity had come in Hohler, Foucher, Castagnetto, and their staffs – and these were all later automatically transformed into diplomatic missions.

The credentials of the Yugoslav Embassy, as I have already mentioned, were dealt with by Kánya, while I was still in Genoa; but when he made his report he did not reveal that there had been a difference of opinion between himself and the newly appointed ambassador. Instead he let me understand that everything would take place according to the established procedure.

It was Kánya's plain duty to inform me that he was planning to depart from the usual practice in such a matter as the presentation of an ambassador's credentials, because any such deviation was not a simple matter of form but a political act for which the ministry would be held responsible. What Kánya had done was markedly unusual. He had decided that those junior members of the new embassy – secretaries and the younger attachés – who had been Hungarian citizens before 1918 would not now be acceptable as staff members of a foreign embassy in Budapest. He had therefore demanded that any such persons – there were two of them – should be changed. The ambassador objected, arguing that such a demand was contrary to all accepted diplomatic practice. Apparently this disagreement had gone on for some time without a solution being found – but I had been told nothing about it.

Then arrived the day for the presentation of credentials. The ceremony was due to begin at eleven o'clock. Horthy, my deputy Ambrózy and the standard-bearer, all in full ceremonial dress, were waiting in the palace for the ambassador's arrival. István Bárczy had left for Pest to collect the ambassador, but Kánya had sent only one car in which there was room only for himself, the ambassador and two members of his staff. Earlier he had sent a message saying that he did not consider former Hungarian citizens, whether of Serbian origin or not, to be acceptable as members of the embassy, and so any such persons should remain at home. Kánya must have imagined that the ambassador, out of respect for the head of state, would find himself obliged to present himself with a reduced suite, and so, by the exercise of this ruse, the question of the disputed attachés would find itself solved. However, the new ambassador told Bárczy that as the Foreign Ministry had not sent the number of cars he had said would be necessary for his staff to be transported to the royal fortress in Buda, he would not be able to present himself to the head of state. He put the whole responsibility for his action on the Hungarian Foreign Ministry and remained adamant, no matter what arguments Bárczy used to persuade him otherwise. One hour after he had been supposed to appear with the ambassador, Bárczy returned empty-handed. The general frustration can only be imagined.

Lajos Rudnay, my cabinet chief, brought news of this to me at lunchtime. Obviously something had to be done at once to prevent our relations with Yugoslavia becoming poisoned by what had just occurred. The ambassador might well take the insult as directed not against himself but against his country, and unless I was going to be able somehow to put matters right at once, endless complications would ensue which could only end in humiliating apologies from our government. There was no question that Kánya's action had no lawful justification. We had ratified the Treaty of Trianon, which had specifically stipulated that all ethnic Serbs living in Banat or Bácksa (both former Hungarian provinces) would now become fully-fledged Yugoslav citizens. Given enough ill-will Kánya's action could easily be interpreted as denial of the treaty's validity by the Hungarian foreign office. It was therefore vitally important that I should speak to the ambassador as quickly as possible so as to make sure that when he made his report to Belgrade he could truthfully say that this delicate affair had been settled to his entire satisfaction.

Accordingly, although I was still convalescent, I sent Rudnay to the ambassador saying I would like to see him at once.

Early that afternoon he arrived. We settled the matter without delay, as soon as I had explained that I had had absolutely no knowledge of Kánya's action and that I deeply regretted that my illness had prevented my handling the matter myself.

My proposal was as follows:

As soon as I was on my feet again I would myself arrange the presentation of credentials to Horthy, to whom I would have already made suitable excuses to prevent his taking offence at the failure to accept his first invitation. As to the question of those attachés who were formerly Hungarian subjects, I too agreed that their appointment was undesirable as it might create the sort of resentment which could be harmful to the amicable relations we were all striving to achieve. I proposed therefore that the gentlemen in question should indeed be presented to the head of state as members of the ambassador's staff, but that immediately afterwards they should return to Yugoslavia and be replaced by others who hailed from the old kingdom of Serbia. As to the future, it was agreed that Belgrade would only send us persons to whose antecedents we could take no possible objection.

The ambassador accepted these proposals, and so this trivial but potentially inflammatory matter was resolved.

About a week later I did indeed direct the ceremony of presenting the ambassador's credentials. One of the two attachés left Budapest at once, and the other shortly afterwards.

This incident shows how even such a personal matter can be smoothed over with goodwill and good manners, despite the lack of an internationally recognized precedent. Of course Kánya could perfectly well have dealt with the matter by telling Mihailovic that he could not give the *Agrément* until the two attachés we considered undesirable had been withdrawn from Budapest. But to give the *Agrément* and then make conditions when it was too late and only to send one car as if the conditions had been agreed and imagine the ambassador would swallow the insult made no sense to me and is hard to understand.

It can only be explained if one is familiar with the ingrained arrogance of those who served the Ballplatz. Their noses were rubbed in it from the day they started as junior clerks. Maybe it was foolish, when a diplomat's job must surely always be to smooth things over, but then in earlier days, when the monarchy was still a great power, she could afford the luxury of being rude to those she considered beneath her. It may have been unreasonable and certainly was expensive, but this was the Ballplatz in the old days. For us to maintain this arrogant tone was, to say the least, harmful. Kánya, of course, had become accustomed to acting in his way when, as a young employee of the Austrian consular service, he had found himself lording it over some small town in the Balkans when the Austro-Hungarian consul stood sky-high on the social scale. Kánya never lost this Viennese arrogance, which had remained unchanged since the days of

Metternich; and, following the Ballplatz tradition, never lost his disdain not only for all inhabitants of the Balkans but also for the Italians. He loathed the northern Germans, held the French to be unreliable and reckless (as many had thought after Sedan); and his contempt was not affected by the fact that Italy had become accepted as a Great Power, that since the Balkan war and, later, the Versailles treaty, both the Greek and Serb kingdoms were no longer mere pawns on the board; while through their own efforts Romania and the new Yugoslavia, which included Serbia, were even now emerging as powers in their own right. Even France, after years of hard struggle, was only now educating her sons with a realistic ideology. Of course, Kánya could not have failed to see all this, but he was too emotionally involved in the old attitudes to understand what it all meant. He was firmly, if perhaps unconsciously, stuck in the belief that all this was temporary and should not be taken seriously as it would not last. As a result he was apt to overestimate the difficulties now being encountered by the new states, to exaggerate the dissatisfaction of the Croats, the Slovaks, of the Ruthenians and, as a result, to take pleasure in personally being in contact with frequently dubious and shady unofficial envoys from our new neighbours.

All this formed one aspect of his odd mentality. However, since there is usually more than one reason for our actions, it cannot explain everything. Kánya's character was such that he took pleasure in annoying or humiliating people. I will mention just one example as proof of what I have said. I once went to see him many years later, and he then told me in a fit of uncontrollable pleasure how he had so enraged the German ambassador that the poor man had almost broken down in his office – and this was in peacetime, when Germany had once more become a power to be feared! His reason for doing such a thing can only be understood or explained if one takes it as a form of mental sadism. It was significant that he could never tolerate anyone near him whom he could not bully or kick around like a court jester.

As Kánya had not told me about his intentions with regard to the Yugoslavian ambassador, so it was only later that I informed him of the solution we had agreed. Kánya said nothing and even appeared to approve, but I could tell he was deeply hurt. He did not dare to protest because he knew that Horthy had been angered to find that Kánya had put him in a situation unworthy of a head of state. Consequently, he said nothing – but from then on I knew he was my implacable enemy and would take his revenge as soon as an opportunity presented itself.

All this made me reflect on something I had been thinking about for a long time: namely that, for two reasons, our ministry of foreign affairs was badly in need of fundamental reform.

The first reason was that it needed to become more homogenous, more united. As it then was, it comprised various very different individuals who had been recruited in a haphazard day-to-day fashion when, in 1918, some sort of Foreign Ministry had hurriedly to be cobbled together. In the circumstances, it was natural that almost anyone with some sort of corresponding experience would be accepted without further enquiry. There were some who had served in the Dual Monarchy's diplomatic corps, others in the consular service, and even several with no experience of foreign affairs who had transferred from some other ministry. The confusion was made even worse by the fact that in the first few months after the war very few suitable candidates – perhaps only three or four – were in Budapest and available for appointment. Kánya, Khuen-Héderváry and others with the right experience were still in Vienna, away in the country, still in the army or even absent as prisoners of war, and so only a few were able to return home when they were most needed. And those who had been recruited so hurriedly under the Friedrich government quickly busied themselves upgrading each other. The strange result had been that by the time the ministry once again became functional those at the top had obtained rank that in no way corresponded to their seniority or diplomatic experience.

As a result of having been formed in such a haphazard fashion, the ministry at that time was made up of several opposing groups whose mutual hostility, however well it might be concealed, was none the less virulent. Side by side in the office were firstly those genuine diplomats with Ballplatz experience (forgetting for the moment those first-comers I have just described), then those from the consular service and finally the civil servants transplanted from other ministries. Some of these people had a little experience of other countries, perhaps due to an Austrian upbringing that had left them steeped in the spirit of the Dual Monarchy, some could even manage a few words of faulty Hungarian, while another group, brought up entirely at home with no notion of anything that transpired outside the country's borders, had no notion of foreign affairs, spoke no language but their own except perhaps a word or two of French, and were completely lacking in any vestige of that solidarity and communal spirit that was the one good legacy of the Ballplatz. And many had none of the social graces that were essential in a diplomatic career abroad.

The second reason why I considered the need for reform so urgent was that, in my view, it had to be made more wide-awake and more nationally minded. This might have been achieved if we could provide the right education and become more careful in the selection of candidates for a diplomatic career. It would also be necessary to make it easier for young men with promise and talent to live comfortably abroad while *en poste*, and this would mean offering from the start a modest but adequate pay structure. The old Ballplatz system of recruiting only rich young men who were able to exist without pay for the first few years was no longer possible for us since, following the king's last *putsch*, the rich young aristocrats no longer came forward as they once had. This was a great loss because such young men, with their command of languages and elegant appearance, would have provided excellent material for a career in diplomacy. Instead they were apt to spend their time in drinking and making-merry. A few came from minor noble families, and those that did were mostly blanks with regard to speaking foreign languages. What we had were mainly the children of senior civil servants, and Kánya modelled the courses for budding diplomats after the Viennese school, but these now badly needed revising as they were no longer in any way adequate.

We would need to find teachers with the skill to inspire the young with enthusiasm for their future career and not fill their heads with the dusty details of such long-forgotten matters as the Peace of Westphalia or the League of Cambrai. Practical knowledge of political science, modern social evolution, overseas commerce and the importance of, for example, cotton and oil were what a budding diplomat now needed to know rather than the petty happenings of the eighteenth century. We had a huge task before us.

When I first accepted the portfolio of foreign affairs and started to become familiar with the machinery of the ministry I was sure I could make a start on these reforms. It did not think it would be so very difficult – until it slowly dawned on me that I would be obstructed in every way by my own colleagues. Success in this sort of venture can only be achieved with the good will of all concerned. This is how, as director-in-chief of the thoroughly demoralized National Opera House, I had managed completely to reform its organization. It is true that, apart from the purely musical side, I did do everything myself. I did all the day-to-day management, I arranged the programme, I drew the costume designs, acted as stage director, supervised the theatre's finances, made contracts with the artists and personnel and defended the interests of the house and its six hundred employees against the onslaughts of the ministry. It had been a tremendous work, and two of my six years' stint as director-in-chief had been spent in pulling the place together.

But there I had been an absolute lord and master. Everyone seemed to want to go my way and, from the prima donna to the stagehands, did what I asked with a smile. I felt they were on my side, and it was characteristic of the atmosphere there that, ten years after I had left them, the chorus asked me for a photograph to put in their dressing room to remember me by[122]. It was indeed a pleasure to work under such conditions.

In the Foreign Ministry things were very different. With only one or two exceptions, I was made to feel that, concealed by the mask of official respect with which I was treated, I was told nothing except what I had specifically asked for, and then only in the most sparing of terms. Everything else, if possible, was kept from me. Occasionally something would come to light of which I knew nothing and of which I had been told nothing. If I required something, of course it was agreed at once – but nothing was done, and when I checked up on the matter, all sorts of excuses would be trotted out. Everything I proposed was sabotaged from the start. It became quite obvious to me that, for the entire personnel of the ministry, the real chief was Kánya, and that I would always be told as little as possible. I tried to make up for this by working harder. Often I would be at my desk all day long and continued until late at night without stopping, ten hours a day or as much as sixteen if there was also a cabinet meeting. I myself composed all the diplomatic correspondence because my colleagues' French was so faulty that it was the only way of ensuring that my meaning would not be distorted. Despite the tremendous amount of work all this involved it was still not enough. Unfortunately, dealing with the problems posed by the Burgenland crisis, the king's attempted *putsch* and the Genoa Conference had meant that I had not been able to get down to starting on more domestic issues. And if I wanted make the foreign office work to my satisfaction, there were all sorts of trivial but still essential things that I had to decide myself. So it was inevitable that, between the great issues of national importance and the minor details of the daily struggle, I could find little time for the reform of the office and its staff.

Many times I felt like losing my temper but, occupied as we were with coping with those great storms that kept breaking over our heads in my first year in office, it was hardly the moment to start wreaking havoc in the office by dismissing my colleagues and then finding replacements for them. This sort of thing could only be attempted when things were calm; and things never were calm. In the spring of my second year I had to go to Genoa, and it would have been absurd to start reforming the ministry just when I was about to be absent. The replacement of ministry staff would have to be supervised personally by me, for it would entail a great deal of pouring oil on troubled waters to still the inevitable frictions and repair the inevitable rifts. Much time was lost because of Genoa and, as soon I got back, by the affair of the Yugoslav ambassador's credentials.

It now became quite clear to me that as long Kánya remained at my side I would be unable to initiate any reforms at the ministry. The section chiefs were all his men. Khuen-Héderváry was imbued with the Ballplatz mentality, and everyone else belonged to Kánya's inner circle. I had two choices: I could either break openly with Kánya, explain the internal office problem to Bethlen and the head of state and arrange to have him pensioned off or I could resign my office.

I could easily have had Kánya dismissed. Horthy was still very angry with him over the affair of Yugoslav ambassador's credentials, while I was quite sure of Bethlen's attachment to me as I was the only one of his friends in whom he had full confidence. The problem was that Kánya's departure would still not have opened the way to reform of the ministry, for my own situation there would not have been changed. I was not sure that Khuen-Héderváry would have stayed on, although it was very possible since he was a well-meaning man with a strict sense of duty. But the other department heads, as well as their immediate juniors, were Kánya's men one and all and so, even if he were to go, my position would remain essentially the same, if not worse, as they would all continue to run to him and take his orders on every little matter that arose. The inevitable result would be two very different wills trying to run the ministry: one mine as the official chief, and the other Kánya's wherever he might be hiding. To achieve anything the section heads would all have to be changed, and who could replace them? Practically none of the more junior staff was sufficiently trained and experienced, but there seemed to be little point in replacing them with anyone new to the foreign office, for such people, however experienced in other ministries, would not be versed in diplomatic procedures which, although they might be only procedures, were still important to the smooth running of foreign relations. I myself was a beginner in such matters, so how could I instruct others? It would mean a tremendous workload if I chose that path; and, after a year and a half of serving my country as foreign minister, I was already tired and suffering from nervous exhaustion.

The other choice was to resign and so avoid the strain of battle; and this is what I chose. I did not want to leave public service, but I wanted to find a field in which I could work in tranquillity. For this reason, I thought of the post of ambassador in Paris, which at that time was the most important one available for a diplomat. It was the time of Poincaré, and France then held the reins of Europe in her hands. For us, Paris was vitally important, and our ambassador there would have a most delicate task, for several enemies of Hungary were firmly ensconced at the Quai d'Orsay. Until then our Paris embassy had been directed only by a chargé d'affaires, as I had not been able to find anyone I thought really suited for the Paris job. I fancy I judge myself objectively when I write that I really was more suited to that post than anyone I knew. Since early childhood I had been brought up immersed in French culture, and no one understood the French way of thinking better than I. My dealings with Barthou were proof of this. Also I had a wide acquaintance in many different circles. The post would be especially interesting to me, since the guardian of the peace treaty terms, the Council of Ambassadors, was based in Paris. The European department of the League of Nations was directed from there, as indeed was everything else that was going on in Europe.

So that was my plan. I told Bethlen what I wanted to do, and he was very reluctant to let me go. Finally he agreed on condition that I should first complete the arrangements for Hungary's admission into the League of Nations and only go to Paris when this had been accomplished. I suggested Daruváry as my successor at the foreign office. He had been *chef du cabinet* to Franz Joseph for many years, and he was then serving as minister of justice. With his lifelong experience at the centre of affairs and long connection with the Foreign Ministry, he seemed to me the best man for the job. Bethlen accepted him at once.

The fact that I would not be able to take up my new post until sometime in October posed a problem as regards our representation in Paris, for the Quai d'Orsay had for some time been pressing us to name a fully-fledged ambassador, and we could not delay much longer. I found the somewhat unsatisfactory solution of naming Praznovsky, who was already chargé d'affaires there, to take over for the few months until I could replace him.

Praznovsky was one of those who had managed to promote himself at the time of the Friedrich government. Now he held the rank of counsellor, which was higher than was justified by his length of service. However, he was a clever intelligent man, and so I had no objections to appointing him ambassador.

I then sent for him and told him of my plan to name him as ambassador to Paris immediately, provided he agreed, as soon as Hungary had been accepted into the League of Nations, to be moved to Prague. This would in no way be a demotion, since he would retain his new rank as ambassador, which in itself was an unheard-of promotion. It was true that, with so little experience, he would carry no weight in Paris and have very little real responsibility, but I looked upon the move as only a temporary arrangement, as did Khuen-Héderváry and Kánya. Praznosvsky accepted my proposition with visible joy and readily agreed to the terms I had outlined. Then we talked of other matters. We had already been thinking of buying a house in Paris, a small private townhouse in the Rue de Berry. We talked about this and about its conversion into an embassy and the costs involved. I promised to come from Geneva to visit Paris and see to all the details myself. We parted in such a friendly fashion that it never occurred to me that Praznovsky would go behind my back to prevent the exchange of posts I had proposed.

Soon after this I found myself preoccupied with all the work needed to prepare for our admittance to the League of Nations.

I held it to be highly desirable that all the formalities should be effected as smoothly and peacefully as possible for our acceptance would in itself symbolize the recognition that Hungary was once again a respectable European nation and was no longer thought of in the pariah role of war criminal, outside the law, which had been so evident at the time of the king's *putsch*.

At that time the prestige of the League of Nations was still without a blemish. Its very foundation had been an immense step forward in international law, the first really important advance since the establishment of the International Court at The Hague. Of course, there were still many drawbacks, and most of these stemmed from the fact that from its inception it was primarily an association of the Victorious Powers, who used it to distribute what had belonged to Germany in the form of colonial mandates to the victors and to spread their authority over the territories of the former Turkish Empire. Through the

League of Nations, the Victorious Powers legalized the cruel conditions of the various treaties of Versailles: for example, the artificial independence of Danzig, the rape of the Saar and the occupation of the Ruhr[123]. But in other matters, such as the question of Vilna, the League could offer no protection to a small nation when its interests conflicted with those of one of the Great Powers[124]. Its organic fault, as it were, was that it always had to give way to power, and if a Great Power objected then the League could not force the issue. It seemed that its ability to arbitrate was limited to enforcing the terms of the peace treaties – and the question of redrawing our frontiers fell into that category.

Nevertheless, it was an important organization.

The presence of the neutral countries, and even more that of the South American states with their growing importance, greatly contributed to reducing tension between the victors and the vanquished, and even in some small matters removing it completely. It was also much to the general good that the Great Powers, now that everything they did was in full view of world opinion, found themselves forced to find benign reasons for some of their less commendable objectives. In those days the prestige of the League of Nations had not yet been destroyed, as it was later to be by its helplessness when faced with Italy's invasion of Ethiopia and Japan's aggression against China.

Much to the advantage of the smaller nations was the fact that the League of Nations then acted much as radio stations were shortly to do. Through it the whole world got to know what was going on. The rights of the minorities were still very uncertain, for the conditions laid down in the peace treaties were so vague and unspecific as to bind no one. Almost the only exception concerned the schedule of rights accorded to the Jews of Poland. All the same, if we brought some minority matter to the attention of the League of Nations, we could sometimes manage to get what we wanted, since the new states did not take kindly to being so publicly called to account for their actions. They did not care to have the eyes of the world upon them. It was possible, by bringing matters up either in the General Assembly or before the Minorities Commission, to find support in the world's press and so, thanks to the pressure of public opinion, arrive at an equitable solution. It was for all these reasons that our formal acceptance as a full member was of such vital importance to us.

At that time there were two matters of outstanding importance that had to be decided as soon as possible. These were the appeals to the international frontier commissions to revise our borders: firstly with Austria and secondly with Yugoslavia. Another matter, although not so important, was to provide an answer to many of the accusations included in the denunciation of Hungary by the *Alliance Israelite.*

Meanwhile I had to prepare our application for acceptance as a member of the League of Nations. We had heard reports that one or two special conditions were going to be imposed upon us. Questions were going to be asked, and doubts expressed. It was all very vague, but it seemed highly probable that Benes, whose hatred of Hungary had flared up again ever since the king's *putsch*, would try to find some impediment to anything we proposed or at least suggest some humiliating procedures to be followed. It was clearly necessary to mobilize every scrap of the goodwill that I had recently worked so hard to build up. Nevertheless, I did decide that if something too shaming were demanded of us then I would withdraw the application rather than agree to any further degradation for Hungary.

As regards the question of our frontiers, I needed to memorize every relevant detail, however small, concerning all questions of geography, hydrography and distribution of population so that no matter what I was asked as a result of the Millerand letter, I would be able to answer with all the facts at my fingertips. I needed to know all the maps and learn vast quantities of statistics by heart. This I did with a good will because all my life I have loved acquiring knowledge and have had the enviable facility to learn quickly. The only matter I found antipathetic was the *numerus clausus*[125]. This had stemmed from a government decision in which I had had no part, but which I might have to defend in an international forum. To prepare for this, I agreed a formula with our government, and this I intended to read out at Geneva.

I set out in the first days of September and took with me a numerous staff. Béla Török, then a counsellor of the embassy and later an ambassador, came as my deputy, and we took Fedor Vest and Villányi as frontier experts. Already waiting for us at the headquarters of the League of Nations was our permanent delegate in Geneva, Zoltán Baranyai.

⤢ Chapter Nine ⤣

It was wonderful to be in Switzerland again and to travel in the shade of giant snow-covered peaks, along the shores of countless lakes and by mountain pastures covered in flowers. Sometimes, from the windows of the train, one could see great distances, spreads of wooden houses with the roofs weighted down with stones, fields full of grazing cows with people busy tending to them: tiny specks in the distance but all beautiful, perfect, as clearly delineated as little Norwegian toys. The most beautiful, for me, is the countryside on the shores of Lac Léman with softly sloping banks and, across the lake, the theatrical backdrop of the Mont Blanc range. It was lovely to see it all: this wise peaceful country where three different peoples with three different languages could make common cause, where there was true brotherhood between people of German, French and Italian race, where the practice of neighbourly love was a reality, and where Christ's teaching of patience with one's fellow men can be seen everywhere. I spent a month in Geneva on this trip and during that time learned a lot about the Swiss with their proud but modest patriotism and that willingness to accept sacrifices that is so characteristic of those who live in this happy land. This happy state was not achieved by accident but stemmed from their own merits and hard work, from their spirit of cooperation, from their common sense and clear-headed pragmatism, and from their imperturbable self-control. At Genève – which, being purely French, is what I suppose I should call it – I stayed at the Hotel Beau-Rivage, although my companions, for economy's sake, stayed at a cheaper and more modest hotel. I would have preferred to have gone there too, but could not do so, as heads of mission must often receive official visits and, since in the eyes of the world a man is judged by appearances, it would have been harmful to my country if I had had to greet callers in some third-rate pension. As it was, I had two small rooms: one for sleeping in and the other for work and receiving visitors.

The Beau-Rivage was then small and elegant and long-established: quite different from the caravanserais of today. It was from here that poor Queen Elisabeth set out on foot to board the ferry and was assassinated on the quayside[126]. The Beau-Rivage then really lived up to its name – 'Beautiful Lakeside'. The windows overlooked the lake, and there was a marvellous view of Mont Blanc whenever that king of mountains deigned to reveal himself. During my stay I saw him just once, for a few minutes only. The rest of the time he was shrouded with dense cloud, although the numerous peaks of the foothills, with their sharply edged sides revealing occasional glimpses of a glacier, were reward enough, especially when also reflected in the dark-blue waters of that crystal lake.

Also installed at the Beau-Rivage were several other heads of mission, principally from the smaller countries, as well as the Japanese and Chinese delegations.

For me the Japanese were the most important because Japan was a permanent member of the Council. And, luckily for me, in their delegation was Mr Onda, then Japanese ambassador in Vienna, whom I knew well as he was also accredited to us. He introduced me to the leaders of the Japanese party and so, being in the same hotel, I was fortunate enough to see them daily at breakfast, exchange greetings with them and often enough indulge in a few words of chat.

The Abbé Seipel, who had succeeded Schober as chancellor of Austria, was there too, and with him was my old acquaintance Count Mensdorff. They had come to Geneva not only for the conference but also in connection with the proposed League of Nations loan. This too proved to be most useful to me, since I was able to do them some favours that were always returned. It can be of great help to get scraps of information in such a way; and Mensdorff, as a result of his long service, had many excellent contacts, especially in English circles.

Among other acquaintances I found in Geneva was a nice elderly Swede, Branting, a socialist who was then their prime minister and who was staying at the Hotel des Bergues with his charming wife, and many others. But the man I was most glad to see was Hanotaux, present as head of the French delegation.

Our first days were spent in getting to know one another, in paying and receiving courtesy visits and in observing the traditional formalities. I paid my visit to the so-called First Committee, which was responsible for proposing new candidates for membership to the General Assembly. The chairman was Count Laudon, the head of the Dutch mission. He was a well-meaning fair-minded man: a diplomat of the old type of *grand seigneur*, with little understanding or sympathy for post-war manners or deceit in negotiation. He was just not made for it, for he was truly a noble-minded man. He assured me we would receive the best possible reception – and he was as good as his word.

The day fixed for my appearance before the First Committee soon arrived. I went trembling with anxiety because of the rumours we had heard before leaving Budapest. I read my initial Declaration in which I affirmed that we would stand by the terms of the peace treaties and that we had nothing but peaceful intentions. After that I expected to be asked some questions, and indeed had prepared my answers knowing that the Czechoslovak delegate would be present. However no one spoke up, and no questions were asked. There was praise for my presentation of Hungary's case, and Laudon was able to declare that the committee unanimously approved our acceptance. This was a great joy to me, and I came away a happy man.

Next day came the surprise. In the official gazette of the League of Nations it was stated that the committee had asked me several questions and then made a number of reservations as regarding our acceptance as a full member of the assembly. There was no mention of the unanimity of the committee in declaring their support for our membership. I went straight to Laudon and demanded a retraction in the next issue of the gazette and a true statement of what had actually transpired. It was obvious to me that Benes must have had a hand in all this, and that what had appeared in the gazette was only the first round in a new offensive against us. However, when I explained this to Laudon, although he agreed that the news published in the gazette had been false, he would not accept that there might have been some malevolent intent behind it. He was so honourable himself that he would not accept even the possibility that the facts had been intentionally falsified – and there the matter rested.

The question of our acceptance came before the General Assembly three days later, and then there transpired exactly what I had foreseen. The Czechoslovak ambassador to Paris rose to speak and, referring to the lying account published in the gazette, attacked Hungary and repeated many of the slanders that had been spread by Benes and printed both in the international press and that of the countries of the 'Little *Entente*'.

On the following day I demanded permission to speak and quickly answered all those accusations as well as re-establishing the truth of what had really occurred at the meeting of the First Committee. Laudon then confirmed the truth of everything I had said. In this way the attack upon us was foiled, but the serenity of our admission had been somewhat spoiled in the process.

At all events, this is how Hungary became a fully-fledged member of the League of Nations. Soon afterwards came the election for the assembly's president, and I mention it because there was an amusing and somewhat touching story linked to it.

At one end of the assembly hall a podium about four or five steps above the level of the floor stretched from wall to wall. At each side sat the secretaries, facing each other. The president's throne-like chair had been set in the centre under a baldaquin supported by four slender pillars. Directly in front of him was the rostrum for those addressing the assembly. This jutted slightly forwards. On it was now placed the ballot box with a narrow slit on top to receive the papers.

The voting took place in an atmosphere of quiet boredom. Once again it was Motta, the Swiss foreign minister, who was elected. The votes were cast in alphabetical order.

When it came to the turn of Romania, we found that a little plump elderly female had been given the task of casting the vote.

Doamna (Madame) Vacarescu was unfortunately so short sighted as to be almost blind. It was not easy for her to find the stairs; and when she had found them and arrived on the podium it was clear that she had completely lost her bearings. First she went up to a secretary sitting at the side and seemed to want to slip her voting paper under his collar. *'Au milieu, Madame! A droit, Madame!'* cried the secretaries. Off to the centre she stumbled and then collided with the presidential chair before trying to push the paper towards his shoulder and then into his ear. The president defended himself as best he might until the poor lady realized she was on the wrong track and succeeded in locating the ballot box. Once there she spent some time looking for the slit; and when she found it and cast her vote she looked around with such a charming smile of relief that we all applauded. She was a very nice woman, highly cultivated, and it was said that when she was young King Ferdinand had once wanted to marry her. Little still remained of her former beauty; but her younger sister, who had accompanied her to Geneva, was the image of Madame Vacarescu when young, and indeed very alluring, especially for anyone attracted to dark-haired women. I went to call on these two several times and was always enchanted by Madame Vacarescu's witty conversation[127].

The most influential department of the League of Nations was undoubtedly the Secretariat. Its chief was Sir Eric Drummond but, as he was also the leading spokesman for its council, he was an extremely busy man and hardly had anything to do with the daily running of his department. Some lesser luminaries decided everything, and these were reputedly in the pay of Benes. That some were not averse to 'presents' I knew from personal experience. It was these men who prepared each day's order of business and provided the working papers for the specialist committees – and who edited the League's official gazette. The false news about the First Committee's handling of our application for membership had been cooked up in this kitchen. In order to get close to them, I managed to become a member of their club. This was arranged by our gifted chargé d'affaires, Baranyai, who had excellent connections and who also introduced me to various other literary and social circles.

Although I never managed to get anywhere with the Secretariat, I soon found myself on terms of intimate friendship with some of the native-born Swiss.

Pre-eminent among these was certainly de Traz, who at that time was editor of the *Revue de Genève*. He was an excellent writer and a most charming man who was related to most of the local patrician families. He received me warmly, and I am sure that our friendship would have developed into a most valuable literary association if he had not died so soon afterwards. Another man with whom I quickly became on the most confidential terms was Monsieur Hensch, who was not only the proprietor of one of the city's principal private banks but also its executive chairman. One day he invited me to lunch with his family. Driving himself, he took me in his car to his villa just beyond Nyon on the road to Lausanne. As we drove, he told me all about how Switzerland's armed forces were run. There, he said, everyone is a soldier and nobody is. Apart from some very small specialist units, there were no professional soldiers. The highest official rank was that of colonel. Hensch, although a banker in everyday life, was also a colonel. He told me that when in 1919 there had been some sort of uprising in Zürich he, as senior officer in the canton of Fribourg, was ordered to restore order. So off he started with his troop, surrounded the trouble centre by a strategic march through the mountains and disarmed the rebellious faction. And when the battle had been won, by strategy rather than by force of arms, he hung up his uniform and went back to being a banker in Geneva. What an amazing country, I thought, where such a thing can happen! Every grown man keeps his weapons and ammunition at home; and, until he is called to the flag, he goes quietly on with his own occupation, be it labourer, shopkeeper, craftsman or business executive. When called up, everyone comes at once – everyone. They do what is asked of them and then they go home, hang up their guns in the closet and become civilians again. There is no martial spirit: soldiering is not an independent career, merely an aspect of service to one's country. I can imagine no other country where this could be possible. Where else would it be conceivable that military arms and ammunition could be kept at home and only occasionally brought out for target practice or when the civilian army was called up for service? Anywhere else there would be a general massacre. To maintain this strict discipline a prodigious and sober sense of duty is required, as well as a feeling for humanity and that unspoken patriotism that is so characteristic of the Swiss people. During the world war so recently ended Switzerland had mobilized its forces to defend its neutral status and had marshalled them along the French and German frontiers. Troops were also stationed on the borders with Austria and Italy. There were no warlike incidents anywhere. The Swiss merely kept watch and waited. If any belligerent happened to stray across the frontier, he would be quietly arrested and interned in a humane and friendly fashion. To a man they were impartial, whether the stranger were on the French or German side. Surely this is evidence of a deeply Christian spirit?

This was not a recent development. It had been the same ever since the Reformation, and I found deeply interesting everything that the Swiss had to teach me during this visit.

In the early days of the reform of the Church the upper cantons were Catholic, while the lower ones were Protestant. Despite this the Catholic cantons raised cattle, cheese and other milk products and sold them to the Protestants, while they in return sent back flour, tanned hides, agricultural implements, even guns and gunpowder. It had been agreed that the wares of one faction would be deposited at a specified border stone and, on the following day the other would bring their counter-value to the same spot. No one cheated; and the two sides never met, for they had realized that, should they catch sight of one another, blood might be spilt and someone might get killed. But commerce was peaceful – and necessary to life. What an admirable spirit! And all this at the same time as those religious wars in which Tilly slaughtered babes-in-arms at Magdeburg during the Peasant's Rising in Germany, when all culture was destroyed and churches burned – together with anyone, of whatever religion, unlucky enough to have sought refuge inside – and when even the crops were set on fire so that the country people would starve to death.

For us the most important issues were now the frontier questions.

We appealed against the new Austrian border largely for the sake of form, since the essential aspects had already been settled at the Venice conference and the king's *putsch* had put an end to further serious negotiation. Still, there were one or two border-line villages whose status had still to be decided.

More important was the frontier with the new Yugoslavia.

By the terms of the Treaty of Trianon the south-western corner of the county of Vas, where only Hungarians lived, had been given to Yugoslavia; as had Murakös, where the inhabitants were Slovenes who hated the Croats and whose capital was Szombathely, which had been left in Hungary. Both these disputed territories depended economically on Hungary, since the Slovenes were cut off by the river Drava (Drau in German), and the inhabitants of County Vas by ranges of mountains. Also the purely Hungarian Ormanság now found itself in Yugoslav Baranya.

To obtain the return of all these diverse territories by application to a committee of the League of Nations seemed to me a hopeless task. The only solution would be if I could come to some arrangement directly with the Serbian foreign minister, Ninçic; so I went to see him.

It was at once clear that Ninçic too favoured our coming to an agreement without reference to the League of Nations. I used the same argument with him as I had with Benes, that is the great moral force of a voluntary agreement. With Ninçic there was also another reason, which was well-known at the time, and that was that Horthy was anxious to settle the question of Szeged with Belgrade, and if we two could somehow get rid of the more contentious border problem, then, as Hungarians had far more in common with the Serbs that with any of our other neighbours – both being bold brave people – there would be no reason to keep us from being good friends.

Our negotiations went smoothly enough and the next day, accompanied by Fedor Vest, I went to Ninçic's apartment to settle the smaller details for, no matter how amicable the general agreement, it is always the minutiae which will determine its ultimate success or failure. This is especially true of an agreement concerning borders for which details of population distribution, water supplies, land-holdings and communications are vitally important. We arrived well armed with maps and statistics.

Ninçic received us, along with two secretaries, one of which I fancy was a military man in civilian clothes, and also the Serbian ambassador to Bern, who had come to Geneva expressly for this meeting.

We quickly came to a full agreement. We divided the issues into two parts. As regards the borders of Bácska and Baranya, we agreed upon an exchange of territory by which Yugoslavia obtained more territory but fewer inhabitants while we retained more people. This was because the part of Baranya to be returned to Hungary was largely inhabited by those of Hungarian origin, who would thereby come back to their mother country. This seemed to me to me more important than holding on to largely uninhabited land just because it had once been ours.

As to the corner of County Vas and Murakös, we agreed to a plebiscite. I had no doubts that this would have a happy outcome for us, for the Hungarian inhabitants of County Vas would vote unanimously to remain Hungarian; while in Murakös most of the Slovenes hated both the Serbs and the Croats so much that they would almost certainly vote for Hungary. It was also very much in their economic interest to do so.

Our discussions were most friendly, although the Serbian ambassador from Bern did his best to make them not so. It was clear that he opposed the arrangement, and at one moment he asked Ninçic to go with him into the next room, whence we could all hear a noisy altercation between them. Ninçic, however, remained firm and announced, as soon as he returned to us, that we could sign the agreement without delay. My secretaries, before leaving the Beau-Rivage, had already drawn up the necessary documents with full details of place names, quota numbers and geographical data (leaving blank spaces only for the places and dates of possible plebiscites). We had done this because, in the case of delicate or difficult negotiations, it always seems wise to be prepared with the necessary draft documents since, if there is any delay, anyone opposing the agreement can use it to disrupt the negotiations.

The Serbian was still rude and ill tempered, and I was astonished that Ninçic should have permitted someone junior to him
to speak like that in the presence of strangers. I would not have
tolerated it for an instant. However: other countries, other customs! Of course, I had not understood what had passed between
them, but several times I heard the name of the Yugoslav prime
minister mentioned and assumed that the ambassador was menacing Ninçic with him. But it was of no moment; the signing was
done and we left in joyous mood.

I went off at once to find Hymans, the Belgian delegate. He
was chairman of the border committee, and I felt it was important that he should first hear of the amicable solution to our
border problems from the Hungarian side, since everyone always
remembers the man who brings good news, and I wanted him to
think of Hungary as a peacemaker. I told him all the essential
details of our agreement and then asked him to postpone the
next meeting of the committee until ratification had arrived from
both governments.

I did not, of course, mention that there might be any doubt as
to whether our government would ratify the agreement. On the
contrary, I emphasized that I was sure the government would
grasp the occasion with joy as showing, in this most delicate of
matters, our desire for peace.

I said 'would grasp' in the future tense; and my reason for this
was that I had already received an answer from Budapest to my
first telegram outlining the agreement reached with Ninçic, and
it had instructed me to sign nothing until the cabinet had
approved the terms. I could not be bound by this, as it would
have been impossible to reach any agreement if everything had
to be subject to a two-day delay while telegrams were exchanged,
especially as on one side no one would have had the chance to
study the texts. There are times when responsibility simply has
to be shouldered and, when something seems to be right, one
must simply go ahead and sign it. Then, if the government, by
now in possession of the full text, disapproves, one resigns and
one's signature automatically becomes null and void. But to wait
for previous permission would be pointless. Anyway, in this situation I was sure that as soon as I spoke to Bethlen, who after all

would have the last word in this matter, he would agree that we had done an excellent piece of work and would give his approval.

I had another reason to make public the intentions of the Hungarian government at that moment. I had hardly left Ninçic's apartment before I was sure that Pasic would very probably try to make trouble. The behaviour of his ambassador to Bern, his provocative manner and passionate quarrel with his own chief of mission, seemed likely to herald another storm, which might well result in objections from the Serbian side. If this were to occur then was it not as well that *my* government should be seen to be wearing the peacemaker's halo?

A few days went by, during which another and more strongly phrased telegram arrived from Budapest demanding again that I sign nothing more without prior consent. Until this was sent, they said, the agreement must be considered invalid, and I was reprimanded for putting my signature to it. I fancy this was the work of Kánya, who sat in my place at cabinet meetings and did everything he knew to belittle whatever I achieved by constantly referring to form and precedent. I passed several very disagreeable days. I had already decided that if necessary I would resign; but it would not be pleasant to have to go back to Hymans and tell him that the Hungarian government had declined to honour the agreement I had signed. However, very soon there arrived from Pasic a telegram instructing Ninçic to denounce the agreement and forbidding him to enter into any discussion on the matter whatsoever. He therefore found himself obliged to declare to the League of Nations that his own government had forsaken him; and so Serbia got the blame for frustrating the agreement.

A few days later the border committee met again.

We sat at a big round table, tightly pressed together, as the frontier specialists also had to be found places. Fedor Vest was beside me. He seemed calm and indeed took part in all our discussions in a completely calm and matter-of-fact manner. No one could have guessed how excited he really was. I was the only one who knew, and that was because, closely pressed together as we were, I could feel his shoulder trembling against mine. I feel it still today when I think about it.

358 *The Phoenix Land*

When Hymans praised us and said a few soothing words about Yugoslavia, I could sense that the general feeling of the committee was becoming sympathetic towards us.

We explained out position with regard to the Muraközs and the little corner of County Vas and asked for a plebiscite there. The Serbian envoy wanted to stick strictly to the terms of the peace treaty, and the decision went against us. It was clear that word had been received from the Victorious Powers – in effect the Quai d'Orsay. We knew already that this would be so. Still, I was pleased that after the meeting many of those present came up to me to say how much they appreciated our conciliatory and understanding attitude.

Ninçic did not attend this meeting. It was clear that he was embarrassed that his government had forsaken him and allowed him to lose face before the League of Nations. Sympathizing with what he must be feeling, I went straight round to see him. When there is trouble is the time when human relations must come first. Ninçic was overjoyed to see me. I told him at once that the collapse of our agreement in no way affected my admiration for him and that I deeply regretted only that the friendly cooperation between our two countries, which had been so clearly adumbrated in the first sentences of the agreement we had signed, could not now be realized as soon as we had hoped. I declared, however, that I still firmly believed in it and would continue to do so. At the end of our talk we agreed to keep in touch, privately and to pass on news of anything that might damage friendly relations between our two countries. If we could do nothing else we would continue to work for a real and lasting *rapprochement* between the Hungarian and Yugoslav peoples.

I left office a few months later; and so did Ninçic. Nothing was to come of our mutual work, and yet I remember him with sympathy and pleasure for he was a man of wide understanding and full of good will.

In mid-September we came to the election of those countries to have seats on the Council of the League of Nations. This was to be the body that took all major decisions, and its composition was therefore of the highest importance. I then heard the alarming news that both England and France were intending to insist on a place for the new Yugoslavia.

For us this would be a dreadful setback, since it would be this Council that would consider any complaints from the ethnic Hungarian minorities in the newly formed or enlarged neighbouring states. Until now such complaints had not met with much sympathy, but at least the Council had been thought of as impartial. That now one of the 'Little *Entente*' countries was to be in the seat of judgement when cases in which her own or her neighbours' minorities were to be decided, and also have the right to make judgements where her own interests were involved, was an unbearable thought.

This caused me many a sleepless night and came at a time when I was already tormented by gnawing personal problems. From the moment I had achieved Hungary's acceptance as a full member of the League of Nations I had been the subject of attack and vilification in our national press: principally, of course, in the Legitimist papers. I was accused of having given away any amount of Hungary's national treasures to obtain that acceptance by agreeing to the most humiliating terms without in return imposing any conditions to preserve the nation's honour. And what was worse, these accusations were made not merely by journalists of no standing but also by no less a figure than Apponyi himself (in an article in the *Budapesti Hirlap*). It was immediately clear to me that if Yugoslavia were to obtain a seat on the Council no one would ever believe that this had not been the price I had agreed to pay for our own admission as a member state. No one would ever believe that I had not had a hand in this and that it had not been part of a bargain struck by me. The slander would stick to me as long as I lived, like a convict's brand, and I could already hear my enemies' shouts of triumph as they roared out calls of 'Traitor!' I was in terrible anguish of mind.

My first move was to call on Edward Wood, the English delegate. I explained to him that it was because of this minority problem that we had to protest against a Council seat for Yugoslavia. He said that he understood our point of view but did not otherwise unbend. I then turned to Hanotaux. He seemed more appreciative but did not yield either, even after we had discussed the matter at length. He stated that it had already been decided. Finding myself in a hopeless situation, I then suggested that, if this could not be changed, and the 'Little *Entente*' was thereby given a permanent advocate in the Council, perhaps France as the traditional defender of the people's rights would accept the role of champion of the minorities and use her powerful voice in defence of the justice of their cause. Hanotaux accepted this most solemnly. Indeed he was a great and noble-minded man. I believe that he only did this for me because he had grown fond of me, and I always think of him with gratitude.

This was a substantial achievement, and I was sure that Hanotaux would keep his word. It also meant that when I became ambassador in Paris I would always be able to count on his support and protection.

Nevertheless, I still considered this only as a second-best arrangement that had been compulsorily imposed upon us. It would still be better if somehow we could bring about the failure of the plan to give a seat to Yugoslavia; and so, although I did not have much hope, this is what I started to work towards.

First I considered what forces I had to contend with, and decided at once that there were three groups where I might muster support. First came the Baltic States, who always stood as one man. With them I had always had good relations. Because of our common Finno-Ugric origins we had always been in sympathy with them, and so I won them over easily. The Finns and Estonians had long looked on the Hungarians as poor relations do on their more eminent cousins. They were proud of the relationship. This meant three votes for us, for Finland brought with her Estonia and Latvia. It was possible that Lithuania would also join us as, since the decision about Vilna, they felt a great resentment against the Great Powers. And so it happened. Now we were four.

The next, and much stronger group, was formed of the South Americans. At that time their leader was Rivas-Vicunna, one of the leading delegates from Chile. He was a dignified man with a great love of truth. I do not now recall how it was that we came to be on terms of confidential friendship. It may well have been that I found him sympathetic at our first meeting, or maybe I found just the words to arouse his sympathy. Perhaps he had first aroused my interest because I had once read that the Chileans still represented the purest Castillian bloodlines since they had never intermarried with the Moorish, Indian or black races. This may all be later rationalization, but whatever it was it is certain that he stood by us most steadfastly. He promised to rally to our side all the other South American countries. He started by inviting me to a dinner where I met all the South American delegates, and he saw that I had the opportunity to talk to each of them individually. As a result, I was able to tell them all sorts of facts about Hungary of which they previously had had no idea. They heard me with great interest, and, since my good friend Rivas-Vicunna had previously spoken well of me to all of them, I did not find it hard to win them to my way of thinking. It was in our favour that they started without any preconceived partisan feelings and indeed found much of the mutual distrust and hatred of the European countries for one another senseless and absurd. This meant that we now had some fifteen or sixteen votes: a tidy number but still not enough.

As there were fifty-two countries represented, I would need twenty-seven votes to be sure of winning.

The third group comprised the Asiatic countries. Their leader was Japan, and so I started to talk to members of the Japanese delegation.

I already knew the Japanese ambassador to Vienna; and I had also read a great deal about Japanese culture. I had always been fascinated by the Far East, and my friend Vilmos Pröhle had taught me a great deal about the Japanese. Ever since the Russo-Japanese War[128] I had learned more from an assiduous reading of the *Illustrated London News*, which for decades had published much about Japan and the character of its people. I was familiar with their unspoken patriotism, and also with the *Bushido* traditions that ruled their daily lives, from how they cut their nails to their acceptance of hara-kiri, the ritual suicide to preserve honour. Perhaps also I have in me, by some process of Mendelian inherited characteristic, an oriental sympathy that allows me more understanding of the Japanese temperament than is the lot of those whose ancestors are of wholly European origin.

The members of the Japanese delegation took all their meals in the dining room of the Beau-Rivage. They ate their lunch at a single long table, while I sat at a small table nearby. It was interesting to watch them. They ate in silence with a mechanical air, almost as if they were still asleep, lazily, and seemingly indifferent to their colleagues' presence. Occasionally they would all suddenly liven up, as if struck by lightning; and this was when a Chinese delegate entered the room. Then their eyes all focussed on him, as they carefully looked to see with whom the Chinaman had come in, with whom he spoke: indeed seemingly taking note of everything about him. This only lasted for seconds before the masks of apparent indifference fell once more into place, and anyone would imagine that they had no interest at all in what went on around them. There was something frightening in this latent invisible alertness.

I became on reasonably good terms with them from our first encounter. I soon discovered that they were interested in my being Hungarian, for they had a keen feeling that Hungarians were in some way related to them. I have no idea if there may be any historical justification for this, although I believe that their country had been invaded in antiquity by Hiung Nuk, and by this conquest the eastern Huns had become the ancestors of the *Daimios,* the ancient Japanese noble caste. This has been denied by certain Indo-Germanic scholars who claim that the Japanese ruling families are descended from Malaysian pirates; but, whatever the truth may be, I can only say that, while in my country this notion of having Far Eastern cousins exists only in the dream-like theories of some 'turanist' scholars[129], it is still widely believed in Japan. This was an asset when I went to see the Japanese delegate.

I started by giving him a resumé of Hungary's recent past. I explained what an injustice it was to brand us as war criminals when there was proof enough that Tisza, then prime minister of Hungary, had strongly protested at Austria's decision to send such an impossible ultimatum to Serbia and had only remained in his post by the order of the old ruler[130]. With exemplary patience he had silently suffered public blame for involving us in a war he himself had worked so hard to prevent. Although he had been no warmonger, it was because people believed the opposite that he had been murdered. Only later, when the records in Vienna had been made public, did the world get to know that Tisza had been forced to remain at his post since he was only too aware that, if he had then made his real views known, the morale of the country would have been shattered, and the ultimate catastrophe would have come all the sooner. He had seen clearly that the loss of the war would inevitably bring with it the dismemberment of his country – and this is indeed what happened. By keeping the secret, he became a martyr to his oath of allegiance and to his sense of duty[131].

The Japanese seemed much impressed by what I had told him of Tisza and then, uttering the greatest compliment a Japanese could give, said: 'For us it is a moral law to endure infamy if it is for the good of our country.'

He then gladly agreed to vote with us on the matter of elections to the Council and promised also to rally the support of China and Siam.

After this visit the Japanese treated me as if I were a fully-fledged Asiatic and soon afterwards asked me to attend an otherwise wholly Asian dinner. The host was Ishii, their chief delegate who was then the Mikado's ambassador in Paris. The entire Japanese, Chinese and Siamese delegations, with most of their wives in national dress, were present. I was the only European.

It was a most interesting dinner not only because of the exotic appearance of the guests. The Chinese women in their national costumes were ravishing. I had already seen them in the hotel, but I had found something droll about their appearance when dressed in European clothes. Mostly rather short, they walked awkwardly in high-heel western shoes. Now they were dazzlingly beautiful. It was not possible to talk to them, although whether this was because they spoke no English or because etiquette forbade them to speak at all I do not know. They smiled but never spoke. On the other hand, the Japanese women – there were only two or three of them – were quite Europeanized. I sat next to the hostess, who was a real beauty; not at all like the diminutive doll-like geishas of popular legend but rather a tall slender woman with an ivory skin that would have been the envy of any elegant European. Her face was narrow, her nose thin, and she held her head high above a tapering neck. In an off-the-shoulder Paris dress she was a ravishing figure who would have stood out in any gathering of the world's most famous beauties. She had a completely cosmopolitan air.

The conversation was in English, as few of the guests would have understood any of the others' languages.

It was soon clear to what extent I had been accepted as one of them. They talked to me unreservedly about their former allies, especially about the English, who were the subject of much criticism. They all believed that they had been made false promises that Australia would be opened to Chinese and Japanese immigrants so as to induce them to support the Allies in the war. Both countries suffered from rapidly increasing populations they could not support at home, and as Australia was so sparsely inhabited they had counted on this promise as a solution to their problems. When the war was won, however, the promise had not been kept, and even America imposed new restrictions on immigration. The Far Eastern countries received no reward, and even access to colonization in Polynesia was denied them. And not only that, but it seemed that there was to be no question of restitution of the huge losses they had incurred. The gist of everything they said was that they no longer believed in the good faith of the countries of Europe.

I enjoyed all this whole-heartedly, especially the fact that the usually reserved and inscrutable Orientals said all this openly to me just as if I were one of them and so could be trusted. For a diplomat this was indeed a great satisfaction.

With four Baltic, four Asian and fifteen South American votes added to our own, we now had twenty-four on our side: close to but not yet quite forming a majority. I still had to look for a few more, so I tackled the Bulgarian and Albanian delegates, and with them I obtained a majority vote that caused the nomination of Yugoslavia to be defeated. If I remember the voting was twenty-six to eighteen. I can still hardly believe it.

There were several especially favourable circumstances at that time. It was fortunate that the election meeting's president was the highly popular old Swede Branting, while it was also undoubtedly in our favour that everyone knew that it was the Serbs who had repudiated my agreement with Ninçic, thus labelling themselves the spoilers of the peace process. There were probably other reasons too, notably that not a few of the neutral countries, led by the South Americans, had grown tired of everything being decided by France and England without prior consultation with anyone else.

All this required nerve-shattering relentless work. It needed a great knowledge of men, or rather of the spirit that guided different peoples. It meant being constantly on the alert to analyse every word spoken to me so that I could put myself in the mental position of the man I wanted to win over. I feel that one of the most important assets of a diplomat is the ability to understand a way of thinking quite alien to one's own. I feel too that maybe it was my experience as a writer that provided me with something of this ability, since all writers must be able to put themselves into the minds of others. It was also to my personal advantage that since early youth I had read widely and, having an excellent memory, retained a multitude of diverse facts, ethnographical and historical, which would at once come to mind when I found myself talking to foreigners, were they Finns, Swedes, Japanese or Bulgarians. I found that having such knowledge of their own countries rejoiced their hearts and, indeed, impressed many of those with whom I had to deal. I even remembered facts about Simon Bolivar gathered from my boyhood reading of adventure stories.

There was another aspect of this affair that surprised me then – and indeed still does – and that was that all my hard work before the election could be done in secret, and that the secret was kept. Neither then nor later did I see the smallest sign that anyone had noticed what I had been doing. I am particularly sure of this as regards the French, who always displayed towards me the greatest goodwill, despite the undoubted fact that, as the nomination to the Council had been put forward by them, they would have been understandably angry if they had known my part in its frustration. This was probably because the French were so sure of themselves that perhaps they had not bothered to wonder what was being whispered in the wings; and perhaps, too, because I had been dealing with diplomats who knew how to watch their tongues. It was an exhilarating experience for me when the voting took place, and we won with an important majority.

All the same it was nerve-racking work for which I paid the price. To remain tautly alert every second, continuously to have to weigh up every sentence – indeed every word – spoken can be grinding toil for anyone. I found myself constantly having to be sure that the words I spoke hit the right note, and at the same time never to lose sight of how the other man's mind worked, how he was reacting and what approach would be most likely to raise an echo of appreciation. And it had to be done with many diverse people, at one moment Spanish and the next Swedish or Japanese, never losing oneself in the Tower of Babel that the League of Nations had become, never forgetting that the Chileans despised the Bolivians, that the Finns were touchy on the subject of their international standing, that with the Dutch one should use only ideological arguments, and that the Lithuanians thrived on hatred. Even so, if this had been all, I could have managed it without any damage to my health.

At the same time there were other matters to attend to, and many small claims to be settled. When the complaint about the *numerus clauses* came before the Council it was my job to defend it even though I had had nothing to do with this purely internal issue. Then Reverchon, the Grand Master of the Geneva Freemasons, came to see me to urge that the Freemasons' lodges in Hungary be allowed to operate freely once more and would also have their funds restored to them. I had to discuss this with him and give him some hope, which put no strain on me as I fully sympathized with his point of view; but at the same time I knew only too well that I could not be of any real help since Horthy detested Freemasonry. Yet, however hesitant I might feel, it would have been impolitic not to give him any encouragement at all since I knew that the League's Secretariat was almost wholly composed of Masons, while a large part of the many delegations was too. After this I had to help Sarah Wertheimstein, sister of Baroness Rothschild, who came to consult me about agricultural reform[132]. I tried to help as best I could. The nice Mrs Snowden was also there. Then there were all sorts of gala dinners and other national and international social engagements which could not be avoided not only because protocol demands one's presence but also because these occasions provided the opportunity for all sorts of useful contacts and confidential exchanges of information.

At this time I found myself effectively working alone, for since Fedor Vest and Villányi had returned home after the frontier question had been settled, only Béla Török remained with me, and, although he was a most talented young man, he had little experience. I was only able really to use him for drafting documents and telegrams and for our reports to Budapest, since much of the work to which I was devoting myself was extremely complicated and could only be undertaken by someone who held all the threads in his own hands.

All this wore down my nerves. I had noticed some time before that my handwriting had become almost illegible, that I was apt to talk too much, and that my temper was all too readily aroused. Also I could hardly sleep. The signs of incipient nervous breakdown became more and more obvious.

What affected me the most – and this is what was finally to cause me to break down – was all the backbiting I received from home. The rejection of the agreement I had made with Serbia over the new Hungarian/Yugoslav frontier question and the stern reproof I had received over this from Budapest, together with many other senseless orders I had been sent but which could never have been complied with, were only made worse by the incessant innuendoes and slanders about me that appeared in the opposition press without the slightest reply from the government papers. I found all this hurtful and humiliating. It is possible I felt it all too much at the time, but it was like an automaton that I made my last efforts to finish my task. After the successful outcome of the voting for the Council seats, my nerves finally gave way.

This happened just when I was due to attend a gala dinner organized by de Traz in my honour. It had been a most kind gesture on his part, but when Bela Török and Zoltán Baranyai came to collect me they found me in such poor state that I had been unable to put on my evening clothes and was in no way fit to socialize with strangers. I felt that at any moment I would collapse physically, and that thousands of ants were running about under my skin! I had immediately to take tranquillizers, speak to no one, lie down and sleep, sleep, sleep . . . It was impossible for me to attend the dinner, which caused me much regret.

After a few days I felt a little better and so, although I should have gone at once to a sanatorium, I wanted to finish my task at Geneva. Luckily, there was nothing really serious that had to be settled, but I still had two speeches to make. These were only statements that had been prepared in advance, which was just as well as I had found that if once I started speaking I said too much, and nothing would stop me. Pál Teleki, in his last days as prime minister, had become just the same before he shot himself.

It was at this moment that I went to Paris to see about the restoration of the little *palais* we had bought for our embassy. In the course of my short stay there I went with Praznovsky to pay a brief courtesy visit to the Quai d'Orsay. I was there only for a few minutes: nevertheless, the Legitimist press at home used the occasion to publish that lying slander about me, which I mentioned earlier.

The restoration of the Rue de Berry house was my last action as foreign minister. After that, I went back to Geneva and waited for the closing of the League of Nations General Assembly. I paid my farewell courtesy visits and thanked all those who had supported me for their help. I went first to Rivas-Vicunna and presented him with the Hungarian Cross of Merit, out of gratitude and also as something to remember me by.

Those were very mixed days for me in the beautiful capital of French Switzerland. Even though it was then that my health broke down completely, I look back on those days with great pleasure, for I still have wonderful memories of that beautiful city.

One of the most marvellous was the view from a lakeside villa. One day I had been invited to a garden party at the house of de Traz's father-in-law. The villa was about ten kilometres east of

Geneva and stood in a vast garden shaded by the wide-spreading foliage of centuries-old oak-trees. The house dated from the end of the eighteenth century and was filled with works of art brought from Paris by the host's forbears who, from father to son, had served in the Swiss Guard of the kings of France. Everything was beautiful and rare and the best of its kind; but the most memorable of all was the view from the garden. I shall never forget it. An emerald-green lawn sloped gently down to the steel-grey water. The lake that day was like a mirror. As it was already late in the afternoon, the lower parts of the mountains on the other side of the lake were in dark shade. The lower peaks, the steep valley-sides and ravines seemed to form a steep wall of shadow, no longer fragmented by shafts of sunlight. Only a few of the highest stood out like claws, showing that there were many of them, high plateaus and crests, one in front of the other, those in the far distance paler than those closer to us. These, however, were only the foothills. Above them were more summits of ice and sparkling snow with, where the sun did not reach, azure streaks almost the same colour as the sky. And then, suddenly, unexpectedly, so dazzling as to appear unreal, defying imagination and as high up as one would look for the stars, shone a blinding white triangle, Mont Blanc itself, dwarfing everything around until it seemed that the highest ranges of the Alps were but little hills beside this mighty monarch. It was a sight to make real the ancient's belief that it was on the highest peaks that the gods lived.

My friend de Traz saw how enchanted I was by this view. The other guests had all departed, but he did not disturb me, and we waited peacefully in the garden for night to fall.

Slowly everything below turned violet-blue, and wisps of grey vapour rose above the surface of the lake. The snow-capped mountains turned to flame, while above them the sky at first turned pale green until the dying orange-red glow of the sinking sun vanished completely to leave both mountains and sky a uniform lilac. As the darkness spread, the bright snow above and the foothills below became as one until, as the night approached, one or two stars appeared. And still there, shining fire-red in the night sky, the glittering triangle of the king of mountains floated serene and alone, unreal in the violet sky like a vision, a holy apparition, triumphant and eternal, the symbol of the all-powerful Lord of All.

Perhaps I had made a mistake in waiting until the General Assembly of the League was finally brought to an end. It might have been wiser to have returned earlier, but then I have always found it difficult not to complete what I have begun and I could not then have known what my enemies were already planning for me. It was so beautiful in Geneva, quieter and more peaceful than elsewhere. Besides this – and although of course I was fully aware that I would be greeted in Budapest with wicked intrigues that would try me sadly – I had another reason for delaying my departure.

Ever since I had first arrived I had been bothered by the fact that there was no sign or memorial to remind us of the place where Queen Elisabeth had been assassinated. In the Alps, as at home, it was customary to erect a cross or a small statue to mark the spot where some fatal accident had occurred, where someone had fallen to their death or been struck by lightning. The Austrian Alps are full of such little wayside shrines – 'martyrs' crosses' they call them – so I thought I would suggest to the city authorities that some mark should show the place where that angelic being, the Great Lady of Hungary who loved us so much, met her death.

My first idea was that a small picture of the Madonna should be fixed to the tree at the foot of which our queen had collapsed; but that did not prove acceptable since it turned out that the City Council did not want anything too conspicuous, partly, I fancy, because they were still somewhat embarrassed that the assassination had taken place in their city. Lengthy discussions followed, and it was finally agreed that they would affix a little medallion, measuring only some six by ten centimetres, to a wrought-iron ring between two of the balusters marking the quayside. It would certainly be inconspicuous but still, for us, a permanent memorial.

I decided to wait for this decision before leaving Geneva. I received it in the last days of my stay.

As soon as I reached home I commissioned Szentgyörgyi to design a bronze medallion. On the front there was a profile of

Queen Elisabeth surrounded by her name and the date of her death; while on the reverse a few words of our eternal gratitude to her. It was very beautiful, but as it was only delivered to me at the beginning of December, a few days before I left office, I handed it over to my successor and charged him to send it on to Geneva, where Baranyai was to arrange to have it put in place. This never happened. About a year later I had to consult one of the ministry's advisers, and I found it on his desk. He had used it as a paperweight.

Back in Budapest, while I had been busying myself with all this, my enemies had profited by my absence to circulate even more damaging reports about me. Before, they had kept to the suspicions of my 'treason'; now it appeared that, with mounting joy, they had spread the rumour that I was going mad, had already lost my reason, even that I was a raving lunatic.

As soon I as I arrived home I went straight to see the prime minister. Bethlen received me warmly, as a friend, and I reported to him on the work I had done at the League of Nations and also told him how it had affected my nervous system. I asked him for permission to take a lengthy holiday so that I could recover my health in some sanatorium, during which time I would prepare for him a detailed account of my mission so that he would have everything on paper.

On this we parted. I did not return to my office in the ministry but went straight to Vienna so as to be on my own.

When I returned I handed in three copies of my report, which gave details of everything that had transpired in Geneva: one was for Horthy, one for the prime minister and the third for the ministry's archive. I made a copy of this, leaving out only the most confidential aspects. I had decided to read this out in parliament, although I later abandoned the idea.

I also withdrew from the appointment to Paris, even though my *Agrément* had already been accorded. It had so happened that Praznovsky had married a rich Frenchwoman and resigned from the diplomatic service, thereby leaving the Paris post unfilled just when we urgently needed an ambassador there. I did not yet feel strong enough for the job, and indeed Bethlen himself asked me to step down. I believe that he had been somewhat influenced by what had been spread around about me.

As it turned out it was to be some time before the Paris post was filled. It was not until the end of January or the beginning of February that Frigyes Korányi arrived in Paris, by which time I was myself fit enough to do the job. So my withdrawal, made for the most selfless of reasons, had achieved nothing. I received a private message from the Quai d'Orsay saying that they would rather have had me than anyone else; but my decision had been taken on 14 December, at the same time as my resignation as foreign minister, so I was no longer in any position to revive the idea. I must also say that the campaign against me, which had been planned in some most influential circles, had soured any ambition I might still have had. Even my report about Geneva, which totally vindicated my actions there, was never read in the House and so received no publicity either then or later. It seemed as if everyone had agreed to maintain a profound silence about everything I had achieved while acting as minister for foreign affairs. They succeeded only too well.

This was the end of my political career in Hungary. If I had wanted it, I could have obtained a seat in the parliamentary elections which were soon to follow; and, if I had set my mind to it, I would probably have acquired considerable influence, since I now had a wide knowledge of the inner secrets of quite a number of contemporary problems – always an advantage in dealing with current affairs. But I felt no desire to do so. I had been a member of parliament from 1901 to 1904 and again from 1910 to 1918, but I had then decided I was not really suited for a parliamentary career. Although I spoke easily in the House, I was never a first-rate speaker and had not striven to be so. On the contrary, I found myself filled with distaste for any form of oratory. Furthermore, I could not bind myself to the party in power, for I found myself opposed to too many things that the government either did or did not do. On the other hand, I did not want to join the opposition either as it would at once have been said of me that I had only done so out of wounded pride: in any case the opposition at that time was as lacking in ideas and firm policy as was the government – as they say in German: '*Dasselbe in Grün*.'

– 'It's just the same, only green.' And so my part in directing Hungary's foreign affairs finally ended there.

All the same, I was twice called in later to give advice and help. On both occasions it concerned the '*optans*[133]'.

This was caused by Romania's manner of dealing with the reform of landownership, especially in the former Hungarian province of Transylvania, and caused no end of dust to rise in those days. It was to poison relations between Hungary and Romania for many years to come. Landowners of Hungarian nationality whose estates had been confiscated received only one per cent of their value in compensation, while it was further decreed that no one of foreign nationality could own land in Transylvania. This last prescription – the law concerning absentee landlords – was a direct violation of the terms of the Trianon Treaty, which specified that all those from the territories to be reallocated to the neighbouring states who opted to retain Hungarian nationality could retain their possessions. The second part of the question concerned the inequality of the land reform conditions as imposed in the Regat – the pre-war 'Old Kingdom' of Romania –and in the provinces now to be acquired from Hungary. While in the Regat owners were entitled to retain a minimum of three hundred hectares, in Transylvania it was reduced to three hundred acres: barely three fifths of the former. And not only that, for Romanian landowners in the Regat who owned several estates in different places were allowed to keep up to three hundred acres of each of their former possessions, while in Transylvania part of only one estate could be retained. All these new dispositions were in flagrant contradiction to the assurances of fair treatment made to the minorities as part of the agreement signed between Romania and the Great Powers. Of course, it had been done because, with very few exceptions, the estates in Transylvania had been held by families of Hungarian origin, and so these new laws had been directed effectively only against Hungarians.

This matter had come up before for me towards the end of my term of office. On 16 August 1922 we put the whole question before the Council of Ambassadors, asking for their intervention to settle the matter according to Articles 53 and 64 of the Treaty of Trianon and Paragraph 3 of the contract affecting the treatment of minorities.

We drew attention to the fact that Romania had based their new decrees on a law introduced in 1917 at Jassy by which all foreign ownership of landed estates had been prohibited. In December 1918 this had been extended to the whole kingdom. We pointed out that this argument was invalid, since Romania did not have the right to apply a law promulgated in 1918 to territory which at that time was not part of Romania, especially after signing the two international agreements by which these new territories were to be acquired. Any existing Romanian law should have been valid only to the extent that it did not contravene these agreements.

The Council of Ambassadors recognized the legality and justice of our argument and at the end of August announced that the proper forum to hear our case was the League of Nations. They also told us what procedure to follow. This is as far as it had gone when I left office.

My successor, in his petition to the League of Nations presented on 23 March 1923, omitted the legal basis for our complaint even though we had originally based our case upon it. He used only the violation of the contract regarding treatment of the minorities, referring to the paragraphs in the peace treaty concerning the *optans* and giving too much importance to the question of compensation, thus, in my opinion, weakening Hungary's case. It seemed to me a mistake for us to insist that the major injustice of the treatment of the *optans* lay in the fact that many former Hungarians had been forced to leave their homes in the new Romania. Presented thus by our foreign office, our case was that the Romanian government first forced the *optans* to leave the country and then at the same time declared them to be absentees. This tempting notion was not correct and soon rebounded on us with a vengeance, since the new Romanian laws had failed to mention that the registration of absentees should not be effective until a year after the ratification of the peace treaty but had instead imposed a much earlier date; if I remember correctly it was either 1918 or 1919. And so our argument, that with one hand they had ejected Hungarian property-owners while confiscating their property with the other because they were absentees, did not hold water. Much stronger arguments could have been: firstly to recall that until the treaty had been ratified the frontiers had remained closed and guarded, and so Transylvanians who had been demobilized in Hungary had been unable to return home; and secondly that the many civil servants who were Hungarian-Transylvanians, owned property in Transylvania and had been expelled before the treaty terms had become valid should have their names removed from the absentee lists. This argument would at least have had the advantage of getting our case more quickly before the Joint Arbitration Tribunal. As it was, we obtained a hearing only after a lengthy and most disagreeable battle.

The strongest part of our case, on which it would have been wiser to base our referral of the matter to the League of Nations, was that the designation of absentees had contravened the terms of the peace treaty as regards treatment of the minorities. We should also have emphasized the difference between the Romanian laws as applied in the Regat and those in Bukovina and Transylvania, which showed only too clearly how these were designed to penalize Hungarian landholders.

Unfortunately, our government decided to concentrate on the issue of compensation.

As I have just written, only the first application to the Council of Ambassadors had been made during my time in office. By the time the answer arrived at the end of August I had already left for Geneva, and so the matter was postponed until after I had returned. However, when I did return, I was not able to work for several months.

I regret this still, because I am sure that if I had then been able to study this question closely, think deeply about it and weigh up all the political implications, and with the experience I had just had of the workings of the League of Nations, I would have been able to propose to our government a different argument and a different way of presenting it; and this would have pre-empted the long unhappy international dispute which followed and which was to make the situation of Hungarians in Transylvania so disagreeable and so difficult.

I was to become involved once more in the problems of the *optans*, but only when I could have no further influence on how it should be handled. The Hungarian government's petition was handed in on 15 March 1923. In mid-April the prime minister telephoned me about the question but not to discuss the strength of our case. Bethlen wanted me to accompany the new Hungarian delegate, György Lukács, to Geneva in a private capacity so that I could make his task easier, partly through my many connections there and partly because of my knowledge of procedure. This was because Lukács would not only be new to Geneva but also because he had had no previous diplomatic experience. My job would be to introduce him to people and help him in all the minor formalities that are so important in diplomatic negotiations. This would be necessary since both Lukács and his legal expert, Gajzágó, were complete novices. I willingly accepted this role of mentor, although I knew such a thing would always be a thankless task.

I accepted willingly for two reasons. The first was that I have always felt strongly that it was my duty, even in small matters, to do whatever I could to serve my country, preserve its good name and promote its best interests. The second was that the mere fact I had been chosen for such a responsible, influential and educational task gave the lie to all those slanders and misrepresentations to which I had been subjected both before and after my resignation – but then unsuccessful Hungarians have always been at their most inventive when it comes to malicious rumour.

I was happy to see again the lovely country beside Lac Léman. I had left in early autumn, desperately unwell; and now that I was well again I was to return in the full splendour of spring.

Now I was to have much more free time. After I had introduced Lukács to all the important people with whom he would have to deal I had little more to do than see that all our missions' courtesy letters were written in correct French. There was a real need for this, since neither of our delegates had an adequate acquaintance with foreign languages. As a result, I became a sort of house tutor, and after the first few days I found myself with little to do except draft official documents and letters in the evenings. This left me free to go where I liked during the daytime.

I took the opportunity one day to pay a visit to Basle, where some of the most important of Holbein's pictures were to be found in the City Art Gallery and also some fine works by the Swiss painters Böcklin and Hodler. I also recall going to Solothurn, home of the Maggi bouillon cube, where the Reinhardt brothers, owners of the factory, had undertaken the princely role of Maecenas. Everything had been built by them – town hall, sports arena, and covered swimming pool – as well as, for their workers, villa-type houses in gardens filled with flowers, where anyone would have been delighted to live. They founded and supported the most exemplary social institutions such as hospitals and what I believe were the first kindergartens in the world. I was particularly drawn to the picture gallery of this remote little town. Already two generations of Reinhardts had been picture-collectors, and the finest of their purchases were displayed in the public gallery they had built. Here were to be found superb works of the Barbizon school, as well as some the best pictures by Swiss painters.

In their own house, freely open for all to see, there were not only paintings by Delacroix, Goya and Manet but also the excellent, yet almost unknown, works of Hodler. It gave me singular pleasure to find in egalitarian Switzerland patrons of art to rival the Medici, the kings of Saxony and Bavaria or, as in Hungary, the Eszterházys. It was indeed proof of a truly cultured people.

Two valued old acquaintances from home were also in Geneva at that time. One was Benedek Jancsó, expert in all matters concerning the problems of minorities; while the other was my good friend and former colleague, Ilyesovics-Illyés, who, as he was originally from the foot of the Carpathians, was now concerned with laying before the League of Nations the complaints of the ethnic Ruthenians, who were being oppressed by the new government of Czechoslovakia.

Although it does not really belong to my narrative, I feel must now include a little tale about these two because at the time it seemed so funny. They are both long deceased so I can tell it today.

Jancsó and Ilyesovics-Illyés were like twins. They were never apart, lived together and went everywhere together. Jancsó had

white hair and was short and fat, while his much thinner friend
was deeply tanned and had black eyebrows as thick as a tooth-
brush. They lived sparingly, for they had very little money, and
their principal amusement was to go for walks, which cost
nothing.

One day there was a charity collection in the town. Groups of
pretty girls roamed the streets with collection boxes, stopping
everyone they met and for each coin dropped in the box they
handed out a paper cloverleaf which could be pinned on. For my
two friends such contributions would have meant a heavy tax on
their slender means. Illyés soon found a solution.

As soon as the first girl approached him, he shouted at her; and
with his flashing eyes, aggressive moustache, mouth opened wide
in a menacing grimace and huge snapping teeth, he was a truly
frightening sight. Even more alarming was the way he would
roar out:

'*Je ne donne rien. Je suis Czechoslovak!*'

The girl nearly dropped dead with fright.

Illyés repeated this with every girl who approached them on
their walk and by this ruse not only saved their money but also
made splendid anti-Czechoslovak propaganda.

The same evening several Swiss friends came up to me
and said: 'How mean those Czechs are! They won't give a *sou* to
charity!'

We laughed a lot about it.

I was intensely curious to know what would happen at the first
session of the Council that was to discuss the plight of the
optans. Benedek Jancsó and I attended it together and found
good places in the public seats, barely ten paces away from the
side of the Council table. From there we had a good view of all
the participants and were able to watch them closely. If I remember correctly it was Balfour who presided. Our delegates, Lukács
and Gajzágó, sat with their backs to us, and Titulescu, who led
the Romanian delegation, was directly facing us.

He was an interesting, if strange-looking man. Clean-shaven,
with wide cheekbones and slanting eyes, he had a marked Asiatic
look. He had greying thick dark hair growing low over his curved
forehead, as one sometimes sees in women. He was very tall with

sloping shoulders, and when I met him for the first time he reminded me of the harem servants I had seen at the funeral of Effendi Ibrahim, the Sultan of Turkey's heir. They too were all exceptionally tall, narrow-shouldered, with feminine-looking foreheads.

All sorts of stories had been told about Titulescu, including that he had endured some accident while still adolescent. Personally I do not believe the rumours, for not only was he a married man, but such gossip was also belied by his tremendous vitality and the sparkling love of battle with which he defended his opinions.

He loved to argue and did it in the French legal manner, which to our eyes always seemed rather showy. He radiated indignation or sorrow or was moved to tears just as the occasion seemed to require. And as he spoke he gestured widely, just as Monnet-Sully used to when playing in *Oedipus Rex*, and from him poured a rush of words, gushing with pathos, roaring, menacing or imploring. That his presence of mind was extraordinary was shown by the way he could instantly exploit any failing in his opponent's argument.

First Lukács read our report. Then, after Titulescu had replied, there followed much argument between him and the Hungarian delegates. This was principally conducted on our side by Gajzágó, who found himself at some disadvantage because of his still faulty command of French. He uttered some awkward phrases, which Titulescu seized upon like a hawk. The whole exchange was like a glossy-skinned shark devouring two small fishes. It was pitiful to watch.

However Titulescu's eloquence was not able to change the predictable outcome. The Council, acting on the advice of the Italian delegate, Salandra, accorded the task of negotiating a compromise between Hungary and Romania to Adatoi, the head of the Japanese delegation.

That was the most we could have hoped for at that stage.

The fatal flaw in the constitution of the League of Nations was that it had no power to enforce its judgements. It could only negotiate and, where the terms of the peace treaties gave a clear direction, it could still only exert moral pressure. Even this depended on the attitude of the Council of Ambassadors simply because only that body was backed by the military force of the Great Powers. At this point it seemed that the question of the treatment of the *optans* was going in our favour. It should also have been to our advantage that a completely neutral judge had been appointed in the person of Adatoi, who, moreover, came from the Japanese delegation where I personally had found so much goodwill and friendly feelings a year and a half before.

As far as I knew, Adatoi had accepted the Hungarian point of view. This, at least, is what Lukács and Gaszágo had been happy to tell me before they returned to Budapest in the blissful belief that the *optans* question had been left in safe hands.

What then happened I do not know, except that a few weeks later I heard that the Japanese had now sided with the Romanians. It seems that instead of staying in Geneva and working to keep the Japanese up to scratch, our people in true Hungarian fashion had gone confidently home to bed, while our opponents went to work on Adatoi.

At any rate, the next meeting was at Brussels on 27 May. Hungary was represented by Imre Csáky and Gajzágó, Romania by Titulescu, and Adatoi was present as arbitrator. Also there were the official secretaries, van Hamel and Mantoux, in their capacities as heads of the legal and political sections of the League of Nations.

On the following day a protocol was drawn up which recorded what progress had been made in the negotiations. It had been cleverly worded, and I believe that the author was Mantoux, who was known to be the trusted friend of the 'Little *Entente*'. The protocol contained no mention of any solution, yet made it clear that Hungary was not objecting to the principle of Romanian land reform, since Romania had the right to make its own internal arrangements on such matters. And, although it did make an appearance elsewhere, there was no reference to the way Romania had modified her contractual obligations.

I only became aware of this in the first days of June when I was summoned to the prime minister's office to attend a conference to discuss how we should deal with this new turn of events. There were quite a lot us present, and they all – Bethlen,

Daruváry, Kánya, Khuen-Héderváry, Gajzágó and Apponyi – blamed Csáky for having signed the protocol. This appeared to have shocked them when the documents revealed his actions, but I personally felt it was unjust to blame him.

It transpired that Kánya had given Csáky an order that in no circumstances was he to allow the conference to break up. Gajzágó related what had happened. On the first day they had argued from morning to night without arriving at any conclusion. At about ten o'clock the following morning Adatoi had summoned the Hungarian delegates to the Japanese Embassy. When they arrived they saw a car drawn up at the front door, laden with luggage. Csáky and Gajzágó were then told that Titulescu would be leaving for home at eleven o'clock. In Adatoi's presence Titulescu showed the Hungarians the protocol document, which had been drawn up overnight. Then Adatoi told them to sign it. At first they demurred, but when Titulescu declared that whatever happened he would be leaving almost immediately and that if they refused to sign, the conference would break up and that it would be their fault. Csáky, remembering Kánya's order, did not dare to take this responsibility and signed.

Although he found himself in a very difficult situation, this whole affair showed once again the impossibility of negotiating in foreign countries with fixed orders from home, for no one can foresee what difficulties may arise once the talks start. It had been quite wrong to give Csáky plenary powers to sign: better for us all if he only had the power to negotiate. He could then have entrenched himself, as I had with Ninçic, behind the ultimate authority of his government's ratification. If that had been done, all this trouble could have been avoided. As it was, the subsequent complications, which were not only disagreeable but also harmful to our country's prestige, stemmed from these two errors. It must be said, however, that the original mistake lay in the manner in which the *optans* question was laid before the League of Nations. This I have already outlined, and this is what I put to the prime minister's conference. Finally it was decided at the meeting that the government would disown Csáky's signature and would inform the League of Nations that it maintained its original position. There was no other way for Hungary if she wanted to continue her fight for fair treatment of the *optans.*

In these chapters I have told the part I was called upon to play in the rebuilding of Hungary. Although it had meant that I had devoted four years uninterrupted work, which had entailed ruining my health by working day and night, I still remember it all with undiminished satisfaction. Even today it gladdens my heart to think that it was I who arranged for Sopron to remain Hungarian, and also that I had played such an significant part in restoring international respect for my country. These achievements gave me the right, I believe, to stand in judgement on the policies, the sins of omission and the foolhardiness which later had such catastrophic effects for the Hungarian people.

Some may think I have gone into too much detail, but although I might have told my tale in a shorter way, with less about myself, it seemed to me essential to relate everything in full, not so much as to vaunt my own actions but because I felt it might be useful to a later generation to be aware of everything that happened, to try to bring to life all the little details of what is involved in a foreign service career as well as to show how diplomatic problems may be solved; and, above all, to grasp how one must adapt to the very different habits of thought in the people with whom we come in contact and how important it is to be prepared to act instantly when suddenly confronted with mishaps no one can foresee.

Hungarians are badly in need of this sort of knowledge, for, as we have no native foreign service traditions, people have come to believe that a diplomatic post is little more than an agreeable way of passing the time, mostly in attending social occasions such as evening parties, balls and festive lunches. They do not know that it is, in fact, one of the most arduous jobs of all, for it entails great responsibility. Once something has been said it cannot be withdrawn, and news of it is at once carried far and wide, creating unforeseen consequences, for we have spoken in the name of our country and those to whom we speak, although we believe them to be friends, can become our enemies overnight. This is especially true for those who represent a small country such as Hungary. Those who represent a Great Power can permit themselves many things. The English say 'My country, right or wrong!' and this is a great saying, not only in the purely patriotic sense in which they are apt to use it but also because it can mean that a powerful nation can change its attitude without doing any harm to itself. A small country, on the other hand, must stick closely to the truth, or it risks being punished a hundredfold. It is vital, therefore, to read between the lines of the drafts of all international agreements so as to be sure they include nothing that does not further the national interest. Lastly, only strict adherence to the truth will benefit one's personal prestige, for that will have a more lasting effect in a diplomatic career than anything else.

❧ Chapter Ten ❧

Having now finally abandoned all diplomatic and political work, I found new interests in artistic matters.

Just at this time Klebelsberg, then minister of education, founded the National Council for Fine Arts with the aim of improving standards, especially in architecture, sculpture and painting. He asked me to be the first chairman, and I believe that he started the organization because at that time I was available for the job. It was, so to speak, tailored to my size. In my youth I had been a painter myself[134]; I was then a pupil of Bertalán Székely. Architecture had always interested me; as Intendant of the State Theatres (1913–1918) I had been responsible for the Opera House and for the transformation of the National Theatre; while in the competition for a design for a commemorative statue to Queen Elisabeth, I had collaborated with my friend Telcs and with Kálmán Györgyi. Our design had been awarded the first prize.

All building work in Budapest was nominally under the authority of the Board of Public Works. As in recent times, its controlling function had become limited to technical and town planning matters, the Council for Fine Arts was now given artistic control of public buildings all over the country. Also falling under its jurisdiction was the organization of national exhibitions both at home and abroad. A further task was to be the founding of local museums in the country towns, for which there was plenty of material – especially in the field of fine arts – reposing in the storage vaults of the national museums in the capital because lack of space prevented their being shown to the public. We were also expected to organize painting and sculpture competitions, arrange the necessary publicity and advise on the state purchase of new works.

I was delighted to be offered this task. It promised to be most interesting, particularly as it gave us the chance to guide public taste. This was just the time when the state was building village schools and guard-posts for the gendarmerie in the country, and the Southern Railway was constructing stations on the Balaton line. People see stations, schools and guard-posts every day, and what they see gives them an idea of what is modern and beautiful and so contributes to the formation of taste. And what they hold as modern and beautiful is what people tend to imitate. It was therefore important for the Council to ensure that every approved design should serve as an example of excellence. We held discussions about this in the section devoted to architectural planning. I was strongly of the opinion that we should not follow foreign ideas; not try to copy the popular German style nor imitate English cottages or Scandinavian workers' dwellings, but rather search out the best and most interesting of our own native models from which we could evolve an internationally recognizable Hungarian style.

We decided to use as a prototype the vernacular style popular at the beginning of the eighteenth century in the country round Vesprém and Komárom on the west side of the Danube, and Miskolc and Tokaj, where the numerous manors and country houses, built mostly with porticos and varied façades, harmonized beautifully with their surroundings.

Among my colleagues were Róbert Kertész, Dénes Györgyi, Medgyaszay and Kocsis – to name but a few – and together we were able to realize many of our ideals. When I visited the country a year or two later I found to my joy that many of the new schools, village halls and guard-posts and railway stations had been built in the style of the sketches we had supplied to MAV (the Hungarian State Railways) and to the ministries of the interior and education. So we had managed to found a school which had influenced popular taste and which made use of local materials.

Our work was both sympathetic and agreeable, as well as being interesting. During that time I met many artists who became my friends. It was also interesting to learn of many things that were not so agreeable: things to which until then I had unfortunately given no thought.

My architect friends drew my attention to the abuse of power and actual swindles that were rife in the award of building contracts arranged by the Board of Public Works.

It was a rule that all contracts for state-sponsored buildings were awarded only after open competitions had been held. On the surface, it appeared that the board observed this ruling, but in its own way. When a substantial building was proposed some five or six large firms were asked to submit tenders; but only those firms that were linked by cartel received invitations with the result that they decided among themselves whose turn it was, and somehow it was always this firm that received the contract – and the more expensive the better. No firm outside the cartel got a look in.

From the many complaints I received from building firms with whom I was on friendly terms, it seemed that this type of corruption would be the easiest to prove. Thinking that it was my duty to inform the government of this, I asked the builders to provide me with full details, which I then took to the minister, József Vass. At that time I truly believed that I would be doing him a favour by telling him of the *'panamas'*[135] going on in his board. Although many people believed him to be a part of it, I found this hard to credit, for Vass was both a professor and a man of the Church. It is true that there had been gossip about him in Budapest, but I did not believe that his official integrity was involved. He had spent his life in the ministry of education as the *Referens*[136] of matters concerning the Catholic Church, and so it did not occur to me that he could have had any knowledge of corrupt dealings in the department for which he was responsible – or so I then thought.

This had been a difficult decision for me personally since I knew well, from my friendship with Klebelsberg, who opposed him in the cabinet, that Vass had been one of those who had taken part in the campaign against me when I had been in Geneva. Nevertheless, I did not allow this to deter me from taking the matter straight to him as I thought it right that he should be the first to hear of accusations levelled against the conduct of the board. After making an appointment by telephone I went to see him in his office. He received me at once with every expression of regard. On entering his office my first impression was one of shock. His room at the ministry was newly furnished and decorated in an elaborately ornate and expensive manner inappropriate and unbecoming to our poverty-stricken country. It was lined with carved oak panelling in the pseudo-rococo taste (or rather bad taste) in which the Budapest decorator, Kozma delighted so much at that time. As soon as I saw it I remembered that I had heard that Vass's own home had been done in the same manner, at enormous expense.

I explained the reason for my visit and handed over the proofs of what I had said. Vass accepted them and thanked me effusively, saying that he would immediately instigate a most rigorous investigation. He made a good impression on me and seemed sincere. He then accompanied me to the very last door, repeating his thanks over and over again until he finally showed me out.

After that nothing . . . and the swindles continued as before. When many weeks had passed, and there had been no sign of any action, and the abuses remained unchecked, I went to see the prime minister and laid everything before him.

Bethlen seemed fairly interested in what I had to tell him, but he had such confidence in Vass that I was sure he would not intervene. It was one of his greatest weaknesses that he had such confidence in all his colleagues that, even when their failings had been made all too clear, he would still keep them on and refuse to believe anything bad about them. The most unselfish of men, he could never bring himself to recognize self-interest in those who served him. He found it difficult ever to part with a colleague, and when he did it was usually only after the man concerned had found some more lucrative post and then made Bethlen believe that the change would somehow benefit the state. As a result, quite a number of his ministers found that they were in their well-paid posts for life; and this was to prove detrimental to his ministry. There can be no doubt that it was a great pity that the prime minister should have had more faith in Vass's integrity than in the facts and figures I showed him. At that time the matter could have been dealt with discreetly and without creating a public outcry. This was to come later when the so-called Dréhr Scandal broke out. Imre Dréhr was the politically appointed Secretary of State of the ministry of welfare from 1925 to 1931. He was accused of being responsible for various '*panamas*' in the ministry and condemned to a term of imprisonment. He committed suicide, as did Hankó-Veress, his section chief. At the height of the scandal Vass also died suddenly, and although it was given out he had had a heart attack, many people believed that he too had killed himself. Nothing harmed the Bethlen government as much as this scandal.

However, there were many pleasanter jobs to be done in the National Council for Fine Arts.

Here I will relate an amusing incident that occurred when two professorial posts fell vacant at the Academy of Fine Arts. Klebelsberg wished to appoint Károly Lyka and Vaszary, both excellent choices, for Lyka was one of our finest art historians, while Vaszary was a painter of considerable accomplishment. He submitted their names to the Regent, but Horthy refused to confirm their appointments, no matter how hard Klebelsberg pressed him. Horthy's reluctance stemmed from the fact that he had two intimate friends, both painters. One was Karlovszky, who had painted his portrait. Karlovszky was a talented artist, if old-fashioned, who hated anything new and who had a most malicious nature. The other was Merész, who also painted in an antiquated manner but who was decidedly second-rate. This last was a frequent guest at the Regent's and, as Horthy in his free time liked to try his hand at water-colours, Merész used to give him pointers on technique and in so doing had become Horthy's tame expert. It was clear that these two had done their best to block Klebelsberg's nominations, especially that of Vaszary. When the minister realized that he was not going to get Horthy's agreement, he asked Oszkár Glatz, the rector of the Academy of Fine Arts, and myself to accompany him to an audience in the Fortress[137].

The first to speak was Klebelsberg, who explained the reasons for his choice in a formal and respectful manner. I followed, speaking more freely since I had known Horthy for many years dating back to the time when we used to shoot together at Szovata when he was still aide-de-camp to Emperor Franz Joseph.

Then Glatz spoke up. He had a merry, good-humoured manner and at once roared out:

'Come on, nominate them, do! I can tell, Vaszary is a great painter. Do listen! You can believe us. We know your Excellency is no painter, so you can't know!'

'Please . . . ' said Horthy, ' . . . I do paint, you know.'

'Well, yes, your Excellency paints, of course . . . but that is not at all the same thing!'

'But I really do paint . . . '

'All right! All right! Of course you do . . . ' replied Glatz, smiling. Then, with a deprecating wave of the hand, he said:

'You do paint, of course! But that isn't the point. We are now talking about real painting. Do please make these appointments. This really is quite a different matter . . . '

Glatz spoke in such an uninhibited and good-humoured way that Horthy started to laugh. Nothing that either his own minister or I had said had had the same effect as Glatz's cheerful sincerity; and Horthy was won over by it. He agreed to nominate our candidates and when we left shook hands with Glatz with marked warmth. This was an instance of the modesty that Horthy used to display before his sycophants flattered him into believing he knew everything and was a great statesman, which later led to megalomania.

After my resignation in the summer of 1923 I went home to Transylvania for the first time since the revolution. It was painful for me, but there was also joy mixed with the pain. I went straight to my lovely home, Bonczhida, and found that everything was just as I had last seen it when I left in 1918[138].

This visit to Transylvania had a great effect on me. It was while I was there that the thought first entered my head that I might come back to my native land for good; and there, far from the world of politics, start to write.

All this was still just a dream, and I was still far from making any definite decision. There were also all sorts of difficulties. Still, this was when the idea was born. Of course, one's decisions are rarely taken for only one reason. Where I am concerned, action is always the fruit of long and profound mental labour and follows much weighing up of the reasons for it, both strong and weak. It gradually became clear to me that I really had almost nothing to do in Budapest. The Council of Fine Arts took up little of my time. I tried several other things, including trying once again to take up painting, but it gave me little satisfaction. I wrote a satirical comedy, *Maskara*, in which I chose the emerging Fascist organization as the object of my mockery. At the same time I still had hankerings for some diplomatic occupation and toyed with the idea of getting a post at some distant embassy. Bethlen hinted at the League of Nations, but this did not appeal to me after my previous experience in Geneva when the Hungarian Foreign Ministry had spent so much time in pulling me this way and that just as a puppeteer treats his marionettes. The Turkish Embassy was then vacant, and I would have gone there willingly. In 1916 and 1917 I had spent a lot of time in the capital, Istanbul, on a cultural and political mission. I got along well with the Turks and felt that my discussions with them had earned me their respect. I still feel I would probably then have done better there than anyone else; but Kánya soon put a stop to that; and it is certain that no ambassador can be properly effec- tive without full support from home. Kánya's ill will would have been an endless source of vexation, and so it was easy for me to draw back from pursuing that idea.

So it was that my dream of returning to Transylvania became gradually stronger and stronger until it finally became a fixed intention. Standing now on the sidelines of political events, I became aware of the insidious growth of a kind of spiritual lethargy in the Hungarian political scene; and this, although barely noticed by most people, played a big part in my ultimate decision. Superficially, there were few signs of this. The League of Nations' loan had given a boost to the economy. Furthermore, the state loans had been followed by private investment. Dollars were pouring into the country, and quite a number of big enter- prises that had access to this new source of funding got them- selves seriously into debt. Although the time of the reform of our national institutions was now over, there were still some impor- tant areas where action was desperately needed: two especially.

The first was in the field of agriculture. The agrarian economy of Hungary was based on wheat production. This worked well under the Habsburg monarchy, for the only great cereal-growing areas within the Empire's borders were the *Alföld* – the Great Hungarian Plain – and the country west of the Danube; and their entire production was sold inside the hereditary lands, with markets in Vienna and even in the Carpathian provinces and Transylvania. The internal customs and excise policy set the prices at a level that made cereal growing profitable. With the new frontiers the situation was completely changed, for now the consumer provinces found themselves outside the country. Hungarian wheat was faced with competition from abroad, and international prices had dropped so low that there was no longer an economically viable market for Hungarian cereals. This was when the so-called '*boletta*' system was introduced. This meant that the combined Hungarian Export Board purchased wheat from the farmers for more than it could be sold abroad. The ultimate deficit to the state was to be met by the treasury. It was intended to be a temporary measure, only to last for the time being. However, to bring it to an end it would have been necessary for the state to act swiftly to encourage better husbandry in some and a move to industry for others. In later years this was achieved in the countryside around Kecskemét. But at that time the ministry of agriculture was not up to the task, and everything stayed just as it was.

The second problem that remained to haunt us was that of land reform. The first plan put forward by the Bethlen government had been too modest, covering only some seventeen per cent of the land available, and failed because those who acquired the distributed lands did not have the cash to exploit them; production fell and, instead of promoting contentment, only discontent followed. Therefore, a year or so after my resignation a new and far more comprehensive plan was evolved which would have had spectacular results if it had not been allowed slowly to peter out. This plan had envisaged that the state would expropriate the land, divide it up and redistribute it, while the former owners would receive compensation in the form of state securities which, being based on the gold standard, would be negotiable abroad, which it was hoped would encourage substantial holders to reinvest in new or existing industries. It was designed to attract the American market, then the world's richest. I do not know who invented this plan, but Bethlen and Horthy were in favour of it. Unfortunately, Bethlen, already overstretched by his myriad responsibilities, could not tackle it alone and did not have one first-rate economist among his close advisers. Valko could have done it, but he soon became foreign minister and anyway was perhaps not aggressive enough for the task, since to fight the opposition of the great landowners needed a man of ferocious energy.

So this plan also failed; and after the World Crash in 1931 no one thought about the matter again[139].

In my view it was the rural Hungarian gentry who were in some measure responsible for this failure to bring about an effective reform of the land. This class had become increasingly influential during the Horthy regime, for the aristocracy had distanced themselves further and further from the government. This, of course, had been largely due to their feelings about the restoration of the monarchy. Their place had been increasingly filled by the gentry, who thus gained much influence with Horthy and his entourage.

And it must be said that the gentry as a class were far more reactionary and opposed to any form of modernization than the aristocrats had ever been. One can say many things detrimental to the Hungarian aristocracy, but it was certain that they never lost their international outlook and so should have been easy to convert to the vital necessity for industrialization.

Notes

1. Of which Miklós Bánffy was Intendant.
2. The office of Ban was equivalent to that of a governor appointed by the monarch.
3. This, as we can see from contemporary photographs, was Empress Maria-Theresia's diamond crown that, according to a note in the treasure house of the Hofburg in Vienna, has not been seen since 1918.
4. Károlyi's version of this visit to Vienna and of the events which follow is significantly different in many respects: see *Memoirs of Michael Károlyi* (Jonathan Cape, London, 1956).
5. Bánffy is here quoting from the account published by the Budapest newspaper *Az Est*.
6. These had been established in the Hotel Astoria.
7. The white aster is usually known as a 'Michaelmas Daisy' in England, while 'aster' is normally kept for the hybrid varieties of this very large genus of plants. Several other historical accounts of this day refer to the 'Michaelmas Daisy Revolution', but the name 'Aster' is more usual.
8. In fact, in October 1914, in the company of a small band of Hungarians who had also been interned in the garrison barracks at Bordeaux, Károlyi was allowed to board a Spanish ship which took them to Venice, whence they went directly to Vienna. The visit to Switzerland took place three years later, in October 1917, when Károlyi attended the Congress of the League for Permanent Peace held in Berne.
9. This is not quite accurate. In January 1918 Imre Károlyi, a prominent banker, published a letter in the press – not a lawsuit – accusing Mihály of being 'half-traitor'. In 1923, when Mihály Károlyi was living in exile in London, it was used as evidence (fabricated, according to Károlyi's memoirs) that led to Mihály's being arraigned for High Treason. Found guilty in his absence (he had already been out of Hungary since 1919), his properties were seized, and he was officially condemned to an exile that, in all, lasted for twenty-seven years.

10. That is, fourteen years after the events here described.
11. The *Kaisers Rock* was the imperial uniform, regarded by the officer caste as a quasi-sacred symbol of their calling that must never be disgraced by word or deed, while the *Portepée Ehre* – literally 'sword-carrier's honour', meaning a gentleman's honour – was a phrase dating originally from the days when all gentlemen, and only gentlemen, wore swords with civilian dress.
12. Although the literal meaning of this German saying is 'How do you take without stealing?' perhaps the sense here is best interpreted as 'How do you remove the best and not be left with the second rate?' or 'If you remove the strong you are left with the weak.'
13. Károlyi does not mention his search for a justice minister but does say: 'I now went, accompanied by the members of the government, to the palace, to take the oath before Archduke Joseph. In the entrance hall we were told that Count Tisza had been murdered in his villa in the Varosliget. The news came five minutes before the swearing-in ceremony and so terrified our future minister of justice that, taking to his heels, he vanished and was seen no more . . . '
14. An exile, stripped of his great possessions, forever wandering in foreign lands, discredited and with little influence. When these memoirs were published in 1932 there would have been few readers who did not know that this is what Bánffy was implying.
15. An incident during the troubled years of the 1848 struggle against the Habsburgs.
16. Led by Lajos Kossuth during the 1848/9 insurrection against Austrian domination.
17. The extensive 'Uj épület' barracks, which were erected in 1786 and pulled down in 1897, covered a vast area which later comprised the Stock Exchange building, Szabadság Square and several streets, as well as banks and other large commercial buildings. In 1850 this was a quiet, almost suburban, quarter that only acquired its later importance after the huge parliament building was completed on the nearby Danube embankment.
18. Countess Katalin Bethlen, wife of Miklós Bánffy's grandfather – also called Miklós – had several daughters, all older than our Miklós Bánffy's father, including Clarisse, who married first Edward Károlyi and then Sándor Károlyi, and Elise who married a Count Berchtold, a relation of Count Leopold Berchtold, the Austrian foreign minister who wrote the infamous Austrian ultimatum to Serbia whose rejection was to bring about the 1914–18 War. Leopold Berchtold's wife was Nadine (sometimes spelt Nandine) Károlyi, another cousin of Mihály Károlyi.
19. Mihály's paternal grandmother, born Countess Caroline Zichy.

20. In the Károlyi palace in Egyetem utca in Budapest. The story goes that he had been sentenced to be hanged but that, to save him that indignity, Caroline Károlyi had smuggled a stiletto to him (hidden in a loaf of bread and carried by a French abbé) with which he wounded himself in the neck and so, as befitted his rank, he was shot instead. The dagger bore the legend '*Ora et semper*' ('Now and always'). It was over his coffin that Caroline is reputed to have issued a terrible curse against the Habsburgs. Years later, when asked why she had never written her memoirs, she replied that she could not write the truth and refused to write lies.

21. During the last quarter of the seventeenth century, a powerful movement in Transylvania, which had formerly been a semi-independent principality, rebelled not only against the imposition of direct Austrian rule but also of the integration of the province in the kingdom of Hungary. 'It was at this time,' state the editors of *The History of Transylvania* (Akadémiai Kiado, Budapest, 1994), 'that the exiles assembled along the Transylvanian border began to be called "*kuruc*". The origin of the expression is uncertain. From the late 1670s a *kuruc* was anyone who took up arms against the Habsburg's rule in Hungary . . . '

22. Bánffy uses here a Hungarian phrase which, literally translated, means 'to grind pepper under their noses!'

23. This is not quite accurate since Mihály Károlyi's great-grandmother had been Georgina de Dillon, daughter of the French general known in Paris as '*le beau Dillon*', and so through her he was related to the Polignacs and many other grand French families. Others of his forebears had extensive French connections, and some of them lived for years in Paris and Menton.

24. It is interesting to note that Mihály Károlyi himself tells how it was his uncle who had first given him Karl Marx's *Das Kapital* as a counterbalance to his early materialistic ideas. He too pondered on how this book had influenced him in ways that would have horrified his uncle.

25. This enormous townhouse still exists and houses the Petőfi Museum as well as a suite of apartments still preserved as they were in the Károlyis' days. The extensive garden is now a public square. The property, confiscated with all the rest of Mihály's holdings in Hungary in the early days of the Horthy regime, was restored to him in 1946 at the same time as the street was renamed Mihály Károlyi utca. After the fall of Communism it regained its original name, which in English means 'University Street'.

26. Károlyi himself only mentions these difficulties obliquely when, in a footnote in his memoirs, he writes that: 'At the last moment, the Soldiers' Council nominated Captain Csernyak as its

representative ... and we were therefore bound to include Csernyak in the delegation, for it would have been unsafe to snub this powerful organization, which would have caused serious trouble at home during our absence.' This is the closest he gets to admitting how limited was his real authority. The suspicion cannot be dismissed that at that stage not even Károlyi himself had noticed.

27. Among them was Baron Hatvany, a leading Jewish newspaper owner, to whom Bánffy refers in some detail in Chapter Eleven.

28. This is, in fact, what was done. The House of Deputies dissolved itself and some time was to pass before it was reconstituted, while the Upper House (the House of Lords) was never to meet again.

29. There is a dramatic description of this event in *They Were Counted*, volume one of Bánffy's Transylvanian trilogy.

30. There is also a full description of this incident in *They Were Counted*.

31. Mihály Károlyi was to write later that the square outside had been packed with people, who cheered as he addressed them from the steps of the parliament building.

32. The ministry of defence building, on one side of the Disz Square near the royal palace, was badly damaged in the autumn of 1944 when it was occupied by German troops and bombarded by the Russians. This battle-scarred ruin has been preserved as a monument to Budapest's suffering during the last stages of the Second World War.

33. The imperial family were not there. On 11 November, after the collapse of the Austrian government, Emperor Karl, with Empress Zita and their children, had secretly left the Hofburg and gone to their private hunting lodge, Schloss Eckartsau on the Marchfeld, a few miles to the north-east of Vienna. There the emperor had signed a brief three-sentence declaration that he resigned his part in the business of state, a document that was later used to justify his enemies' claims that he had abdicated. It was from Eckartsau that, on the evening of 23 March 1919, the imperial family embarked on the imperial train with a small escort of British soldiers and left for Switzerland. They were never to see Vienna again.

34. In *They Were Found Wanting*, volume two of Bánffy's Transylvanian trilogy, he writes: 'But *Mannestreue*, that old German tradition that a man must be as good as his word, did not apply only to the glamour and chivalry of medieval knights: heroism and self-sacrifice could be just as noble in the grey obscurity of ordinary people in a little country town.'

35. The Congress of Vienna in 1815 was the largest gathering of heads of state and/or their leading ministers that Europe had ever

known. It was convoked to reorganize Europe after the first defeat
of Napoleon. Prince Metternich, in whose study Bánffy was now
to find himself, was foreign minister to Emperor Francis I, a post
he held from 1809 to 1848 (see Harold Nicolson, *The Congress of
Vienna*, 1946).

36. Now the site of Berlin's principal airport.
37. Revenge, that is, for their defeat by Prussia in 1870.
38. Which may be taken as meaning 'any little gain is better than
    none'.
39. At Radun, which was in German territory until it became included
    in the newly re-created Poland after the 1914–18 War.
40. Princess Blücher was no more a British spy than that other
    beautiful Englishwoman married to a German aristocrat: Daisy,
    Princess of Pless. Both women spent the war years in Germany
    and both were occasionally to suffer from the same malicious
    gossip, although this seems to have been completely baseless. Both
    of these ladies, although loyal to their own country, were equally
    loyal to that of their husbands.
41. Béla Kun's short-lived Communist republic in Hungary.
42. After leaving the Theresianum in Vienna, Bánffy had studied with
    the famous Budapest painter Bertalán Székely before studying law
    at the University of Kolozsvár. Amongst other works of his that
    still exist are a quantity of his designs for costumes and scenery at
    the Budapest opera. His daughter still possesses a self-portrait
    and a painting of her mother – the actress Aranka Varady – as
    Shakespeare's Ariel. The painting of Bánffy used as a frontispiece
    for *They Were Found Wanting* and *They Were Divided* in Arcadia
    Books' edition of the Transylvanian trilogy is a copy of Bánffy's
    own self-portrait.
43. '*Rapin*' can mean either a student or a second-rate painter. It is
    unclear which of these two meanings Bánffy intended.
44. The Dutch title *Jongheer* is the equivalent to that of baron.
45. This little bust has survived, rescued by the family from the
    Bánffy house in Budapest when it was occupied by the Russian
    army in 1944. It resembles the larger than life-size marble bust by
    Strobl at present lent by Katalin Bánffy-Jelen to the Budapest
    Opera, where it stands in one of the grand tier foyers beside the
    great stair. Katalin Bánffy-Jelen presented Mrs Mendlik's clay
    maquette to Gábor Koltay after he had been responsible for the
    reissue of Miklós Bánffy's great Transylvanian trilogy – *Erdélyi
    Történet* – in one deluxe volume in Budapest in 1993.
46. A comprehensive account of the events leading up to the departure
    of the emperor and empress and their family is given in Gordon
    Brook-Shepherd's *The Last Habsburg* (Weidenfeld & Nicolson,
    London, 1968), which also quotes extensively from the diary of

Lieutenant-Colonel Strutt, who was at their side at Eckartsau, who was responsible for the arrangements, and who also accompanied the party on the King-Emperor's royal train.

47. The English journalist was Ellis Ashmead-Bartlett, who only gave a brief mention of what followed in his perceptive and sympathetic account of Hungary's plight, *The Tragedy of Central Europe* (Butterworth, London, 1923), but who does not reveal anything of his own involvement. The affair is recounted in greater detail in Owen Rutter's 'authorized' biography of Admiral Horthy, *Regent of Hungary* (Rich & Cowan, London, 1939); and, although it varies slightly from Miklós Bánffy's account, it also has no hesitation in stating that Ashmead-Bartlett netted £60,000 for his help, which explains Bánffy's cryptic comment: 'although not only as a favour'.

48. The nearest translation of the original Hungarian would be 'black market currency'.

49. A month or so earlier Count Julius Károlyi – a distant cousin of Mihály Károlyi – had formed a right-wing 'national' government in Arad to provide a rallying point for all those Hungarian patriots who opposed the rule of Béla Kun and the spread of Communism. Archduke Joseph, who had been appointed *homo regis* by King Karl at the time of the October Revolution, took on the duties of head of state, with Julius Károlyi as prime minister and Admiral Horthy as minister of war and commander-in-chief of those elements of the army which had remained loyal to the dynasty. This 'national' government had soon moved its headquarters to Szeged, out of reach of the threat posed by the occupying Romanian army.

50. These districts lie in the Burgenland and were to be given to Austria under the terms of the Peace Treaty. The exiled officers' plans were in effect for a pre-emptive strike before Hungary was dispossessed of yet another part of her former possessions. The whole matter is discussed by Bánffy in his posthumous memoir *Twenty-Five Years 1945*, which forms the second part of this current volume.

51. In English in the original.

52. Bánffy is referring here to the revolution in October 1918, described earlier in this book.

53. The Szeged 'national' government, which Bánffy has already mentioned in this text, would eventually lead to Admiral Horthy assuming the office of Regent.

54. The Austrian armed police: militia stationed in country districts to maintain order.

55. Under pressure from the Allies, Béla Kun was forced to resign on 1 August. He then took refuge in Vienna.

56. Don Livio, Prince Borghese, later also the eleventh prince of Salmona (1874-1939).
57. It was from this town that the ex-emperor and empress were to embark on their journey into exile in 1922.
58. The total defeat of the French by the Germans at Sedan in 1870 had brought about not only the fall of the Second Empire and the departure of Napoleon III but also the loss of Alsace-Lorraine and other humiliating terms exacted by Berlin.
59. The White Terror was a disgraceful chapter in Hungarian history when the new nationalist government, soon under Admiral Horthy, led to a series of atrocious acts of revenge intended to wipe out forever any lingering traces of the Communist regime.
60. Meaning 'Tall House', this sounds somewhat ludicrous to Hungarian ears.
61. In 1925 it was discovered that a huge quantity of forged French francs had been printed inside the Military Cartographic Institute. Deeply implicated, and finally found guilty of planning the fraud was Prince Lajos Windischgrätz, a prominent member of the Legitimist Party, who admitted responsibility but later claimed he had done this solely to protect the prime minister and other highly placed personages. His disingenuous apologia for this and other somewhat dubious activities are to be found in his autobiographical *Helden und Halunken*, which was translated into English as *My Adventures and Misadventures* (London, 1965).
62. This ban applied only to delegates from the defeated nations.
63. To Hungarian ears his name sounded like the Magyar word meaning 'sleepy'.
64. Where Bánffy owned some farmland.
65. The ancestral palace of the Esterházys at Galanta seems to be one of the models for the fictional castle of 'Jablanka', which figures extensively in the second and third volumes of *The Writing on the Wall*. One of Miklós Bánffy's great-grandmothers was Agnes Esterházy.
66. The 1848 Party was formed by supporters of the 1848 uprising in Hungary that fought against the absolute rule of the Habsburgs and domination by Austria.
67. Meaning 'Sooty' in Hungarian.
68. The shooting at Surány was famous and has been described by Bánffy in an important scene set at 'Jablanka' in the trilogy.
69. Miklós Bánffy had cousins in almost every part of the country just north of the Great Hungarian Plain.
70. There is an echo of this sad memory in the closing pages of *They Were Divided*, the third volume of *The Writing on the Wall*, when Balint Abády watches a batch of enthusiastic young recruits singing happily as they march off to their own destruction.

71. Three of Hungary's most revered patriots.
72. On 29 August 1526 King Louis II of Hungary was defeated by the forces of the Sultan Suleyman I. The king and the greater part of the Hungarian army lost their lives in the battle; and, although the Turks briefly retreated, by 1541 the area they controlled reached as far as Buda.
73. From the mid-seventeenth century in the person of the emperor of Austria.
74. King Stephen I, who founded the Arpád dynasty in 996, was the first monarch of a united Hungary. Their rule lasted for some three hundred years. Many of the noble families of Hungary and Transylvania claim descent from the Arpád kings.
75. The two treaties of the Peace of Westphalia in 1648 brought an end to the Thirty Years' War, which had devastated central Europe in the first half of the seventeenth century.
76. In fact, following the defeat and expulsion of the independent King Frederick, husband of the Winter Queen, Elizabeth Stuart, sister of England's Charles I, Bohemia was incorporated into the Habsburg domains, and a new and stricter constitution imposed in 1627.
77. The complications of the struggle against the Habsburgs at the time when Hungary was also menaced by the Turks are described in full in *History of Transylvania*, issued by the Budapest Akadémiai Kiadó in 1994.
78. In western Hungary near the Austrian border.
79. This happened in 1684, the king of Poland being John III Sobieski. The first Holy League had been proposed by the Pope in 1569 and ratified by Spain, the Papacy and Venice in the summer of 1571, just four months before the decisive defeat of the Turks at the Battle of Lepanto.
80. Count Miklós Esterházy was Palatine when, in 1627/8, he discussed with Archbishop Péter Pázmány the prospect of launching a war against the Porte from Transylvania.
81. Ferenc Deák's period of influence was the troubled times of the 1848 revolution that led, finally, to the 1867 compromise, incorporating many of the principles of Hungarian independence which he had declared to be essential and unchangeable.
82. Baron von Bach became effective ruler of Hungary after the suppression of the 1848 revolution by the Habsburgs. The terror his rule inspired was only brought to an end in 1867.
83. There seems to be some confusion here. A note in the Hungarian edition states that this Prince Teck was a brother of Queen Mary who had once been proposed as a husband for one of Archduke Joseph's daughters. This is clearly unlikely since both brothers had been married years before the war. They had given up their

German titles in 1917 when the elder was created Marquis of
Cambridge and the younger Earl of Athlone. Lord Cambridge's
son was not married until 1923 and was no longer entitled to call
himself Prince Teck. Lord Athlone had no son. Who then was this
Prince Teck?

84. *The House of Teck* by Louis Felbermann (London 1911).
85. These lines appear in English in Bánffy's text.
86. Friedrich's dubious activities, and also later at the time of the
affair of the forged French francs, are described from a different
point of view in Prince Lajos Windischgrätz's memoirs, which
were published in an abridged English translation in 1966.
87. Colonel Léhar was later to show that his real allegiance was to the
exiled monarch. He played a double role at the time of King Karl's
second attempt to regain the throne of Hungary in October 1921,
while Sigray was also to play a double role at the time of King
Karl's *putsch*. His activities then, and also during the affair of the
forged French francs, are also mentioned by Windischgrätz.
88. This line appears in English in Bánffy's text.
89. The term used to denote the traditional military tunic.
90. Whenever a new monarch was required for a newly emergent
country, the procedure generally accepted by the Great Powers
was to select some young European princeling who at that time
held no official post. The belief in the suitability of any person of
semi-royal or royal status was not always justified.
91. Elise Berchtold seems to have been the model for one of Bánffy's
more sympathetic characters in the trilogy.
92. This is actually a mistake on Bánffy's part. The Venice
Municipio then occupied, and still does, the two twelfth-century
Romanesque palaces of the Loredan and Farsetti families.
93. His name was Richard Oppenheimer. This, however, is not the
British Colonel Oppenheimer who figures in Chapter Eight of
From My Memories.
94. Viktor Ranzenberger and Gyula Ostenburg. They commanded
the reserve gendarme battalions in Sopron and Torony.
95. This conversation took place on 16 October. Windischgrätz reveals
that 'towards the end of August' King Karl had told him that he
was at that time planning 'a fresh trip to Western Hungary to the
loyal troops under Lehár and Osztenburg'. So much for Sigray not
knowing what was in the wind!
96. Windischgrätz writes that Bethlen had agreed that his speech at
'a national memorial service' would include the statement that it
was the policy of the government to recall Hungary's crowned
apostolic king. This seems to be what Andrássy and other loyal
supporters of King Karl had reported to him, but which had not
been strictly accurate. Windischgrätz also writes that the

'Emperor and Empress' had precipitated their arrival in Hungary on the strength of a favourable report from Rakovszky, Sigray and Lehár!

97. The Czirákys were closely related to many of Hungary's most influential aristocratic families.

98. A possible further reason may well lie in the fact that Countess Sophie Chotek, who became the morganatic wife of Archduke Franz Ferdinand and who was assassinated at Sarajevo with her husband, had formerly been a lady-in-waiting to Archduke Friedrich's wife, Isabella. It seems to have been Zita's influence that was responsible for the new Emperor Karl's demotion of Archduke Friedrich from the head of the Austro-Hungarian army in 1917.

99. This looks like an inadvertent mistake in view of the larger numbers already mentioned.

100. This phrase appears in English in Bánffy's text.

101. In his memoirs, Prince Windischgrätz gives his own somewhat disingenuous apologia for his part in these events and what was to follow.

102. The Budapest editors suggest that here Bánffy really means Soós.

103. Not far from the city centre.

104. Then one of the outlying suburbs of Budapest.

105. There seems to be some confusion here between the jurist Guyla Térfy and Béla Térfi who became minister of agriculture later that year.

106. The property of Count Ferenc Esterházy. Tata itself lies a few miles from Kómarom on the Danube and on the main road to Austria.

107. Windischgrätz's version is that 'a group of Horthy adherents under Colonel Simenfálvy made a surprise attack in the middle of the night and arrested all the principal personages'!

108. This was claimed by Windischgrätz to have been said to *him* by Briand in Paris sometime before the Treaty of Trianon had even been signed – this was 4 June 1920, some ten months before the first *putsch* in April 1921.

109. Near Lake Balaton in western Hungary.

110. This is Bánffy's wording. The context here suggests he means the Council of Ambassadors.

111. The king, who was not strong and suffered from periodic bouts of ill health, was to die there the following year.

112. The translators have a copy of one of these photographs found among the Bánffy papers deposited at the Ráday Institute in Budapest.

113. This was László Bárdossy, who declared war on the USA on 13 December 1941.

114. The old imperial Austro-Hungarian Foreign Ministry in Vienna.
115. The double sovereignty of the head of the Habsburg house as king of Hungary and emperor of Austria.
116. Shortly after Bánffy's return from the Genoa this series of twenty-one coloured caricatures was published in Leipzig under the title *Fresques et Frasques*. The originals were hung in a special room in Bánffy's house in Budapest and are now preserved in the Radáy Institute along with what remain of Bánffy's papers.
117. He was later given a peerage.
118. One of Bánffy's principal tasks had been to obtain the Great Powers' approval for negotiating a revision of Hungary's new frontiers as soon after the conference as possible.
119. In 1848.
120. As a landowner in Transylvania, Bánffy was able to obtain dual Hungarian and Romanian nationality. This dual nationality was to be of much use to Bánffy when, in 1943, he went to Romania to try and persuade that country to join with Hungary in signing a separate peace with the Allies. These negotiations were to fail because of disagreement over the future of Transylvania.
121. Bernini's *St Theresa* is actually in the left transept and has always been an object of controversy. Even Baedeker referred to it as 'notorious'. There are altar-pieces by Domenichino, Guercino and Guido Reni, but if Bánffy was near the Bernini it is not surprising that he noticed nothing else.
122. Bánffy is still remembered with affection and respect at the Budapest Opera House. Some forty-five years after his death in 1950, a tribute to his enterprise and achievement during his period as Intendant was still being printed in the programme and, in 1994, at the invitation of his current successor, his daughter Katalin unveiled a marble bust of Bánffy by his friend, the famous sculptor Strobl, in the foyer of the theatre.
123. Danzig (Gdansk) the Baltic port of Poland, was made an internationally administered zone after World War I, while the German industrial region of the Saar was placed under League of Nations jurisdiction, only to be returned to Germany in 1935. The Ruhr was occupied by France until 1925 when she withdrew.
124. Both Poland and Lithuania claimed the city of Vilna. The Soviet Union supported the Lithuanian claim, and the League of Nations, under French pressure, supported that of Poland. The city was to remain Polish until 1939 and is now the capital of Lithuania.
125. In 1920 an infamous decision had been made to limit the number of Jewish students entering universities to six per cent of the intake.
126. On the afternoon of 10 September 1898, the Empress Elisabeth (Queen of Hungary) was walking from the Hotel Beau-Rivage,

accompanied by Countess Sztaray, to board the steamer for Caux, where she planned to spend a few days. Edward Crankshaw in *The Fall of the House of Habsburg* writes: 'a young man hurried towards them, barred their path, leapt at the empress and stabbed her violently and swiftly in the breast. Elisabeth fell to the ground as the young man rushed headlong away. But, with help, she got to her feet, was dusted down, refused to go back to the hotel, said it was nothing and resumed the walk to the steamer. Countess Sztaray had to help her up the gangway, but she did not collapse until she had set foot on deck; then she sank down and died. The young man was Luigi Lucheni, an Italian builder's labourer, twenty-six years old.'

127. In the spring of 1890 Hélène Vacarescu, a young Romanian aristocrat was the favourite lady-in-waiting to Queen Carmen Sylva of Romania. The queen soon saw that the shy young Crown Prince Ferdinand had fallen in love with the girl and did everything she could to further the romance. She omitted, however, to tell King Carol, and when, in the spring of 1891, the king was told he exploded with anger and forbade the match, insisting that his nephew would have to marry a royal princess or give up being his heir. Ferdinand gave in, and the queen, with Hélène in tow, left for Venice, where Pierre Loti, hearing the story, wrote his novel *L'Exilée* about them. It was banned in Romania, and in little over a year's time the crown prince married Queen Victoria's granddaughter, Princess Marie of Edinburgh, later to become Queen Marie of Romania. Hélène Vacarescu never married. For many years she lived in Paris where – rich, scholarly and witty – she spent a useful and popular life devoted to a variety of social, literary and political activities. See *Marie of Romania* by Terence Elsberry.

128. Between the years 1904 and 1905 Japan had inflicted a heavy defeat upon Russia.

129. The 'turul' is the heraldic bird of Hungary.

130. That is, Emperor Franz Joseph.

131. Bánffy was present in the government party headquarters the day the Serbs rejected the Austrian ultimatum. In the penultimate chapter of *They Were Divided* there is a moving description of Tisza refusing to appear on the balcony to acknowledge the cheers of the crowd who 'could not have known that Tisza was opposed to the war. No one knew, except those who had attended the king's council meetings. On the day that the ultimatum had been decided, Tisa had at once resigned. He had remained in office only because ordered to by the monarch himself. He had resigned because he thought that by so doing he would be able to modify the harsh terms of the ultimatum; but when he had found that his

struggle would be in vain and that he would never be able to bring
Berchtold and Conrad to his way of thinking, he had decided to
stay, as he knew that he alone was strong enough to hold the country together at such a critical time. At the express wish of the king
he had agreed to keep his opposition secret, principally because he
knew that Hungary's newfound unity would be shattered if it were
known what he really felt. So he accepted responsibility for a war
he had fought hard to prevent. Out of a sense of duty he had
accepted a task he loathed, the task of organizing a war knowing
well what it would mean. He accepted it in silence, a silence that
lasted until his death.' When the clamour has died down, and the
book's hero prepares to leave, he sees Tisza sitting alone. 'There
the man sat, in a deep armchair, not speaking to anyone, with a
dark expression on his face and teeth clenched. What a tragic face
the man had! Abády was startled and he sensed at once that there
must have been some deep compulsion to explain why he had
refused to speak, why he had rejected all appeals from his followers, why he could not allow himself to go out and make a speech
and allow himself to be cheered . . . he knew he could not intrude,
so he turned away and went home. But he never forgot the moment
he had seen him there, sitting in silence in the deep armchair with
his legs crossed, his thick-lensed glasses making his eyes seem so
much larger, a bitter crease on his forehead, and even more bitter
lines reaching down each side of his face. He had sat there motionless, staring ahead of him as if all he could see was the fate of his
country . . . '

132. The Hungarian Wertheimstein family had estates at Nagyvárad,
soon to become transferred to Romania and renamed Oradea.
There is, however, a small mistake here. Rose's husband, the
Honourable (Nathaniel) Charles Rothschild, was the second son of
the first Lord Rothschild. He died before his elder brother, who
had succeeded as the second Lord Rothschild, and so the title
missed a generation, and it was Nathaniel Charles' son who succeeded his uncle.

133. '*Les optans hongrois*' was the term used in the Treaty of Trianon to
denote all those residents of the Hungarian territories which were
to be handed over to the neighbouring states but who chose to
retain their Hungarian nationality. Derived from the French
'*optan*' – a person who makes a choice – it was adapted into
Hungarian as '*optan(s)*'.

134. And not only in his youth. His daughter still possesses a small self-
portrait showing Bánffy in early middle age, which shows considerable mastery of his medium; as do the caricatures and the
costume and set designs for the Budapest Opera now in the Ráday
Institute. His coloured design for the decoration of the altar for

King Karl's coronation in 1916 is still displayed in the Treasury of the Matthias Church in Buda.

135. *'Panama'* in Hungarian means 'swindle'. It is derived from the notorious corruption that brought about the liquidation of the first Panama Canal Company in 1889.

136. Regulator or arbiter.

137. Regent Horthy had his quarters in the Royal Palace in the old fortress of Buda.

138. The great castle of Bonczhida, some twenty-nine kilometres north of Kolozsvár, was one of Transylvania's grandest country houses. Destroyed after World War II and now utterly ruined, it lives on in Bánffy's detailed descriptions of the castle of 'Dénestornya' in the first volume of his Transylvanian trilogy. After we had completed this translation of Bánffy's memoirs, the Translyvanian Trust started a full-scale restoration; when completed the castle will be used as a centre for cultural studies, including modern methods of restoring old buildings. The work of the Transylvanian Trust has been considerably helped by the Prince of Wales, whose practical interest has been manifested by the provision of English architects and specialists. This would have given great pleasure to Miklós Bánffy himself, who would doubtless be gratified that an apartment is being prepared for the use of his family.

139. That is, until the post-war Communist government expropriated all the agricultural holdings they could lay their hands on.

Glossary of Names and Places

Ady: Hungarian poet who had been closely associated with Mihály Károlyi at the time of the October Revolution.

The Duke of Alba: Commander-in-chief of the armies of King Philip II of Spain and Regent of the Netherlands when largely Protestant Holland formed part of the Habsburg domains in the sixteenth century. Waged a bloody war in a vain attempt to eradicate Protestantism in the Netherlands.

Archduke Albrecht (1897-1956): A fervent admirer of Germany and the Nazi Party.

Count Gyula Andrássy (1860-1929): Member of the Hungarian parliament, a Legitimist leader and political opponent of István Bethlen and the Horthy administration. Mihály Károlyi's father-in-law, he was also an art collector of some distinction.

Mihály Apaffy I: Prince of Transylvania from 1665 until 1690.

Count Albert Apponyi (1846–1933): From 1892, he led the Hungarian Party and was minister for religion and education from 1906 to 1910 and from 1917 to 1918. A leading advocate of free schooling, he attracted the animosity of several minority groups. He led the Hungarian delegation to the Paris peace talks and fought hard to achieve revision of the treaty terms. He was the leading speaker of the Legitimist Party in parliament in the post-war years.

Lord Asquith (1852–1928): The Earl of Oxford and Asquith. Liberal politician, held several ministerial posts and was prime minister from 1908 to 1916.

Gül Baba: Muslim holy man who is said to have been present when Budapest was taken by the Turks in 1541 and who afterwards planted a rose garden on the hill that bears his name to this day. His small octagonal mausoleum was used for a time as a Christian chapel but was restored to its original condition in 1961. It commands a fine view of the Danube.

Lord Arthur Balfour (1848–1930): Statesman and politician, prime minister of Great Britain and several times British delegate at international conferences. Later created an earl. His languid manner concealed an exceptionally acute brain. Piers Brendon, in his *Eminent Edwardians*, wrote: 'Balfour had the sang-froid of an iceberg.'

Zoltán Baranyai (1888–1948): Historian, diplomat and jurist. In 1920 the Hungarian government had created a non-official secretariat at the League of Nations in Geneva. It was headed first by Mihály Réz (1878–1921) then by Baranyai.

Jean Louis Barthou (1852–1934): Headed the French delegation at the Genoa conference. He was prime minister of France in 1913 and minister of defence and justice between 1921 and 1922. In 1934, as foreign minister, he was active in building up France's defences against the threat posed by the rise of the Nazi Party in Germany. In the autumn of that year he was assassinated in Marseille.

Lajos Batthyány: Hungary's first constitutional prime minister, executed by Franz Joseph in 1849.

Tivadar Batthyány: Liberal politician, one of the founding members of the National Council, once a friend and collaborator of Károlyi's but who afterwards was to back away from him.

Józef Bem: Polish soldier of fortune who had become a general in the Transylvanian uprising against the Habsburgs. In December 1848 he reoccupied Kolozsvár, but in August 1849 he was forced to surrender and, with twelve other generals and several hundred others, was executed by order of Emperor Franz Joseph.

Eduard Benes (1884–1948): Nationalist Czech politician. Under Habsburg rule, he agitated for the independence of Bohemia and was later rewarded by the Western powers with ministerial posts in the newly formed Czechoslovak Republic, of which he became prime minister in 1921 and president of the republic in 1935. A lifelong enemy of Hungary.

Philippe Berthelot (1866–1934): French foreign office minister who played an influential part in the discussions on the border changes decided at the peace talks that followed the First World War.

Bessarabia: Territory annexed by Russia in 1812, seized by Romania in 1918 and restored to Russia in 1947.

Count István Bethlen: Member of an old aristocratic family that for centuries had furnished the once semi-independent province with its rulers and political leaders. He was born in 1874 and in 1945 was imprisoned by the new Communist regime. Bethlen was one of Transylvania's most influential politicians. Like Bánffy, he had a dream of one day restoring some degree of autonomy to Transylvania but was finally frustrated by the inexorable terms of the peace treaties that followed the First World War. He died in 1947.

Vilmos Böhm (1880–1949): Defence minister under Károlyi and commander-in-chief of the army under Béla Kun. He fled the country in 1919, returning only after the Second World War when he accepted diplomatic posts, including that of ambassador to Sweden. He then fell out with the post-war Communist government and never returned to Hungary.

General George Boulanger (1837–1891): French minister of defence from 1886 to 1887 and headed a reactionary revolt against the French republic in 1889.

Ionel Bratianu (1864–1927): Leader of the Romanian National Liberal Party – Partidul National Liberal – who was prime minister of Romania five times between 1909 and 1927, when he was succeeded by his brother. His party was supported largely by big business and concentrated on modernizing Romania's backward economy. A leader of pro-Allied opinion in Romania, he was later largely responsible for his country entering the war in 1916 on the Allied side. Later he sent Romanian troops to help oust the Béla Kun regime and then to occupy a large slice of Hungarian territory.

Aristide Briand (1862–1932): French foreign minister for many years and later prime minister. Queen Zita's brothers deceived themselves if they fancied that Briand supported the return of the King-Emperor Karl either to Hungary or Austria. He seems to have politely pronounced himself sympathetic to the exiled Habsburgs but had never been so rash as to pledge French support for their restoration.

Lord Bryce (1838–1922): Politician, historian, attorney at law and professor at Oxford, British ambassador in Washington from 1907 to 1914. Viscount Bryce spoke in the House of Lords about the unjust decisions of the treaty of Trianon.

Budweis: Formerly in the Austro-Hungarian Empire, now in the Czech Republic more than two hundred kilometres north of Vienna.

Prince Castagnetto (1879–1923): Member of the Neapolitan Caracciolo family, Italian ambassador in Budapest from 1920 to 1923.

Lord Robert Cecil (1864–1958): Lawyer and conservative politician, son of Lord Salisbury, represented Britain at the Paris peace talks.

Gyorgyi Vasilievich Chicherin (1872–1936): Senior soviet minister from 1918 to 1930, was signatory to the Brest-Litovsk treaty.

George Benjamin Clemenceau (1841–1936): Radical French politician. He was prime minister from 1906 to 1909, during which time he was responsible for the separation of church and state. He was again prime minister in 1917 and presided over the peace talks, where he proved to be one of the most implacable enemies of Germany and Austria-Hungary. This earned him the nickname of 'the Tiger'.

Count Czernin: Austrian foreign minister in 1914 and responsible for persuading the aged emperor into signing the fatal ultimatum which was then delivered to Serbia and resulted in the declaration of war. He had done this by informing Franz Joseph that the Serbian army had already crossed the Drava and so was invading Hungarian territory. This was not in fact true. He was a supporter of Archduke Franz Ferdinand, heir to Austria-Hungary since the suicide of his cousin the archduke Rudolf, and who had collected around him in the Belvedere palace in Vienna what many people considered a sinister cabal whose ultimate aim was to incorporate all the Balkan states under the aegis of the Habsburg monarchy. The plots woven in the Belvedere palace form the subject of a seminal subplot in Bánffy's *The Writing on the Wall*.

Géza Daruváry (1866–1934): Bánffy's successor as foreign minister from 1922 to 1924.

Friedrich Ebert (1871–1925): German politician, leader of the Social-Democrat Party between 1913 and 1919 and president of the so-called 'Weimar Republic' between 1919 and 1925.

Tibor Eckhardt (1888–1972), Press spokesman for the provisional government in Szeged in 1919, head of the press department under Teleki's government between 1920 and 1921, president of the Independent Smallholders Party in 1932.

János Erdélyi (1863–1930): As his name suggests, a native of Transylvania, he was principal envoy of the Romanian government at the Budapest discussions concerning the transfer of Transylvania to Romanian sovereignty.

Empress Elisabeth, Queen of Hungary: Wife of Emperor Franz Joseph. Spent much time in Hungary, loved the Hungarians and spoke their language, and was much beloved by them.

Count Tamás Erdödy (1868–1931): His memoirs, *Die Memoiren des Grafen Tamás von Erdödy Habsburgs Weg von Wilhelm zu Briand Vom Kurier der Sixtus-Briefe zum Königsputschisten von Paul Szemere und Erich Czech* were published in 1931.

Mihály Esterházy (1884–1958): Member of parliament from 1910 and Mihály Károlyi's envoy to Switzerland between 1918 and 1919, distant cousin to Bánffy and a close friend.

Móric Esterházy: Cousin and close friend of Miklós Bánffy.

King Ferdinand of Bulgaria: Known to the world as 'Foxy' Ferdinand, scion of the family of Sax-Coburg Goth, king of Bulgaria from 1908 to 1918, died 1948.

Luigi Facta (1861–1930): Head of the Italian government from February to October 1922.

Fiume: A port on the Adriatic, formerly part of the Austro-Hungarian Empire. It was renamed Rijeka when ceded to Yugoslavia by the Treaty of Trianon in 1920 and is now in the independent republic of Slovenia.

Maurice Foucher: Became high commissioner in Budapest in 1920. He was recalled to Paris after King Karl's second *putsch*.

General Franchet d'Esperey: French officer, commander-in-chief of the Allied forces based in Belgrade when the war came to an end.

István Friedrich (1883–1951): Hungarian politician. In 1919 he assisted in the plot to oust the Peidl government and then tried to form a government of his own which was not recognized either by

Admiral Horthy or by the Western powers. He joined the exiled king in his attempts to return and then became one of the founders of the Legitimist Party.

Gerbeaud: Founder of the most famous café, pastry and confectionary shop in Budapest which bears his name and whose doors are still open today. The chocolates are as good as ever. There is a moving scene in *They Were Divided*, the last book of Bánffy's trilogy, which is set in Gerbeaud's in 1914.

Gödöllo: Former Habsburg summer residence not far from Budapest.

Gyula Gömbös (1886–1936): Pro-fascist president of the Hungarian Defence Union in 1919, defence minister from 1929 to1936.

General Görgey: One of the 1848 rebels. Hopelessly outnumbered and surrounded, surrendered to the Tsarist army at Világos as he knew his men would be more humanely treated by the Russians than they would have been by the Austrians. With hindsight there is no question that this was the only sensible course and saved many lives, but he was nevertheless considered to be a traitor by many Hungarians.

Count János Hadik: Briefly prime minister in the troubled days at the end of October 1918. He does not seem to have inspired much confidence either in the young king or, for that matter, in Mihály Károlyi who was to succeed him in office.

Albert Hanotaux (1853–1944): French politician and historian, twice minister for foreign affairs. He was in office when Madagascar became part of the French empire and played an important part in the formation of French West Africa. He frequently represented France at the League of Nations.

Lajos Hatvany (1880–1961): Rich Hungarian banker and newspaper owner, author of several works who also edited a five-volume collection of papers concerning the great poet Petöfi. Was a member of the National Council in 1918. Left Hungary on the fall of Communism. Although politically active at the time of Károlyi's socialist republic, he receives only two brief and unflattering mentions in the Károlyi memoirs. He was much disliked by Bánffy.

Baron Julius von Haynau: Austrian military commander principally responsible for savage reprisals against those who had taken part in the 1848 revolution. It was his order to execute thirteen generals that earned Emperor Franz Joseph the nickname, so full of hatred: 'The Old Hangman in Vienna'.

Iván Héjjas (1890–1950): a well-known figure of the White Terror. It seems he must also have understood some German, as he served in the nineteenth Imperial Regiment.

Ferenc Herczeg (1863–1954): Much respected Hungarian writer and friend of Bánffy's.

Géza Herczeg (1888–1954): Edited the *Nap*, *Magyar Hírlap* and *Az Ujság*. In 1918 he was head of the press department under Mihály

Károly. Later he worked in Vienna for the Neue Freie Presse. After a time he went to live in America.

The Abbé János Hock: With Károlyi and others, was a founder member of the National Council, much disliked and distrusted as a self-seeking demagogue by Miklós Bánffy but much admired by Mihály Károlyi, who described him as 'a brilliant orator'. On 16 October he became president of the National Council, a post which Károlyi resigned, having been appointed Minister-President. Like Károlyi he was later to find himself an exile from Hungary.

The Hofburg: The vast imperial palace in the centre of Vienna.

Sir Thomas Hohler (1871–1946): English diplomat. Held posts in Constantinople, Saint Petersburg, Cairo, Tokyo, Mexico and Washington, chief commissioner in Budapest from 1919, ambassador from 1921 to 1924. Friendly with Admiral Horthy.

Sir Esmé Howard (1863–1939): British diplomat and philanthropist. In 1926 he became ambassador to Washington.

Alexander Petrovich Isvolski (1856–1919): At various times Russian ambassador to the Vatican, to Belgrade, to Munich, to Tokyo and to Paris. Russian foreign minister from 1906 to 1910.

Jassy: Capital of the former principality of Moldavia that had been incorporated within the then principality of Romania in 1866. The inhabitants included many of Magyar origin and since becoming a province of Romania there had been several distributions of land to the peasantry. This continued after Romania was elevated into a kingdom in 1879.

King John I of Hungary: Lost his throne after only a year to the rival claimant, Archduke Ferdinand of Habsburg, who, seeing John I's weakness in the face of the Turkish threat and the fact that he had been deserted by those Hungarians and Transylvanians who had put him on the throne, invaded Hungary in 1527 and was immediately crowned with St Stephen's Crown, which had been used less than a year before for King John himself.

Archduke Joseph: Cousin of the emperor who made his home in Hungary. He lived at Poszony (now Bratislava) in what was then northern Hungary and is now the Czech Republic. Countess Sophie Chotek, who was his wife's lady-in-waiting, afterwards morganatically married Archduke Franz Ferdinand and was assassinated with her husband at Sarajevo in 1914.

Emperor Franz Joseph (1830–1916): Succeeded to the thrones of Austria and Hungary at the age of seventeen in 1848 and was on the throne during the troubled times of the Hungarian revolution of 1848. For many years he was still hated by those with memories of Austrian oppression. From 1867, when the *Ausgleich* (Compromise) was promulgated, the empire of Austria-Hungary became known as the 'Dual Monarchy' since the monarch in his own person was emperor of Austria and king of Hungary. From that date, the two countries had their own parliaments, prime ministers and civil servants, and only foreign policy, the banking systems and the armies were integrated under one banner. His only son, Crown Prince Rudolf, committed suicide at Mayerling in 1889, and his wife, the beautiful but wayward Empress Elisabeth, was assassinated in Geneva in 1898. This was not the end of his tragedies: in 1914 his heir, Archduke Franz Ferdinand, was assassinated in Sarajevo by a Serbian terrorist, an event that swiftly led to the outbreak of general European war in 1914. Thereafter, the succession to the Dual Monarchy of Austria-Hungary feel to another nephew, Archduke Karl.

Ferenc Julier (1878–1946): Hungarian strategist, successor to Stromfeld as Chief of General Staff under the Communist regime.

Kálmán Kánya, (1869–1945): Hungarian Foreign Office official, served as ambassador to Mexico before the First World War and in the 1920s and 1930s was successively chief secretary of the foreign office, ambassador to Berlin and finally foreign minister. No friend to Bánffy.

King Karl I (1887–1922): Crowned in the first part of these memoirs, he left the country in 1918 and was the last monarch of the Austro-Hungarian Empire.

Jongheer van Karnebeek: Dutch foreign minister.

Julius Károlyi (1871–1947): Foreign minister from 1930 to 1931, and prime minister from 1931 to 1932.

Count Mihály Károlyi (1875–1955): Hungarian politician, cousin of Miklós Bánffy, member of parliament from 1901, president of the Independent Party from 1913. Before World War I broke out he declared his support for British and French attitudes. He was against Hungary's participation in the war and also the policies attributed to Count István Tisza. He became president of the Hungarian Republic in January 1919 and shortly afterwards, with the rise of Communism, left Hungary to live in the West and only returned in 1946. For a short time he accepted representative diplomatic posts. From 1949 until his death in 1955, he lived in Paris.

Baron Sándor Károlyi: Commander-in-chief of the armies of Ferenc Rákóczi II, Prince of Transylvania, who had revolted against the Habsburgs in the last years of the seventeenth century. Rewarded for his services to the dynasty with huge grants of land and the title of Count. Rákóczi, on the other hand, was exiled. The peace of Szatmár in 1711 ended the rebellion and confirmed the Habsburg rule over Transylvania. In his memoirs Mihály Károlyi comments wryly that his family owed their immense wealth to the Habsburgs and finally lost it because of the part he played in their downfall.

Sándor (Alexander) Károlyi: Count Károlyi Mihály's great-uncle and second husband of his grandmother Clarisse, who had first married

Edward Károlyi, Mihály's grandfather. She was aunt to Miklós Bánffy. They lived at the vast manor house of Föth, some nineteen kilometres northeast of Budapest (still preserved and now used as a school for orphaned children). The great library of this house, where Mihály did all his early reading (see*Memoirs of Michael Károlyi*, Jonathan Cape, London, 1956) is the setting for an important scene in *They Were Counted*, the first volume of Bánffy's Transylvanian trilogy.

Kaszino Club: The aristocrats' club, now pulled down, which stood on the corner of Lajos Kossuth utca and Museum korut. Its entrance was directly in front of the former entrance to the Hotel Astoria, which still flourishes and which figures in Bánffy's account of the October Revolution in 1918.

Count Kaunitz (1711–1794): Distinguished statesman under Empress Maria Theresia.

Kecskemét: Agricultural province eighty-five kilometres south of Budapest, which boasts Hungary's largest orchards, produces thirty per cent of the country's wine and the famous Kecskemét apricot brandy.

Count Sándor Khuen-Héderváry (1881–1947): Hungarian politician and diplomat, held various ministerial posts and was ambassador in Paris from 1934 to 1940.

Count Kunó Klebelsberg (1875–1932): With István Bethlen organized the party of National Unity in 1919. Minister of the interior from 1921 to 1922, and minister of education and religion from 1922 to 1931, he was influential in the reform of the educational system and the establishment of village schools. He created Hungarian Institutes in Vienna, Berlin and Rome.

Lajos Kossuth (1802–1894): Hungary's greatest revolutionary patriot, born into an old but untitled family of minor landowners in northeastern Hungary. He became known early as a talented and ardent political journalist with strong Liberal views for which he was imprisoned in May 1837. Soon after his release he became editor of the *Pesti Hirlap*, the most prominent Liberal newspaper, a position he used to further the aims of all those who advocated such radical reforms as abolishing all remaining traces of feudalism and the taxation of the nobility. This soon led to open opposition to Habsburg rule from Vienna. He became a member of parliament in 1847. By 1848 he had become the acknowledged leader of the Hungarian revolution whose aim was complete political independence from Austria. When, by 1849, the Hungarian insurrection had won many successes, he made a public declaration stating that 'the House of Habsburg-Lorraine, perjured in the sight of God and man, had forfeited the Hungarian throne' for which he earned the lifelong hatred of the young Emperor Franz Joseph. After the surrender of General Görgey at Világos, the insurrection was effectively at an end, and

Kossuth fled to Turkey. Eventually, after a period of exile in England, where he was fêted as a great patriot, he went to Italy and was to die there, in Turin. His body was taken back to Pest where he was buried amid the mourning of the whole nation.

Béla Kun: Hungarian Communist leader whose rise to power in 1919 had brought about the flight of Mihály Károlyi. His repressive rule lasted only until the autumn of 1919.

Philip László: Hungarian painter who made an international reputation principally in London during the first part of the twentieth century.

Karl Liebknecht (1871–1919): Leader of the 'Spartacus League' workers revolutionary movement.

David Lloyd George (1863–1945): Radical British politician. He became leader of the Liberal Party, a position he held until his death. He held several ministerial posts and was prime minister from 1916 to 1922. He represented England at the peace talks in Paris and in several subsequent international conferences.

Cesare Lombroso, 1839–1909: Eminent Jewish-Italian criminologist, professor of psychiatry, forensic medicine and criminal anthropology and author of several seminal works on those and related subjects.

Louis Loucheur (1872–1931): Industrialist, French minister for rearmament and reconstruction from 1917 to1920, member of French delegation to the peace conference.

Márton Lovászy (1864–1927): Liberal Hungarian politician, member of the National Council in 1918 and one of Mihály Károlyi's ministers. He was to become minister of war under Friedrich.

György Lukács (1865–1950): Former editor of the review *Monarchy*. Became leader of the Revisionist Party in 1927.

Ramsay MacDonald (1866–1937): Became England's first Labour prime minister in 1924 and again from 1929 to 1937.

Iuliu Maniu (1873–1951): Leader of the Romanian National Party, several times prime minister of Romania.

Friar George Martinuzzi (1482–1551): Bishop of Várad and later governor of Transylvania, played a leading role in trying to unite Hungary in the troubled times of John I.

Professor Tomás Masaryk (1850–1937): Founded the Czech People's Party under the Austro-Hungarian monarchy in 1900. He was leader of the Czech People's Party in Paris from 1916 and later, president of Czechoslovakia from 1918 until 1935.

Count Mensdorff (1861–1945): Cousin of King Edward VII and was immensely popular during his time as ambassador in London.

Count János Mikes (1876–1943): Archbishop of Szombathely at the time of King Karl's two attempts to regain his Hungarian throne. A colourful character and a lifelong monarchist, he was well known to Bánffy as a fellow Transylvanian.

Andor Miklós: A well-known newspaper proprietor.

Miskolc: An industrial town in north-east Hungary.

Ferenc Molnár: Internationally renowned novelist and playwright.

Monnet-Sully: Nineteenth-century French actor known for the exaggerated theatricality of his performances.

Traian Mosoiu (1868–1932): Commander of the Romanian army of occupation and in 1920 minister of defence in Bucharest.

Field Marshal Pál Nagy (1864–1927): Commanded the Miskolc garrison and was called to Budapest after Rezsö Willerding had refused to take up arms against King Karl during the second *putsch*.

Lord Newton: Spoke about the Hungarian question in the House of Lords on 20 March 1920. He visited Hungary in 1921 and was the leading figure in an organization called the Oxford League for Hungarian Self-Determination. Friend and supporter of István Bethlen.

Parád: Area in the Tatra hills some one hundred kilometres east of Budapest.

Nicola Pasic (1846–1926): Serbian statesman and several times prime minister of Yugoslavia.

Ivan Fiodorovich Paskievich (1782–1856): Duke of Warsaw, led the Russian armies that invaded Transylvania in 1848, chief of staff to the Imperial Russian army in 1849.

Gyula Peidl (1873–1943): Hungarian politician. Joined Social-Democratic Party in 1909 and emigrated soon after his brief spell as prime minister in 1919. His government lasted six days, and on 6 August a *coup d'état* by the National-Clerical Party made István Friedrich prime minister and named Archduke Joseph as Regent of Hungary.

Raymond Poincaré (1869–1934): After holding several ministerial posts, he became president of France from 1913 to 1920.

Caserio Princip: Killed Archduke Franz Ferdinand at Sarajevo, thus precipitating the start of World War I.

Vilmos Pröhle (1871–1946): Professor of linguistics and an expert on the Far East. Bánffy and István Bethlen helped finance the publication of his *From the East* in 1922. A National Christian Unity Party member of parliament, he resigned as a result of the party's attitude to King Karl. Author of a Turkish grammar and editor of an anthology of Japanese literature.

Pál Prónay (1875–1945): Lieutenant-colonel in the Hungarian army, was forced to retire from active service after his support for King Karl's second *putsch*.

István Rakovszky (1858–1931): politician in the People's Party, active during the opposition coalition from 1906 to 1910, president of the first National Assembly from 1920. He and Gratz arrived in Sopron on Thursday 20 March, where King Karl appointed a new 'government' with Rakovszky at its head.

Walter Rathenau (1867–1922): Industrialist, writer and politician. Appointed foreign minister in January 1922 and assassinated later the same year.

Prince René of Bourbon-Parma: Born 1894, the twelfth child and fifth son of Robert, Duke of Parma. He was brother to the Queen-Empress Zita. One of Prince René's older brothers, Prince Sixtus, born in 1886, was well known to have played a prominent part in acting as his brother-in-law's envoy during secret talks with the Allies when the war was at its height.

Vilmos Röder (1881–1969): A colonel at the time of King Karl's second *putsch*, Röder went on to head the department of strategic planning and was later Chief of General Staff from 1930 to 1935 and minister of defence from 1936 to 1938. He was one of Bethlen's most trusted supporters and at the end of the Second World War, at the Crown Council in 1944, it was he who advised on the ceasefire arrangements.

Johannes Schober (1874–1924): Chief of police in Vienna from 1918, chancellor from 1921 to 1922 and from 1929 to 1930, foreign minister from 1930 to 1932.

Count Antal Sigray (1879–1947): Much in evidence in 1922 when King Karl made his second attempt to return to Hungary and regain his throne (see Chapter Six of Bánffy's *Twenty Five Years [1945]* in this volume). He was a lifelong supporter of the Legitimist cause. In 1943 he openly advocated the withdrawal of Hungary from its alliance with the Axis and in revenge, was arrested by the Germans and sent to the concentration camp at Mauthausen. After his release, he left the country and died in New York in 1947.

Sándor Simonyi-Semadám (1864–1946): Briefly prime minister in 1920. Retired from politics in 1922.

Colonel Tihamér Siménfalvy: A member of several extreme right-wing organizations. Admiral Horthy had great confidence in him.

Slovensko: Province of Hungary awarded to the new State of Czechoslovakia the Treaty of Trianon.

Field Marshal Jan Smuts (1870–1950): South African soldier and liberal politician, Prime Minister of South Africa from 1919 to 1924 and again during the Second World War. Close friend of Winston Churchill.

Károly Soós (1869–1953): Served in Austro-Hungarian army, promoted to general and field marshal. Served as Chief of General Staff and minister of defence in 1920. Commanded army of the south.

Spandau: Berlin's military headquarters and principal barracks situated about ten kilometres northwest of the city centre.

Aurél Stromfeld (1878–1927): prominent left-wing politician with a distinguished army background.

István Szabó of Nagyatád (1863–1924): Founder of the National Independent and Holders Party in 1909, which led to the formation

418 *Glossary of Names and Places*

of the National Smallholder's Party in 1919. After the fall of Communism, he became finance minister and later minister of agriculture. He was largely responsible for the 1920 law that distributed land to the peasantry.

The Szeklers: A race of disputed origin but with largely Magyar traditions and language who had settled in Transylvania some time in the Dark Ages, and who formed an important section of the (then) Hungarian community in the population of that province. They were fiercely anti-Romanian, claiming to have come there centuries before immigration was to bring many Romanian peasant families seeking refuge from the Turkish domination of what was in 1866 to form the independent principality (and from 1881, kingdom) of Romania with an appointed German sovereign, Prince Charles of Hohenzollen-Sigmaringen. The Romanians claim descent from the Dacians of Roman times, and the whole question of the origins of the several ethnic groups in Transylvania has for many years been the subject of bitter dispute between scholars of Magyar and Romanian origins.

Szovata: Located in Transylvania, 152 kilometres south of Kolozsvár – now Cluj – with hot and cold salt lakes.

Count Pál Teleki (1879–1941): Born of an ancient Transylvanian family, geographer and scientist, president of the Society of Turan, 1913, foreign minister and minister for agriculture in Count Gyula Károlyi's government founded in Szeged to combat Communist rule in Budapest. In 1920 he again became foreign minister and then, in 1921, prime minister. He worked hard for the revision of the Treaty of Trianon, opposed the growing influence of the Soviet Union and was one of the first Hungarian politicians to recognize the threat posed by the Nazis. Appointed once more to the office of prime minister in 1939, he killed himself when Hitler tried to make Hungary enter the war on the German side.

Kálmán Thaly (1839–1909): Poet and historian. He wrote about the *'kuruc'* spirit and helped create the national veneration for Rákóczi's part in the 1848 freedom fight. He founded the Hungarian Historical Society and the magazine *Centuries*.

Imré Thököly: one of Transylvania's greatest and most successful military leaders. Earned the admiration of France and other opponents of the Habsburgs and played a decisive part in attaining a measure of independence for Hungary in the late seventeenth century.

Viorel Tilea: Romanian diplomat. His posthumous memoirs, *Envoy Extraordinary* (Hagerstown Press), were edited by his daughter Ileana Tilea in 1998. His unpublished correspondence – some of it with Bánffy – shows that the two men had become friends.

István Tisza (1861–1918): Several times prime minister of Hungary. Although opposed to the war, he kept this office at the request of Emperor Franz Joseph and was assassinated in 1918. Bánffy gives a sympathetic portrait of this most honest and upright of Hungarian politicians in his trilogy, *The Writing on the Wall*.

Nicolae Titulescu: Romanian ambassador in London in 1922 and foreign minister from 1927 to 1936. His compatriot, the diplomat Viorel Tilea, refers to Titulescu in his posthumous memoirs, *Envoy Extraordinary* (London, 1998) as 'a wise and highly respected statesman who had avoided being embroiled in local politics yet was often a foreign minister in reserve'. In 1934 he was responsible for establishing diplomatic relations between Romania and the USSR.

Tokaj: Located at the centre of the district producing Hungary's most famous wine of the same name. Pope Pius IV expressed his appreciation of it at the Council of Trent (1545–1563) at which the Roman Catholic Church planned the Counter Reformation. King Louis XIV of France is recorded as saying: 'Tokaj is the wine of kings and the king of wines.'

Alexandru Vajda-Vojvod (1872–1950): One of the leading figures of the Romanian National Front in 1918, prime minister from 1919 to 1920 and from 1932 to 1933. He was a Transylvanian landowner of ethnic Romanian origins with property not far from the Bánffy castle of Bonczhida.

Colonel Vix: Commander of the French Military Mission, which then occupied Hungary, and was all-powerful. He was a real thorn in the flesh to Mihály Károlyi, who was later to write of him that he turned down all Károlyi's requests but not those from 'Germanophile' members of the *'ancien régime'* who 'busied themselves with drawing up unfavourable reports on the new Hungary, reports which Colonel Vix . . . was only too pleased to forward to Versailles'.

Warnemünde: A small port on the Baltic just north of Rostock.

Kaiser Wilhelm II (1851–1941): Grandson of Queen Victoria and Emperor of Germany from 1888 until the end of World War I, when he abdicated and went to live in retirement at Doorn in Holland. Known to all Englishmen as 'The Kaiser' and much hated as being responsible for the war.

Queen Wilhelmina: Queen of Holland from 1890 to 1948 when she abdicated in favour of her daughter Princess Juliana.

Thomas Woodrow Wilson (1856–1924): From 1913 to 1921 he was president of the United States, and entered the war on the Allied side in 1917. He was present at the peace talks in Paris which led to the Treaty of Trianon in 1920, but his Fourteen Points, which were just and moderate, failed to be incorporated into the final draft of the treaty, due largely to the Allies' desire for vengeance against Germany and Austria-Hungary.

Empress Zita (1892–1989): Princess of Bourbon-Parma. Married to Archduke Karl in 1911. He died in exile in 1922, while she went on to survive him by over fifty years.